HITLER'S
PANZERS

HITLER'S PANZERS

THE LIGHTNING ATTACKS
THAT REVOLUTIONIZED WARFARE

DENNIS SHOWALTER

BERKLEY CALIBER, NEW YORK

THE BERKLEY PUBLISHING GROUP
Published by the Penguin Group
Penguin Group (USA) Inc., 375 Hudson Street, New York, New York 10014, USA
Penguin Group (Canada), 90 Eglinton Avenue East, Suite 700, Toronto, Ontario M4P 2Y3, Canada
(a division of Pearson Penguin Canada Inc.)
Penguin Books Ltd., 80 Strand, London WC2R 0RL, England
Penguin Group Ireland, 25 St. Stephen's Green, Dublin 2, Ireland (a division of Penguin Books Ltd.)
Penguin Group (Australia), 250 Camberwell Road, Camberwell, Victoria 3124, Australia
(a division of Pearson Australia Group Pty. Ltd.)
Penguin Books India Pvt. Ltd., 11 Community Centre, Panchsheel Park, New Delhi—110 017, India
Penguin Group (NZ), 67 Apollo Drive, Rosedale, North Shore 0632, New Zealand
(a division of Pearson New Zealand Ltd.)
Penguin Books (South Africa) (Pty.) Ltd., 24 Sturdee Avenue, Rosebank, Johannesburg 2196,
South Africa

Penguin Books Ltd., Registered Offices: 80 Strand, London WC2R 0RL, England

This book is an original publication of The Berkley Publishing Group.

The publisher does not have any control over and does not assume any responsibility for author or
third-party websites or their content.

Copyright © 2009 Dennis Showalter
Maps by Jay Karameles, Olórin Press
Book design by Tiffany Estreicher

FIRST EDITION: December 2009

Library of Congress Cataloging-in-Publication Data

Showalter, Dennis E.
Hitler's Panzers : the lightning attacks that revolutionized warfare / Dennis Showalter.
p. cm.
Includes index.
ISBN 978-0-425-23004-6
1. Germany. Heer—Armored troops—History—20th century. 2. Tanks (Military science)—
Germany—History—20th century. 3. World War, 1939–1945—Tank warfare. 4. World War,
1939–1945—Germany. 5. Hitler, Adolf, 1889–1945—Military leadership. 6. Lightning war—
Germany—History—20th century. 7. Military art and science—Germany—History—20th century.
I. Title.
D757.54.S56 2009
940.54'1343—dc22
2009017551

PRINTED IN THE UNITED STATES OF AMERICA

10 9 8 7 6 5 4 3 2 1

CONTENTS

GERMAN CAMPAIGN IN THE WEST, 1940

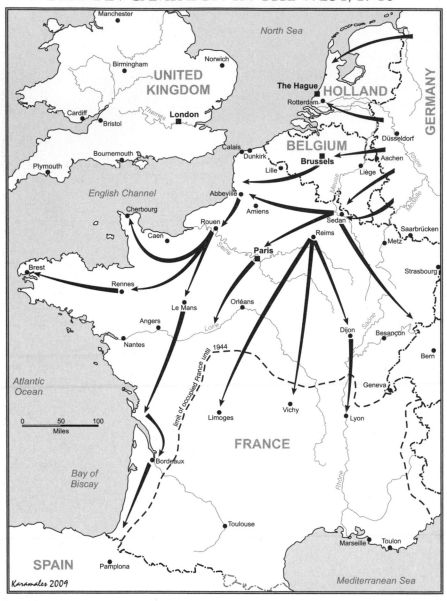

GERMAN INVASION OF SOVIET UNION, 1941–1942

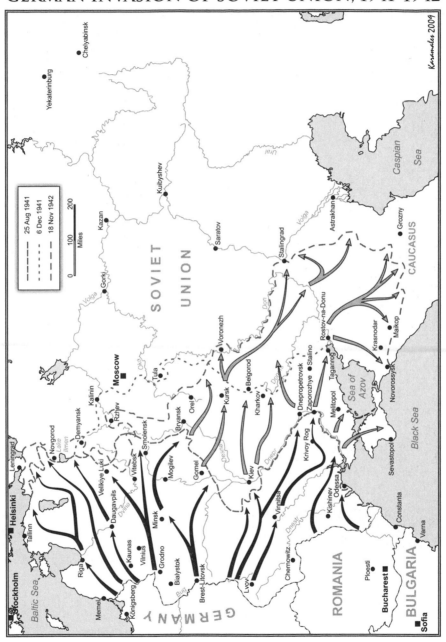

CAMPAIGNS IN NORTH AFRICA

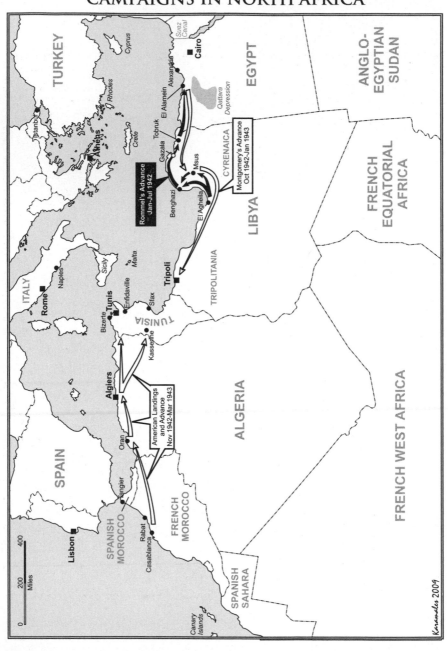

EASTERN FRONT, 1943–1944

THE EASTERN FRONT, 1944–1945

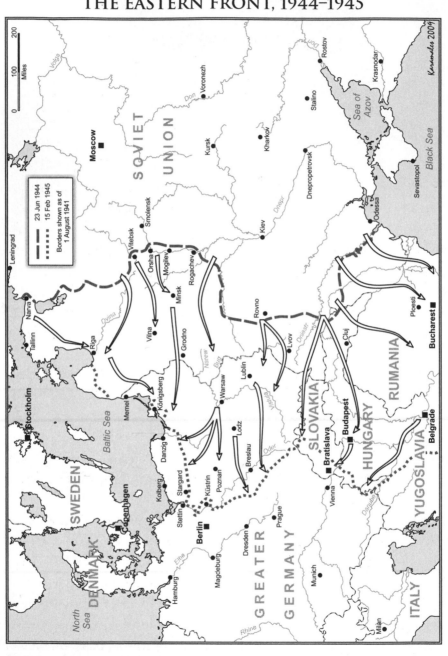

INTRODUCTION

THE GERMAN ARMY of World War II continues to attract reader attention. Academic studies and military analyses, general-reader narratives and coffee-table picture books, all jostle for places in bookstores and on bookshelves. Central to history and myth alike are the armored forces: the tanks and assault guns, the motorized infantry, and the supporting arms of the panzer and panzer grenadier divisions of the army and the Waffen SS. They were the heart of the army's fighting power and the core of its identity from the first days of victory in 1939 until the Third Reich's downfall in 1945.

The panzers have inspired a correspondingly rich literature. Works on doctrine, tactics, and equipment stand alongside studies of the panzers' place in the German way of war and the history of war in the twentieth century. In darker contexts scholars present the panzers' contributions to an ethic of fear and force that permeated Germany and its army before the rise of National Socialism transformed apocalyptic ideology into genocidal reality.

General, comprehensive discussions of Hitler's panzers have been understandably lacking. This book puts panzers at the center of three interfacing narratives. It presents the panzers' contributions to the development of mechanized war and armor technology, their influence on the role of the army in German culture and society, and their role in the Third Reich's conduct of World War II—militarily and morally.

The massive body of printed and archival sources available on each of these subjects can provide a multiple-entry footnote for every paragraph and for many individual sentences. I have appealed to reader-friendliness,

eschewing a reference apparatus in favor of occasionally naming someone whose contribution to a particular issue demands acknowledgment.
For simplicity's sake I have taken several other shortcuts as well. German
ranks are given in American equivalents—including the mouth-filling
titles of the Waffen SS. I reduce to a minimum the italicization of
already complex German vehicle and weapons designations. All units
of all armies follow the same terminology unless otherwise noted. Thus
British or French armored units titled squadrons and regiments usually
become companies and battalions.

The consistent use of "approximately" and "about" when giving
vehicle strengths in particular reflects the fact that those numbers often
varied widely, literally from day to day, given the effectiveness of the
workshops and recovery crews. Exact statistics are correspondingly
likely to mislead—which was not infrequently the intention of compil-
ers seeking to increase their inventory by exaggerating shortages.

This is a story as much as a history. It is shaped by research and by
four decades' worth of memories and anecdotes acquired from listen-
ing to the men who were there on both sides. It addresses deeds and
behaviors that defy conventional explanations, positive and negative. In
the kaleidoscope that was the Third Reich, the same institutions, the
same persons, the same man, could show a near-random set of faces.
Which were masks and which realities? Throughout this project I have
sought counsel from another soldier, who asks that when his story is
told, "nothing extenuate, nor set down aught in malice." In telling the
tale of Hitler's panzers, there are worse mentors than Othello.

Authors' acknowledgments are tending to match those of the Acad-
emy Awards in length and fulsomeness. Without intending to slight
anyone, I thank the students of Colorado College, who after over forty
years keep me having too much fun to retire. And I thank especially the
office staff of the history department: Sandy Papuga and Joanna Popiel.
The book is dedicated to them, for more reasons than they know.

CHAPTER ONE

BEGINNINGS

SEPTEMBER 15, 1916, began as a routine day for the German infantrymen in the forward trenches around Flers on the Somme—as routine as any day was likely to be after two and a half months of vicious, close-gripped fighting that bled divisions white and reduced battalions to the strength of companies. True, an occasional rumble of engines had been audible across the line. But the British had more trucks than the Kaiser's army, and were more willing to risk them to bring up ammunition and carry back wounded. True, there had been occasional gossip of something new up Tommy's sleeve: of armored "land cruisers" impervious to anything less than a six-inch shell. But rumors—Scheisshausparolen in Landser speak—were endemic on the Western Front. Then "a forest of guns opened up in a ceaseless, rolling thunder, the few remaining survivors . . . fight on until the British flood overwhelms them, consumes them, and passes on. . . . An extraordinary number of men. And there, between them, spewing death, unearthly monsters: the first British tanks."

I

IMPROVISED AND POORLY coordinated, the British attack soon collapsed in the usual welter of blood and confusion. But for the first time on the Western Front, certainly the first time on the Somme, the heaviest losses were suffered by the defenders. Reactions varied widely. Some men panicked; others fought to a finish. But the 14th Bavarian Infantry, for example, tallied more than 1,600 casualties. Almost half were "missing," and most of them were prisoners. That was an unheard-of ratio in an army that still prided itself on its fighting spirit. But the 14th was one of the regiments hit on the head by the tanks.

Shock rolled uphill. "The enemy," one staff officer recorded, "employed new engines of war, as cruel as effective.... It is necessary to take whatever methods are possible to counteract them." From the Allied perspective, the impact of tanks on the Great War is generally recognized. The cottage industry among scholars of the British learning curve, with descriptions of proto-mechanized war pitted against accounts of a semi-mobile final offensive based on combined arms and improved communications, recognizes the centrality of armor for both interpretations. French accounts are structured by Marshal Philippe Petain's judgment that, in the wake of the frontline mutinies of 1917, it was necessary to wait for "the Americans and the tanks." Certainly it was the tanks, the light Renault FT-17s, that carried the exhausted French infantry forward in the months before the armistice. Erich Ludendorff, a general in a position to know, declared after the war that Germany had been defeated not by Marshal Foch but by "General Tank."

In those contexts it is easy to overlook the salient fact that the German army was quick and effective in developing antitank techniques. This was facilitated by the moonscape terrain of the Western Front, the mechanical unreliability of early armored vehicles, and such technical grotesqueries as the French seeking to increase the range of their early tanks by installing extra fuel tanks on their roofs, which virtually guaranteed the prompt incineration of the crew unless they were quick to abandon the vehicle. Even at Flers the Germans had taken on tanks like any other targets: aiming for openings in the armor, throwing grenades, using field guns over open sights. German intelligence thoroughly interrogated one captured tanker and translated a diary lost by another. Inside of a week, Berlin had a general description of the new weapons, accompanied by a rough but reasonably accurate sketch.

One of the most effective antitank measures was natural. Tanks drew fire from everywhere, fire sufficiently intense to strip away any infantry in their vicinity. A tank by itself was vulnerable. Therefore, the German tactic was to throw everything available at the tanks and keep calm if they kept coming. Proactive countermeasures began with inoculating the infantry against "tank fright" by using knocked-out vehicles to demonstrate their various vulnerabilities. An early frontline improvisation was the geballte Ladung: the heads of a half dozen stick grenades tied around a complete "potato-masher" and thrown into one of a tank's many openings—or, more basic, the same half dozen grenades shoved into a sandbag and the fuse of one of them pulled. More effective and less immediately risky was the K-round. This was simply a bullet with a tungsten carbide core instead of the soft alloys commonly used in small arms rounds. Originally developed to punch holes in metal plates protecting enemy machine-gun and sniper positions, it was employed to even better effect by the ubiquitous German machine guns against the armor of the early tanks. K-rounds were less likely to disable the vehicle, mostly causing casualties and confusion among the crew, but the end effect was similar.

As improved armor limited the K-round's effect, German designers came up with a 13mm version. Initially it was used in a specially designed single-shot rifle, the remote ancestor of today's big-caliber sniper rifles but without any of their recoil-absorbing features. The weapon's fierce recoil made it inaccurate and unpopular; even a strong user risked a broken collarbone or worse. More promising was the TuF (tank and antiaircraft) machine gun using the same round. None of the ten thousand TuFs originally projected were ready for service by November 11—but the concept and the bullet became the basis for John Browning's .50-caliber machine gun, whose near-century of service makes it among the most long-lived modern weapons.

When something heavier was desirable, the German counterpart of the Stokes mortar was a much larger piece, mounted on wheels, capable of modification for direct fire and, with a ten-pound shell, lethal against any tank. The German army had also begun forming batteries of "infantry guns" even before the tanks appeared. These were usually mountain guns or modified field pieces of around three-inch caliber. Intended to support infantry attacks by direct fire, they could stop tank attacks just as well. From the beginning, ordinary field pieces with ordinary shells also proved able to knock out tanks at a range of two miles.

In an emergency the large number of 77mm field pieces mounted on trucks for antiaircraft work could become improvised antitank guns. These proved particularly useful at Cambrai in November 1917, when more than a hundred tanks were part of the spoils of the counterattack that wiped out most of the initial British gains. They did so well, indeed, that the crews had to be officially reminded that their primary duty was shooting down airplanes. As supplements, a number of ordinary field guns were mounted on trucks in the fashion of the portees used in a later war by the British in North Africa.

If survival was not sufficient incentive, rewards and honor were invoked. One Bavarian battery was awarded 500 marks for knocking out a tank near Flers. British reports and gossip praised an officer who, working a lone gun at Flesquieres during the Cambrai battle, either by himself or with a scratch crew, was supposed to have disabled anywhere from five to sixteen tanks before he was killed. The Nazis transformed the hero into a noncommissioned officer, and gave him a name and at least one statue. The legend's less Homeric roots seem to have involved a half dozen tanks following each other over the crest of a small hill and being taken out one at a time by a German field battery. The story of "the gunner of Flesquieres" nevertheless indicates the enduring strength of the tank mystique in German military lore.

Other purpose-designed antitank weapons were ready to come on line when the war ended: short-barreled, low-velocity 37mm guns, an automatic 20mm cannon that the Swiss developed into the World War II Oerlikon. The effect of this new hardware on the projected large-scale use of a new generation of tanks in the various Allied plans for 1919 must remain speculative. What it highlights is the continued German commitment to tank defense even in the war's final months.

That commitment is highlighted from a different perspective when considering the first German tank. It was not until October 1916 that the Prussian War Ministry summoned the first meeting of the A7V Committee. The group took its name from the sponsoring agency, the Seventh Section of the General War Department, and eventually bestowed it on the resulting vehicle. The members were mostly from the motor transport service rather than the combat arms, and their mission was technical: develop a tracked armored fighting vehicle in the shortest possible time. They depended heavily on designers and engineers loaned to the project by Germany's major auto companies. Not surprisingly, when the first contracts for components were placed in November, no fewer than seven firms shared the pie.

A prototype was built in January; a working model was demonstrated to the General Staff in May. It is a clear front-runner for the title of "ugliest tank ever built" and a strong contender in the "most dysfunctional" category. The A7V was essentially a rectangular armored box roughly superimposed on a tractor chassis. It mounted a 57mm cannon in its front face and a half dozen machine guns around the hull. It weighed 33 tons, and required a crew of no fewer than eighteen men. Its under-slung tracks and low ground clearance left it almost no capacity to negotiate obstacles or cross broken terrain: the normal environment of the Western Front. An improved A7V and a lighter tank, resembling the British Whippet and based on the chassis of the Daimler automobile, were still in prototype states when the war ended. A projected 150-ton monster remained—fortunately—on the drawing boards.

Shortages of raw material and an increasingly dysfunctional war production organization restricted A7V production to fewer than three dozen. When finally constituted, the embryonic German armored force deployed no more than forty tanks at full strength, and more than half of those were British models salvaged and repaired. Material shortcomings were, however, the least of the problems facing Germany's first tankers. By most accounts the Germans had the best of the first tank-versus-tank encounter at Villiers Bretonneaux on April 24, 1918. British tankers, at least, were impressed, with their commanding general describing the threat as "formidable" and warning that there was no guarantee the Germans would continue to use their tanks in small numbers.

In fact, the German army made no serious use of armor in either the spring offensive or the fighting retreat that began in August and continued until the armistice. In the ten or twelve times tanks appeared under German colors their numbers were too small—usually around five vehicles—to attract more than local attention. The crews, it is worth mentioning, were not the thrown-together body of men often described in British-oriented accounts. They did come from a number of arms and services, but all were volunteers—high-morale soldiers for a high-risk mission: a legacy that would endure. Europe's most highly industrial-ized nation nevertheless fought for its survival with the least effective mechanized war instruments of the major combatants.

In public Erich Ludendorff loftily declared that the German high command had decided not to fight a "war of material." His memoirs are more self-critical: "Perhaps I should have put on more pressure: perhaps then we would have had a few more tanks for the decisive battles of 1918. But I don't know what other necessary war material we should have had to cut short." For any weapon, however, a doctrine is at least as impor-tant as numbers. In contrast to both the British and the French, the German army demonstrated neither institutional nor individual capac-ity for thinking about mechanized war beyond the most immediate, elementary contexts.

II

THE SAME POINT can be made about the Second Reich's general approach to mobile warfare. The existence of a specific "German way of war" remains a subject for debate. Robert M. Citino, the concept's foremost advocate, describes its genesis in a Prussian state located in the center of Europe, ringed by potential enemies, lacking both natu-ral boundaries and natural resources. Unable to fight and win a long war, Prussia had to develop a way to fight front-loaded conflicts: short, intense, and ending with a battlefield victory leaving the enemy sufficiently weakened and intimidated to forgo a second round.

The Western world has developed three intellectual approaches to war. The first is the scientific approach. The scientists interpret war as subject to abstract laws and principles. Systematically studied and properly applied, these principles enable anticipating the consequences of decisions, behaviors, even attitudes. The Soviet Union offers the best example of a military system built around the scientific approach. Marxism-Leninism, the USSR's legitimating ideology, was a science. The Soviet state and Soviet society was organized on scientific principles. War making was also a science. The application of its objective principles by trained and skilled engineers was the best predictor of victory.

The second approach to war is the managerial approach. Managers understand war in terms of organization and administration. Military effectiveness depends on the rational mobilization and application of human and material resources. Battle does not exactly take care of itself, but its uncertainties are best addressed in managerial contexts. The United States has been the most distinguished and successful exemplar of managerial war. In part, this reflects the country's underlying pragmatism: an ethic of getting on with the job. It also reflects a historical geography that, since the Revolution, has impelled America to export its conflicts—in turn making administration a sine qua non. As demonstrated by the disasters suffered by Harmar and St. Clair in the 1790s to the catastrophe of Task Force Smith in 1950 Korea, without effective management, successful fighting has been impossible.

The Germans developed a third approach: understanding war as an art form. Though requiring basic craft skills, war defied reduction to rules and principles. Its mastery demanded study and reflection, but depended ultimately on two virtually untranslatable concepts: Fingerspitzengefühl and Tuchfühling. The closest English equivalent is the more sterile phrase: "Situational awareness." The German concept incorporates as well the sense of panache: the difference, in horsemen's language, between a hunter and a hack, or in contemporary terms, the difference between a family sedan and a muscle car.

Prussia's situation did not merely generate but required the tactical orientation of its mentality. This is in direct contrast to the United States, whose fundamental military problems since at least the Mexican War have been on the level of strategy and grand strategy: where to go and how to sustain the effort. The actual fighting has been a secondary concern, which is why so many of America's first battles have been disasters. Prussia, on the other hand, was unlikely to recover from an initial defeat. This was the lesson and the legacy of Frederick the Great. Its reverse side was the sterility of victories won in vacuums: by the end of the Seven Years' War, Prussia was on the point of conquering itself to death.

As a consequence, Prussian theorists, commanders, and policy makers were constrained to develop a second, higher level of warmaking: the operational level. "Operational art" is usually defined in general terms as the handling of large forces in the context of a theater of war. The Germans incorporated a specific mentality emphasizing speed and daring: a war of movement. This involved maneuvering to strike as hard a blow as possible, from a direction as unexpected as possible. It depended on, and in turn fostered, particular institutional characteristics: a flexible command system, high levels of aggressiveness, an officer corps with a common perspective on war making. "We must strive," wrote military theorist Friedrich von Bernhardi in 1912, "to gain a victory as rapidly as possible at the decisive spot by concentration . . . and then take advantage of it with the utmost energy . . ."

As Citino emphasizes, the German way of war had nothing to do with miles per hour—in principle. Practice was another story, especially over the course of the nineteenth century. As industrialization and bureaucratization enabled increasing armies' size, as technology facilitated their concentration in the theater of war, the new German Empire kept pace. In 1914 its armies took the field without a hitch. At the other end of the military spectrum, Germany boasted Europe's best-trained infantry and its most effective artillery. What it lacked was the mobility necessary to complete strategic movements like the great sweep through Belgium, and to develop the tactical victories won on the battlefield.

That limitation was more than a consequence of the dominance of firepower and the undeveloped use of internal-combustion engines. It involved a gap in the German way of war: neglect of operational mobility. Like its counterparts, nineteenth-century Prussian cavalry had been essentially a tactical instrument. In the Wars of Liberation, it had been deployed by regiments and brigades. In the Wars of Unification, 1866 and 1870, larger formations had been only organized on mobilization. Despite demonstrating all the disadvantages of improvisation, this remained unchanged in 1914.

The German cavalry division of 1914 was a potentially effective combined-arms team. Its six regiments, 4,500 troopers, had twelve field pieces and a half dozen mobile machine guns as organic fire support. They depended on horses but were by no means helpless on foot. Regiments were extensively trained in marksmanship and skirmishing. Officers did not ignore the potential of dismounted fire action. The division had its own bridging train, and even a radio detachment. Most divisions either had attached or could call on a battalion or two of Jäger. These elite light infantry formations included a cyclist company, a machine-gun company, and a small motor transport column whose ten trucks could be used to shuttle infantry forward, much like the truck companies attached to US infantry divisions in World War II.

Could firepower and mobility compensate for a lack of endurance? The question was never addressed. Alfred von Schlieffen, author of the great offensive plan implemented in 1914, had insisted on strong cavalry forces on the flanks. Instead, half the cavalry of Germany's active army was directly assigned to infantry divisions. Of the ten cavalry divisions deployed on the Western Front in 1914, five were deployed to cover the advance in such unlikely cavalry country as the Vosges and the Ardennes. One need not assume that German cavalry that was utilized as an early version of the Soviet operational maneuver group would have somehow averted stagnation. The high force-to-space ratios of the Western Front, combined with the overwhelming superiority of firepower over mobility, and protection, would, in all probability, have ended in something approximating the race to the sea and the development of trench warfare no matter what the Kaiser's horsemen did or did not do. What is significant is the cavalry's acceptance of its limitations. Comprehensively rethinking the use of existing organizations to improve flexibility and maximize striking power proved to be beyond the collective imagination of the cavalry as well as the high command.

The German cavalry went to war in 1914 all too conscious of its fragility. Apart from the effects of long-range, rapid-fire weapons, devastatingly demonstrated in the Wars of Unification, the cavalry's self-image was of a specialized arm, demanding a spectrum of skills that required an extra, third year of service from peacetime conscripts. It was an equal shibboleth in the mounted arm that effective cavalry could not be improvised, and therefore the existing force must be carefully husbanded—not kept in the "bandbox" Lord Raglan proposed for British cavalry during the Crimean War, but in no way expendable like common infantrymen. Between 1871 and 1914, cavalry doctrine focused on reconnaissance and screening. These missions offered a chance to salvage the mythology of the *arme blanche*, albeit on a reduced scale. Charges en masse might be obsolete. German horsemen focused instead on the charge en petite: riding at the enemy in traditional style but at troop and squadron strength.

As early as 1905, automobile engineer Paul Daimler demonstrated a surprisingly advanced prototype armored car at the autumn maneuvers. It was dismissed as lacking practical utility. A couple of improvised armored trucks were attached to each cavalry division and used for fire support. Equally improvised detachments of machine-gun crews and riflemen in commandeered civilian cars did useful service occupying bridges and road junctions in advance of the horsemen. In 1915 the General Staff developed specifications for a purpose-built armored car. The resulting models carried two or three machine guns and were well armored for the time. One later model even had a radio. The cars also possessed rear steering positions, enabling them to reverse out of tight spots. That last was a useful quality, given the bulky shapes and high weights that rendered them visible on roads and limited their cross-country mobility to a point near zero.

In the war's first year, both fronts saw their share of what an earlier generation of horse soldiers called "hussar tricks" of low-level derring-do. In Poland, cavalry played an important role in the breakout from Lodz in November 1914 and division-strength raids periodically disrupted Russian communications and Russian equilibrium. The limited Russian road network, however, inhibited the use of the cavalry beyond the hit-and-run level. German generals also increasingly used their mounted troops to plug gaps in what was never a continuous front. Men and mounts alike were worn down for marginal advantages. In the West, beginning in 1915, the Germans cold-bloodedly reorganized their cavalry divisions as semi-mobile infantry or dismounted them altogether.

The fledgling air arm benefited disproportionately from these policies. The future Red Baron, Manfred von Richthofen, was not the only disgruntled troop officer who grumbled that he "had not gone to war to collect cheese and eggs," and took to the skies instead. But when the German army mounted its final great offensive in March–April 1918, the limits of its infantry-artillery base grew increasingly obvious. The Germans could not develop their initial advantage in the war's decisive theater. They could break into Allied defenses, and they could break through them. They could not break out.

In one sense Ludendorff's often-derided concept of "punch a hole and see what develops" resembles Erich von Falkenhayn's concept for the 1916 attack on Verdun. Both were ultimately focused on the level of policy: Do so much damage that France in one case, and the Allies in the other, would be impelled to negotiate. When the coalition withstood the shock at policy levels, translating tactical victory to the operational level became decisive. It was not only that Germany lacked the force structure to make even a token effort. From Ludendorff down, no one with serious authority had a paradigm, a template, for making that transition. The oft-cited absence of a decisive operational/strategic focus for the offensive reflected two years of learning how to wipe out Allied gains by devastatingly successful local counterattacks whose decisive points were usually obvious. The vaunted storm troopers eventually first exhausted their bag of tactical tricks, and then exhausted themselves. The specially prepared "attack divisions" were bled white as Allied railroads and trucks reinforced critical sectors before the Germans could advance through them on foot. The result was stalemate, leading to exactly the kind of drawn-out fighting retreat that German planners and thinkers had predicted meant catastrophe, and then to final visions of an apocalyptic last stand in the Reich itself.

There were exceptions. Small detachments of armored cars served in Russia and Romania. One AFV (amored fighting vehicle, the general name and abbreviation for any form of battlefield armor) even found its way to Palestine, where it engaged in a brief firefight with two of its British counterparts before being abandoned by its crew. An improvised "assault group" formed around an infantry battalion that was riding requisitioned supply trucks bounced Romania's Iron Gates in 1916 and held off a division until relieved. A cyclist brigade played a key part in the rapid overrunning of Russia's Baltic Islands in 1917. The postwar Freikorps that fought in the Baltic used armored cars as assault vehicles against the Bolsheviks and, on one occasion, combined them with a truck-mounted rifle battalion in a counterattack. It was, however, General Hans von Seeckt who moved the German army from Sitz to Blitz.

III

AN ARISTOCRAT AND a Prussian Guardsman, General Hans von Seeckt fit none of the stereotypes associated with either. Educated at a civilian Gymnasium rather than a cadet school, he had traveled widely in Europe, visited India and Egypt, and was well read in contemporary English literature. During the war he had established a reputation as one of the army's most brilliant staff officers. Having made most of that reputation on the Eastern Front, he was untarnished by the collapse of the Western Front, and a logical successor to national hero Paul von Hindenburg as Chief of the General Staff in the summer of 1918. In March 1920 he became head of the army high command in the newly established Weimar Republic.

Seeckt disliked slogans; he disliked nostalgia; he rejected the argument, widespread among veterans, that the "front experience," with its emphasis on egalitarian comradeship and heroic vitalism that was celebrated by author-veterans like Ernst Jünger and Kurt Hesse, should shape the emerging Reichswehr. Instead he called for a return to the principle of pursuing quick, decisive victories. That in turn meant challenging the concept of mass that had permeated military thinking since the Napoleonic Wars. Mass, Seeckt argued, "becomes immobile. It cannot win victories. It can only crush by sheer weight."

Seeckt's critique in part involved making the best of necessity. The Treaty of Versailles had specified the structure of the Reichswehr in detail: a force of 100,000, with enlisted men committed to twelve years of service and officers to twenty-five. It was forbidden tanks, aircraft, and any artillery above three inches in caliber. As a final presumed nail in the coffin of German aggression, the Reichswehr's organization was fixed at seven infantry and three cavalry divisions: a throwback to the days of Frederick the Great. Whatever might have been the theoretical hopes that the newly configured Reichswehr would be the first step in general European disarmament—when, presumably, the extra cavalry would give tone to holiday parades—Germany's actual military position in the west was hopeless in any conventional context. In the East, against Poland and Czechoslovakia, some prospects existed of at least buying time for the diplomats to seek a miracle. Seeckt's Reichswehr, however, faced at least a double, arguably a triple, bind. It could not afford to challenge the Versailles Treaty openly. It badly needed force multipliers. But to seek those multipliers by supporting clandestine paramilitary organizations depending on politicized zeal was to risk destabilizing a state that, though unsatisfactory in principle, was Germany's best chance to avoid collapsing into permanent civil war.

Seeckt's response was to develop an army capable of "fighting outnumbered and winning." Among the most common misinterpretations of his work is that it was intended to provide cadres for a future national mobilization. Almost from the beginning the Reichswehr developed plans for eventual expansion. These plans, however, were based on enlarging and enhancing the existing force, not submerging it in an army prepared to fight the Great War over again. The manuals issued

in the early 1920s, in particular the 1921 field service regulations titled
Fuehrung und Gefecht der Verbundeten Waffen (Leadership and Employment of Combined Arms) emphasized the importance of the offensive.
The Reichswehr, Seeckt insisted, must dictate the conditions of battle
by taking the initiative. It was on the offensive that the superiority of
troops and commanders achieved the greatest relative effect. The leader's
responsibility was above all to maintain pace and tempo. He must make
decisions with minimal information. Boldness was his first rule; flexibility his second. Doctrine and training alike emphasized encounter battles:
two forces meeting unexpectedly and engaging in what amounted to a
melee—a melee in which training and flexibility had a chance to compensate for numerical and material inferiority. Even large-scale attacks
were envisaged as a series of local combats involving companies, squads
and platoons finding weak spots, creating opportunities, cooperating ad
hoc to exploit success.

General-audience writings like Friedrich von Taysen's 1921 essay
on mobile war also stressed what was rapidly becoming a new—or
rediscovered—orthodoxy. Machines, Taysen declared, were useless
unless animated by human energy and will, when they could contribute
to the rapid flanking and enveloping maneuvers that alone promised
decision in war. Two years later he restated the importance of fighting spirit and warned against allowing infantry to become addicted to
armor support.

Taysen's soaring perorations on "Germanic limitlessness" and "living
will" were a far cry from Seeckt's practical approach. They nevertheless
shared a common subtext: the centrality of mobility in both the figura-
tive and the literal senses. The Reichswehr had to be able to think faster
and move faster than its enemies at every stage and in every phase. Paradoxically, the banning of cutting-edge technology facilitated cultivating those qualities by removing the temptations of materially focused
faddism. Elsewhere in Europe, J. F. C. Fuller and B. H. Liddell-Hart
depicted fully mechanized armies with no more regard for terrain than
warships had for the oceans they traversed. Giulio Douhet and Hugh
Trenchard predicted future wars decided by fleets of bombers. French
generals prepared for the "managed battle" structured by firepower and

controlled by radio. The Red Army shifted from an initial emphasis on proletarian morale to a focus on synergy between mechanization and mass as ideologically appropriate for a revolutionary state.

In sober reality, not until the end of the 1920s would the technology of the internal combustion engine develop the qualities of speed and reliability beyond the embryonic stages that restricted armored vehicles to a supporting role. Aircraft as well were limited in their direct, sustained contributions to a ground offensive. Wire-and-strut, fabric-covered planes with fragile engines, even the specialized ground-attack versions developed by the Germans, were terribly vulnerable to even random ground fire. Artillery, despite the sophisticated fire-control methods of 1918, was a weapon of mass destruction. In that context the Reichswehr cultivated its garden, emphasizing human skills—a pattern facilitated because much of the process of maintaining effectiveness involved preventing long-service personnel from stagnating as a consequence of too many years spent doing the same things in the same places with the same people.

The cavalry in particular emerged from its wartime shell. The treaty-prescribed order of battle gave it an enhanced role faute de mieux. The mounted arm was forced to take itself seriously in the tasks of securing German frontiers and preserving German sovereignty. Further incentive was provided by tables of organization, internal organizations that authorized one cavalry officer for two of his infantry counterparts. There were fewer opportunities to withdraw into nostalgic isolation—everyone had to pull his professional weight. As early as spring 1919, a series of articles in *Militär-Wochenblatt*, the army's leading professional journal, dealt with the army's projected reconstruction and included two articles on cavalry. Maximilian von Poseck, the arm's Inspector-General, argued that in the east, large mounted units had been effective for both reconnaissance and combat, and mobile war was likely to be more typical of future conflict than the high-tech stalemate of the Western Front.

The Reichswehr's cavalry cannot be described as taking an enthusiastic lead in Germany's military mechanization. Its regimental officers initially included a high percentage of men who had spent their active service in staffs or on dismounted service, and who were now anxious to get back to "real cavalry soldiering." In the early 1920s Seeckt consistently and scathingly criticized the mounted arm's tactical sluggishness, its poor horsemanship, and its inaccurate shooting, both dismounted and on horseback. Too much training was devoted to riding in formation—a skill worse than useless in the field, where dispersion was required. Horses did not immediately become "battle taxis." Lances were not abolished until 1927—a year earlier, let it be noted, than in Britain. Neither, however, did the cavalry drag its collective feet, or pursue horse-powered dead ends with the energy of their European and American counterparts. After 1928, through judicious juggling of internal resources, each Reichswehr cavalry regiment included a "Special Equipment Squadron" with eight heavy machine guns and, eventually, two light mortars and two light cannon—a significant buildup of firepower, achieved without doing more than slightly bending treaty requirements.

The cavalry also benefited from the absence of institutional rivals. There was no air force to attract forward thinkers and free spirits. Germany had no tank corps, no embryonic armored force, to challenge the horse soldiers' position and encourage the narrow branch-of-service loyalties that absorbed so much energy on the mechanization question in France, Britain, and the United States. Instead, German cavalrymen were likely to find motor vehicles appealing precisely because they were deprived of them.

German and German-language military literature of the 1920s projected the development of a genuine combined arms formation. While details varied, the core would be three horse-mounted brigades—a total of six regiments, each with a machine-gun squadron. These would cooperate with an infantry battalion carried in trucks, a cyclist battalion, and an independent machine-gun battalion, also motorized. Fire support would be provided by a battalion each of horse-drawn and motorized artillery. With a detachment of around a dozen armored cars, a twelve-plane observation squadron, an antiaircraft battalion, an engineer battalion, and signal, medical, and supply services, this theoretical formation combined mobility, firepower, and sustainability to a greater degree than any of its forerunners or counterparts anywhere in Europe.

In the delaying missions that were generally recognized as probable in a future war's initial stages, the division could keep an enemy off balance by its flexibility, with its brigades controlling combinations of other units in the pattern of the combat commands of a US armored division in World War II. Offensively the division could operate independently on an enemy's flank, and behind the kind of rigid front line projected throughout Europe by French-influenced doctrines, disrupting movement by hit-and-run strikes or, in more favorable circumstances, developing and exploiting opportunities for deeper penetration.

Though their concepts could be tested temporarily in maneuvers, these divisions were impossible to create under the original provisions of Versailles. The initial direct impulses for motorization and mechanization instead came from a source no one would have been likely to predict. The Versailles Treaty allocated each infantry division a Kraftfahrabteilung, or motor battalion. As this organization developed it was not the orthodox supply formation most probably envisaged by the Allied officials who structured the Reichswehr, but rather a general pool of motor transport. The hundred-odd men of a motor company had access to two dozen heavy trucks and eleven smaller ones, six passenger cars, four buses, seventeen motorcycles, and two tractors. Treaty interpretation even allowed each battalion a complement of five wheeled armored personnel carriers. These *Gepanzerter Mannschaftstransportwagen* resembled those used by the civil police, without the twin machine-gun turrets, and could carry a rifle squad apiece. With that kind of vehicle pool on call, it was a small wonder that as early as 1924, units conducted on their own small-scale experiments with organizing motorcycle formations, and provided dummy tanks for maneuvers. The motor battalions were also responsible for the Reichswehr's antitank training—a logical assignment since they controlled the only vehicles able to provide hands-on instruction.

The motor transport battalions' practical support for operational motorization was not necessarily a straw in the Reichswehr's institutional wind. A front-loaded, offensively minded Prussian/German army had traditionally regarded logistics as unworthy of a real soldier's attention. Under the Kaiser, train battalions had been a dumping ground and a dead end for the dipsomaniac, the scandal-ridden, the lazy, and the plain stupid—the last stage before court-martial or dismissal.

That heritage probably had something to do with the assignment in 1922 of one Lieutenant Heinz Guderian to a staff post in the 7th Kraftfahrabteilung in Munich. Guderian had a good enough war record as a signals and intelligence officer to be assigned as the army's official representative to the Iron Division in the Baltic. But instead of strengthening General Staff control of that unruly formation, he supported its de facto mutiny in the fall of 1919. Initially transferred to command an infantry company, a punitive measure common for General Staff officers with blotted copybooks, Guderian's superiors described his new assignment as a positive career move that would improve his professional breadth. Guderian saw it as a further demotion. But given the highly limited opportunities for ex-lieutenants in the civilian economy of 1919 Germany, Guderian finally decided to report to the 7th after all.

His commanding officer was Lieutenant Colonel Oswald Lutz. Lutz had begun his career in the railway troops, then, during the war, shifted to motor transport, eventually becoming its chief for the 6th Army. An enthusiastic supporter of tank development, Lutz had also considered wider aspects of motorization. Serving in the postwar Truppenamt—successor to the forbidden General Staff—in the Weapons Office and then the Inspectorate of Motor Troops, he spearheaded a reconceptualization of the Reichswehr's approach to the use of motor vehicles in general and tanks in particular. He insisted on expanding the initial emphasis on technology to include the study of tactics. Lutz also pestered civilian designers to develop prototype specialized vehicles, the artillery tractors and the half-tracks, with front wheels for steering and caterpillar tracks in the rear for cross-country mobility, that some of his officers were considering as complements to specialized fighting vehicles.

Again, this process was facilitated by circumstances. Guderian's story of the senior officer who told him trucks were there to haul flour ("Mehl sollt ihr fahren!") is almost certainly apocryphal. As the Reichswehr settled into its peacetime stations its vehicles were, however, likely to be underemployed. During the war, shortages of gasoline and rubber had increasingly restricted the use of trucks even for basic supply purposes. A century earlier, advocates of railroads had depicted a Germany made invulnerable by troops shuttled behind steam engines. Now a new potential form of strategic/operational mobility was attracting notice. The Reich's steadily improving road system had even the state railway service investing in buses to supplement its locomotives. Even conservative officers saw the prospects—and career advantages—of eventually establishing a transport force that could quickly shift regiments, perhaps even divisions, to threatened sectors and regions.

In the winter of 1923–24, Reichswehr maneuvers incorporated cooperation between motorized ground troops and simulated air forces. In 1925, the 1st Division in East Prussia included armored cars, motorized artillery, and dummy tanks in its maneuver orders of battle. Such exercises highlighted the Reichswehr's limited achievements in motorization. They also offered opportunities to consider problems as they arose—and foreign observers noted the Germans seemed well able to correct mistakes involving motor vehicles. In 1924, the motor troops were made responsible for monitoring developments in tank war and preparing appropriate training manuals.

Motorization received a further institutional boost when, in 1926, Colonel Alfred von Vollard-Bockelberg took over as branch Inspector General. He expanded and transformed the branch officers' course from a focus on technical details of maintenance to a program incorporating, and then emphasizing, tactical studies. It would eventually become the Armored Forces School. In 1929, an improvised motorized "reconnaissance and security battalion," drawn primarily from the 6th Motor Battalion, took the field for maneuvers. In 1930, the 3rd Motor Battalion was completely reorganized as a fighting formation, including mock-up tanks and antitank guns as well as the more orthodox mix of trucks, cars, and motorcycles. By then a new armored personnel carrier was coming on line, based on a four-wheel civilian truck, with a cupola-mounted machine gun enabling it to double as an armored car. And Bockelberg gave the branch a new name. Henceforth it was titled Motorized Combat Troops.

IV

IN JANUARY 1918, as part of the preparation for the great offensive, Ludendorff's headquarters issued the *Guide for the Employment of Armored Vehicle Assault Units*. It described their main mission as supporting the infantry by destroying obstacles, neutralizing fire bases and machine-gun positions, and defeating counterattacks. Because tanks by themselves could not hold ground, the document emphasized the closest possible cooperation with infantry. Tank crews were expected to participate directly in the fighting, either by dismounting and acting as assault troops, or by setting up machine-gun positions to help consolidate gains. In fact the tanks and infantry had, for practical purposes, no opportunity to train together—a problem exacerbated by the continued assignment of tank units to the motor transport service. In action, the tanks' tendency to seek open ground and easy going clashed fundamentally with the infantry's doctrine of seeking vulnerable spots. Nothing happened to change the infantry's collective mind that tanks were most effective against inexperienced or demoralized opponents.

The widespread and successful Allied use of tanks in the war's final months made a few believers. In the first months after the armistice, before the Republic's military structure was finally determined, critics suggested the German army had seriously underestimated the tanks' value. After Versailles made the question moot in practical terms, theoretical interest continued.

Much of this was conventional, repeating wartime arguments that tanks were most effective in creating confusion and panic, in the pattern of antiquity's war elephants. Positive theory on the use of tanks closely followed contemporary French concepts in projecting a first wave of heavy tanks acting more or less independently, followed by a second wave of lighter vehicles maintaining close contact with the infantry. But in contrast to the French, who saw tanks as the backbone of an attack, the Reichswehr's infantry training manual of 1921 warned against the infantry laming its offensive spirit by becoming too dependent on armor.

These positions were in good part shaped by the tanks' existing technical limitations. In particular they were considered too slow and too unreliable to play a central role in the fast-paced offensive operations central to Reichswehr tactics. At the same time, German military thinkers and writers, Seeckt included, recognized that even with their current shortcomings, tanks had a future. The trailblazer here was Ernst Volckheim. He had been a tank officer during the war, and afterward returned to his parent branch. In 1923 he was assigned to the Reichswehr's Inspectorate for Motor Troops. That same year he published an operational history of German tanks, affirming armor's continuing technological development and its corresponding importance in any future war. "If tanks were not such a promising weapon," Volckheim dryly asserted, "then certainly the Allies would not have banned them from the Reichswehr!"

Above all, Volckheim argued, tanks were general-service systems, able to engage any objective and move in many different formations. In that way, they resembled the infantry more than any other branch of service. The tanks' future correspondingly seemed to lie with emphasizing their basic characteristics: speed, reliability, and range. In contrast to a general European predilection for light tanks that focused on improving their mobility, Volckheim saw the future as belonging to a medium-weight vehicle built around its gun rather than its engine. In a future war where both sides had tanks, speed might provide some initial tactical opportunities. The tank with the heaviest gun would nevertheless have the ultimate advantage.

The next year Volckheim published two more books on tank war. One repeated his insistence that tanks would develop to the point where infantry would be assigned to support them—a hint of the rise of the panzer grenadier that was near-heresy in an army focused on infantry as the dominant combat arm. Volckheim's second book went even further, projecting the future main battle tank by asserting that technology would eventually produce a family of armored vehicles specially designed for particular purposes. Equipped with radios, exponentially faster, better armed, and with more cross-country ability than anything even on today's drawing boards, they would in fact be able to operate

independently of the traditional arms—an echo of the theories of
Volckheim's British contemporary, J. F. C. Fuller. He admired as well
the designs of American J. Walter Christie, which could be switched
from wheels to tracks as needed.

Volckheim was also an officer for the working day. First detached
to the Weapons Testing School at Doeberitz, in 1925 he was promoted
to First Lieutenant and assigned to teach tank and motorized tactics
at the infantry school at Dresden. From 1923 to 1927 he also published
two dozen signed articles in the Militär-Wochenblatt, the army's
long-standing semiofficial professional journal. Most of them dealt
with tactics of direct infantry support by setting problems and presenting solutions. An interesting subtext of these pieces is the scale of armor
Volckheim's scenarios usually presented: an armor regiment to a division, a battalion supporting a regiment.

Volckheim also addresses the subject of antitank defense—a logical response to the Reichswehr's force structure—and some of the best
were published in pamphlet form. Volckheim recommended camouflage, concealment, and aggressive action on the part of the infantry,
combined with the forward positioning of field guns and light mortars
to cover the most likely routes of advance. Unusual for the time, Volckheim also recommended keeping tanks in reserve, not merely to spearhead counterattacks but to directly engage enemy armor as a primary
mission.

Volckheim, with the cooperation of *Militär-Wochenblatt's* progres-
sive editor, retired general Konstantin von Altrock, made armored warfare an acceptable, almost fashionable, subject of study in the mid-1920s
Reichswehr. Initially most of the material published in *MW* translated or
summarized foreign work. By 1926 most of the articles were by German
officers, both from the combat arms and—prophetically—from the
horse transport service as well. Fritz Heigl's survey of world developments, *Taschenbuch der Tanks* (Tank Pocketbook), whose first edition
appeared in 1926, was widely circulated. Its successors remain staples of
chain bookstore and internet marketing.

The Reichswehr's Truppenamt, often described simply as the successor to the treaty-banned General Staff, was actually formed from

its predecessor's Operations Section. Reorganized into four bureaus—operations, organization, intelligence, and training—and more streamlined than its predecessor, the Truppenamt shed responsibility for the kind of detailed administrative planning that had increasingly dominated the prewar General Staff. That was just as well, for while the methods might be transferable, the fundamental reconfiguration of Germany's security profile demanded fresh approaches.

On the specific subject of armored warfare, the intelligence section monitored foreign developments in tactics and technology systematically enough to issue regular compilations of that material beginning in 1925. German observers took careful notes on postwar French experiences with combining horses and motor vehicles, new material such as half-tracks, and patterns of armor-infantry cooperation. They noted as well the British maneuvers of 1923 and 1924, observing in particular the appearance of the new Vickers Medium, whose turret-mounted 47mm gun, good cross-country mobility, and sustainable speed of around 20 miles per hour made it the prototypical modern tank. English was the fashionable foreign language in the Reichswehr, and Britain was an easier objective for short-term visits. And German officers regularly visited a United States whose army was more willing than any European power to show what they had. In objective terms that was not very much, and most of it existed as prototypes and test models. But the German army offered three months of subsidized leave as an incentive to improve language proficiency, and America offered attractive possibilities for travel and culture shock.

In 1924 Seeckt ordered each unit and garrison to designate an officer responsible for acting as an advisor on tank matters, conducting classes and courses on armored warfare, and distributing instructional materials. These included copies of Volckheim's articles, Heigl's data on foreign tanks, and similar material issued by the Inspectorate of Motor Troops. The armor officer had another duty as well: to serve as commander of dummy tank units in the field. Seeckt ordered that representations of state-of-the-art weapons, especially tanks and aircraft, be integrated into training and maneuvers. Tanks in particular must be represented as often as possible in exercises and maneuvers, to enable practicing both antitank defense and tank-infantry cooperation in attacks. Troops were to practice both tactical motor movement and firing from the treaty-sanctioned troop transports. Reports from the annual maneuvers were to include "lessons learned" from operating with mock armored vehicles.

By the mid 1920s the Truppenamt was moving doctrinally beyond the concept of tanks as primarily infantry-support weapons and organizationally by considering their use in regimental strength. In November 1926, Wilhelm Heye, who the previous month had succeeded Seeckt as Chief of the Army Command, issued a memo on modern tanks. Heye wore an upturned mustache in the style of Wilhelm II, but that was his principal concession to Germany's military past. Like Seeckt, he had spent a large part of the Great War as a staff officer on the Eastern Front. In 1919 he had been in charge of frontier security in East Prussia, and from 1923 to 1926 commanded the 1st Division in that now-isolated province. Heye argued that technical developments improving tanks' speed and range had repeatedly shown in foreign maneuvers, especially the British, the developing potential of mechanization. Operating alone or in combined-arms formations, tanks were not only becoming capable of extended operations against flanks and rear, but of bringing decisive weight to the decisive point of battle, the Schwerpunkt.

During the same year, Major Friedrich Rabenau prepared a detailed internal memorandum for the Operations Section. Rabenau was an established critic of the heroic vitalist approach to modern war and its emphasis on moral factors such as "character." He went so far as to argue that future armies would depend heavily on a technically educated middle class and technically skilled workers. Now he synthesized developments in mobility with the concepts of the Schlieffen Plan. Schlieffen's grand design, Rabenau argued, had failed less because of staff and command lapses than because its execution was beyond the physical capacities of men and animals. Comprehensive motorization would enable initial surprise, continuing envelopment, and a finishing blow on the enemy's flanks and rear. Rabenau's ideas, widely shared in the Operations Section, percolated upwards. A directive in late 1926 asserted that not only could tanks be separated from foot-marching infantry, they could best be used in combination with other mobile troops—or independently. In 1927, section chief General Werner von Fritsch went on record to declare that tanks, in units as large as the British brigades, would exercise a significant influence at operational as well as tactical levels.

V

HEINZ GUDERIAN EVENTUALLY did such a good job overstating his role in the development of Reichswehr thinking on armor that those who correct his exaggerations run a certain risk of going too far in the opposite direction. Guderian's fondness for the first person singular should not obscure his early investigations of armored vehicles' possibilities— or his early addressing of those possibilities in the context of Germany's defeat in the Great War. He developed—or perhaps more accurately enhanced—a reputation for clarity and forcefulness, recommending for example that instead of the currently popular hybrids, cavalry divisions should be entirely mechanized. In 1924 his exile ended when he was transferred to the staff of an infantry division as an instructor in military history and tactics.

Guderian's approach was unusual even in a German army more open than most to learning from negative experiences. His classes focused on defeat—specifically, defeat caused by failure to innovate. Guderian ascribed that as much to intellectual rigidity as to technical indifference. He argued, for example, that "shock power" was considered prior to 1914 to depend on infantry attacks with cold steel. During the Great War it came to depend on artillery fire. That was still the case in France. But the guns moved too slowly and took too long. Shock was force multiplied by impulsion; both elements were important. Victory required bringing fire against the enemy quickly, through maneuver. And that, Guderian increasingly asserted, meant mechanization—specifically, fast-moving, gun-armed tanks.

As a teacher Guderian was an acquired taste whose allusive approach and sardonic sense of humor alienated as well as inspired. But he was a dynamic lecturer who took advantage of the opportunity to read widely in German and foreign literature on armor's current developments and future prospects. The division commander, himself interested in motorization's prospects, had worked with Guderian in the past and was willing to give him his head. In 1927, freshly promoted to major, he was assigned to the Truppenamt's Operations Section, in principle to study the development of motor transportation for infantry. That same year, Fritsch was replaced as section head by General Werner von Blomberg, whose interest in motorization ranged from replacing the infantry's bicycles with motorcycles to preparing training schedules for theoretical tank regiments.

It was scarcely surprising that the Operations Section focused obsessively on the British maneuvers held that summer. These exercises centered on an Experimental Mechanized Force built around armored cars and medium and light tanks, and including a temporarily motorized machine-gun battalion, a field artillery battalion, a battery of light infantry guns, and an engineer company, all truck-transported. The section reported extensively on the maneuvers themselves and provided translations and summaries of the major journalistic commentaries, especially those by Fuller and Liddell-Hart. The statement of British Chief of Imperial General Staff Sir George Milne that future armored forces would be able to strike up to three hundred miles into an enemy's territory struck particular chords. Guderian credits the post-maneuver *Provisional Instructions for Tank and Armored Car Training* with providing the theoretical basis for a developing German armor doctrine. The work was summarized, and then translated—no great feat of intelligence, since it was available on the open market.

Even—or better said, especially—in the Reichswehr, theory required testing. Banning weapons and limiting numbers enhanced the risks of abstraction, postulating developments and concepts beyond the attainable and the sustainable. New models of dummy tanks appeared on the maneuver grounds. The originals had usually been wooden frames mounted on bicycles or pushed around by a couple of soldiers. By 1928 the firm of Hanomag was delivering motorized mock-ups that could cross terrain at fair speeds. That summer, Vollard-Bockelberg used them in a small-scale exercise reflecting British tactics by deploying the model tanks in three waves: two to break through to the enemy artillery zone and into his rear; the third to support the infantry directly.

By 1930 all the motor battalions conducted similar exercises built around dummy tanks and wooden antitank guns.

In April 1931, Oswald Lutz was appointed Inspector of Motor Troops. He requested as his chief of staff Heinz Guderian, freshly promoted to lieutenant colonel. In 1931–32, the team planned and conducted a series of upscale exercises involving entire battalions of dummy tanks with supporting infantry and artillery. For Lutz the "supporting" adjective was central. Tanks were now the key weapon on the modern battlefield. Infantry, artillery, engineers and aircraft played essentially supporting roles. Tanks therefore should carry out independent missions, as opposed to being tied down to the infantry. Independence in turn required mass; using tanks in anything less than battalion strength diluted their shock effect and rendered them disproportionately vulnerable to antitank defenses. Finally, Lutz insisted on surprise as a critical force multiplier. Surprise involved more than the timing if an initial attack. Tanks should advance in echelons and on a broad front, constantly shifting the focus of their movements in order to confuse the defender. But Lutz was no advocate of the all-armor approach; instead, he stressed the importance of cooperation. In particular the infantry must closely follow the tanks to exploit the initial shock of armor, and trust to the tanks for fire support instead of looking to the rear for artillery or waiting for their own heavy weapons.

On the technical side the development of armored vehicles had continued after the armistice. Initially this focused on wheeled vehicles for internal security purposes. The design capacity to do more remained. The question from the military perspective was how best to work with industry to enhance that capacity and develop state-of-the-art designs without flagrantly violating the terms of Versailles. By the mid-1920s the solution had been worked out, less on paper than by winks, nudges, and gentlemen's agreements. The Truppenamt would prepare specifications.

Interested companies would produce designs and prototypes for study and testing. That process would continue until it somehow became feasible to begin production openly.

The first concept of the Weapons Office in 1925 was cutting-edge: a 16-ton vehicle with a top speed of 25 miles per hour, 14mm of armor overall, and a turret-mounted short 75mm gun. Three firms—Krupp, Rheinmetall, and Daimler-Benz—responded, two with a long history of arms production, the third specializing in motor vehicles. None gave the project high priority; all found it more difficult than expected to transform sketches and figures into a functioning weapons system. The half dozen prototypes available by 1929 were most useful as showcases for developments in automotive technology, engines, and suspension systems, than as practical field designs. Though it took only half the time to develop and present their prototypes, the same could be said for the Truppenamt's second proposal, submitted in 1928. This was a light tank, seven and a half tons, carrying a turret-mounted 37mm high-velocity gun, slightly faster and carrying a bit less armor than its larger stablemate. As a fig-leaf concession to Versailles, the designs were given the subtle cover names of "large tractors" and "small tractors."

If the Reichswehr's theories of armored war owed heavy debt to Britain, its tank designs channeled France in their armament and in the concept behind the paired designs. The heavier vehicles would directly support and cooperate with infantry. The lighter ones would lead attacks and act as tank destroyers. The French reversed the order, but the thinking was similar.

The Reichswehr pursued other avenues as well. With great reluctance, Lutz abandoned his hopes for a Christie-type wheel/track tank as attention shifted to developing armored cars. During and after the war, German designs were characterized by heavy armor and armament but correspondingly poor off-road capacity. In 1927, the Inspectorate of Motor Troops submitted contracts for prototypes—this time to three firms with histories of successful heavy-truck design: Daimler, Buessing, and Magirus. Since the beginnings of industrialized war in the nineteenth century, the Prussian/German army had been reluctant to rely on single suppliers. The results here justified the multiple tenders, providing the technical basis for the eight-wheeled armored cars that would guide and lead the panzers across most of Europe a decade later.

Taking the test models to the field posed a different set of problems. After the war, Germany sold the design of its projected light tank to Sweden, and one of its designers also relocated. The vehicle went into service in a modified form in 1921, and gave enough satisfaction that the Swedish army and government remained open to further cooperation. Economics reinforced technology. In 1920, the major heavy-machinery firm of Landsverk was on the edge of bankruptcy. Working through a Netherlands company, the German company Gutehoffnungshütte Aktenverein purchased half the stock, and by 1925 owned more than 60 percent of it. Landsverk continued to turn out trucks and tractors, and railroad and harbor equipment. It also developed a sideline: producing armored vehicles. German engineers, technicians, and designs played significant roles in the process, and some of the resulting vehicles were eventually exported as far afield as Ireland. Despite regular low-level exchanges of personnel and concepts, however, as far as the Reichswehr was concerned, Sweden's society was too open for much more than the military tourism that in 1929 allowed Guderian, as the guest of a Swedish armor battalion, to actually drive a tank for the first time.

Looking eastward suggested better prospects since, due to the Treaty of Rapallo in 1922, Weimar Germany and Soviet Russia had frequently made common cause, brought together by their shared status as outlaw states. For German soldiers the vast, impenetrable Soviet Union offered opportunities to circumvent Versailles in relative obscurity. Their Russian counterparts saw Germany as a source of technical modernization. Preliminary planning for military cooperation began in 1920, expanded after a secret clause of Rapallo allowed Germans to train in Russia, and culminated in 1939 with an agreement to establish schools for chemical, aircraft, and armor development.

The tank school at Kazan, on the lower Volga, was considered sufficiently important by the German government to pay its expenses, with the Soviets responsible for on-site maintenance. From its beginnings in 1927, however, the school suffered from conflicting expectations. Stalin hoped to use German expertise to develop the USSR's tank and tractor industries. The Germans were at best conflicted about facilitating the creation of a high-tech army in a Bolshevik state. The tank models the Reichswehr had promised remained stuck on the drawing boards. Germany's political opposition, especially the Social Democrats, consistently probed and challenged the Soviet connection. The Soviets, suspicious in principle of any capitalist state, found it difficult to believe the technical and political difficulties could not be resolved by making a few judicious examples. When they showed how that could be done in the Shakhty Trials of engineers accused of "wrecking" the Soviet economy, the German government temporarily drew back in the face of what it regarded as a provocation.

At the Reichswehr's urging, the project was resumed. Things went slightly better on the ground, even though the Russian share of the enterprise was under not the Ministry of Defense, as might be expected, but the NKVD, the police force of the Soviet Union. Actual training did not begin until 1929. Soviet ideologues and Russian patriots argued that a revolutionary republic had little to learn from foreign aristocrats. German professionals tended to dismiss the Russians as retrograde. Most of the training was done on the models and variants of "tractors" shipped by twos and threes into the USSR. The Russians did provide thirty of their own tanks, and when the British allowed arms sales to the USSR, some of their improved mediums were added to a mix large enough for battalion-scale exercises. The Russians, in the process of developing their own armored doctrines, were more concerned with the technical side, pressing for a level of cooperation that would include manufacturing German tanks under German supervision in Soviet factories. That prospect was too ambitious for a Reichswehr reasonably content with a status quo that enabled selected officers to observe Russian maneuvers and inspect Russian tank units, allowed others to take and teach the courses, and not least gave firms actually or potentially involved in armored vehicles design and manufacture to expose engineers and administrators to the Kazan experience. Eventually, fifty-odd officers participated as students and instructors in the Kazan programs. They gave the Reichswehr a core of men with hands-on experience that proved disproportionately valuable in the 1930s.

Kazan's actual curriculum does not seem particularly innovative compared with the soaring visions of the Truppenamt that reflected a continued—arguably a developing—debate over just what came next. As interest in mechanization developed, officers from other branches, or with broader perspectives, diluted the initial intensity. A 1929 article in *MW*, for example, used the 1917 Battle of Cambrai as a springboard to describe modern tanks as having three missions: cooperating with infantry in the initial breakthrough, overrunning enemy artillery before it could react, and then completing an operational breakthrough. The author recommended using as many as five waves of armor, including reserves. A *Guide to Leadership and Battle*, published by a Reichswehr major in 1929, spoke of tanks and other forbidden fruits, aircraft and heavy artillery, as army-level tools to tip the balance at the decisive point. Cavalry divisions were described as combinations of horse, cyclist, and motorized elements supported by armored cars and, when necessary, by tanks as well.

A rapidly increasing body of similar literature took a similar position: somewhere in the middle, accepting as a given that tanks would play a major role in future wars but uncertain of exactly how that scenario would develop. The 1929 edition of a standard handbook for officers of all arms, issued by the Training Section, described tanks as having two missions: cooperating with the infantry and operating independently—with the caveat that they should not get too far ahead of the main force. How far was too far? In the final analysis, the Reichswehr simply lacked the practical experience with real tanks to make any reasonable choices. That was about to change—and change massively.

Another kind of change was underway as well. Particularly during the tenure of Kurt von Hammerstein-Equord as chief of the Truppenamt and then of the Army High Command from 1930 to 1934, war games became increasingly theoretical, dispensing with realistic troop levels and postulating artificial political conditions in order to expand the learning experience of the game situation. This abstraction encouraged wider acceptance of the concept that quality, particularly when enhanced by technology, could overcome numbers. The issues of mobility, surprise, and concentration of force that had initially been key to tactical survival became the basis of power projection at the operational level. The Reichswehr in the early 1930s did not withdraw to the airy empire of operational dreams. Hammerstein-Equord insisted on the distinction between "studies" that had to be grounded in reality and war games designed to enhance the vision and capacity of future field commanders. Staff training stressed that victory depended on the offensive, and that the offensive was the product of a mind-set emphasizing surprise, deception, and, above all, courage to take risks against odds.

Such concepts were best nurtured in an environment where the kinds and levels of friction inevitable in maneuvers conducted on large scales with conscript forces did not exercise a sobering impact. In the fall of 1930, the Reichswehr maneuver amounted to a full-fledged mobilization exercise. All ten divisions were included in the scenario, though for the sake of economy most were represented by their staff and intelligence sections. The maneuver nevertheless featured full telephone and radio nets, a postal service, and all the rest of a modern administrative system. It also incorporated simulated tank forces. The maneuver's purpose was to test commanders and senior staffs. The emphasis was on challenging "fog and friction" by speed, maneuverability, and flexibility. The fast pace and complex scenarios resulted in high levels of confusion, duly noted by foreign observers. But the resulting melees in a sense reflected the outcome sought by a developing German doctrine for combat against superior forces: jump down their throats and kick them to death from inside.

The Reichswehr's developing skill in motorized operations at both theoretical and practical levels was further highlighted in the maneuvers of September 1932, held in the area of Frankfurt an der Oder. The respective commanders would be heard from again. Their names were Gerd von Rundstedt and Fedor von Bock. Blue, the defending force under Rundstedt, had two cavalry divisions and only a single infantry division. Bock's Red invaders, intended to represent Poles, included an entire cavalry corps, with cyclists and motorcyclists, motorized artillery, and motorized reconnaissance elements. The combat vehicles and the motorized formations were almost all simulated. Results were mixed, particularly when horses and motor vehicles attempted to cooperate directly. But the speed and scope of the exercises impressed all observers. Some motorized units advanced 300 kilometers in three days—a pace unmatched since the Mongol invasions of the Middle Ages. It would have been difficult to transform the Reichswehr into a defensively oriented force—even had a government with the will and power to do so existed.

The army's prospective mechanization was hardly a closely guarded secret. In a public lecture to a patriotic organization, Defense Minister Wilhelm Groener described a future army with a fully motorized cavalry, a developed system of antitank weapons, and a force of light and medium tanks able to support infantry and operate independently. This was by now a standard boilerplate. But considered in a wider context, it might seem surreal—along with this entire chapter. A German army expressly forbidden the use of aircraft and armored vehicles nevertheless systematically investigates, analyzes, and begins to implement in exercises the techniques of modern war. Instead the present text repeatedly refers to foreign observers taking notes at Reichswehr maneuvers, but does not mention their filing any specific charges of violating the terms of Versailles. Just what was going on?

Weimar Germany was a sovereign state. Its soldiers could not reasonably be prevented from speculating on the nature of the wars they might have to fight. When the issue came up, German spokesmen made a convincing case that the very circumstances of German disarmament required the Reichswehr to be highly cognizant of possible threats it could not match directly. In practical contexts, moreover, the Germans kept well to the treaty's terms. The few dozen imitations and improvisations that took the field for a few days each autumn were hardly fear-inspiring, and were quickly dismantled. The collaboration with the Soviet Union was likewise known to the Allied agencies responsible for enforcing the armistice terms. Their combined contributions to Germany's military system were correctly judged as marginal.

From the perspectives of France and Britain and from the perspective of the League of Nations as well, standing on details was considered counterproductive when compared with the prospects of drawing Weimar Germany into a general program of European disarmament.

In 1927 the Foreign Office successfully negotiated the withdrawal of the Inter-Allied Control Commission, which since 1919 had supervised the nuts and bolts of disarmament. The diplomats saw this as a step toward national security in an international context. The Reichswehr considered it an opportunity to pursue and expand its programs in preparation of a bigger future. In the years that Adolf Hitler was coming to power in Germany, the Reichswehr would establish the foundations for a Wehrmacht that developed into a uniquely formidable instrument of war.

CHAPTER TWO

MATRICES

GERMANY BECAME AN official member of the League of Nations' Preparatory Commission on Disarmament in 1926. The adjective, not the noun, was the key word in that body's title. Its history is a story of gridlock. German policy makers were by no means secretive or cynical. They insisted openly and emphatically that collective security depended on equality of armed forces at mutually acceptable levels. That meant revision of Europe's status quo not necessarily on Germany's terms, but in Germany's favor. Reducing numbers and limiting weapons—particularly the "offensive" weapons like tanks and aircraft, so often excoriated by disarmament advocates—could only improve Germany's relative position.

I

DISARMAMENT OFFERED OTHER prospects. By the mid-1920s the Reichswehr was internationally admired for the quality of its personnel, the level of its training, and not least its high morale. Its numerical weakness limited its operational worth against its neighbors' exponentially stronger conscript forces. Reducing those armies' numbers would highlight the advantages of a professional, long-service force. And it would be the Reichswehr that possessed the advantage of direct experience with such a system.

By the mid-1920s Germany's military helplessness in practical contexts was beyond reasonable denial. In the east, man for man and company for company, the Reichswehr might be exponentially superior to Polish conscripts. But what if the Poles kept coming until the Germans ran out of ammunition? German plans involved creating local volunteer forces as a second line. But the probable survival time of an SA Standarte or a Stahlhelm detachment against a Polish battalion in the open field was measurable in hours—perhaps minutes. In the west, the Ruhr occupation of 1923 and the bloody record of contemporary French imperialism from Syria to Morocco indicated that anything like the civilian-based *Volkskrieg* (People's War) advocated by some enthusiasts might salvage German national honor, but at a price neither politicians nor soldiers were willing to consider.

A Truppenamt war game in the winter of 1928–29 was set in the context of a two-front war with France and Poland—hardly an illogical scenario. Even with allowances for Poland keeping strong forces to watch its Soviet frontier, even by incorporating projected possible augmenting of the Reichswehr's force structure, the most favorable outcomes involved delaying actions fought in a militarily hopeless cause.

The Reichswehr was not "militaristic" in the sense made famous by Alfred Vagts. Its generals were not content to supervise drills, organize parades, and conduct elaborate exercises with simulated armies. The conclusion that increasingly permeated senior Reichswehr leadership was nevertheless simple and startling. Because Germany could not wage war, war must be avoided. As a corollary, revising Versailles by abrogating its disarmament clauses was likely to make Germany's last condition worse than its first. A program of military expansion designed to raise the republic's armed forces to the levels of even Poland or Czechoslovakia was likely to have a general ripple effect: an arms race forcing Germany into a competition it had no chance of winning, a stern chase to nowhere. Even before the onset of the Great Depression, there was no practical chance that Germany's voters would underwrite such a policy in the absence of a tangible, immediate threat.

Substantive concessions on the issue of arms limitation would not have guaranteed European stability. They did offer a window of opportunity for continued, positive German participation in a modified treaty framework. But any serious steps to restoring Germany's military strength in any parameters ran directly counter to France's continued commitment to maintaining its security directly, through its own armed forces and a system of alliances. With economic and diplomatic independence increasingly becoming the new European order, with an increasingly factionalized polity influenced by increasingly strong anti-war sentiments, France was essentially unable to move toward a compromise with Germany on arms control even if the will to do so had existed.

By 1930 even internationally conscious Reichswehr personalities like Groener were growing frustrated by a policy seeming to offer nothing but indefinite postponements. The long-projected plans for expanding the Reichswehr to a 21-division force were made increasingly comprehensive. An initial Aufstellungsplan of April 1931 and a Second Armaments Program in early 1932 provided for assembling essential material: uniforms, personal gear, rifles, and machine guns. By 1933 about two-thirds of the hardware was in place. It was, however, easier to produce equipment than to find men. The Great War veterans as a class were getting long in the tooth for service in the combat arms. The Restructuring Plan of November 1932 offered placebos: integrating police units and volunteer home guard formations, enlisting a few thousand men for three-year terms, encouraging men to volunteer for a few weeks' elementary training. An alternate prospect—and a corresponding challenge—was, however, emerging. And it was here that the army began finding common ground with the emerging National Socialists.

The Nazi Party has been compared by scholars to almost every possible human organization, even medieval feudalism. The one adjective that cannot be applied is "patriarchal." Hitler's public persona was that of leader, elder brother, perhaps even erotic symbol, but never a father. Change—progress—was the movement's flywheel. Nazi nostalgia found its essential expression in domestic kitsch. It had no place in military matters. The Reichswehr and the "Movement"—die Bewegung, as the Nazis preferred to be known—thus had the common ground of

emphasizing a commitment to the future rather than a vision of the
past. Hitler's initially enthusiastic wooing of the soldiers was based on
his intention of using them first to consolidate his hold over both the
Nazi party and the German people, then as the standard-bearers of ter-
ritorial and ideological expansion until they could safely be replaced
by the SS. The Reichswehr for its part also saw the Nazis as means to
an end, albeit the more pedestrian one of increasing the armed forces'
resources.

National Socialist views of war differed in important, arguably
essential respects from those of the Reichswehr. But on such subjects as
anti-Marxism, anti-pacifism, and hostility to the Versailles Treaty, the
military's values were not incongruent with those avowed by Nazi theorists and propagandists. Those positions were also respectable across a
broad spectrum of Weimar politics. Germany wanted normalcy in the
years after 1918, but was unable to achieve it at the price of abandoning the illusions and delusions of the Great War. The gradual turn to
Nazism that began in the late 1920s, represented a "flight forward," an
effort to escape that cognitive dissonance, as much as it reflected a belief
in the Nazis' promises to make things better.

The Reichswehr was not a fascist coup or a right-wing conspiracy
waiting to happen. From its inception, the Reichswehr had regarded
itself not as an independent player but a participant in a common
national enterprise based on rearmament and revision. Refusal to iden-
tify the armed forces directly with the Republic facilitated the transfer
of loyalties from the Empire. It enabled avoidance on one hand of the
problems of a Soviet model of military professionals reduced to technicians while commissars wielded real power and, on the other, of the
risks of saddling Germany with an officer corps of mercenary technocrats. Yet as the gulf between soldiers and politicians widened, as the
Republic's crisis deepened with the depression, few officers saw their
responsibilities to the state in any but the narrowest terms. The results
of the war game of December 1932, with its predictions of domestic
collapse should Nazis and Communists combine against an overextended, outnumbered, and probably outgunned Reichswehr, were presented with a kind of malicious pleasure that reflected more than simple

anti-republican sentiment. It suggested instead a fundamental detachment from a "system" that remained fundamentally alien to an army
with its own independent, comprehensive ties to state and society.

In the early 1930s, Germany was being swept by a wave of popular militarism and quasi-militarism, extending across the political and
cultural spectrum. The Communists' Red Front Fighters' League, the
Social Democratic Reichsbanner, the right-wing Stahlhelm, and above
all the National Socialist SA attracted increasing numbers of young men
who thought they were tough and were willing to prove it. Beer mugs,
lead pipes, and an occasional knife were not likely to intimidate external enemies. But however much Reichswehr planners and Reichswehr
officers might dislike the revolutionary premises underpinning these
organizations, the possibilities inherent in bringing storm troopers into
uniform and under army discipline were too enticing to be ignored—
to say nothing of the corresponding risks of leaving them to their own
devices and those of their leaders, including Adolf Hitler.

The Reichswehr understood better than any army in Europe or the
world that total war and industrial war had generated new styles of
combat and new methods of leadership. The officer no longer stood
above his unit but functioned as an integral part of it. The patriarchal/
hegemonial approach of the "old army," with professional officers and
noncommissioned officers (NCOs) parenting youthful conscripts and
initiating them into adult society, was giving way to a collegial/affec-
tive pattern, emphasizing cooperation and consensus in mission performance. "Mass man" was a positive danger in the front lines. What
was necessary was "extraordinary man": the combination of fighter and
technician who understood combat both as a skilled craft and an inner
experience. The street brawlers of 1931–32 were promising raw material
for a new military order. In passing, those would be exactly the qualities
eventually cultivated in the panzertruppen.

Mechanization temporarily receded into the background with the
Nazi seizure of power in March 1933. Or perhaps, better said, it was
subsumed in the metastasizing of German armed forces under the Nazi
New Order. One of Hitler's first acts as Chancellor was to appoint
General Werner von Blomberg as Minister of Defense on January 30,

1933. This reflected a wider bargain—Hitler openly acknowledged the Reichswehr as the leading institution in the state, and promised to initiate a general rearmament program. In return, the Reichswehr relinquished its long-standing responsibility for maintaining domestic order, giving Hitler a de facto free hand in Germany's "restructuring."

The next three or four years were the golden age—at least in public—of what Hitler called the "two pillars" rhetoric: the assertion that the armed forces and the Nazi movement were the twin foundations of a reborn Germany. Internationally, after a few months of smoke and mirrors, Hitler withdrew Germany not only from the Disarmament Conference but from the League of Nations in October 1933. In December he decided to triple Germany's peacetime army to a strength of 300,000. Its 21 divisions would form the eventual basis for a field army of triple that number. The mission of that force was described as conducting a defensive war on several fronts with a good chance of success.

A long-standing critic of Groener's position, Blomberg supported rearmament in a specifically military context. He was correspondingly willing to accept both the internal strains placed on the newly renamed Wehrmacht by forced-draft expansion and the international challenges posed by its precondition: the reintroduction of conscription. Hitler's breaking of the SA's power in June 1934 seemed to offer fundamental proof of the Führer's good faith. By March 1935, when Hitler declared "military sovereignty," the Truppenamt was projecting a peacetime force of 30 to 36 divisions, increasing to 73 on mobilization. By July the newly rechristened General Staff planned for a peacetime establishment of 700,000 by—a strange coincidence—October 1939. By 1936 the army's projected war footing was 3,737,000 men in 103 "divisional units"—a force profile comparing favorably with France's mobilized strength.

The Wehrmacht's plans and projections heralded and structured the takeoff of a growth that rapidly became its own justification and eventually outran both financial resources and production capacity. It also initiated an increasingly fierce competition with a newly created air force and a resurgent navy. In those contexts, theater was everything. And the army was not behindhand in showing off its bag of tricks. Oswald Lutz organized Germany's first tank unit on November 1, 1933. *Kraftfahrlehrkommando Zossen* consisted of a single skeleton company with fourteen "tractors." Another 150 chassis for training drivers were delivered in January 1934. In July, Lutz was appointed head of the new Kommando der Panzertruppen (Armored Forces Command), with Guderian still his chief of staff. By November the original company had been expanded into a two-battalion regiment, with a second created at the training ground of Ohrdruf.

Adolf Hitler might have run for office in good part on the strength of his wartime service as a muddy-boots infantryman. But the Führer also had a predilection for high-tech displays. Hitler's use of airplanes in his later election campaigns was as much for show as for convenience. His speeches approached the level of sound and light shows. And his fondness for muscle cars and fast driving was familiar. In early 1934, accompanied by Hermann Göring, he made what probably began as a routine inspection of new equipment. Guderian instead put on what later generations of soldiers would describe as a dog-and-pony show. For a half hour he showed off a motorcycle platoon, a platoon of the 37mm antitank guns just coming on line, a couple of armored car platoons, and the pièce de résistance: a platoon of the new training tanks. Chassis only, with no turrets, no armament, they nevertheless impressed the Führer. Guderian quotes him as repeatedly exclaiming, "That's what I want! That's what I want to have!"

Did Hitler actually see the military possibilities of these few dozen small vehicles? More likely he was taken by their potential for reinforcing his comprehensive propaganda campaigns, domestic and foreign, in the same context as his admonition to Göring that numbers of planes took precedence over their types and combat value. Certainly he did nothing specific to expand the armored force as such. The High Command and the General Staff took care of that on their own. In 1934, as the original seven Reichswehr divisions began to triple themselves, their motor battalions produced fourteen antitank battalions and seven motorized reconnaissance battalions. The 1st and 2nd Cavalry Divisions

took delivery of several hundred motor vehicles. The 3rd not only traded
in its horses altogether, but came under command of the Inspectorate of
Motorized Combat Troops.

That last was the result of a suggestion made by one of the army's
rising stars. Then-Brigadier General Walther von Reichenau is best
known as one of Hitler's early open sympathizers among the Reichswehr's senior officers. He was also interested in motorization, and as
an artillery specialist was concerned with keeping even an embryonic
armored force from becoming too much a thing in itself. As chief of
the Wehrmachtamt, he was in a position to influence policy. It was the
kind of gesture Lutz welcomed as one of the preliminary steps intended
to produce an armored force of three divisions, plus two or three independent tank brigades, by the end of 1938.

On July 1, 1934, the Inspectorate of Motor Combat troops was reorganized. The Inspectorate for Army Motorization was made responsible
for overall supervision of the process. The Motor Combat Troops Command would control the projected panzer divisions, in effect becoming
a corps-level field command. Lutz assumed command of both agencies;
his ambitious amanuensis Heinz Guderian became Motor Combat
Troops Chief of Staff—a fast-track posting, if the holder could develop
it. Lutz had no doubts.

II

THE PROJECTED GERMAN force structures were hardly unique. France's
horsed cavalry divisions were not very different from the German
models. Contemporary Polish mobilization plans projected mobile or
"mixed divisions." In the course of the decade, Austria, Czechoslovakia,
Romania, and Bulgaria would collect their respective tank and motorized elements into ad hoc "fast divisions," though these reflect available
forces rather than any real doctrine. But the German stress on mobility,
deep penetration, envelopment, and initiative was original. It reflected
growing institutionalization of the concept that future campaigns would

be decided at neither tactical nor strategic levels, but in the previously vaguely defined intermediate sphere of operations.

The question nevertheless remained: How did mechanization best fit into the army's overall rearmament program? Arguably the central figure in providing an answer was Ludwig Beck, Chief of the Truppenamt (which resumed the name of General Staff in 1935) from 1933 to 1938. His post made him responsible for considering and integrating mechanized mobility into German military planning. His character and temperament created two sets of myths. That of the lesser world, fostered in particular by Guderian in his widely read memoirs, depicts Beck as conservative to the point of reaction on the subject, committed to mass armies in the old style, with no understanding of armor technology and no concept of using tanks except as infantry support. From the greater world of Beck's growing distrust of Hitler, escalating as early as 1938 into active opposition, comes the hypothesis of his resistance to the Führer's aggressive foreign policy, including an attempt to retard development of the mobile forces that were its primary instrument.

Both interpretations are misleading. No less than the rest of the senior officer corps, Beck supported rearmament and revision of the Versailles treaty—ultimately by force. The question was, what kind of force. On one hand Beck carefully studied British and French developments in tank technology and armor doctrine, in particular the works of Leo Geyr von Schweppenburg, military attaché to Britain, who discussed the concepts frequently with Liddell-Hart and other leading politicians and soldiers. Schweppenburg observed the British armor maneuvers of 1932 and 1934, submitting detailed and enthusiastic reports. Beck supplemented these with his own analysis of the British experience—particularly the continuing problems of controlling armored forces larger than a small brigade.

In June 1935, before the initial field exercises of the original panzer division, Beck conducted a staff ride based on a counteroffensive by no fewer than three panzer divisions, plus infantry, against a Czechoslovakian attack in the region of the Erzgebirge. The nature of the terrain stacked the deck; it was little surprise that Beck described tanks as weapons of opportunity, best employed in limited sectors. He also stressed the importance of all-arms cooperation. He asserted that once the front was broken, armored formations could operate effectively, perhaps decisively, on enemy flanks and in the rear areas.

That was about as close to a mainstream position as could be found in the Wehrmacht. Beck was willing to prognosticate—a staff exercise in 1936 was built around an entire armored army. In practical terms, however, he implemented a policy of general mechanization. The three panzer divisions discussed earlier would, by September 1939, be complemented by 36 more tank battalions primarily intended for infantry support—a ratio of one battalion per infantry division of the projected army. Beck also planned to motorize some infantry divisions, partially motorize others, and create light mechanized divisions more or less on the French model. These policies were implemented in 1936. In a technical context, Beck pushed for the development of medium tanks and for an even heavier "breakthrough" model.

This comprehensive approach was, in terms of army politics, a way of encouraging cooperation by spreading the wealth. In the same context it provided for healthy competition: a broad spectrum of approaches to a fundamentally new means of making war. No one really knew, for example, how antitank techniques and technologies would develop relative to the tanks' capacities. Beck was correspondingly willing to let other states—those that could afford errors—take the lead in major institutional and doctrinal innovation.

Beck's approach to armored-force development also reflected a general concept of rearmaments progressing by measured stages in a context of limited resources, human and material. Effective cadres for training and command could not be conjured from thin air and 100,000 men. The German auto industry had developed to serve specialized markets, and would take time to adjust to large-scale manufacturing of military vehicles. In 1939 there was still no system for converting the industry to war production. Steel and oil, the panzers' bone and blood, were in short supply and high demand. Heinz Guderian's brand of optimism on that issue was well enough; perhaps even desirable, in an officer with limited responsibilities. Beck and the General

Staff had to plan for the army—and consider as well what to do if those plans did not survive the proverbial first contact with an enemy.

Requiring consideration as well was the possibility of a preventive strike by Germany's neighbors—perhaps a preemptive one, given Hitler's increasingly assertive foreign policy. Infantry divisions were like municipal bonds. They were a safe military bet: easily raised, trained, and equipped; providing no original threats. And should the armored-force enthusiasts be proven correct, the separate tank formations could readily be combined into divisions and replaced in turn by new creations.

In October 1934, the army issued a table of organization for an "experimental armored division." Built around the Zossen and Ohrdruf tank regiments, the formation included a motorized brigade with a motorcycle battalion and a two-battalion "light rifle regiment"; an antitank battalion with 36 towed 37mm guns and eventually a battery of 20mm self-propelled antiaircraft cannon; a reconnaissance battalion of motorcycles and armored cars; and an artillery regiment with two battalions of 105mm howitzers, one truck-drawn and the other self-propelled. The 3rd Cavalry Division provided troops and cadres for what, on October 15, 1935, officially became the 1st Panzer Division. It took the field for the first time in August, and encompassed 13,000 men, more than 4,000 wheeled vehicles, and almost 500 tracked ones, at the Lüneberg maneuver grounds near Münster in Westphalia.

Lutz took personal charge of an exercise that still depended heavily on simulation and imagination. Tanks were in short supply relative to theoretical strengths and types. Radio allocations were incomplete. The division commander, Maximilian von Weichs, had been directly reassigned from the 3rd Cavalry Division, and retained a horseman's perspective. Many of the junior officers and enlisted men also came from freshly converted cavalry regiments. Training beyond crew levels was still a work in progress. But the former troopers were keen. When Army Commander in Chief Werner von Fritsch demanded the division execute a 90-degree turn to meet a theoretical flank attack, the movement was completed in just under 90 minutes, with a minimum of loose ends.

Fritsch was suitably impressed, and Lutz's report was appropriately enthusiastic. The tanks covered an average of 600 kilometers, with only

27 breakdowns—a good sign of fundamentally sound design and manufacture. Tanks must be used in masses and organized in large formations.
Single battalions or regiments could only succeed against limited objectives. Should armor be designated specifically for infantry support—a
policy Lutz criticized—it must be organized in brigade strength. In that
context, Lutz recommended a tank brigade of three two-battalion regiments as optional. This would give the division a total of more than 500
tanks—an excessive number by later standards, but arguably defensible
when most of the available vehicles in the near future would be armed
with nothing more lethal than rifle-caliber machine guns.

Lutz's concept of using tanks in masses reflected more than
Reichswehr-era theory. He and Guderian had visited the Soviet Union
in 1932, and had kept abreast of intelligence reports on Soviet tank and
vehicle production. Guderian considered the Red Army to be leading
the world in mechanization. His criticism of the relatively inflexible
Soviet concept of three distinct missions—close infantry support, breakthrough, and deep penetration—was acknowledged in Lutz's assertion
that the combination of a tank brigade and a motorized brigade, the
two complementing each other, enabled the division to perform a broad
and changing spectrum of tasks.

No less relevant for the panzer arm's development was the assertion
that, especially in combat, radio was by far the best means of rapid, secure
communication among motorized formations. Commanders therefore
needed armored command and signal vehicles, because they must be
at the head of their units. That final statement was not merely a challenge to, but a denial of, the Great War model of command exercised
from rear-echelon communications centers. It was no less a significant
modification of Helmuth von Moltke the Elder's familiar aphorism that
"no battle plan survives contact with the enemy." Future commanders of
mobile, mechanized forces would be in a position to make, remake, and
implement plans reflecting changing situations.

Lutz's report confirmed the Army High Command's earlier decision to create two more panzer divisions. It stressed the importance of
creating divisional headquarters as soon as possible in order to provide
guidance as men were assembled and equipment delivered. Command

of the 2nd went, predictably, to Guderian. The 3rd's commanding officer was Ernst Fessman, a cavalryman by branch but with experience commanding both a motor battalion in the Reichswehr and the first tank brigade in 1934–35. As for the deployment of the new formations, Guderian recommended, presumably with Lutz's concurrence, that one panzer division be stationed in Berlin and one in Weimar. These would be responsible for defending Germany's east. The third division should be deployed in the region of Würzburg-Bamberg to provide defensive strength against the French. The three projected independent brigades should also probably be located with a view to their operational employment in western Germany.

This in-house memorandum goes against both the long-standing theoretical approach of concentrating armored forces in mass and the long-standing myth of the panzer arm as the mailed fist of Nazi aggression. At this stage Germany was still seriously vulnerable, and the very success of Lutz's 1935 exercise highlighted that vulnerability. How best to counter attacks spearheaded by similar large armored formations? The standard recommendation was "offensive defense": strategic/operational delaying actions conducted at the tactical level by mobile ripostes, in particular outflanking movements, once the infantry had taken some of the edge off enemy armor.

German divisions had a total of 72 antitank guns, half assigned to regiments, half pooled in a divisional battalion, all motorized—a flexible and formidable force in an essentially horse-powered formation. The gun itself, a Rheinmetall-designed 37mm piece, had been under development since 1925, and in small-scale production since 1928. With its original spoke wheels replaced in 1924 by pneumatic tires, it was a handy and mobile weapon, highly effective against the kinds of tanks currently in foreign service and well suited to the tactics of shield and sword in a combined-arms context.

"Offensive defense" reflected—perhaps viscerally—the postulate that Germany's major probable enemies would be slow-moving (the French) or slow-thinking (the Poles). In slightly modified form it would emerge again in the aftermath of Stalingrad. It was nevertheless a dead-end option—not least because the style and nature of Hitler's foreign policy was making it increasingly obvious at the army's higher levels that any trouble Germany got into would require self-extraction. The international community was hardly likely to be forthcoming and benevolent toward a systematically antagonistic Reich.

At the same time new types and families of armored fighting vehicles were entering service. The centerpiece was the Panzer I. Its genesis was the 1932 purchase of a vehicle from Britain. The Vickers-Carden-Lloyd was what was called a "tankette": a turretless one- or two-man vehicle, more of a machine-gun carrier than anything else but easy to manufacture and, above all, cheap. The initial German intention was to use the chassis to mount a 20mm cannon in a revolving turret. When that proved too heavy, two light machine guns were substituted. The first prototypes were delivered by Krupp in February 1934. Four months later a satisfied army ordered an initial production run of 150, and then doubled it.

Originally the Panzer I had been viewed as a temporary measure, a training vehicle and nothing more. But when the better-armed and armored versions expected to replace it encountered developmental troubles, the little hybrid became an operational vehicle. Between October 1937 and September 1939 its numbers remained stable at around 1,450. The definitive Panzer I weighed a little under six tons, had a two-man crew, and armor protection good only against small arms. It also had two less-visible qualities that were to impact the panzer arm for half its combat existence. Each vehicle carried a radio and mounted a powerful, reliable engine, giving it a top road speed of 25 miles per hour. "Train as you fight" was a long-standing mantra in the German army. It might be said as well that a new weapons system is like a first lover: the experiences, good and bad, remain vivid. The peacetime tankers who began as corporals and lieutenants were formed in their concepts of armored war not only by doctrine and training, but by the cracker boxes in which they learned the hands-on aspects of survival: communications and mobility to set up and get out of "shoot-and-scoot," and "hit 'em where they ain't" tactical situations.

The Panzer II was another consequence of the retarded development of heavier models. Its specifications were issued in July 1934, and the winning design was submitted by Maschinenfabrik Augsburg-Nuremberg (MAN)—a newcomer to the armaments field, a choice reflecting in part the army's commitment to involving as many firms as possible in the production process.

Inexperience on all levels had a price. It took MAN longer to manufacture even preproduction models; the engineers and the soldiers constantly meddled with the design. Not until 1937 did mass production begin. The basic version, Models A, B, and C, weighed in at a little under nine tons, was armed with a 20mm turret cannon, and had a range of around 125 miles and a road speed of around 25 miles per hour. Models D and E had their tracks and suspensions modified to enable speeds up to 35 miles per hour, but at a significant sacrifice of cross-country performance.

Panzer II models supplemented rather than replaced Panzer I in a rapidly expanding armored force. By the outbreak of war, more than 1,200 were on line as stablemates of the smaller vehicles. Their stopgap character was recognized from the beginning. Mechanical reliability, ease of operation, and long range could not compensate for a main armament primarily effective against soft-skinned vehicles. If the type had a future it was in reconnaissance, not combat. Wehrmacht designers and planners instead projected a standard tank battalion of three companies armed with effective armor-piercing guns and one company with larger-caliber weapons.

The Panzer III represented half of that future. Its design orders were first issued in 1935, and for security purposes it was initially designated "platoon commander's vehicle." The first four prototypes, offered by four different firms, were tested in late 1936. The winner was Daimler-Benz, but the contract proved a mixed blessing. The original specifications were for a tank weighing 15 tons and capable of 25 miles per hour. Daimler made the weight by limiting the armor to Panzer II levels, and adapted a suspension system from its civilian vehicles that restricted the speed to 20 miles per hour. The result was more tinkering. A reworked suspension and a more powerful engine improved the speed even when the armor was increased to as much as 30mm, offering reasonable protection against large fragments from artillery shells and glancing hits from antitank rounds. The design's final weight was 19.5 tons—still well below the 24 tons that were the limit of German field bridges.

All this took time. The Panzer III went through no fewer than four type designations before the Model E was considered sufficiently refined to manufacture in some numbers. Even then the first general-production version of the tank was one letter later. The Mark F went into production in September 1939—just too late for the Polish campaign.

The same could not be said, albeit just barely, for its designated partner. The Panzer IV would remain in production throughout the war. The most numerous and the most versatile tank the Wehrmacht developed, it is also usually considered one of the world's classic armored vehicles, a strong contender for Top Ten status in any comparative listing. Its origins were unpretentious. The Weapons Office wanted armaments firms to gain experience designing and producing heavy tanks. Lutz and Guderian had from early days seen the need for a support tank. The result was a project for a "battalion commander's vehicle" of 24 tons—the bridge weight limit—mounting a 75mm gun, which was really a howitzer, only 24 calibers long. Dubbed by its crews as the "cigar butt" and other, cruder names involving length, its high-explosive and smoke shells were intended to provide for close support—not only for tanks but for their accompanying infantry. In the war's early years, however, a three-inch shell exploding on or near a tank could do significant damage—not least to crew morale. The Panzer IV would acquire from its early days an enduring reputation as a formidable opponent.

The Panzer IV suffered from an embryonic armament industry's lack of experience producing even moderately large tanks, and from an increasingly overstrained manufacturing capacity. Only about 200 were on inventory by September 1, 1939. That was enough, however, to begin allocating a company to each battalion, and to test the three-to-one combination initially proposed by Lutz and Guderian. The design withstood prototype testing admirably. The Panzer IV's suspension matched its eventual 20-ton weight, and was so reliable it became standard for all the later versions. Its superstructure was proportioned generously enough to allow for up-gunning. Its turret was electrically powered, improving exponentially the chances of getting off the first shot so often decisive in mobile war. Add standard frontal armor of up to 50mm, with 20mm on the sides and rear, plus a reliable Maybach engine giving a top speed of 20 miles per hour and a 100-mile range, and the Panzer IV was a crew's delight when it began entering unit service in 1938.

The panzer force was taking delivery of a wide variety of other armored vehicles as well. Among the most significant, and probably the most overlooked, was the armored command vehicle. Lutz's insistence that commanders of mobile forces must command from the front implied a need for an appropriate mount. The early tanks were too small and cramped to allow for the additional, still-bulky signal apparatus, and for an extra man to operate it. In 1938 the first versions of a converted Panzer I made their appearance. The turret was replaced by a fixed superstructure, a signaler was added, and the interior reconfigured to accommodate a table, map boards, and most important, two radios: one to communicate with the unit's tanks and one to keep in touch with higher headquarters. They were cramped and inconvenient, but the equipment worked—and they looked enough like ordinary tanks not to offer obvious targets. Around 200 were available for the Polish campaign, where they proved key links in the communications network that gave the Wehrmacht its nervous system.

In the German concept of mobile war, wheels were only marginally less important than tracks. That said, the first example was unimpressive: an open-topped scout car built on a civilian truck chassis, with a two-man crew, 8mm of armor, and a light machine gun. Entering service with the cavalry, by 1939 it had devolved to the infantry's reconnaissance battalions as one step above bicycles. Next step was a two-step: the development and introduction of the Leichter Panzerspähwagen Sonderkraftfahrzeug (SdKfz) 221/222—a Teutonic mouthful that translates as Armored Reconnaissance Car Special Purpose Motor Vehicle 221/222, and thankfully shortens simply to Armored Car 221/222. The latter, definitive version began joining reconnaissance battalions during 1938. A four-wheeled, five-ton vehicle, with a 20mm cannon or a light antitank rifle in an open-topped turret and a two-man crew, it could do 50 miles per hour on roads, half that across country, thanks to its four-wheel drive and a relatively powerful engine. The 222 was popular in service and easy enough to manufacture that a number were exported to Nationalist China, where it was also well liked.

The 222 is best understood as an upscale version of the Daimler scout car coming into British service about the same time. It could gather information but was ill-suited to fight for it. Apart from that, the German army had enough of a tradition of heavy wheeled vehicles to encourage the simultaneous development of the SdKfz Heavy Armored Car 231—Six-Wheeled. The 231 could trace its origins to a civilian-developed vehicle whose initial version was too heavy and too expensive. Rejiggered into a six-wheel design built, initially, around a Daimler-Benz truck chassis, the 231 first entered service in 1932. Its ancestry was both visible and problematic. It looked like a civilian automobile, in that unlike the 222, its engine was up front and vulnerable even given the well-sloped 14.5mm armor. At almost six tons, the weight was too heavy for the chassis, and the suspension was a constant source of concern despite the good road speed of 40 miles per hour. Like the 222, it was easy to manufacture—a thousand were created by the time production ceased in 1935. But even more than the Panzer I, the Armored Car 231 was used as a training vehicle and relegated to second-line service as fast as a replacement could be made available.

That replacement kept the designation, but was an entirely different vehicle: an eight-wheeled, rear-engineered design built on a Buessing-NAG chassis. It could do over 50 miles per hour on roads, 30 miles per hour off road. With dual steering, all-wheel drive, and independent suspension, its cross-country capacity even through sand and mud exceeded any wheeled, armored vehicle in any army, despite its relatively heavy weight. Its turret-mounted 20mm cannon and 15mm armor were adequate for the scouting mission that was its fundamental purpose, and from its first entry into service in 1938, the Achtrad "eight-wheeler" was popular with its crews. The complexity that made it difficult and expensive to manufacture was an acceptable tradeoff, especially given the increasing quality of unit-level maintenance in the Panzer arm. The new 231's major tactical drawback was its size. At seven feet eight inches and 8.3 tons, it was not exactly suited for "sneak and peek." For "shoot and scoot," however, the Achtrad was unmatched during the war's first half, and its size enabled the inclusion of a radio system that added "communication" to its long list of positives.

The 222 and 231 spawned a long list of modifications. Most were specialized radio vehicles. The 222 in particular was too small to carry both a radio and a cannon. Its near-sister SdKfz 223 was distinguished by a smaller machine-gun turret and carried a third crew member. Both six- and eight-wheel versions of the 231 also had radio versions with frame aerials. These, perhaps because of their distinctive appearance, are disproportionately featured in illustrated works despite their relatively small numbers.

This is one of the points in the narrative where it is tempting to dive into the permutations and modifications of design and armament that give Hitler's panzers their enduring appeal to buffs, hobbyists, and rivet heads. There are, for example the various artillery tractors that kept the guns within supporting range of the tanks. There is even a half-track motorcycle, initially developed to tow the 37mm antitank gun. Space and discipline combine, however, to take us forward to the last major family of armored vehicles that Germany took to war in 1939—half-tracks.

The SdKfz 251 stands with the Panzer IV at the focal point of Wehrmacht armor. Its only rival for "best of its kind" was its US army counterpart. It was a bit of a military afterthought. German infantry had regularly ridden trucks to the combat zone during maneuvers since the Reichswehr years. In the early days of the armored force, motorcycles were so popular that five of the nine rifle companies in a panzer division's rifle brigade rode them. Trucks and cycles, however, shared common problems: high vulnerability and limited off-road capacity. On the other hand, the panzers' commitment to the principle of close tank-infantry cooperation was reinforced by the experiences of both sides in the Spanish Civil War, when tanks operating alone in broken or built-up terrain proved highly vulnerable to infantry who kept their heads. In a 1937 exercise, the modified civilian two-wheel-drive trucks assigned to the motorized infantry performed so badly that Guderian, still a mere colonel, directly challenged the army's commander in chief, Werner von Fritsch, to remedy the situation.

"Had my advice been followed, we would now have a real armored force" were bold words, often cited to prove Guderian's professional conviction, his moral courage, and his arrogance, depending on the author's perspective. In fact, exercises and maneuvers were historically regarded as high-stress situations where such outbursts were more or less predictable, and Fritsch had a known high tolerance for young enthusiasts. Guderian, moreover, was widely understood as Lutz's protégé (an alternate German word is *Protektionskind*, "favorite child"). In short, he got away with it.

In concrete terms, Lutz and Guderian pressed for the development of an infantry-carrying vehicle with sufficient cross-country mobility to accompany tanks into action, and with enough armor and firepower to allow the crew to fight from it, if necessary. Such a vehicle had to meet two external requirements. It had to be cheap, and it could not interfere with tank production. That ruled out prima facie any kind of full-track design. Trucks were disqualified because any reasonably armored version would be heavy enough to overload suspensions and to lack off-road capacity. The answer came from the artillery—and indirectly from France.

Even before World War I, truck companies on both sides of the Atlantic had been experimenting with replacing rear wheels with some sort of track in order to lessen ground pressure and improve mobility in mud, snow, and sand. Most prominent in this effort was French engineer Adolphe Kegresse, whose successful conversion of some of Russian Tsar Nicholas's autos inspired the Putilov armaments works to consider a project for military half-tracks. After the war the French firm of Citroën developed several civilian versions, staging well-publicized desert crossings in North Africa and central Asia and attracting the particular attention of a French army still engaged in Morocco and southern Algeria.

From the later 1920s, half-tracks made up a steadily increasing percentage of France's military motor vehicles. Initially and primarily used as artillery and engineer vehicles, they found their way to the mounted troops as well. The French cavalry division as reorganized in 1932 had 150 armored versions as reconnaissance and combat vehicles. Another hundred, unarmored, carried the men and weapons of the battalion of *Dragons portés* (motorized dragoons) newly created for each mounted division.

With such an example so ready at hand, as early as 1926 the Reichswehr's Weapons Office began preparing its own design for half-track tractors. Daimler-Benz began working on a production version in 1931; by 1936, a series of vehicles from one ton to eighteen tons were on the drawing boards or in the field, mostly as artillery tractors. That reflected, in passing, the artillery's continued reluctance to accept the urging of the Lutz/Guderian school and fully mechanize the panzer divisions' fire support by developing self-propelled mounts. This was more than commitment to branch self-interest and a tradition of towing guns into battle. Tracked vehicles were still fragile relative to the weight and the recoil of even a light field piece like the standard 105mm howitzer. In addition to probable effects on accuracy, a breakdown took the gun out of action as well. Not until well into the Cold War would even the US army abandon towed guns as standard divisional-level weapons.

On the bright side from the panzers' perspective, Hanomag's three-ton tractor seemed well suited to carry a rifle squad. The armored chassis was provided by Büssing and the fit, if not perfect, was close enough for government work. At eight tons, with between 8 and 15mm of armor and mounts for two light machine guns, the 251 was tough and durable, eventually serving as the mount for a bewildering variety of weaponry. Tracks extending to nearly three-fourths of the chassis, plus a sophisticated steering system, compensated for an unpowered front axle and gave the vehicle better cross-country abilities than its US counterpart and eventual rival.

The technical hair in the soup of the 251 was its complexity. It may be argued as well that neither the infantry nor the panzers sufficiently internalized the need to emphasize rapid, large-scale production. The first A-model versions did not begin service trials until 1939, and there would never be enough of them to equip more than one battalion in all but a few favored panzer divisions.

Production delays bedeviled as well the 251's smaller cousin. The SdKfz 250 developed out of a growing mid-1930s belief that reconnaissance was too vital an element of mobile war to be trusted to existing combinations of motorcycles and armored cars. At times it might be necessary to fight for information; at times it might be necessary to traverse rough ground to secure information. The solution was a half-sized half-track built on the chassis of the 1-ton artillery tractor. At 5.4 tons, with up to 14.5mm of armor, an open top, and a six-man crew, the 250 could move at almost 40 miles per hour, cover 300 miles on a single fueling, and, when necessary, put a few boots on the ground to search, destroy, and provide fire cover. It would not see service until 1940, but eventually it would prove almost as versatile a weapons platform as the 251. And its description completes the first tranche of Wehrmacht armor.

III

THE STORY OF the SdKfz 250 segues neatly into the institutional development of the armored force in the second half of the 1930s. On March 15, 1936, a Weapons Office memorandum allocated three missions to the armored force: supporting the infantry attack, providing antitank defense, and carrying out independent operations in cooperation with other motorized troops. But other ideas were also percolating through the military system. The cavalry in particular had been hemorrhaging men and talent. Five of its eighteen regiments had already been transformed into tank, motorized, or motorcycle units. The rest were shedding squadrons for the new antitank and reconnaissance battalions. The Wehrmacht had plans to retain horse cavalry on mobilization, but it would take the field assigned by squadrons to infantry divisions. Small wonder that increasing numbers of talented and/or ambitious junior officers were seeking their future in the mechanized units.

The cavalry had been the army's social elite since the days of the Great Elector. Even in the Reichswehr years its officer corps included a high proportion of landed gentry: vons and von und zus. Its continuing influence had been highlighted by Maximilian von Weichs's seamless move into command of the Wehrmacht's first and only armored division. To respond to the march of progress was one thing; to fade ignominiously away was quite another.

Military considerations shaped the cavalry's behavior as well. German strategy was, as noted above, still predicated on the defensive. In that context there seemed to be a valuable operational role for a modern force able to perform a screening function, initially engaging and channeling an enemy while the panzer divisions lurked in reserve as a final argument. And should, as expected, the national strategy eventually require a military offensive, then mechanized reconnaissance, screening, and pursuit would be even more necessary. The argument was sufficiently persuasive that in August 1937 the Army Command informed Lutz that instead of creating additional panzer divisions, it planned to create the first of three "light divisions" in the fall of 1937.

The short lives and undistinguished careers of these formations has somewhat obscured their intended character. Though used as such in the Polish campaign, they were not panzer divisions manqué. Nor, as is sometimes asserted, were they a direct response to the French army's new light mechanized divisions. Their closest analogs are the armored cavalry regiments introduced in the US army's order of battle during the Cold War era to provide mobility, firepower, and shock action at the operational-level cutting edge. The missions were strikingly similar: reconnaissance and screening, plugging gaps in the line, conducting delaying actions, quickly occupying vital sectors, and, finally, pursuit and overtaking of retreating enemy forces.

The light division's norm was three "cavalry rifle battalions" and a "cavalry motorcycle battalion," one or two reconnaissance battalions built around motorcycles and armored cars, and a three-company light

tank battalion eventually to be equipped with the later, fast models of
the Panzer II. Internal signs of the division's mission were the trans-
porter vehicles issued to the tank battalion to facilitate operational
mobility and save wear on the tanks. The number of machine guns in
the rifle battalions was about double that of standard infantry—a useful tactical force multiplier in either defense or attack. Externally, no
one could mistake the light divisions' retention of the cavalry's yellow
branch color as opposed to the pink of the panzer divisions. Nor could
anyone mistake the creation of a separate corps command to supervise
their training and development.

At the other end of the spectrum, the infantry was also brought
under the mobile-warfare tent. It was increasingly clear that mechanization as such was having to compete with a broad spectrum of other
rearmament initiatives, in the context of a regime that considered "prioritization" something of a swear word. The three authorized panzer
divisions risked being submerged in a growing sea of foot-marching,
horse-powered infantry—the exact kind of mass army the Reichswehr's
institutional mentality was conditioned to avoid.

On January 30, 1936, Beck recommended motorizing four infantry
divisions. It was quick, it was cheap, and it was doable in the contexts
of industrial production and manpower procurement. Beck described
motorized divisions as necessary for rapid-approach marches and surprise movements, to provide mobile reserves for the high command,
and as a counter to aerial interdiction of rail transport. Significant as
well was the French army's 1935 decision to motorize no fewer than
seven of its first-line divisions. Armies resemble the fashion industry in
their susceptibility to trends, and health aficionados in their quest for
symmetry.

The Lutz/Guderian pressure persisted, and the heritage of fifteen
years' worth of theoretical consideration on the prospects of large-scale
mobile war remained active. In May the General Staff described motorized divisions as having the same capacity as their standard counterparts,
but with an added capacity for rapid movement and maneuver. Suitable as mobile reserves, presumably for defensive purposes, motorized
divisions could also be concentrated in mobile armies, presumably for

offensives at the operational level in combination with the light and panzer divisions.

Like the light divisions, the new motorized divisions received their own corps headquarters. They also kept their original branch color: white. Otherwise, they were not exactly given a lot of thought. Four standard infantry divisions simply turned in their horses for trucks, motorcycles, and a dozen armored cars. They did have one tactical advantage over their French counterparts. For mobility, the French division's infantry depended heavily on a Groupement of trucks attached for each move. The German trucks were organic down to company/platoon level—a major difference in flexibility even if the trucks were essentially road-bound and highly vulnerable even to small-arms fire.

IV

THE SOLDIERS WERE confident that once Germany's young men changed their brown shirts and Hitler Youth uniforms for army Feldgrau, their socialization away from National Socialism would be relatively easy. The relevant virtues the Nazis preached—comradeship, self-sacrifice, courage, community—had been borrowed from the army's ethos. The army knew well how to cultivate them from its own resources. The new Wehrmacht had new facilities. Barracks with showers and athletic fields, plenty of windows, and amåple space between bunks were a seven days' wonder to fathers and uncles who had served under the Empire. Leave policies were generous, and applied without regard for rank. Food was well cooked and ample. In the field, officers and men not only ate from the same kitchens; they used the same latrines. Uniforms looked smart and actually fit the wearers—no small matters to young men on pass needing to make quick impressions.

As the army expanded, its conscripts were motivated, alert, and physically fit to degrees inconceivable in all but the best formations of the Kaiser's day. The fact that military service had been restricted gave it a certain appeal of the transgressive, the forbidden, something generally attractive to adolescent males. Thanks to the eighteen months of compulsory labor service required of all seventeen-year-olds since 1935, the new recruits required a minimum of socializing into barracks life, and were more than casually acquainted with the elements of close-order drill.

The army was still the army, and NCOs had lost none of their historic set of tools, official and unofficial, to "motivate" recalcitrants and make them examples for the rest. Even more than in the Reichswehr, however, officers and noncommissioned officers were expected to bond with their men, leading by example on a daily basis. One anecdote may stand for many experiences. A squad of recruits was at rifle practice. The platoon commander asked who was the best shot among them and offered a challenge: "Beat my score and you can have an early furlough." At the end of three rounds, the private won by a single point—by grace of a lieutenant who knew how to lose without making it obvious. When the wheels came off in a combat situation, such officers seldom had to order "Follow me!"

German army discipline by British or American standards allowed harshness as a norm, and as the war went on, it escalated to large-scale draconic brutality quite apart from any alleged "Nazification." Military service, however, had for more than a century been a major rite of passage for males in Prussia/Germany. That aspect not merely survived under the Weimar Republic, it acquired something like mythic status—again, in good part because service was so limited. Contemporary conscripts in France, Belgium, and Poland, to say nothing of the Soviet Union, were likely to have a substantially different perspective. An easy rite of passage is a contradiction in terms, but under Prussian kings and German emperors, the army's demands had generally been understood as not beyond the capacities of an ordinarily fit, ordinarily well-adjusted twenty-year-old. Exceptions were just that. And in the Weimar years, a near-standard response of older generations across the social and political spectrum to anything smacking of late-adolescent malaise or rebellion was along the lines that what the little punks needed was some shaping up in uniform.

That mentality arguably echoed another facet of late-Weimar public opinion involving a closed institution: a growing obsession with crime, and a corresponding attack on the prison system as a rest cure for criminals. The latter criticism grew more vitriolic, especially on the Right, as the depression imposed greater hardships on ordinary citizens. By the time the Nazis took power, demands for stricter treatment of prisoners, and especially rigorous policies toward "incorrigibles," were firmly in place. The Nazis were pleased to oblige.

The recruits who began occupying the new barracks and filling the ranks of new units when conscription was formally reintroduced in 1936 thus found themselves in a comprehensive environment supporting compliance, cooperation, and participation. At this stage the more extreme ramifications of both army discipline and Nazi ideology were usually fringe manifestations, affecting the kinds of outsiders usually generated by male bonding groups. And the armored force benefited disproportionately from the new military order. Service in the panzers was a particular plus for those young men who may not have been part of a motorized society but who were nevertheless eager for the opportunity. Anticipating one's draft notice gave some freedom to choose one's branch of service. The prewar armored force never lacked for volunteers.

Most of the sixteen weeks of basic training was done in the traditional fashion: by units, with recruits arriving at the depot in time-honored fashion. Their initial processing, however, differed to a significant degree from both pre-1914 practice and the patterns in contemporary conscript armies. While not ignoring experience, aptitude, education, and even social class, the German sorting and screening system paid close attention to what later generations would call personality profiles. Determination, presence of mind, and situational awareness were the qualities most valued, not only with an eye toward prospective candidates for NCO stripes and officers' commissions—both vital for a rapidly expanding army—but as the foundation of an effective soldier.

German initial training was much more than simple hut-two-three-four. It can be compared to a combination of the US army's basic training and its Advanced Infantry Training, informed by the Marine Corps mantra of "every man a rifleman." This reflected an understanding gleaned from the trenches of the Western Front: The infantry is the army. It takes the highest percentage of casualties. Its moral and physical demands are the greatest. A soldier who cannot meet them is less than an effective soldier no matter his level of technical proficiency.

When new soldiers were formally sworn in, it was often in the presence of a flag, or a weapon symbolizing branch of service; in the panzer regiments, a tank. From there they moved into a mix of specialized instruction and field training. The former was the easiest. Crewmen were chosen for particular positions according to abilities demonstrated early in training. By 1940, the standard tank crew was five men: commander, gunner, loader, driver, and radioman. There was some cross-training, but tankers were expected to emphasize development of specialized skills: the crew was a team, a community, with everyone sharing everyday tasks of repair and housekeeping.

The fact that relatively few recruits were familiar with motor vehicles of any kind was in some respects an advantage. They had no inappropriate civilian habits to unlearn when it came to driving. They developed impressive skill at maintenance; one of the unremarked qualities of the armored force was an ability to keep its vehicles running at company levels through most of the war. Gunnery training was excellent, and as muzzle velocities and ranges increased, was supported by some of the war's best optical equipment. German tank marksmanship was formidable from 1939 to 1945, a fact affirmed by any enemy who faced it.

Technical proficiency was only one side of the coin. Training at all stages emphasized direct, small-unit cooperation among tanks, infantry, engineers, and antitank gunners. *Truppenführung*, the army's basic doctrinal manual, was published in 1933–34 as *Heeresdienstvorschriften (Army Regulations) 300*. Its introduction described war as subjecting the soldier to "the most severe tests of his spiritual and physical endurance." Combat involved an unlimited variety of situations, changing frequently and suddenly and impossible to predict or calculate in advance. It also involved the independent will of the enemy. Misunderstandings and mistakes were to be expected. Overcoming them depended more on character than intellect. And character in the context of combat meant, above all, will.

That principle held good for all ranks, general to private. The days of *Kadavergehorsamkeit* (corpselike obedience) were long past—if indeed they ever existed. The question of nature versus nurture did not significantly engage the Wehrmacht. Long before Leni Riefenstahl celebrated Hitler's version of the concept, the armed forces acted on the principle that a soldier's will was essentially a product of cultivation. Drill was presented as a means to develop the reflex coordination of mind and body. In contrast to the practices in most Western armies, conscript or volunteer, troops trained day or night, at immediate notice, in all weather, under conditions including no rations. Combat conditions were simulated as closely as possible through the extensive use of live ammunition. An indelible part of German military lore was the "massacre of the innocents" in 1914, which described thousands of German youths, so badly trained that many could not even load a rifle, being shot down by British regulars they could not see. "Never again!" was the motto of the senior NCOs, who even before the war constantly reiterated that the minor hardships and vague risks of training were nothing compared to the reality of the front lines.

Casualties in training, while not exactly processed as routine, were nevertheless accepted as necessary, not least as a reminder of the dangers of carelessness and stupidity. During World War I, the German army had to grapple with the problems posed by fatalism. The belief that death was essentially random was logical enough in trench warfare. It also diminished situational alertness. The Reichswehr and then the Wehrmacht sought, in contrast, to inculcate both the belief that situations could be mastered and the skills to master them. Acquiring those skills, it should be noted, involved the systematic application of intellect. The modern German soldier was not conceived in the semi-mystical image of the Great War "front fighter," as depicted by Ernst Jünger—transcending the challenge of industrial war by moral force. His was a synergy of warrior and technician—not the will keeping the intellect, but the two acting in a dialectic of combat to manifest the "character" described in *Truppenführung*. The combination of faith and works was as formidable in a military context as in a spiritual one.

In the course of the war, an army fighting under increasingly desperate situations would turn voluntarily to National Socialism as a motivator. In prewar years, the case was somewhat the reverse, in accordance with a tradition, dating to the Second Empire and continuing in the Reichswehr, of keeping "party politics" out of the barracks. The generals' initial concern that the new Wehrmacht would be swamped by successive intakes of committed National Socialists proved exaggerated. In part that reflected the movement's relatively short existence as a major social and political force. Four or five years were, as a rule, sufficient to put no more than a Nazi patina on existing viewpoints and values. At this stage, moreover, many of the values and qualities the army sought to cultivate were more or less congruent with both some elements of National Socialism and some attitudes at least accepted, if not affirmed, in German society at large.

In those contexts neither the army's everyday routines nor the fundamental values and intentions underlying them were likely to be challenged in principle on any more than an individual basis. That reflected as well the Wehrmacht's fundamental homogenization. Unlike its Imperial predecessor, it had no identifiable minorities: no Poles, no Alsatians, no Jews. The system of regionalized recruiting and replacement, sustained whenever possible throughout the war, put men with similar backgrounds and accents together, at least as the core of a particular unit. This meant that, as a general consequence, a soldier was less likely to be singled out as "the hillbilly," "the guy from Brooklyn," or as any other member of the "all-American squad" of war-movie mythology. A man had to single himself out, whether by attitude or behavior. Apart from any "pack instinct" allegedly hard-wired into male biology, the consequences were usually sufficiently unpleasant that a committed teenage Nazi was as likely to curb his enthusiasm for Hitler's New Order as a sloven was likely to "learn to keep his rifle and himself just so."

V

ONE OF THE more interesting phenomena since 1945 has been the development in the West, the US in particular, of a mythology depicting the German army of World War II as a "clean-shield" force fighting first successfully and then heroically against heavy odds, simultaneously doing its best to avoid "contamination" by National Socialism—a "band of brothers" united by an unbreakable comradeship. That concept of comradeship is arguably the strongest emotional taproot of what John Mearsheimer memorably dubbed "Wehrmacht penis envy." Soldiers and scholars outside Germany have consistently cited "comradeship" as a major explanation of the "fighting power" the Reich's opponents found so impressive. In American interpretations, German comradeship also serves as a counter to the flaws of a replacement/rotation system that during World War II, Korea, and Vietnam, was based on individual assignments. One under-analyzed reason for the relatively high morale sustained by US ground forces in Iraq seems to have been the adoption of unit rotation.

After 1945, for German veterans, comradeship became the war's central justifying experience—in good part by default. Few were willing to admit they had fought for Hitler and his Reich. The concept of defending home and loved ones was balanced, and increasingly overbalanced, by overwhelming evidence that the war had been Germany's war from start to finish. What remained were half-processed memories nurtured over an evening glass of beer, or at the occasional regimental reunion: memories of mutual caring, emotional commitment, and sacrifice for others. Traditionally considered to be feminine virtues, these human aspects of comradeship made it possible for the soldier to come to terms morally and emotionally with war's inhuman face—the destruction and the killing—and to come to terms as well with the nature of the regime his sacrifices had sustained.

Comradeship as understood in modern armed forces can be traced to the Revolutionary/Napoleonic era. It owes something to the extension of medieval ideals of chivalry to the common soldier in a context of general war. In the American Civil War, both sides presented themselves as fighting "for cause and comrades." During World War I, the concept of "frontline comradeship" or "comradeship of the trenches" emerged—particularly in Germany—as a means of distinguishing those who had been "out there" from others whose war had been fought in the rear echelons, or at home in the factories and on the farms.

Soldiers of all countries, especially those recruited and organized on a regional basis, bonded naturally as a response to the unfamiliar horrors of the trenches. Frontline routines generated small relational groups based on affinity, proximity, and experience. These were, above all, survival mechanisms: a man physically or emotionally alone on the Western Front was a dead man, or a shell-shock case waiting to happen. The German groups developed affective as well as instrumental functions. More than their French or British equivalents, they functioned as surrogate families. Nurturing functions that civil society assigned to women were assumed by "men supporting men." The case of Adolf Hitler indicated that these "trench families" could make room as well for eccentric cousins.

Thomas Kuehne interprets comradeship as a major source of the large-scale participation of "ordinary men" in what became the ordinary crimes of the Third Reich. Neither ideology nor fear motivated that behavior. Nor was it a primary consequence of war's brutalizing effect. Instead, Kuehne argues convincingly, German soldiers longed for Gemeinschaft, the spiritual community described since the Enlightenment in glowing terms by intellectuals, Romantics, and not least politicians. Soldiers sought direct, personal Gemeinschaft even more in the context of Nazi promises that turned to dross as the bombs fell and the casualty lists grew.

The ad hoc, constantly renewed and reconstructed communities resulting from constant heavy losses were in part held together by the few old hands who set the tone and passed on the traditions. Newcomers not only seeking but needing to belong in order to survive physically and mentally sought out and affirmed the collective's values. "Good" was defined as anything that strengthened the community. Kuehne asserts that in order to be accepted as a man among men, soldiers were ultimately willing to participate in activities forbidden by religion, by civil law, and even by the army itself. The highest prestige was enjoyed by the most open denier of norms—any norms. Doubts, scruples, and inhibitions were experienced before and after the collective behavior that affirmed the group against external challenges—and usually experienced privately.

Such considerations were, however, far in the German army's future during what seemed the endless summers of the mid-1930s. A significant reason for the relative absence of this kind of reflection in military circles was the sheer amount of activity and stimulus involved in the Wehrmacht's exponential expansion. There was so much to do and so much to learn, not only for the annual intakes of recruits but for officers and NCOs admiring their new badges of grade and rank. A high private from the old Reichswehr who was not sporting at least a Feldwebel's pips and tresses was a near-anomaly. Career lieutenants and captains blossomed within months into majors and colonels, with even higher ranks on their horizons. This was more than simple careerism. It was a chance for brave work in one's chosen career. To do good and to do well simultaneously is an enticing prospect. Promotions, moreover, frequently involved transfers to a different branch of service, where different skill sets and different requirements kept men busy staying abreast of the curve.

Nowhere were those patterns stronger than in an armored force coming into existence with the speed and force of an emerging volcano.

Between 1936 and 1938, the panzer division also began taking on the internal form later made familiar in World War II. The original Lutz/ Guderian division included too many tanks to control effectively. With much chopping and changing, the number was gradually reduced to around 350 in two two-battalion regiments. Each battalion had four companies with four platoons of five Panzer Is or IIs. And platoon training was the bedrock of panzer tactics.

There were four standard platoon formations: "one behind the other" for route marches, the "double rank" of commander followed by two pairs in approach marches, the "line" of four tanks with the commander in front for assembly, and finally the distinctive "wedge," which was actually a V-formation with the commander—again—at the tip and two tanks spread out on either side of him. Company and battalion formations were essentially larger versions of the standard four. Effective enough to take the panzers through six years of war, they were simple enough to execute—once everyone knew how.

The guiding tactical principle was attack by fire and movement: platoons and individual tanks supporting each other, and in turn supported by motorized infantry, artillery, and engineers—an integrated combat team. Tank-against-tank combat was not considered something to be sought, merely an aspect of the overall mission. Its success depended on hitting first with superior firepower, and, like every other aspect of armored warfare, that situation was best created by seizing the initiative through maneuver. The faster the attack, the stronger the shock and the quicker the primary mission completed. A defeated enemy was to be pursued relentlessly, with every effort made to cut off his retreat and finish him on the spot.

Advance planning was likely to be limited. For commanders, that meant keeping orders brief and flexible. It meant informing every subordinate, down to the junior ranks, of the essentials: mission, forces, positions; cooperation with supporting elements; what to do once the initial objectives were achieved.

On exercise fields and maneuver grounds the principle of "sweat saves blood" was translated in the panzer divisions into thrown tracks, breakdowns, disrupted communications, lost directions, smashed fingers—and blistered ears when senior officers and NCOs evaluated the results. But from the panzer divisions' beginnings, another ethos developed as well—a hands-on, unit-level recognition that mistakes were not merely normal but necessary. Commanders who operated from a "no-defects" mode were denying subordinates the opportunity to cultivate the situational awareness that would enable them to survive in combat, and the initiative that would enable them to triumph. A tanker looking over his shoulder for orders was a dead man walking.

Nor did it hurt morale when the tankers received a distinctive black uniform for dress and walking-out. It was partly derived from the black coveralls worn as duty uniforms for obvious reasons. At this point, black in German military culture did not yet have a sinister aura. It was rather a positive reminder of the uniforms worn by many of the volunteer units that fought against Napoleon: young, enthusiastic heroes willing to die for freedom. And old-time *Panzermänner* generally affirm that "tanker black" was a definite social asset in the bars and cafes.

VI

THE SPANISH CIVIL War appeared to consign much of this to that airy empire of dreams Heinrich Heine had described as the Germans' true home. Its operations were characterized by the use of tanks both episodically and in small numbers. While occasionally as many as fifty or sixty might appear at one spot, fifteen or twenty was the usual norm on both sides. Rough terrain and poor roads limited movement. Poorly trained infantry eschewed the risks of staying close to tanks; the things drew fire. Not surprisingly, tanks proved disproportionately vulnerable to antitank guns—especially the light, handy 37mm types just coming into widespread use. When tanks did manage a local breakthrough, their next move usually involved turning around and fighting back to their own lines. Even the apostle of mobility, B. H. Liddell-Hart, concluded that the lessons of Spain were that the defense was presently dominant, and that few successes had been gained by maneuver alone. The French and Russian armies came institutionally to similar conclusions. So did most of the rest of Europe.

The widespread negative judgments on tanks may have reflected as well the image of the war, assiduously promulgated on the Left, as a struggle between Spain's common people and its "establishment." In that context the tank invited definition as a quintessential Fascist weapon. Songs and stories consistently described tanks and aircraft pitted against "guts and rifles," with the latter combination ultimately triumphant. Within armies, even hard-shelled social and political conservatives might well take heart from this apparent reaffirmation that men, not machines, determine victory.

The Germans nevertheless continued on their pre-Spain course. It has been suggested that they did indeed react to the difficulties encountered by the Spanish and Italians in effectively employing armor. Instead of deciding the thing was impractical, however, they concluded that "of course these people can't do it." Robert M. Citino offers a more nuanced paradigm when he states that the Spanish Civil War was not a proving ground and "the Spaniards were not guinea pigs." The Germans on the ground had neither the numbers of tanks, nor the tank technology, nor the degree of control to impose any of their ideas on the Nationalist high command in a systematic fashion. In contrast to the aircraft of the Condor Legion, the crews of the three dozen Panzer Is initially sent to Spain in October 1936 were restricted to training missions and observation—at least in principle. In fact, the tankers, whose strength eventually increased to three companies, regularly spent time at the front and were regularly rotated back to Germany. Their commander, a future general but then merely Major Wilhelm Ritter von Thoma, personally led the Nationalist armored attack on Madrid in November 1936, and claimed to have participated in 192 tank engagements.

The men coming back from Spain were an invaluable conduit of lore from the sharp end to the grass roots of the panzer regiments. The wider results of their experience were summarized in a General Staff report of March 1939. The Nationalists, the document concluded, never used tanks in strengths larger than a company, and then only for infantry support. The corresponding restrictions on their movement made light tanks in particular vulnerable to even rudimentary antitank defenses. That, in turn, enhanced the need for gun-armed vehicles. Whenever possible, the Soviet tanks used by the Republicans were salvaged and welcomed for their high-velocity 45mm guns. And there was good reason for the German armored force's emphasis on unit morale and individual moral fiber. The report mentioned that an initial enthusiasm for armored service among the Spaniards quickly evaporated when it became known what the inside of a burned-out tank looked like. By the end of 1938, rumor described captured Russian tanks as being crewed by pardoned criminals or men given a choice between prison and making a single attack in a tank.

This was hardly sufficient data to justify completely revamping the Wehrmacht's approach to armored war. German professional literature regularly featured warnings against overemphasizing the Spanish experience. In more practical terms, the armor lobby was by now too firmly entrenched to be dislodged by internal means.

Higher-unit training in the peacetime panzer divisions continued to emphasize maneuvering and controlling tanks in large numbers. On June 1, 1938, the panzer divisions got their own manual, *Richtlinien für die Führung der Panzerdivision*. Emphasis on combined arms had not yet produced the closely integrated battle groups characteristic of the war's later years. Instead the pattern was the panzer regiments leading and the motorized infantry acting in support, somewhat along the lines of the British armored divisions of 1943–44.

To a degree, that reflected the progress of training: Tank and motorized formations had to become comfortable in their own skins before they could begin to work in genuinely close harmony. But teething troubles notwithstanding, in the fall maneuvers of 1937, the 3rd Panzer Division put on an impressive show, breaking the enemy flank, successfully assaulting a bridgehead from the rear, then shifting again to disrupt logistics and headquarters systems—all in close cooperation with Luftwaffe elements.

Armored force theorists made a correspondingly forceful case for the concentration of the panzer divisions into a corps, and the concentration of that force at the operational Schwerpunkt, the vital spot, of the opening campaign. Heinz Guderian's 1937 book *Achtung—Panzer!* is widely credited with structuring and popularizing that perspective. The book was in fact written on the recommendation of Lutz, who sought to make armored warfare's case in a public context. It was derivative, a compilation of Guderian's previous lectures and articles, but made up in conviction what it lacked in cohesion. Never lacking in an eye to the political sector, Guderian cited the Four-Year Plan, controlled by Hermann Göring, to support the argument that Germany would soon be able to produce enough synthetic fuel and artificial rubber to be freed from its current dependence on imports. He quoted Hitler's affirmation of "the replacement of animal power by the motor [which] leads to the most tremendous technical and consequently economic change the world has ever experienced."

Guderian's concluding peroration that "only by providing the army with the most modern and effective armaments and equipment and intelligent leadership can peace be safeguarded" resonates ironically in the context of Hitler's 1938 purging of the army high command and his subsequent reorganization of the armed forces' command structure, culminating in his assumption of supreme command. The book, however, was widely discussed, and sold well enough to pay for Guderian's first car—an amusing sidebar given his support for motorization.

Armored force doctrine and training placed increasing emphasis on ground-air cooperation. The long-standing myth that the Luftwaffe was essentially designed for close support of the land forces has been thoroughly demolished by, among others, James Corum and Williamson Murray. During World War I, the German air force had nevertheless paid significantly more specialized attention to ground support than its Allied counterparts. The Germans developed armored, radio-equipped infantry-contact machines for close reconnaissance. Used in twos, threes, and larger numbers, German *Schlachtstaffeln* (battle squadrons), each with a half dozen highly maneuverable two-seater Hannover or Halberstadt attack planes, proved devastatingly effective at shooting in attacks from the summer of 1917. In the later stages of the 1918 spring offensive, aircraft were used to parachute ammunition to frontline infantry. The experience of being on the receiving end of tank-infantry cooperation at the hands of the BEF in the war's final months drove home the lesson: close air support was a good thing for an armored force.

During the Weimar years the Reichswehr worked closely with the civil aircraft industry and the civilian airlines to keep abreast of industrial and technological developments. Under the guidance of Hans von Seeckt, German officers developed intellectual and doctrinal frameworks for air war in general and air-ground cooperation in particular. As early as 1921, regulations stressed the importance of using attack aircraft in masses against front lines and immediate rear areas. Maneuvers used balloons to represent forbidden aircraft, and emphasized unit-level anti-aircraft defense with machine guns and rifles in lieu of the banned specialized weapons. In Russia, from 1925 to 1933, the air school at Lipetsk successfully functioned as both a training base for pilots and a testing ground for aircraft.

The initiation of full-scale rearmament and the creation of the

Luftwaffe as an independent service temporarily combined to take air and ground on separate paths in the mid-1930s. Luftwaffe theorists accepted using fighters for direct support of ground forces as a secondary mission, but emphasized the greater importance of interdiction behind—well behind, as a rule—the fighting front. That attitude began to change as reports from the Spanish Civil War highlighted not merely the potential but the ability of aircraft to have a decisive effect on ground operations—especially against troops poorly trained, demoralized, or even temporarily confused. Nationalist or Republican, it made no difference.

Luftwaffe officers were increasingly expected to know army tactics and doctrine; to participate directly in army exercises and maneuvers as air commanders; to instruct the army in the nature and missions of air power. At the focal point of the new relationship was the armored force. Luftwaffe doctrine insisted air support must be concentrated at decisive points, not dispersed across fronts and sectors. This concept meshed precisely with the panzer commanders' emphasis on concentration, speed, and shock.

Implementation took three forms. One was the creation of specialized tactical reconnaissance squadrons assigned at corps and division levels, and the parallel development, from field army headquarters down to panzer divisions, of a system of air liaison officers to report ground-force situations to air officers commanding the supporting reconnaissance squadrons and the antiaircraft units.

The Luftwaffe's second contribution was close support. As early as the 1937 maneuvers, an entire fighter group, 30 aircraft, was placed at the disposal of a single panzer division. The obsolescent Henschel Hs 123 biplane, a failure in its intended role as a dive-bomber, found a second identity as a ground-attack aircraft whose slow speed and high maneuverability made its strikes extremely accurate. The Junkers 87 Stuka dive-bombers, deployed in small numbers to Spain, manifested near pinpoint accuracy and had a demoralizing effect out of proportion with the actual damage inflicted. Given the right conditions, it seemed clear that a few Stukas could achieve better results than entire squadrons and groups of conventional bombers. Throughout 1938, Stukas and Henschels exercised with panzer formations in an increasing variety of tactical situations. In the air and on the ground, the same conclusion was being drawn: Close air support, especially in the precise forms normative for dive and attack planes, could become "flying artillery fire," bringing the tanks onto initial objectives and keeping them moving not merely at tactical but perhaps operational levels as well.

No less significant was the Luftwaffe's third contribution: the development of a maintenance and supply system mobile enough to keep pace with the armored columns and keep the relatively short-ranged close support aircraft in action even from improvised airfields. Turnaround time and sorties mounted are better tests of air-power effectiveness than simple numbers of planes. It would be a good few years before the panzer divisions would have to wonder where the Luftwaffe was. It would be striking just ahead of them.

Colonel Hans Jeschonnek was appointed Luftwaffe Chief of Staff in February 1939. A bomber officer with—limited—unit experience, he nevertheless recognized both the importance and the difficulty of integrating close air support to ground operations. He understood as well the desirability of keeping air assets under Luftwaffe control—not as easy as it might seem even with Göring as chief, given the army's historically dominant position in Germany's military system. Jeschonnek's response was to organize a specialized ground-support force. In the summer of 1939 he began consolidating the Stuka groups into a *Nahkampfdivision* (close-combat division). Its commander was Wolfram von Richthofen, cousin of the Red Baron, who had extensive Spanish experience and was among the Luftwaffe's leading dive-bomber enthusiasts. Eventually the division would expand into a full and famous corps. But with more than 300 first-line combat aircraft on strength in September 1939, it was already the world's largest and most formidable ground-support air element.

The panzers experienced the differences between the most rigorous maneuvers and the least demanding field conditions in March 1938. That was the month when Hitler bullied the right-wing government of Austria into accepting Anschluss, or union, with the Third Reich—a more fundamental violation of the Versailles settlement than rearmament had been. He convinced the rest of Europe to accept it through the application of diplomatic smoke and mirrors. The 2nd Panzer Division was ordered to join the Wehrmacht forces assigned to occupy the Reich's new province. The new mobile forces had deliberately been held back from earlier "flower occupations" of the Rhineland and the Saar. Now Guderian had two days' notice to march his division from its garrison in Würzburg the 250 miles to the soon-to-be-former border, and then enter Vienna in presumed triumph.

The result was one of the most monumental compound fiascoes in the entire history of mechanized operations. Guderian, a master at presenting himself in the best possible light, could find nothing good to say about the inadequate planning, inadequate maintenance, and inadequate logistics that left broken-down tanks stranded on every major road out of Würzburg and constrained the survivors to refuel from obliging Austrian filling stations whose low-octane gas fouled engines so badly that many vehicles required major overhauls at the end of the march. Perhaps it was just as well that the division remained in Vienna once the garrison-shifting generated by the Anschluss was completed. In any case, Guderian stood at Hitler's side when the Führer spoke in his hometown of Linz, and basked in his pleasure at the sight of the tanks the mechanics were able to keep going.

Hitler's instructions of May 1938 for the Wehrmacht to prepare for an invasion of Czechoslovakia escalated the prospects of a general war Germany had little chance of winning. Ludwig Beck resigned as Chief of the General Staff in August. His successor, Franz Halder, inherited the outlines of a generals' plot to seize Hitler's person as soon as he issued orders for an invasion of Czechoslovakia. Some senior army officers, including Beck, had grown sufficiently dubious about the risks of Hitler's freewheeling foreign policy in the context of Germany's still–incomplete rearmament that they had developed plans for a "housecleaning." These plans involved eliminating Nazi Party radicals, restoring traditional "Prussian" standards in justice and administration, and putting

Hitler firmly under the thumb of the military leadership. Should that last prove impossible and the Führer suffer a fatal accident—well, no plan survives application, and the state funeral would be spectacular.

Whether anything would have come of it remains a subject of speculation. The agreements secured from Britain and France at the Munich Conference of September 1938 left Czechoslovakia twisting in the wind, and hung any potential military conspirators out to dry. Czechoslovakia's western provinces, the Sudetenland, were ceded to the Reich without a shot fired. Those who had urged caution on the Führer were correspondingly discredited.

These events had less direct impact on the armored force than might have been expected. On an operational level, the main problem was seen as breaking through formidable Czech border defenses—a task for infantry, artillery, and aerial bombardment that brought more conventional generals to the fore of planning. Internal attention was further diverted by a major reorganization. In addition to forming the corps headquarters authorized for the light and motorized divisions, the former Mobile Combat Troops Command became XVI Corps, with the three panzer divisions under its direct command. Three new divisions were added to the order of battle. The 4th Panzer Division formed at Würzburg to replace the 2nd. The 4th Light Division was built around elements of the former Austrian army's Mobile Division in Vienna. And in November, the 5th Panzer Division was organized at Oppeln, in Silesia, with many of its recruits coming from the newly annexed Sudetenland.

A number of the tank battalions already existed as separate formations, part of Beck's program for providing direct support to infantry divisions. The restructuring nevertheless meant more rounds of reassignments and promotions. The three mobile corps were assigned to a new army-level command created in 1937: Group 4, under Walther von Brauchitsch—the stepping-stone to his appointment as commander in chief of the army a few months later. Lutz briefly commanded XVI Corps, then was put on the retired list in 1938. This has been described as a forced retirement, a response at higher levels reflecting criticism of the way the armored force seemed to be developing as an army within the army.

This argument is supported by Brauchitsch's character and branch of service. He was an artilleryman, and while a solid professional, was neither a forceful personality like Guderian nor a smooth operator in the pattern of Lutz. Lutz's removal from the scene, however, can also be interpreted in wider contexts, as part of a housecleaning of senior ranks reflecting both Hitler's desire for more malleable generals and the High Command's belief in the need for fresh blood.* Lutz was one of those who had openly questioned the Führer's policies as excessively risky. Lutz was also sixty-two, the same age as Gerd von Rundstedt, also retired in 1938—arguably a bit over the line for field command in the kind of war he had done so much to create. Lutz was unlikely to step down of his own accord, though allowing him to learn of his new status from a newspaper article was unmistakably déclassé.

The appointment of Guderian as Lutz's successor in command of XVI Corps also suggests that Lutz was not singled out for removal on either political or professional grounds. The German army, like its counterparts before and since, had an ample number of sidetracks for officers identified with mentors who made career-ending slips. But in 1938 the Inspectorate of Motorized Combat Troops and the Inspection for Army Motorization were combined into a single agency with the mouth-filling title of Inspection Department 6 for Armored Troops, Cavalry, and Army Motorization (In6). Its focus was to be on nuts and bolts: training, organization, technology. At the same time, an Inspectorate of Mobile Troops was established to develop doctrine and tactics, supervise the schools, and advise both the army high command and In6 on the operational aspects of mobile war. The post was offered to Heinz Guderian.

---

* Another element of the reorganization was Hitler's creation of the Oberkommando der Wehrmacht (Wehrmacht High Command), in theory superior to the Army High Command, and intended as its rival—a common pattern in the Nazi regime. In practice it functioned as his personal advisory board. After 1940, OKW was given responsibility for an increasing number of "secondary" war theaters; by 1942, only the Eastern Front remained under direct control of the Army High Command. Since that theater absorbed most of the panzers for most of the war, for the sake of clarity, "High Command" refers to the army authority in this text unless otherwise noted.

The appointment had a back story. The new Inspectorate seems to have been Brauchitsch's idea. Hitler approved. Guderian initially turned down the post on the grounds that it lacked any real authority; he could only make recommendations. When Hitler informed him that his advisory responsibility meant that, if necessary, he could report directly to the Führer in his capacity as Commander in Chief of the Wehrmacht, Guderian changed his mind. A promotion to *General der Panzertruppen* (Lieutenant-General) further sweetened the deal.

This account has been challenged by Guderian's friend, General Hermann Balck. Balck describes a cabal involving Brauchitsch and the General Staff to kick Guderian upstairs, or at least sideways, in order to minimize the effect of what was considered his "tunnel vision" on the subject of army motorization. Some support for that unverifiable hypothesis is offered by Guderian's initial assignment in the new mobilization scheme: command of a second-line infantry corps in the western theater. In 1940, Erich von Manstein would receive a similar assignment for the same reasons: as an obvious slap on the wrist, and as a warning against excessively close contact with the Führer. In Guderian's case, however, that contact was a bit too valuable to waste, given the growing indications that one of the Third Reich's alleged "two pillars" was significantly overtopping the other.

At least that seems to have been the opinion of Brauchitsch's successor as commander of Group 4. Walther von Reichenau stood out among the army's generals as an admirer of Hitler, and assiduously cultivated his own back channels to the Führer. He was unlikely to seek to choke off Guderian, especially since the two men were much alike in aggressive temperament and blinkered vision.

Guderian's driving energy was immediately put to use. Lutz was no weakling, but his chief talents had been as a negotiator and a facilitator. The panzer divisions suffered from constant teething troubles, expected and unexpected. The senior formations were still very much works in progress. In a 1938 exercise, the staff of the 1st Panzer Division created a foul-up beyond the generous tolerance for maneuver mistakes. Perhaps energized by Hitler's presence, Guderian not only blasted the regiment's officers but ordered some punitive transfers "to encourage the rest." Guderian also struggled mightily with the cavalry in an effort to wean them away from a historic commitment to screening and reconnaissance. On the technical side, Guderian iterated and reiterated the importance of radio communication—increasingly with aircraft as well as vehicles. Though initially unable to provide every tank with a transmitter, he did make sure each had a receiver.

With the occupation of the rump Czech state in March 1939, Guderian and the armored force simultaneously acquired a windfall and a problem. The windfall reflected Bohemia's history as a center of arms design and manufacture under Habsburg rule. The Czechoslovak government cultivated that heritage, and in the 1930s produced two state-of-the-art designs. The TNHP 35 weighed a little more than 10 tons with 35mm of armor on the front and 16mm on the sides. It could do 25 miles per hour on roads, was high-maintenance but easy to operate, and, best of all, carried a high-velocity 37mm gun. The TNHP 38 was even better. At 10 tons with 25mm of frontal armor, it was more maneuverable than the 35, carried the same 37mm gun, and on the whole was roughly equal to the Panzer III, which was still backed up on German production lines.

The Germans' initial problem was adapting their new tanks to Wehrmacht requirements. The armored force took over about 200 of what were rechristened the 35(t), for Tsechoslowakei, and began the extensive modifications necessary, particularly in radio equipment, to make them suitable for German service. The 38(t) was just coming into production when the Germans marched in and began testing the design. In May 1939 the Weapons Office contracted with the Czech factory to manufacture 150 of them. They were the first of a long line of 38(t)s that would serve throughout the war in a variety of roles. None, however, would be ready for service by September 1, 1939.

On the organizational side, on November 24, 1938, von Brauchitsch issued a sweeping directive for the development of the army's motorized forces. It projected a final goal of nine panzer divisions, to be met by converting the four light divisions in the fall of 1939. Each army corps would have a motorcycle battalion; each field army would receive a number of motorized reconnaissance battalions. Independent armored brigades were projected as well, to support conventional infantry divisions or cooperate with motorized ones—the latter a possible foreshadowing of the panzer grenadier divisions. Finally, a number of independent companies equipped with "the heaviest kind of tanks" would support infantry attacks against fortifications.

On April 1, 1939, the General Staff ordered the creation of four new panzer divisions—effective, ironically, on September 19. In practice, that meant raising and training the tank units and supporting formations necessary to upgrade the light divisions. At the same time, the armored force was allocating the revamped Czech tanks and the Panzer IIIs and IVs also beginning to enter service. As if that was not enough, the panzers were increasingly drafted for display purposes; parades in Berlin and other German cities were designed to impress not only foreign observers but a German population that cheered Hitler's bloodless victories and yet retained a vivid collective memory of World War I.

Whatever the tanks may have provided in terms of intimidation and reassurance, Guderian and his generals were less than pleased at the waste of time and energy. The fall maneuvers, however, were expected to compensate. For the first time the armored force was to take the field in strength: XVI Corps would control three panzer divisions, the 4th Light Division, and a motorized division. Deploying that force would require implementing the first stages of mobilization for the units involved. To test the concept of the air-ground combat team on a similar scale, the Luftwaffe would provide its new tactical support force. The exercises were never held. Instead, on September 1, 1939, the panzers went to war for real.

VII

THE CRITIQUE OF mass war developed in German military thought after 1918 had never excluded numbers, per se. Its goal had been the eventual creation of a force able to achieve decisive tactical and operational results initially, thus avoiding the spiral of escalation forcing Germany into a war of attrition—exactly the kind of war the professional soldiers had warned for years and decades that Germany had no chance of winning. The army that took the field, however, was the product of improvisation. The steady pace originally projected by the General Staff and the High Command was submerged by a rearmament that rapidly became its own justification and increasingly outran available human and material resources. Even after the Blood Purge of 1934 eliminated the possibility of using the SA as the basis for an alternative military system, the army continued to fear dual loyalty in an increasingly Nazified society. Total war of the kind Hitler seemed willing not merely to risk but to affirm remained, in strategic terms, the wrong kind of war for Germany. And in social and political contexts, a mass war involving the German Volk was likely to benefit the Nazis far more than the soldiers.

Since the Napoleonic Wars the Prussian/German army had stressed the desirability of a high average quality. The General Staff developed as a leaven to the officer corps as a whole, rather than a self-absorbed elite. In operational terms, one regiment, division, or corps had been considered as capable as any other. When reserve divisions were organized on a large scale as part of the run-up to World War I, they were structured as far as possible to the active army's norms, and from the beginning were used in the same way as active formations. In 1939, however, most of the divisions were formed by *Wellen* (waves), each with differing scales of equipment, levels of training, and operational effectiveness. Now in planning for war, the army was constrained to develop a hierarchy of dependability, with the peacetime divisions of the "first wave" at its apex—and the mobile divisions at the apex of the first wave.

That situation offered the army a political and military window of opportunity. The tactical, doctrinal, and institutional concepts developed by the Reichswehr and refined after 1933 provided the prospect of decisive offensive operations executed not by a small professional army but by specialized technocratic formations within a mass. High-tech force multipliers favored developing an elite group; not in the racial/ideological sense of the emerging Waffen SS, not even an elite element depending on personnel selection like the paratroopers of the British and US armies, but a functional elite, based on learned skills. Its professionalism would enable the employment of ways of war, inapplicable by homogenized mass armies in the pattern of 1914–18, that would bring victories despite the institutional weaknesses of the new Wehrmacht— and despite any signs of clay feet or cardboard spine Germany's Führer might show along the way.

CHAPTER THREE

TRIUMPH

For YEARS THE Polish campaign of 1939 was widely described as the first test of blitzkrieg, "lightning war." Then soldiers and academics began to question both the nature of the campaign and the existence of the concept. German scholars in particular have been at pains to discredit and deconstruct the concept of blitzkrieg—to a point at times suggesting Kafka's hunger artist, who rejects admiration for his self-destructive behavior. Reduced to its essentials, the critique of blitzkrieg is that the German victories of 1939–40 were not consequences of doctrine or planning. They developed from a series of accidents and coincidences reflecting operational improvisations born of the necessity to avoid a drawn-out war of attrition, and responding to strategic imperatives generated by the essentially random nature of the National Socialist regime. Far from being a German concept, blitzkrieg was in fact a term coined in the West, first used in *Time* magazine and introduced to the German army secondhand. Hitler himself as late as 1942 dismissed it as "Italian phraseology."

I

The INTERACTING DECONSTRUCTIONS have in turn generated opportunities for reconstruction. Blitzkrieg was certainly not a comprehensive principle for mobilizing Germany's resources for a total war waged incrementally. Nor was it a structure of concepts like Air Land Battle or counterinsurgency, expressed in manuals, taught in schools, and practiced in maneuvers. The word itself had appeared now and then in German military writing since the mid-1930s, not in a specific sense but to refer to the kind of quick, complete victory that was at the heart of the army's operational planning, and a central feature of its doctrine and training. Nor was the context always positive. Just before the outbreak of war, one critic affirmed that the chances of a blitzkrieg victory against an evenly matched enemy were zero.

To say that blitzkrieg was an ex post facto construction nevertheless makes as much sense as to assemble the components of a watch, shake the pieces in a sack, and expect to pull out a functioning timepiece. The most reasonable approach involves splitting the difference. On one hand, blitzkrieg is a manifestation of Bewegungskrieg, the war of movement, the historic focus of Prussian/German strategic and operational planning that Seeckt and his contemporaries sought to restore after the Great War. On the other hand, blitzkrieg gave a technologically based literalness to an abstract concept. Bewegungskrieg had always been more of an intellectual construction than a physical reality. It involved forcing an enemy off balance through sophisticated planning creatively implemented in a context of forces moving essentially at the same pace. In blitzkrieg the combination of radios and engines made it possible for an army literally to run rings around its enemy—if, and it was a big if, its moral and intellectual qualities were on par with its material.

The Polish campaign helped shape that concept. Considered in hindsight, Case White, the cover name for the invasion of Poland, seems a classic example of what the Germans call "a made bed." Much of the terrain was ideal for mobile operations: large stretches of open country with neither formidable natural obstacles nor man-made ones like the hedgerows of Normandy. The weather cooperated. September was unusually dry—a boon in a country where paved roads were few to an invader whose off-road capacities were limited. The Polish army depended on the muscles of men and horses for mobility. It had around 600 tanks, but most of them were counterparts of the Panzer I, and most of those were attached by companies to the cavalry brigades. Strategically, German occupation of the rump state of Slovakia left Poland enveloped on three sides—yet the Polish army was deployed along its frontiers in a pattern similar to the one Napoleon sarcastically suggested was best suited to stop smuggling.

That positioning reflected domestic factors. Poland, much like West Germany during the Cold War, could not afford to abandon large parts of its territory without devastating consequences for the national morale on which its conscript army's effectiveness depended. It reflected as well the defensible—and accurate—conclusion that even without the non-aggression pact with Germany, whose negotiation had hardly been a secret, the Soviet Union could be expected to seek direct profit from a German-Polish war.

In sum, Poland had no prospects of waging anything like a long war successfully. Its only prospects lay with its French and British allies. That, in turn, ironically placed Poland in a position similar to that of Prussia in the autumn of 1806, when it did not have to defeat Napoleon, just bloody his nose and set him back on his heels until the British guineas and Russian bayonets that were the Fourth Coalition's real strengths could be brought into play. German planners, with vivid memories of the World War I blockade and well aware of France's "Anaconda plan" of total mobilization for total war, were correspondingly committed to a war from a standing start. Overwhelming Poland as quickly as possible would change the military dynamic—and might just change the international dynamic as well, if Hitler could pull off another of his high-wire stunts.

Reduced to basics, the "decisive point" of Case White rested with Army Group South: three armies coming out of Silesia and Slovakia. Army Group North's two armies attacked from Pomerania and East Prussia. The strategic intention was a breakthrough of the Polish cordon followed by a double penetration: a pincers movement on a Schlieffenesque scale, the tanks meeting somewhere around Warsaw and then separating again, one part turning inward toward the Vistula River to finish off the trapped Polish main force, the other continuing to the Bug River to screen the decisive battle and secure against such contingencies as Soviet treachery.

The projected campaign generally resembled pre-World War I planning and specifically replicated the Austro-German offensive into Russian Poland in October 1914. Despite significant tactical successes, that operation ultimately failed. There was only one way for the German army to achieve its objective operationally: keep moving. Army Group South had the peacetime army's three mobile corps headquarters, four panzer divisions, all four of the light divisions, and two motorized divisions—around 2,000 tanks. Army Group North had the newly organized 10th Panzer Division, a provisional division built around a panzer brigade, and a corps of one panzer and two motorized divisions under Heinz Guderian—around 500 tanks, but with lesser distances to cover.

Army Group South broke through and drove northeast, bypassing defenses, striking into the Poles' rear to cut communications and block retreats, supported by Stuka dive-bombers whose precision strikes were neither disrupted from the air nor challenged from the ground. The Stukas had increased their repertoire by adding a propeller-driven siren to each strut of their fixed landing gear. The eldritch screaming of these "Trumpets of Jericho" reinforced the conviction, affirmed by virtually everyone ever under dive-bomber attack anywhere, that the plane was aiming at him personally.

That did not mean the Poles collapsed. Nor did they act, contrary to one report, as though German tanks were still made of wood and cardboard. The panzers and motorized infantry of Army Group North found breaking out was hard to do against local counterattacks and the determined resistance of cut-off troops with no place to go. It was in this sector that the legend of cavalry attacking tanks with lances was born—courtesy of some Italian journalists who listened to shaken German survivors of the actual event. On September 1, a Polish lancer regiment stumbled on elements of a German battalion in a clearing, charged, and took them by surprise. Then a few German armored cars appeared and shot the lancers to pieces. But that incident, among others, shook the 2nd Motorized Division badly enough that its commander briefly considered retreat until brought up short and sharp by Guderian.

The panzers' initial fighting in the northern sector featured the kinds of logistical, tactical, and communications lapses predictable for any untested formations in the first days of any war. Guderian's lead-from-the-front approach led to interventions in the chain of command that confused his subordinates. Nevertheless, by day five of the offensive the tanks and trucks of Army Group North were on their way to Warsaw. Hitler himself came forward to see the results, and the one-time infantryman was suitably impressed when Guderian showed him Polish artillery positions overrun and destroyed by tanks.

On October 15 the spearheads of XIX Panzer Corps, now reinforced by the 10th Panzer Division, reached Brest-Litovsk, far into the Polish rear. Army Group South's 4th Panzer Division reached the outskirts of Warsaw as early as October 8, but lost half its tanks attempting to break into the city. The general advance was further delayed by a desperate Polish breakout attempt that caught the German left flank along the Bzura River. But the panzers shifted their axis of advance 180 degrees in twenty-four hours with an ease belying their lack of experience. Stukas and conventional bombers hammered Polish concentrations. The counterattack collapsed in a welter of blood and the mobile forces swung back toward Warsaw to link up with Guderian.

On September 17, the Red Army crossed Poland's eastern border with a half million troops. That ended any Polish hopes for continued resistance on the far side of the Vistula—hopes in any case dashed by the refusal of the Western allies to make more than a token effort to relieve the German pressure. Only Warsaw remained unconquered and its defenders cashed out high, inflicting heavy casualties despite continuous air and artillery bombardment, both characterized by disturbingly high levels of inaccuracy. German propaganda spoke of an eighteen-day war. Army Group South, which bore the brunt of the fight for Warsaw, lost more men in the second half of the campaign than in the first two weeks, a dry run for the serious work. Warsaw capitulated on September 27. On October 5, Hitler reviewed a victory parade through the devastated city. The last organized Polish force fought off the 13th Motorized Division for four days before surrendering at Kock on October 6. Poland was kaput. What remained was establishing the new border with Russia, organizing the occupation of the Reich's latest conquest, and evaluating performances.

To a degree, unusual after such a decisive victory, the German army applied an "iron broom" to doctrine, training, and command. The artillery was criticized for hanging too far back and for being unresponsive to the rapidly changing requirement of modern battle. The infantry came under fire for a general lack of aggressiveness and flexibility and for too often waiting for the guns, the tanks, and the Stukas to do the work instead of pressing forward with their own resources. Officers at all levels were reminded of the need for maintaining situational awareness, for maintaining calm in what seemed a crisis, and, above all, for seizing the initiative in every situation.

The panzers came off unscathed by comparison. Prior to September 1, questions had remained as to how well the methods and material of mobile warfare would actually work in the field. A month later, there seemed no doubt: The combination of tanks, motorized troops, and aircraft could not only break into and break through an enemy front; they could break out, with decisive effect. Breaking regiments and battalions into combined-arms battle groups, usually based on the tank and rifle regiments but reconfigured to meet changing tactical and operational situations, was generally validated. The difficulties of practical implementation even against what quickly became episodic resistance were noted, but described as susceptible to training and experience.

That did not mean fine-tuning could be neglected. The armored force reported a loss of just over 200 tanks—under 10 percent of the total committed, and that figure is the one most often cited. Recent research by Polish scholars in German records indicates that almost 700 tanks were written off at one time or another from all causes. About 550 of those were either total losses or beyond the ability of unit workshops to repair. These statistics reflect a demanding operational environment, one that encouraged neglecting vehicle maintenance because of crew and unit stress and fatigue. They reflected the relative fragility of the Panzer Is and IIs that formed the bulk of the armored force. And they reflected the determined local fights, often to the last man, made by Polish troops using everything from satchel charges, grenades, and antitank rifles to field guns firing over open sights, in the pattern of the First World War.

In the long run, actual losses were inconsequential. No one with any responsibility seriously considered the light tanks as anything but stopgaps. On mobilization, each tank battalion had left one company behind as a depot. In the panzer divisions, one of the remaining three companies was supposed to be equipped with Panzer IIIs and IVs. Delivery problems meant only the 1st and 5th Divisions came close to that standard. The light tanks were left on their own—contrary to prewar doctrine and expectation. Absent projected support from the high-velocity gun of the Panzer III and the 75mm of the Panzer IV, light tanks depended even more than anticipated on speed and maneuverability. A light tank halted for any reason was wearing a bull's-eye. A light tank challenging a barricade risked winding up on its side. A light tank engaging antitank guns was pitting hope against experience. It was first-rate crew training—but the hard way.

Tactically, frontline reports uniformly insisted on using tanks en masse, by battalions at least. Even when needed for direct support of infantry, tanks should never be distributed in less than company strength. Panzer officers also consistently complained of the motorized infantry's inability to keep pace, and more or less delicately suggested that advancing under fire was not a particular strong point. Some suggestion of the infantry's problems in that regard comes from the war diary of the 35th Panzer Regiment. Describing the initial fight for Warsaw on September 9, it refers to truck-borne infantry taking cover under heavy small-arms fire as their unarmored vehicles went up in flames. The diary does not refer to any direct support provided by tanks that were having their own troubles that day. "Avoid built-up areas" was solid panzer advice, eventually forgotten in the rubble of Stalingrad. Solid as well was the recognition that the motorized troops at least needed more in the way of organic supporting weapons and, if possible, a general issue of armored half-tracks.

The panzers took with them into Poland another legacy. After 1933, generalized concepts of the "East" as an object of German manifest destiny, long present in the general culture, were integrated with National Socialist conceptions of the East as "living space." Soldiers were informed that they were the vanguard of Germany's destiny, with the missions of conquering the new territory and governing the primitives who inhabited it. "I'm looking for hard men," Hitler declared to his adjunct. "I need fanatical National Socialists. See to it that such men are brought forward."

The Führer had plenty of prototypes. From the early days of September 1939, negative, derogatory attitudes toward Poles and Jews informed the army's official reports, its private correspondence, and its public behavior. Troops used Nazi jargon to describe the people as "subhuman" or "inhuman"; junior officers and enlisted men showed consistent willingness to initiate reprisals, to implement terror, to translate vague authorizations to establish local security into fists and boots, summary executions and firing squads.

The Prussian/German army had a history—it might be said a culture—based on risk and violence, fear and force. World War I had shown German units were likely to assume any surprise attack was initiated by the civilians. A report from 4th Panzer Regiment, for example, describes priests "disappearing" into a village church "as soon as panzers appeared.... Signals were immediately observed from the church tower. Then machine guns opened fire on us." Two well-placed rounds from a Panzer IV solved that particular tactical problem. The social/cultural one remained. Fast-moving armored formations were disproportionately likely to come under unexpected fire. Erich Hoepner, commanding XVI Panzer Corps, ordered "the most severe measures" against "partisans." On September 4 and 5, troops of his 1st Panzer Division responded by shooting a number of male civilians, apparently in the belief that someone in the village had fired on them. Elements of 1st Panzer killed more civilian men and destroyed as many as 80 farms in another village in reprisal for a Polish counterattack—presumably assuming the civilians had somehow participated. In the aftermath of the collapse of the Bzura counterattack pocket, the 4th Panzer Division was involved in a number of killings of Polish civilians and of soldiers who were legally prisoners of war by the terms of the local surrender.

Examples can be multiplied, though not yet ad libitum. Compared to the rear-echelon "Action Groups" that followed the army, and to a

Waffen SS that was at this stage far more dangerous to civilians than to anyone with a gun, the panzers' shield might even be described as relatively clean. Their behavior nevertheless went well beyond first-battle jitters involving quick triggers or misunderstood gestures or a straggling soldier officially surrendered who still had his rifle.

II

DEAD POLES WERE quickly forgotten, if they were thought of at all. Though there had been no significant tank-versus-tank engagements during the Polish campaign, German planners were aware that against the French and British, they would face superior numbers, better armed and armored vehicles, and not least stronger antitank defenses. As the Wehrmacht began the process of deploying westward, the armored force underwent a major restructuring.

First to go were the light divisions. Field experience confirmed the prewar decision to concert them to panzer formations. While they had generally performed well enough on the move, lack of tanks proved a major handicap whenever it came to fighting. Adding a company of mediums was unlikely to remedy the problem. Instead they were renumbered as the 6th through the 9th Panzer Divisions and given a two-battalion tank regiment (a single battalion in the case of the 9th). Increased production of Panzer IIIs and IVs resulted in new tables of organization as well. In February 1940 every tank battalion was authorized two light companies, each with two platoons of Panzer IIs and two of Panzer IIIs, and a third "medium" company with a platoon of five Panzer IIs and two platoons totaling seven Panzer IVs; more larger tanks would be issued as they arrived.

That was the theory. In fact, the new tanks trickled in during the winter and spring of 1940. The gap was filled in part by delivery of the 38(t). Around a hundred each went to the 7th and 8th Panzer Divisions (the 6th had the older 35(t)); the other seven divisions had German vehicles, including a significant number of Panzer Is—around a hundred in

the 3rd, 4th, and 5th. The next campaign would still be a light tank operation, with all the accompanying implications for better and worse.

In one respect the tanks would be even lighter than desired. The
Panzer IIIs coming into the battalions were models E and F, with 30mm
of frontal armor and the highest standard of reliability in the armored
force. The gun, however, was the original 37mm. The Weapons Office
and the armored force alike had originally wanted a heavier piece. A
50mm/42-caliber gun was available; the tank's turret and turret ring
had even been designed to mount larger weapons, but retooling would
reduce production at a time when every tank counted. Only a few of the
up-gunned versions would see action in the western campaign.

Experience in Poland indicated that the motorized divisions were
too large to be controlled in mobile operations. Each shed a regiment,
usually transferred to a panzer division organically short of infantry. The
Cavalry Rifle Regiments and the reconnaissance formations of the former light divisions were reorganized to panzer division standards with
some anomalies—including the troopers' pride that kept them wearing cavalry yellow branch insignia instead of donning infantry white.
Armored half-tracks remained part of Heine's "airy empire of dreams"
for all except a few companies in the 1st, 2nd, and 3rd Panzer Divisions—
the privilege of seniority.

As long as the infantry rode trucks, battle group system or no, they
would be thrown sufficiently on their own resources to make organic
support weapons vital: medium mortars, 37mm light infantry guns,
37mm antitank guns. In contrast to the foot-marching infantry, these
were usually assigned to battalions. That in turn gave regimental headquarters more time to train in handling combined-arms formations, as
opposed to using attached tanks as generic close support. The rifle companies and battalions, for their parts, intensified assault training, working independently and with the divisional pioneers to break the way for
the tanks and then keep pace with them as they advanced.

A few other mobile formations existed as well. Two battalions of
Panzer IIs converted to flamethrowers were authorized in the spring
of 1940. The 40th Panzer Battalion for Special Purposes was organized
with three companies of Panzer Is and IIs and a few experimental types

for the invasion of Denmark and Norway. A two-regiment motorized brigade participated in the Danish phase of the operation. Far more significant was the appearance of the Grossdeutschland Regiment. Its ancestor was the Berlin Security Battalion, originally formed under Weimar to safeguard the government and showcase the Reichswehr. In 1937 it was expanded to regimental strength. Recruited, like the former Prussian Guard, throughout the Reich, it was considered a corps d'elite and in 1940 it included four battalions. Three were standard motorized infantry. The 4th, prefiguring later developments in the motorized infantry, was a support battalion with an infantry gun company, an anti-tank company, and something entirely new: an assault gun battery of six self-propelled 75mm mounts.

The assault gun was a product of exigency: a substitute for the heavy tanks projected in the 1930s for direct infantry support; and a consequence of branch rivalry in the German army. Had rearmament progressed in the systematic fashion envisaged by the General Staff and the High Command, or had Hitler adjusted his diplomatic offensive more closely to Germany's military capacity, assault guns might well never have existed. Their institutional patron was the artillery. Responding to the nascent armored force's call for tanks to be concentrated under its command, Germany's gunners argued that infantry support would inevitably suffer. Experience indicated that weapons in a different branch-of-service chimney were all too likely to be totally elsewhere when needed.

During World War I, the artillery had responded by forming specialized "infantry gun batteries," armed with modified field guns—an approach unique to the German army. There had never been enough of them, and in the 1920s the Reichswehr had developed two purpose-designed infantry guns, one 75mm and the other 150mm—the same caliber as the standard medium howitzer. Introduced in regimental gun companies, they were useful but disproportionately vulnerable, especially at close range. Their crews, moreover, wore infantry-branch white, and the cannon cockers saw themselves being relegated to third place in the combat arms pecking order.

In 1935, Erich von Manstein, newly appointed head of the General

Staff's Operations Section, prepared a memo consolidating previous discussions and recommending the development of a self-propelled "assault gun" to work directly with the infantry, with each division having its own battalion. What the gunners described, and what the Weapons Office turned into a development contract in 1936, was to a degree a throwback to the original Allied tanks of World War I: a vehicle with a low silhouette for concealment "not to exceed the height of a standing man," all-round armor protection, and a 75mm gun with both high-explosive and armor-piercing capacity. Putting those requirements together made a turret impossible; the gun would instead be mounted in a fixed superstructure with a limited traverse of 30 degrees. Initially, as in the later US tank destroyers, the top was open to facilitate the observation considered necessary for tactical effectiveness at infantry ranges. Before going into production, however, the vehicle was given a roof and a panoramic sight enabling it to employ indirect fire. After all, assault guns were artillery weapons.

Guderian, the armored force's designated pit bull, argued that the concept was a mistake. Turreted tanks could do anything assault guns could do; the reverse was not the case. A subtext amounting to a main text was that the projected assault gun would use the chassis of the Mark III tank and the gun intended for the Panzer IV. Guderian and his tanker colleagues were not placated by projections indicating that rising production would avert serious competition for chassis. A disproportionate number of officers in senior army appointments had begun their careers in the artillery—Fritsch, Beck, and Halder, among others. It has been suggested that a "gunner mafia" thwarted Guderian out of branch rivalry. More to the point was the fact that the light tanks that were expected to become surplus as the IIIs and IVs entered service were too small and fragile to carry a three-inch gun even in a hull mounting, while the artillerymen wanted every active infantry division to have its assault gun battalion by the fall of 1939.

In practice, assault guns never became a high-priority item. The first soft-steel experimental models were not completed until 1938. The first production run was only 30, and those were not delivered until May

1940. Only a half dozen six-gun batteries saw action in France. Later orders placed in early 1940 were for only 120 vehicles—hardly evidence of either branch or institutional commitment to the concept. Not until the Sturmgeschütz III proved its worth beyond question did the contracts expand and the assault gun begin to take its place beside the panzers in Wehrmacht history and military lore.

Light tank chassis were nevertheless good for something. The towed antitank gun was still considered satisfactory as the backbone of antitank defense. The army's offensive mind-set, however, encouraged active defense to the point where the initial title of *Panzer Abwehr* (tank defense) was changed prewar to *Panzerjäger* (tank hunter). The 37mm gun was easily handled, but against the up-armored tanks coming into service, its days were numbered. The more powerful designs on the drawing boards were also significantly heavier. But the Czech army had possessed a very effective 47mm antitank gun and the armored force had an increasing number of Panzer Is becoming surplus to requirements. Remove the German turret, mount the Czech gun behind a three-sided shield, and the result was the first tracked, armored antitank gun to enter service. The design was patchwork and its numbers were small, but as with the assault gun, its relative success in 1940 made the 47mm Panzer I combination the first in a long line of similar improvisations in all armies.

In the interim between the fall of Poland and the attack on France, the armored force confronted another kind of technological problem. How best could the commander of a mobile formation built around the internal-combustion engine be at the critical point of a battle while at the same time continuing to command his whole force effectively? The panzer division included an "armored radio company," but its vehicles were as a rule attached to division and brigade headquarters. Events in Poland had demonstrated the practical limits of radio communication under field conditions. "Leading from the front" invited the dispersion of effort as commanders seeking to exploit presumed opportunities wound up directing isolated actions that eventually devolved to skirmishes with limited tactical results. Guderian's familiar mantra *"klotzen, nicht kleckern*" ("slug, don't fumble; keep focused on an objective") was sound enough. The problem was implementation.

Erwin Rommel, newly appointed commander of the freshly minted 7th Panzer Division, addressed the problem by developing a mobile headquarters based on an electronic command system mounted in a cross-country vehicle: a network of radios allowing him to contact both subordinate formations and his own main headquarters. He sought as well to develop a common way of doing things—not as a straitjacket, but rather as a framework for structuring the behavior of subordinates in the constant emergency that was the modern mobile battlefield. Commanders at all levels were to exercise independent judgment, with the division commander using his sense of the battle and the information provided by his headquarters to select points of intervention, ideally to refine and complete the efforts of the men on the spot.

Rommel made clear to his senior staff officers that he depended essentially on them to process and evaluate information in his absence, and to act on it, should that seem necessary. By later American standards, German divisions had small headquarters whose officers were relatively low ranking. That reflected exigency more than principle; the army after 1933 was never able to keep pace with its own expanding need for troop staff officers. The often-praised "lean and mean" German structure meant everyone worked constantly. Vital information could be overlooked by busy men. Fatigue and stress led to errors in judgment and to problems of communication as tired, frustrated alpha-male subordinates snapped pointlessly at each other. Especially in a mobile division, success depended heavily on a commanding general willing to support the decisions of even junior staff officers in whose ability, toughness, and loyalty he had confidence.

There was only one Rommel, who in the 1940 campaign would deliver arguably the most outstanding division-level command performance in modern military history. But in every panzer and motorized division, men with similar perspectives were assuming senior posts. Friedrich Kirchner of 1st Panzer Division, the 6th's Franz Kempf, the 10th's Friedrich Schaal, and their counterparts were not water-walkers. But they were solid professionals, able to get the best out of subordinates. Some began as gunners, some as infantrymen, and some wearing cavalry yellow. What they had in common were high learning curves, fingertip situational awareness, and emotional hardness unmatched even in the Red Army. The combination would prove consistently formidable, no matter the operational considerations.

The greater question in these interim months was how the mobile formations could best be used. At division levels the accepted pattern for an initial deployment was a wave formation with tanks leading. The rifle brigade and usually the pioneers formed the next echelon, then the artillery. The reconnaissance battalion scouted ahead, looking for enemy forces and alternate routes of advance. The attack itself went on in a relatively narrow front, no longer than a thousand yards. As a rule, the tanks led, regiments abreast or one following the other, each responsible for overwhelming a particular element of the defense. Their moral effect was considered on a par with their physical impact, both combining to carry the division through enemy defense by mass, shock, and speed. The motorized battalions, supported by the antitank battalion and the pioneers, would clear pockets of resistance along the line of advance, consolidate captured ground, and prepare to hold it against counterattacks until summoned to catch up with the tanks and repeat the process. The reconnaissance battalion would move into the lead, three or four miles ahead of the tanks, supported when necessary by the motorcyclists. The artillery supported the whole operation with direct or indirect fire as necessary—or as possible. The guns were expected to keep pace with the tanks, which waited for no one.

The major development after the Polish campaign involved using armored forces to conduct the initial breakthrough even against prepared defenses. On February 7, at a war game held in Koblenz, Guderian proposed concentrating the armored forces for a drive across the Meuse River around Sedan, then expanding the bridgehead northwest toward Amiens. The Chief of Staff insisted on a measured buildup, waiting for the infantry before seeking to exploit the initial success. A month later, a second war game evaluated the same issue. This time the pressure from on high for using infantry to force the crossing was even stronger. Guderian and XIV Panzer Corps commander Gustav von Wietersheim responded that the proposed conservative employment of the armor was so likely to produce a crisis that they could have no confidence in a high command that ordered it.

These kinds of war games were intended to generate spirited debate with no hard feelings. But when two experienced senior generals flatly declared "no confidence" in a plan, it was the closest thing possible to saying "get yourself another boy." This partly manifested the panzer troops' new confidence. Arguably it also reflected a persisting sense at senior command levels that, for all their retraining, the foot-powered infantry of 1940 might not be the soldiers their fathers were in 1914. This was the time of the new men of the German army: the panzer troops.

The army faced a related problem: growing shortage of motor vehicles. As early as 1938, maintenance personnel had to cope with a hundred different models of trucks. That number had been reduced, but on the outbreak of war, confusion was restored by the commandeering of thousands of trucks directly from the civilian economy. Polish roads— or the absence of them—had been hard enough on the panzers. Supply columns had suffered losses in some cases more than 50 percent, many of them permanent. By 1940, write-offs had reached a point where the General Staff was considering replacing some trucks in infantry divisions with horse-drawn vehicles. Small wonder in such contexts that the concept of putting the mobile forces up front increasingly permeated thoughts about the coming campaign.

III

THE GENESIS OF the German strategic plan against the Western allies is familiar. Hitler wanted the Western campaign to begin immediately after the fall of Poland. The initial date of November 12 was a compromise with a High Command reluctant to mount an offensive under any circumstances. Its foot-dragging produced no fewer than 29 postponements and a concept for Case Yellow, the Western offensive, that involved sending 75 divisions, including most of the army's mobile formations, into the Low Countries to engage the main Anglo-French strength in what was expected to be an encounter battle in central Belgium. Even before Hitler became directly involved in the planning process, this unpromisingly conventional proposal was generating increasing criticism. It incorporated no proposals for destroying enemy armed forces, speaking rather of creating favorable conditions for future operations. The High Command's thinking seemed to go no further than punching a hole and seeing what developed. In that sense their proposal owed more to Ludendorff's abortive 1918 offensive than the Schlieffen Plan to which it has often been compared.

Interwar theorists of independent armored warfare like Fuller and Liddell-Hart tended to stress disruption—paralysis—as an end in itself. Cut an enemy's nervous system and all that remained was rounding up the demoralized and hungry masses. By contrast, the High Command's plan anticipated the kind of hard fighting that made decisions dependent on contingencies—including a solid probability of defeat at the hands of Allied armor. It required little more than back-of-the-envelope calculation to determine that the force-to-space ratios created by the proposed operation would invite exactly the kind of head-on engagements the army's mechanized elite was ill-configured to fight. The consequences of defeat, or even stalemate, somewhere in Belgium were hardly likely to have involved strengthening either Hitler's domestic position or Germany's chances for victory.

German doctrine, both generally in the army and specifically in the armored force, was based on destroying enemy forces by breaking their will and their ability to resist. That was the principle of Vernichtungs-schlacht, too often tendentiously translated as "battle of annihilation" and then interpreted literally. That was also the basis of the alternative concept put forward by Erich von Manstein, then-chief of staff to Army Group A. Manstein's proposal was intended as much to provide a central role for his commanding general, Gerd von Rundstedt, as to furnish a program for victory. His projected thrust through the Ardennes would transform Rundstedt's army group from a secondary player to the campaign's focal point. Broken terrain made the option a risk—but a calculated risk, taking maximum advantage of the principal German force

multipliers: leadership and technology. Hitler, disgruntled by his generals' conventionality and angered by a security breach that put copies of
the original plan in Allied hands, took advantage of Manstein's temporary presence in Berlin to discuss his ideas. A few days later he issued
a new operational plan: a Sichelschnitt ("sickle cut") through northern
France that would eventually put seven of Germany's ten panzer divisions under Army Group A.

The intelligence service's conviction, repeatedly tested in war gam-
ing, was that the French and British high commands would respond
slowly to that kind of surprise. Since 1933, generals and politicians on
both sides of the English Channel had failed to understand German
intentions and German decision-making processes. Instead they had
grown accustomed to putting unexpected events into preconceived
models, from a postulate that Hitler ultimately would not risk war to
a belief that Germany would attack in Belgium because it suited the
Allies' book that it do so. Both common sense and thinking outside the
box were sacrificed to habit—and in the case of the French, to logic.
Allied intelligence provided more than enough evidence to turn eyes
to the Ardennes in the spring of 1940. Instead, the Allies believed what
they needed to believe about the German operational plan, and kept on
believing it during those few crucial days when the German spearheads
sliced across their rear toward the Channel.

Had Allied leaders anticipated a major offensive through the
Ardennes even as a contingency, it is almost inconceivable that the
catastrophe of 1940 would have taken place as it did. Indeed, the alternative of a French victory parade down Unter den Linden was a real
possibility. France in 1940 was arguably in less danger of moral collapse
than a Germany whose public morale was in good part a consequence
of what seemed Hitler's unbroken string of rabbit-out-of-the-hat successes. German soldiers as well as French ones panicked on the battlefields of 1940. Many of the shortcomings in training and equipment
France faced in the 1930s had been addressed and overcome or moder-
ated by the spring of 1940. The British Expeditionary Force (BEF) had
done a good deal to improve its effectiveness since its initial deployment across the Channel. The Allies had "equipment for victory": pow-

erful air forces, a fully motorized BEF, and around 3,500 tanks, many of them superior to the lighter models still predominant among the 2,300 German ones. And the French expected to win when the fighting started. The French army may have been less effective than its enemy on the tactical level, and its commanders on the whole may have been a cut below their German counterparts. However, nowhere in French circles or among France's allies was there serious doubt of the French ability at least to stop any German offensive in its tracks. That kind of confidence is itself a force multiplier not to be despised.

The Germans thus benefited disproportionately from an obliging enemy. An obliging enemy is not an enemy that makes mistakes, but rather one that behaves as though the opposition prepared his orders. "Obliging," however, is not a synonym for "stupid." Chief of Staff Franz Halder was won over by Sichelschnitt at least as a calculated risk preferable to the existing alternatives, but realized its success depended on keeping the Allies' attention focused on the Low Countries. German military planners' focus on tactical and operational levels at the expense of strategy and policy has been so often repeated it has become a shibboleth. Halder and his subordinates were well aware that the Netherlands were reluctant to cooperate militarily with anyone—even neighboring Belgium. Belgium had begun developing a defensive line facing Germany at the start of the war. It also briefly deployed its army on both the French and German frontiers, and the government had repeatedly emphasized the worthlessness of any Allied assistance that arrived after Belgium had been invaded and devastated, as had been the case in 1914. Immediate and convincing Allied commitment in the face of a German initiative was correspondingly imperative. The dynamics of any battle fought in Belgium would change significantly should Belgian involvement be less than enthusiastic, to say nothing of the probable consequences of the non-participation of Belgium's two dozen divisions.

How, then, to keep the Allies convinced that what they wanted to do was also operationally necessary? The developed German plan used almost a third of the armored force as bait. The 9th Panzer Division, with the fewest number of tanks, would cooperate with the Luftwaffe's paratroopers and the army's air-landing division to strike the

Netherlands in a "shock and awe" operation. Two panzer and a motorized division under Army Group B would provide the mobile core of
an otherwise foot-powered thrust into Belgium. A chess player might
speak of a knight's move, a bullfight aficionado might think of a matador's cape. But the other half of the knight fork, the sword delivering the killing blow, was Panzergruppe Kleist. Five armored and three
motorized divisions, plus the Grossdeutschland Regiment, would pass
through the Ardennes and force their way across the Meuse River into
northern France. An entire antiaircraft corps was folded into the Panzergruppe to compensate for fighter planes with other assignments.
Its right flank would be covered by another two-division panzer corps
under Hermann Hoth.

The operation was still high-risk. It involved more than 130,000
men and more than 1,500 armored vehicles—many of both nose-to-tail
from the border all the way back to Koblenz. No tank-and-truck force
approaching that size had ever been deployed before. Could it fight
through a forest, breach prepared defenses, and cross a major river without sacrificing its fighting power?

As much to the point, could Panzergruppe Kleist keep out of its
own way once the fighting started? Ewald von Kleist was a cavalryman
whose first experience with armored troops had been as a corps commander in Poland. He had done well enough handling two panzer divisions, but his current assignment reflected less his operational skill than
his emotional steadiness and mental toughness. He had a reputation for
bringing subordinates to his point of view without pulling rank. If the
Panzergruppe was the Schwerpunkt of Case Yellow, the Schwerpunkt
of the Panzer Group was Guderian's XIX Corps. "Der *schnelle Heinz*"
("Hurrying Heinz"), as the men called Guderian, far overshadowed
the other two corps commanders in terms of talent and charisma. They
would take their leads from Guderian. He could make the sickle cut
work—but like a fine-tuned engine, he needed a governor to prevent
overheating. That was Kleist's job, much as in World War I Hindenburg
had acted as the nitrogen to Ludendorff's oxygen in the duo's best days.

Army Group A's headquarters rejoiced in its new role but was less
pleased with the instrument for achieving it. Nothing like Panzergruppe

Kleist had ever existed in the German command structure. Armies and corps, yes, but a "group" was generally understood as a temporary organization for secondary missions. Rundstedt left no doubt that the Panzergruppe as a concept was on trial by keeping it organically subordinate to one of his field armies during the campaign. This was anything but a vote of confidence, and proved a constant source of confusion, friction, and bad temper. It also served to galvanize Kleist's professionalism and his professional ambition.

Since the First World War, French military authorities had routinely described the Ardennes as impenetrable to armored vehicles—"Europe's best tank obstacle," in the words of French commander in chief Maurice Gustave Gamelin. The impenetrability was not taken literally, but the French were convinced that even a full-scale offensive would take no fewer than five days—more likely nine—to push through the Ardennes, and about two weeks to attempt a crossing of the Meuse. Prewar intelligence reports of German intentions to attack through the Ardennes were processed as referring to no more than a secondary offensive. Initial reports of massive tank columns seemingly everywhere in the forest were dismissed as first-battle jitters. Besides, even if the Germans made it through the trees, they would surely be stopped by the river.

In Belgium, Army Group B did its job to near-perfection. A day's initial delay due to blown bridges only encouraged the Allies to rush into Belgium and assume defensive positions along the Dyle River, reinforcing and supporting the Belgians. It was according to plan—the Dyle Plan. French generals and staff officers were students and creatures of a doctrine emphasizing the importance of a firepower and management. They had no intention of playing to the German army's obvious strength by seeking an encounter battle of the classic sort, as opposed to using armor in defensive contexts along a line offering a shorter and stronger position than the one defined by the Franco-Belgian frontier.

Arguably the Germans' greatest success at the strategic level, however, was achieved in Holland. Gamelin was committed to—one might say obsessed with—fighting as far away from French soil as possible. In pursuit of that design, he had reconfigured the employment of the mobile strategic reserve created with considerable effort during the 1930s.

Originally it was projected that reserve would be deploying around Reims for use against a German invasion anywhere from Switzerland to the Low Countries. The final "Breda Variant" of the Dyle Plan, adopted in November 1939, projected using it, organized as the 7th Army, to drive into Holland and extend the left flank of an Allied position Gamelin expected would stop the Germans in their tracks—or close enough to that for military purposes. And then one would have most of Belgium to establish a killing ground for the managed battle that would decide the war.

Instead German airborne and motorized forces already well stuck into Holland enmeshed the French mobile reserve in a morass of streams, woods, and soft ground. And when, on May 16, 1940, Britain's new premier Winston Churchill asked, "Where is the mass of maneuver?" the French could only reply, with a suitably Gallic shrug, *"Aucune"* ("There isn't any").

One of the overlooked ironies of 1940 is that the 7th Army's initial staging area was close behind the Ardennes. Whether the elite 1st Light Mechanized Division, two first-line motorized divisions, and four infantry divisions committed in the event to the Breda Variant could have stemmed the tide flooding out of the Ardennes on June 12 is debatable. But they would have helped—and matters could hardly have been any worse for their presence.

Army Group A pushed through the Ardennes undeterred by air strikes that proved unexpectedly vulnerable to small-arms fire, and barely detained by bicycle-riding Belgian Chasseurs Ardennais and French cavalry divisions whose horse-mounted and motorized regiments proved an unfortunate mix of "manure and gasoline." French and Belgians achieved some impressive local successes. Confusion developed regarding operational zones and lines of march, with the 1st and 10th Panzer Divisions in particular briefly getting tangled. The Germans nevertheless drove relentlessly. Advance elements were constantly rotated, with fresh crews brought up on trucks to take over tanks in place. The Germans took hair-raising chances. On the first day of the attack, 400 men of Grossdeutschland were successfully airlifted behind Belgian lines in 100 light airplanes, German counterparts of the Piper Cub. The

Germans improvised almost at random, finding fords under fire when bridges blew up almost beneath the treads of the lead tanks. It required not nine days, not five, but only three for the mechanized spearheads to emerge from the forest and roll toward Sedan.

Kleist, the old cavalryman, might be a few miles per hour behind the pace of modern war, but he knew opportunity when he sensed it—or perhaps when it was forced upon him. He differed with Guderian about the exact axis of the attack and its precise timing. Nevertheless, on May 12, Kleist informed Hitler that he proposed to "bounce" the Meuse—cross it with his own resources even though most of his artillery was still tangled in the Ardennes. The High Command responded by allocating its heaviest tactical hammer—Wolfram von Richthofen's retitled VIII Air Corps, 300 Stukas, and 40 ground-attack biplanes with a crack wing of Messerschmitt 109s—as escorts to reinforce the effort. Altogether, 1,500 aircraft would support the crossing: Stukas, bombers, and fighters.

Guderian's spearheads reached the Meuse late on the twelfth and spent the night organizing assembly areas. The main event began on the thirteenth. The narrative framework is familiar: middle-aged French reservists, poorly trained and motivated, hammered into the ground by dive-bombers and artillery; German infantry improvising crossings, knocking out surviving positions as pioneers bring up bridges and ferries for the tanks; French communications cut, French artillery immobilized, and finally, French infantry cracking and panicking as the panzers sliced into their country's heartland.

Up close and personal, the story was different. French infantry withstood a long day under air attacks whose scale and intensity made even the Germans say "hell had broken loose." French artillery stopped the Germans in their tracks on the far side of the Meuse until midafternoon. French machine guns shot up rubber boats and their occupants. The XIX Panzer Corps attempted six major crossings on May 13. Three failed completely. Not until dawn on the fourteenth did the first tanks cross the Meuse. In the interim the infantry, as always, took heavy losses in what became essentially a storm trooper fight in the style of 1918: taking pillboxes with a combination of minor tactics and major courage against defenders who failed to read the script calling for them to run away. It was satchel charges and grenades at close quarters, pistols, sometimes bare hands. The Stukas set the table, but May 13 was the Day of the Rifleman—the lieutenants and sergeants and rear-rank privates of Hermann Balck's 1st Regiment, of Grossdeutschland and their counterparts who took XLIV Panzer Corps over the river at Monthermé and opened the way for Hoth's divisions further north at Dinant. Never again would panzer commanders—successful ones at least—treat the truck-riders and motorcyclists as a supporting cast.

By the morning of May 14, the panzer divisions had torn a hole 50 miles wide in the French lines. It was a tactical opportunity and an operational one—if the Germans could develop it. Guderian demanded a breakout. He did not want to lose time building up the bridgehead— and giving the French a chance to contain it. Better to keep moving, despite resistance from the rear as well as the front. Guderian wanted at least a 12-mile bridgehead as a first step. Kleist was satisfied with five miles, and made it an order. He had ample company. Halder noted in his diary that Hitler was "frightened by his own success, afraid to take any chances." The High Command in principle favored exploiting victory, designating the Somme as the next objective, but sought as well to control the pace of the advance. Rundstedt was sufficiently worried about the prospects of a French counterattack that when he visited Guderian's commands post on the fourteenth, he insisted Kleist's directive must stand. A solid shoulder beat a broken neck.

Guderian had nothing if not the courage of his convictions. His intention was to leave 10th Panzer Division and Grossdeutschland to secure his southern flank, pivot 1st and 2nd Panzer southwest, then west, link up with XLIV Panzer Corps, and keep going. He issued the appropriate orders on the evening of the fourteenth. Around midnight Kleist confirmed them—and for two more days ran interference with his superiors. This was "mission tactics" in the true sense: a subordinate as yet without relevant orders acting on his own situational awareness, supported by the next echelon of command. Ewald von Kleist did not lack professional courage. His head no less than Guderian's was on the chopping block—perhaps literally—should anything go irreparably wrong. And the operational analysis of Panzergruppe Kleist handsomely acknowledged that Guderian's "unauthorized measures . . . resulted in a great success . . . for the entire course of operations and averted a major threat."

Much of the thanks was really owed to 10th Panzer and GD. By nightfall on the fifteenth, the Germans were in defensive positions on the high ground around the village of Stonne. Infantry forward, anti-tank guns in support, the panzer brigade in reserve: it reads easily on paper. On the ground it was the consequence of the first day of a battle both sides compared to Verdun. Stonne changed hands seventeen times between the fifteenth and the seventeenth of May as desperate Allied air strikes on the Meuse bridges were accompanied by equally desperate French efforts to break through to the river on the ground.

The main counterattack was built around the 3rd Armored Division. These were new creations, designed to be part of the "managed battle" as opposed to conducting independent operations. They had only a single battalion of infantry. Their logistic support was limited. But with four tank battalions, including two of B-1s more heavily armed and armored than anything in the German order of battle, a *division cuirassée* was reasonably suited to an at-all-cost effort—especially when, like the 3rd, it was paired with a first-rate motorized division and under the command of France's leading light in peacetime armored maneuvers.

In the end, the French effort fell prey to order-counterorder-disorder. General Jean-Adolphe Flavigny had since noon on the twelfth to prepare the operation. He folded when confronted with the real thing in one of those command disconnects that occurs in any transition from peace to war, yet is virtually impossible to predict specifically. Flavigny's intention was to stop the Germans, and only then attack: managed battle epitomized. But the 3rd Armored, which had been organized only in March, was handicapped by comprehensively bad staff work centered on fueling problems. French tanks were seriously short-legged compared to the German ones; range was a low-priority consideration in *bataille conduit*. Flavigny had planned to attack before noon on the fourteenth.

He postponed until the fifteenth, and then postponed again, when his divisional commanders reported a general attack would be impossible because of the dislocation of their formations.

Flavigny, in sharp contrast to Guderian, did nothing to take control. Instead French resources were frittered away in company-and battalion-scale lunges toward Stonne that nevertheless gave the Germans all they could handle. The B-1s, weighing in at more than thirty tons, heavily armored, with a turret-mounted 47mm antitank gun and a 75mm in the hull, frightened some of Grossdeutschland's infantry into blind panic, and with good reason. One B-1 took 140 hits—all ricochets—and accounted by itself for more than a dozen German tanks. Another caught a column of German infantry and literally overran them, entering Stonne with blood on its tracks.

The antitank gunners held their ground as their 37mm rounds bounced away like tennis balls. Only by waiting for a close-range shot at the more vulnerable sides, a near-ultimate exercise in nerve and discipline, did the Germans manage to knock out or discourage enough of the B-1s to maintain the moral balance of a fight that eventually turned Stonne into a tank graveyard, with more than fifty of them—French and German—derelict in the streets and on the outskirts.

There was nothing wrong with French heart. The failures lay in command and communications systems that left tanks, infantry, and artillery putting in small-scale, uncoordinated attacks, which eventually gave the Germans time to support and relieve the mobile troops with infantry from the follow-up waves. The straight-legs repulsed final French efforts at Stonne as the tanks and trucks turned westward with the rest of Guderian's corps.

Abraham Lincoln once described a Union general as reacting to defeat "like a duck hit on the head." The metaphor applies equally well to French commanders trying to decide what to do next as the Germans poured across the "impassable" Meuse. Again the French fought well at the cutting edge, with some of the finest performances given by their African and North African soldiers. On May 15, at a village called La Horgne, a brigade of Spahis—Algerian and Moroccan cavalry still riding horses—held up part of the 1st Panzer Division for eight hours.

Balck, no stranger to close combat, later declared that rarely did he see men fight as well as these, who stood to the last for France and for honor.

Much of the key to the French dilemma lies in a noun in the above paragraph. "*Part*" of the German division was blocked—one of its two battle groups. The other group was able to keep moving. So was the rest of XIX Panzer Corps, as the French proved unable to concentrate forces sufficient to block the spearheads, let alone counterattack them effectively. "A day late and a hundred francs short" comes to mind as another trope for a French High Command still expecting the main German attack through Belgium as the panzers drove dead into France, toward ground hallowed by the Great War, and deep into the Allied rear.

IV

THE PANZERS FACED problems in their own rear. When XLI Panzer Corps had difficulty breaking out of its bridgehead around Monthermé, Rundstedt ordered the task turned over to infantry. Kleist turned Nelson's blind eye, the 6th Panzer Division overran the last French positions, and its commander turned loose an improvised battle group. Its tanks and motorcyclists, a battalion of each, covered 35 miles in five hours. The former cavalrymen drove through and over French formations that were unable to believe the Germans were where they were, and were unable to react to their presence. Eighth Panzer Division came up the next day and finished the job. When the shooting was done and the prisoners interrogated, the Germans discovered XLI Panzer Corps had destroyed the French 2nd Armored Division, which had been caught in the process of moving into position and hamstrung by a series of contradictory orders. Rundstedt's headquarters backed off and restored Kleist's freedom of movement—at least until next time.

Further north, Hermann Hoth's XV Panzer Corps had the original mission of covering Kleist's right flank by passing through the Belgian Ardennes and crossing the Meuse around Dinant. More than its French counterpart, the terrain was a nightmare of hills and valleys, unimproved regional roads, and trails leading nowhere in particular. But the Belgians defended only a few of their obstacles. Allied aircraft were conspicuously absent. Hoth, a former infantryman whose men nicknamed him Vati (GIs would have called him "Pop") knew how to "pick 'em up an' put 'em down," whether boots or treads; and he had Erwin Rommel. In three days the 7th Panzer Division advanced almost 60 miles. Make them keep their heads down; go through them and past them; mop them up: it was blitzkrieg *pur*. Hoth gave Rommel his head: cross the Meuse and keep going. With the bridges at Houx and Dinant blown, motorcyclists used a weir and a lock gate, both unguarded, to get a foothold on the west bank. Rubber boats carried across a company's worth of reinforcements by the time the defenders came fully alert, a little before daybreak on May 13.

As casualties mounted under French artillery and machine guns, Rommel started a fresh wave of riflemen across the Meuse—and took a place in one of the leading rubber boats, to find himself caught in a French tank attack. He ordered the infantry to open fire with rifles and machine guns. With bullets glancing off their armor and sparks and fragments ricocheting through firing ports, the tanks fell back. Returning across the river, the general lent a hand with building a ferry heaving timbers while under fire in waist-deep water. He was first across in his command vehicle. Not only did Rommel seem to be at every vital spot exactly when he was needed; to the men of 7th Panzer Division, he seemed as well to be bulletproof.

By the early morning of May 15 the crossing was secure, a pontoon bridge was in place, and 7th Panzer Division's combat elements were ready to roll. Rommel established a "thrust line" on the division's maps, divided into sectors. To call in air support or artillery fire, all Rommel needed to do was refer to one of the sectors. The recipient's job was to note the target area, bring it in, and keep it coming. By the elaborate standards of the Great War, this was near-random improvisation. The division's artillery commander was nevertheless delighted to be able to provide the kind of instant support that artillery had been able to deliver when guns galloped into battle behind six-horse teams.

Rommel rode with the leading tanks—into a counterattack by two of the French army's best divisions: 1st Armored, with its two battalions of B-1s, and 4th North African, which included a number of long-service professional soldiers, among the best fighting men in France. The French had had a long, hard day on the fourteenth. Advancing through swarms of refugees, constrained to move at slow speeds and in low gear, their fuel tanks were nearly empty and their crews tired. For convenience their commanders bivouacked in the open to await the gasoline trucks. No one bothered to dispatch even a few motorcyclists to screen the roads to the east.

Seventh Panzer Division took the French by surprise. Panzer IIs and 38(t)s concentrated on the thinner side armor of the French tanks, on ventilators, tracks, and suspension systems. The Panzer IVs used high-explosive rounds against the fuel trucks that began arriving just as the German attack started. Coordinated resistance foundered as French tank commanders found their radio batteries had been run flat. Crew after crew ceased fire, waving rags and handkerchiefs from their turrets to indicate surrender. Thirty-five tanks, including 19 heavy Char Bs, went under in a matter of minutes.

Leaving the rest of 1st Armored to the just-arriving 5th Panzer Division, Rommel led his own tank regiment westward at forty miles per hour. By the end of the day the panzers had reached the edge of the northern extension of the Maginot Line. Officers and men from rear-echelon French units, confused and shaken, were surrendering in masses, responding to any orders they received, even if the language was German and the content was "Drop your weapons! Hands up." Seventh Panzer Division nevertheless found heavy going on the seventeenth, grinding through the fortified zone against stubborn resistance that seemed to intensify as the day waned. The moon was up and the long European twilight had set in by the time the last roadblocks were cleared, and Rommel saw his chance. There was still enough light for the panzers to drive forward and break out. A risk, yes—but preferable to a night's delay and an enemy further reinforced.

The tanks rolled forward in a long column, impelled by the hammering of their own guns, picking up speed as the confidence of the lead drivers increased. French soldiers and refugees abandoned the road for its ditches. No time for prisoners—just fire a few bursts as warning and deterrent. An occasional brief position report to his increasingly confused, increasingly anxious division headquarters was Rommel's only contact with the rear. Still no resistance—and then it was clear that 7th Panzer Division was through the Maginot Line and on its way to the Sambre River.

By then the tactical situation had dissolved into chaos. Seventh Panzer Division's men and vehicles intermingled with refugees and soldiers, some anxious to surrender and others looking for a chance to fight. Rommel personally led an improvised battle group of tanks and motorcyclists through Avesnes and into Landrecies, where an intact bridge over the Sambre pointed the way deep into the rear of the Allied forces in Belgium. The 7th Panzer Division had advanced more than 50 miles, made a night march unprecedented in the history of armor, captured 10,000 prisoners and 100 tanks—and recorded losses of 35 dead and 59 wounded.

By the standards of the campaigns of Frederick the Great, the Wars of German Unification, and the trenches of 1914–18, the achievement was almost beyond comprehension—but not beyond exploitation. At midnight orders came through from Hoth: continue the attack, direction Cambrai. On May 18 the 25th Panzer Regiment, with its fuel and ammunition replenished and most breakdowns repaired, shot its way into Cambrai across country where during the Great War advances had been calculated in hundreds of yards and casualties counted in tens of thousands. And then Hoth ordered a halt.

Hoth's caution was more than conditioned reflex. Rommel's was not the only panzer division running miles ahead of the rest of the army. The 6th was keeping pace, its columns tangling with Guderian's until the two generals worked out the routes of advance. By now the three divisions of Guderian's corps were even deeper into France than their stablemates, though the advances in miles had not been as far. Seen in hindsight, this was the beginning of nonlinear operations, with gaps in one's front less important than forward progress, and flanks best covered by keeping the enemy confused and off balance. To Guderian and Rommel, speed was the new mantra; rapidity of movement and thought was the key to modern battle. The panzer force was capable of commanding itself all the way to the English Channel. Seen on a map, however, the panzer spearheads looked like fingers thrust out from a hand—and were correspondingly vulnerable to being seized and broken one by one. As early as the fifteenth, Rundstedt considered halting the motorized forces rather than risk even a local defeat that might throw the German advance off balance. He had his staff prepare a stop order just in case. Then the army group commander received a call from the Wehrmacht High Command, Hitler's mouthpiece: shut the panzers down.

Hitler may not have given that order personally, but during a visit to Rundstedt's headquarters on May 17, he emphatically supported it. A successful counterattack, he declared, might encourage both the Allied generals and their politicians. Rather than a helter-skelter push to the English Channel, a solid defensive shoulder in the south should be the next step. The Führer, for the first time since assuming power, encountered overt, coherent, and cohesive resistance among the soldiers. Chief of Staff Franz Halder executed a neat political flanking maneuver, first convincing the Army's commander in chief, Walther von Brauchitsch, to order the offensive renewed, then confronting Hitler to insist the panzers' southern flank was not a problem. Hitler, according to Halder's diary, raged, screamed—and in the end, acquiesced.

Early on May 17, Kleist took a plane forward to pick his own bone with Guderian. The day before he had issued an order establishing a stop line, only to learn Guderian's spearheads were already more than 20 miles beyond it. Apart from the winds starting to blow from above, for Kleist the question was exactly who was commanding the panzer group. Guderian's conscience for once was clear. He had only received the order after midnight, correctly believed it outdated, and acted accordingly. Kleist upbraided Guderian in language more expressive than polite. Guderian's equally heated reply concluded with a request to be relieved. Kleist accommodated him, then wisely left before someone said something that could not be overlooked. Rundstedt immediately restored Guderian to his command with a slap on the wrist requiring him to keep his headquarters temporarily in place. Guderian got around that by using telephones instead of radios. Kleist had no serious problem with the decision. Guderian had forced his hand, but he was soldier enough to sense a developing opportunity. Hermann Hoth also recognized hot dice when he saw them—especially when they came up "promotion," as the High Command on May 17 created Panzer Group Hoth from XV Corps and XVI Corps redeploying from Belgium.

That put what amounted to Germany's entire mobile force—nine panzer and four motorized divisions and several smaller formations, plus elements of the still-embryonic Waffen SS—under Rundstedt's command for a killing stroke: a drive to the English Channel that would cut off the British Expeditionary Force and an entire French army group still facing east and north, still embedded deep in Belgium.

The Germans owed that situation to the panzers. Army Group B might have been a strategic matador's cloak, but its operational sword was tempered steel. The XVI Panzer Corps headquarters had long experience handling tanks, and Erich Hoepner was second only to Guderian as a panzer general. A cavalryman who was an early supporter of mechanization, he commanded 1st Light Division, took over XVI Panzer Corps from Guderian before the Polish campaign, and showed the kind of skill making it possible to overlook a well-known distaste for Nazism. Hoepner's two divisions—3rd Panzer Division from Berlin-Brandenburg and 4th Panzer Division, with its home base in Würzburg—were first-class, well-trained, experienced men manning a total of more than 600 tanks, including 130 Mark IIIs and IVs. Hoepner could also call on the ground-attack specialists of VIII Air Corps, and on the 300 bombers and 500 fighters as the other Luftwaffe units supporting the army group.

The panzers' immediate and most formidable opposition was the French Cavalry Corps of General Rene Prioux. Its core was the 2nd and 3rd Light Mechanized Divisions. On paper these formations resembled the panzer divisions, each with two tank and three motorized battalions, and a total of around 240 tanks. Sixty of them were light vehicles armed only with machine guns and distributed among the dragons' ports. Ninety more were 12-ton Hotchkiss H35s and H39s. Though well armored, the older models carried only a short-barreled 37mm gun dating back to the Great War, which was essentially useless against armor.

The H39 had a modern 37mm gun, but 3rd DLM had only two dozen of them. The remaining 90 French tanks, however, were better than anything in the German stable—better, arguably, than anything in any army's order of battle in 1940. The SOMUA S35 had its design faults: radios only for platoon commanders and a one-man turret forcing the tank commander to serve also as gunner and loader—multitasking ahead of its time. It also featured a well-shaped cast hull—albeit in two pieces riveted together—armor that reached a maximum of more than 50mm, internal fuel tanks giving its 21 tons a range of 150 miles and a maximum speed of 23 miles per hour, and best of all, a high-velocity 47mm turret-mounted main gun, able to outrange any German tank and penetrate its armor from any angle.

Five years of war would demonstrate that in armored war, quality could go far to compensate for numbers. "Quality" however, was more than statistics. It involved training and doctrine. The SOMUA was slow coming on line, thanks in good part to chronic labor troubles in a unionized, Communist-influenced armaments industry. Ideally the light mechanized divisions would have had twice as many SOMUAs as they did. Only about 250 were available by June 1940, with corresponding effects on crew and unit training. That was especially true in the 3rd Division, which had only been organized in January. French concepts for using the DLMs initially reflected the traditional cavalry missions of reconnaissance and screening. By 1939 more attention was paid to offensive capabilities, but these involved exploitation rather than penetration. From the High Command's developing strategic perspective, the optimal initial use of the light mechanized divisions was to cover the move into Belgium. Advancing rapidly and independently, they could conduct a cape-and-sword defense against a projected German armored spearhead as the main force deployed behind them.

That kind of close synergy among doctrine, force structure, and strategic planning is usually and legitimately praised highly in military writing. In 1940 it comprehensively structured the behavior of Prioux and his troopers—for good and ill. Their specific mission was to screen the "Gembloux gap," a 25-mile-wide stretch of country free of significant natural barriers and only partly screened by rudimentary, hastily constructed tank obstacles. Then, the final orders ran, they were to hold until the motorized divisions could establish a defense line. Hold until the morning of May 14.

Rene Prioux had nothing of Joachim Murat or Jeb Stuart in his professional makeup. He was too worried about the Luftwaffe and his own lack of air cover to undertake even the limited spoiling attacks originally enjoined by his superiors. The result was a head-on, two-day encounter battle that began around the village of Hannut on May 12. In a fashion prefiguring the behavior of Israeli armor in the early days of the 1973 Yom Kippur War, 4th Panzer Division attacked with more energy than tactical sense, and took heavy losses from French artillery fire and armored ripostes. The SOMUAs in particular, boldly handled in company strengths, proved an unpleasant surprise as the greenhorns of 3rd Light Mechanized Division came away victors on points from a good day's work. Fuel shortages also hampered the German deployment to the point that Hoepner, instead of continuing to probe opportunistically for weak spots, decided to reorganize, resupply, and mount a two-division set-piece attack the next day.

A ball-peen hammer is a good tool. A nine-pound sledgehammer is also useful. Guderian might have done it with more finesse, but beginning a little after noon on May 13, 3rd and 4th Panzer Divisions, around 560 tanks all told, struck 3rd Light Mechanized Division on an eight-mile front. There was bitter fighting in defended villages, with riflemen clearing strong points and tanks bypassing them whenever possible. Survivors of disabled French tanks fought on with pistols against armor plate. A captain of the 35th Panzer Regiment described two observers in a water tower engaging tanks with rifles until "shot full of holes like sieves." It was not until around 3 PM that the German tanks reached open ground, only to face a series of armored counterattacks. French tanks seemed to be everywhere at once, bypassing the panzers and engaging the infantry, forcing the tanks to turn around and bail out their comrades. The close-gripped, seesaw fighting featured small German armor-piercing shells ricocheting harmlessly off French turrets and hulls. The 6th Panzer Regiment and a company of antitank guns hit every tank in a retiring French column with everything in the inventory, including 75mm rounds. The vehicles just kept moving, with one crew eventually counting 15 antitank hits and 42 bullet scars.

The tactical differences were coordination and cooperation. The Germans fought in combined-arms teams, with towed antitank guns supporting the panzers under a consistently effective air umbrella. The French fought exposed to the sky, in compartments, each arm on its own. The German tankers fought by battalions; the French never went beyond company levels. Even individual French tanks often failed to support each other. Their lack of radios required at least one company commander to transmit orders by running from tank to tank under fire. Their small turrets in practice made tank commanders no more than gunners once combat was joined.

The 3rd DLM, moreover, fought alone against superior numbers. The 2nd Light Mechanized Division remained in its positions all day, facing front and fixed in place by German infantry, force-marched forward. As the Germans freed themselves from the melee and resumed their advance, Prioux, his local reserves exhausted, ordered a withdrawal to the main positions by now established around Gembloux. The cavalry corps had done its job; no reason remained to risk an elite force in an isolated forward position.

When losses were tallied, 3rd DLM had accounted for 160 German tanks at the cost of around 100 of its own. It was true that the Germans held the field, and so were able to recover and repair a good many of their losses. It was true as well that casualties had been absurdly light by Great War standards—only 150 total in the entire 4th Panzer Division. Nevertheless the consciousness of superiority recorded in the corps war diary did not translate to immediate pursuit in a deepening twilight, where all tanks seemed to look alike.

For Erich Hoepner it had been a good day's work. Committing his panzers en masse had paid off despite the losses. German tanks might be inferior in a stand-up fight, but their mobility and the skill of their crews and commanders had set the stage for the next scene: breakthrough at Gembloux. Preliminary orders went out at 3 AM; the French spent the next 18 hours executing a fighting retreat that tied the panzers in knots and completed the cavalry's delaying mission. Instead of overrunning the gap before the French could assume the position, Hoepner's corps confronted a solid defense line manned by three first-class divisions: 1st Moroccan and 1st and 15th Motorized Divisions, with Prioux's tanks deployed by battalions in their rear. A few tentative probes were so strongly received that Hoepner ordered his advanced units to fall back and prepare for a coordinated corps-scale attack the next day.

The resulting engagement of May 15 was the first time the panzer divisions were used to break through a major, prepared defensive position. Both division commanders led with riflemen going in afoot under air and artillery cover, the panzer regiments following closely either to meet enemy armor or exploit the expected breakthrough. Matters unfolded differently. A French army proverb says, "Algerians are men; but Moroccans are lions." From the first exchange of shots, the men from the Atlas Mountains proved a match and better for 4th Panzer Division's infantry. The tanks suffered no less in trying to carry the riflemen forward against gun positions the Luftwaffe failed to find, let alone silence. Particularly disconcerting was the heavy loss of Mark IVs, brought forward for their guns but all too vulnerable to antitank fire. By 4 PM nothing resembling a breakthrough was in sight, and 4th Panzer Division's commander suggested an attack the next day would have no better prospects given the same conditions.

The 3rd Panzer Division initially held its tanks farther back, but also wound up committing them piecemeal to support the infantry against resistance no less determined and no less effective than that confronting the 4th Panzer Division. Results were no better. The Berliners ground forward slowly, a company here and a battalion somewhere else, against constant counterattacks. Late-evening reports that the defenses had finally been breached were unconvincing. Hoepner decided instead to continue the attack the next day, but to replace the panzers with two infantry divisions, presumably better suited to the nature of the fighting and certainly more expendable. The decision proved moot as on May 16 the French withdrew, finally reacting to the breakthrough at Sedan. Hoepner's panzers followed briefly then redeployed as part of the drive to the Channel.

The fighting around Gembloux tends to be overshadowed by the more dramatic events to the south. Tactically, Hannut had shown the worth of spearheading an attack by using tanks in masses, even against superior material. Gembloux indicated the limitations of that approach against an organized defense. The panzers might well have broken through and broken out in another day or two. But on the morning of May 14, 4th Panzer Division reported only 137 tanks ready for action—less than half the authorized strength. Third Panzer Division reported as many as a quarter of its tanks out of action. Even with top-grade field repairs, these were not statistics calculated to inspire trying the same thing again. Crew morale might be as high as the officers said, but there were limits to the number of times men shot out of one tank could simply be assigned to another.

Operationally, the panzers had inverted French doctrine by keeping the Cavalry Corps fixed in place instead of the other way round. On the night of May 14, Gamelin considered pulling it out of the line and turning it against the right flank of the German spearhead coming from Sedan. It was a mission well suited to the DLMs' tactics and training—before the losses inflicted by the panzers, and before the corps was integrated directly into the Gembloux position. Instead the cavalrymen were ingloriously drawn into the general retreat to Dunkirk, just like any second-line foot-marching division caught in one of history's greatest envelopments.

The panzer groups' operational mission was clear: drive northwest between Arras and the Somme, then cut off the Allied forces withdrawing from Belgium. But by now Halder, in the best opportunistic tradition of the General Staff, was considering swinging the bulk of the panzers south into France, fulfilling the original Schlieffen Plan by means of the internal-combustion engine while Army Group B, reinforced by the rest of the armor, mopped up what remained north of the penetration. Hitler, still anxious for the security of the southern flank, rejected this prospect out of hand in favor of halting the mobile forces west of Arras and giving the infantry time to close up.

Meanwhile the panzers rolled on and their opposition dithered.

General Alphonse Georges, commanding the French Northwest Front, collapsed in tears when informed of the breakthrough at Sedan. Gamelin called for a decisive counteroffensive against a German spearhead whose vulnerability increased with every mile it traveled. A newly organized armored division commanded by an obscure colonel with something of a reputation as a military theorist, nibbled at 1st Panzer Division's rear echelons on May 17. But Charles de Gaulle was unable to work a miracle. A report from 1st Panzer Division described a lone B-2 trundling down the road with no obvious intention, shrugging off repeated hits from Panzer IIIs. "We observed that our [37mm shells] were not penetrating," sagely noted the company commander. The French vehicle was then engaged by a 20mm antiaircraft gun and by pioneers and infantrymen with hand grenades. Nothing. The captain then took on the B-2 from the rear with three Panzer IIIs. At around 250 yards the purportedly armor-piercing rounds continued to bounce harmlessly off the turret and the rear plates. The French responded by shooting up a passenger car, and then abandoning the tank and surrendering when a 37mm round—finally, one might add—knocked out the engine.

This event epitomized the nature of the Allies' response to Sichelschnitt. Either formations assigned to counterattacks shed pieces on the way, or the mission was given to improvised forces lacking the cohesion to develop any local success they might gain. Gamelin was dismissed with ignominy on the nineteenth. His replacement, seventy-four-year-old Maxime Weygand, planned a pincer attack on both sides of the breakthrough. The southern arm never got beyond the preliminary orders stage. An attempt to mount a corps-strength attack from the north on May 22 was seen off essentially by the Luftwaffe alone. British Expeditionary Force commander John Vereker, Viscount Gort managed to assemble two British tank battalions, a couple of infantry battalions, and some field and antitank guns on the old World War I battlefield of Vimy Ridge, with ephemeral promises of French support and concrete orders to strike the Germans when they came within range.

The resulting counterattack gave Rommel and 7th Panzer Division a few bad quarters of an hour around Arras on August 21. The operational effect was the military equivalent of throwing a handful of boiled peas at a wall. But whether gallant thrust or forlorn hope, the move focused what Roland Friesner describes as a "flank psychosis," a "crisis psychosis" that produced a layered controversy in the German high command.

V

AT 2 AM on May 21, 1940, the first German troops reached the Channel coast, west of Abbeville. Appropriately enough they were infantrymen, from 2nd Panzer Division's 2nd *Schützen* Regiment. If any aspiring classicists in the ranks cried "Thalassa!" in imitation of Xenophon's 10,000 Greeks, history is silent. Second Panzer Division had advanced 60 miles that day. More than a million men—the entire BEF, a Belgian army that had fought better than anyone expected, a French army group plus bits and pieces of several more—were cut off in Flanders, 80 or 100 miles at best from the coast that offered a still-ephemeral salvation. The German infantry that would decisively close the corridor were still advancing. A lot of ground remained free from German boots or treads. But real-world prospects for a successful mass breakout to the south were finished.

Guderian for one had no doubts. He proposed to turn his divisions north, to the channel ports: 1st to Calais, 2nd to Boulogne, and 10th to Dunkirk, and the sooner the better. In desperation the British threw sacrificial garrisons into Calais and Boulogne. But the road to Dunkirk, designated as the main evacuation port, lay virtually open for 10th Panzer Division—or rather, it did until Kleist responded to high-echelon anxiety over the abortive British attack at Arras by pulling the division into reserve.

Not until May 22 was Guderian allowed to resume his advance. By then the British had settled in. It took 2nd Panzer Division three days of street fighting to take Boulogne. Calais held out until the twenty-sixth in one of the campaign's epic stands. By then the nerves of Hitler, and those senior generals still awaiting the grand Allied counterattack, were strained to breaking point. The situation was not helped by the Führer's recurrent presence at various field headquarters, his anxieties trailing like a cloak. The panzer generals, the bit between their teeth, wanted to press the attack. Army Group A preferred a brief halt to sort out the mobile forces and allow the infantry to catch up and secure the corridor opened by the tanks. Halder and the High Command advocated a bold advance in a strategic context—arguably even the "Schlieffen option" mentioned earlier. Hitler sought a *Verschnaufpause*, a breathing space, partly to evaluate a situation that had outrun even his imagination, but also to demonstrate that he was supreme commander in practice as well as by title.

The situation was tinder for what Carl von Clausewitz called "friction." Kleist provided the spark when, on May 23, he complained to Rundstedt that his group was so dispersed and had suffered such heavy losses, including more than half its tanks, that it was too weak to mount an attack against strong forces. Halder dismissed the message as an attack of nerves. Rundstedt, however, responded by shutting down the panzers for a day, with the advance to resume on the twenty-fifth. The High Command in turn reassigned both panzer groups to Army Group B—as drastic a reaction as possible short of ordering Rundstedt's outright relief. Order, counter order, disorder—and in the midst of it, Hitler appeared at Rundstedt's headquarters. He promptly reversed the transfer orders, which had been issued without his knowledge. He then declared himself completely in agreement with Rundstedt's perspective. Army Group A at 12:45 PM confirmed the shutdown of the panzers. Hitler complemented this with a directive establishing the next objective as the destruction of Allied forces in Flanders. He also gave Rundstedt a free hand in the conduct of operations—a factor that had significant consequences.

Halder on one end, and Kleist and his commanders on the other, reacted with varying combinations of fury and bewilderment. Even Guderian, seldom at a loss for words, declared himself speechless. Efforts by Halder and Brauchitsch to change the Führer's mind were predictably futile. Noteworthy in that context is Hitler's reiterated denunciation of what he described as challenging his authority by transferring the panzer groups without permission. That was arguably more significant than such generally cited factors as hope for peace with Britain, worry about the boggy Flanders terrain, concern with sparing the panzers for future operations, or even desire to give Hermann Göring and his "National Socialist Luftwaffe" the glory of finishing off a trapped enemy. Not until May 26 did Hitler rescind the "halt order"—and even then only at Rundstedt's urging. By that point it was hours too late to make a difference.

Gerd von Rundstedt gave Hitler all the backup he needed by using his free hand to hold the tanks firmly under his thumb. Only on the morning of the twenty-fifth did he allow Kleist and Hoth to change his mind. Not until the morning of the twenty-seventh were panzer divisions able to shift from refueling, repairing, and relaxing to combat readiness—with, just possibly, a slight loss of cutting edge. In that interval the German infantry were unable to reach Dunkirk before the withdrawing troops established a defensive perimeter stronger than anything at Sedan or Gembloux, and even more resolutely manned. The Luftwaffe was unable to shut down the evacuation, as overcast skies and calm seas facilitated movement off the beaches. Nor were the panzer divisions exactly eager to come to grips with Dunkirk's defenses. Writing darkly of tank strength reduced by half and soft, rain-saturated ground impassable for those remaining, even Guderian recommended Dunkirk be left to the infantry and artillery while the panzers refitted for the coming battle of France.

This did not represent some sudden change of heart or loss of confidence. For Guderian, timing and momentum were the keys to mechanized victory. Both had been lost. Continuing to play out the changed scenario was more reckless than folding the hand and awaiting the next round of play. His sudden apparent pessimism silenced those voices still talking of an all-out armor-tipped effort to break through the Allied perimeter. The tankers more or less contentedly turned south, leaving an unanswered question: Could the Dunkirk evacuation have been prevented, or even significantly disrupted, had the Führer and his generals ridden a hot hand and kept the tanks rolling towards the beaches?

Wars may not be won by evacuations. It is nevertheless incontestable that the way Dunkirk was evacuated contributed vitally to Britain's continuing the fight. Not only did the country's only significant force

of trained soldiers survive to fight again; they returned in archetypi-
cally British fashion: brought home by the Royal Navy and the British
people, in organized formations, ready at least in public "to have another
go." Dunkirk lent moral and material substance to the famous image of
a defiant Tommy proclaiming, "Very well, then! Alone!" What might
have been the reaction had Britain confronted a demoralized rabble of
stragglers and survivors?

The BEF of 1940 did not lack courage. But initiative, flexibility, and
tactical skill were not among its strong points. Hew Strachan accurately
describes it as "outthought and outmaneuvered." The rains that softened
the ground around Dunkirk did not begin to fall until after May 24.
Had the panzers caught up with the British retreat, it is not too difficult
to imagine replications of the situations created after the breakthrough
at Sedan, of men giving up the fight from simple confusion. The risks
were clear, but Hitler's Reich and German blitzkrieg had in common a
bottom line of opportunism. Eventually both would decay into choos-
ing what seemed to be the easy way as a preferred option. And in that
context it is worth remembering the words of another soldier, this one
from the seventeenth century, James Graham, Marquis of Montrose:
"He either fears his fate too much/Or his deserts are small/That puts it
not unto the touch/To win or lose it all."

Such apocalyptically gloomy thoughts were far from the minds
of most of the tankers, privates to generals, taking position for Case
Red, the conquest of France. The high command's assumption that the
French no longer possessed any significant reserves produced a decision to distribute the panzers across the sectors of Army Groups B and
A, using infantry and artillery to secure multiple simultaneous breakthroughs, then directing and combining mobile forces as opportunities
for exploitation developed.

Despite the short time available, the French had established
a solid defense in depth along the Somme and Aisne, integrated by
checker-boarded strong points based on farms and villages. Many units
had been ordered to hold *sans esprit de recul*—to the finish. They fought
with grim determination and improved finesse. Crossing the rivers cost
the Germans time and lives. Stuka strikes had limited success neutral-

izing mutually supporting networks, as opposed to knocking out individual positions. But once the zone of resistance was penetrated, there was nothing much behind it—certainly nothing that could stop panzers on the loose.

The French were still in the process of reconstructing their shattered mobile divisions when the Germans struck. Army commanders continued to distribute their remaining tanks by battalions, so closely behind forward positions they were easily bypassed. Britain provided its only armored division: around 300 rivet-shedding deathtraps that broke down about as quickly as German gunners could disable them. German armored columns fanned out across central France, overcoming dozens and hundreds of small-scale stands by improvised task forces, brushing aside counterattacks by "provisional companies" of surviving tanks from broken units and "independent companies" equipped with tanks fresh off production lines. Their monuments were a few helmet-topped crosses alongside country roads.

Rommel's 7th Panzer Division had been dubbed the "ghost division" for its speed and flexibility: "Now you see it, now you don't." The Ghosts went cross-country to capture Le Havre, set an army record by advancing more than 160 miles in a single day to seize the city and fortress of Cherbourg in an urban blitz, and finished the war on its way to the Spanish frontier. Third Panzer Division reached Grenoble. Second Motorized finished the campaign in the Loire Valley. The chief laurels of Case Red, however, fell to Guderian. Given his own panzer group of four armored and two motorized divisions, he shouldered his way across the Aisne, then swung southwest in the rear of the Maginot Line, isolating the area as Wilhelm Ritter von Leeb's infantry-based Army Group C attacked the fortifications from the front. In the autumn of 1939, Manstein had discussed forcing the French to fight on the wrong side of their vaunted fortifications. On June 16, Guderian—who, parenthetically, was officially under the command of 12th Army—made the concept work. He swung his tanks and riflemen 90 degrees east for a broad-front thrust into Alsace. Executed so smoothly that its difficulty has gone unnoticed, the movement completed the encirclement of almost a half million French soldiers in the historic battleground and killing ground from Nancy to Belfort. That other elements of the panzer group reached the Swiss border the next day was a bonus for the journalists—and for Hitler, who at first refused to believe the dispatch. And all of this was achieved, moreover, without the massive air support Guderian enjoyed in the breakout from Sedan.

In those contexts it made little difference that Italy entered the war on June 10, or that Paris, declared an open city by a fugitive government, was occupied—by a straight-leg infantry division—on June 13. Marshal Philippe Petain, aged hero of the Great War and newly appointed prime minister, requested an armistice on June 17, while something remained to be salvaged. On June 22 the agreement was signed, in the same railroad car that had been used for the armistice of 1918. Adolf Hitler lacked an ironist's subtlety, but he had a keen sense of history.

CHAPTER FOUR

CLIMAX

For Hitler's panzers the summer of 1940 was a time of high celebration. The sun had never shone so brightly—literally, in the near-perfect weather, and metaphorically in the favors showering from an ostensibly grateful Führer. The tankers were not yet sufficiently well positioned to share in the cornucopia of gifts, decorations, and promotions at the very top that produced so many new field marshals that Rundstedt grumbled his new rank had been cheapened. They nevertheless finished well up in the victory sweepstakes. Kleist, Guderian, Hoth, and Hoepner were all promoted *Generaloberst* (General) with the same date of rank: July 19.

With a major expansion of mobile forces in the works, opportunities were opening at every level of command from division to platoon. The two Armored Troop Schools at Münster and Wuensdorf were well into their wartime stride as officer training establishments. Cadets were assigned after basic training with their unit—if they had no combat experience—followed by eight weeks of officer training. The branch school provided sixteen weeks of specialized technical and tactical instruction. Cadets then returned, usually to their original units, for a probationary period prior to being commissioned. In contrast to the Americans and to some degree the British, the German army believed that anyone unable to command and lead those he had served among as an enlisted man was unlikely to make a good officer. At higher levels there were training courses for new battalion commanders, second chances for salvageable officers with blotted copybooks, and useful training and staff appointments for those a bit long in the tooth or slow in reaction to be useful for field operations

Napoleon once said soldiers are led with baubles. For officers with "sore throats," army slang for anyone seeming interested in the higher decorations worn around the neck, Rommel and most of his senior counterparts were as generous with recommendations as the High Command was in accepting them. And many an enlisted *Panzermann* could return home on a hero's furlough with an Iron Cross on his chest.

The price of all this? Around 700 tanks permanently lost—most of them obsolescent, eminently expendable Panzer Is and IIs. Fewer than 50,000 killed in the entire Wehrmacht during the whole campaign. In most of the mobile units, losses had been low enough to foster nostalgia for absent friends rather than mutual speculation on who would be next.

The tankers stood down. Fifth and 7th Panzer Divisions prepared desultorily for an invasion of England that the High Command projected as a large-scale river crossing. The project was treated with appropriate seriousness at regiment and company levels—which is to say the Landser generally enjoyed themselves splashing in the water and messing around with boats. Other divisions, like 4th and 10th Panzer, drew duty in occupied France: deferential men, accommodating women, and ample sightseeing. Still more fortunate outfits went home promptly: 3rd Panzer to Berlin and 9th to Vienna, where their receptions were a good deal more enthusiastic than they had been when marching out in 1939.

I

IN THE FALL of 1940 Adolf Hitler had the opportunity to consolidate rule over a European empire unmatched since the days of Napoleon. Norway, the Low Countries, and northern France lay under German occupation. The government of Vichy France was eager to assume the role of a client state. Mussolini's Italy and Franco's Spain were vulnerable to German pressure. Nazi influence in the Balkans grew by the week. Josef Stalin still "trusted" his treaty partner to continue acting like a capitalist. Rational calculation, which excluded the Winston Churchills and Charles de Gaulles, allowed only one conclusion: the Third Reich was here to stay, at least for the foreseeable future. That conclusion had been shaped by the Wehrmacht—specifically its panzer divisions.

Blitzkrieg essentially meant convincing participants and observers—one's own side and the home front included—that enemies faced inevitable and humiliating defeat. In a technological age, that no longer meant man-to-man physical superiority as it had in the Middle Ages, or even at times in the trenches of the Western Front. It spoke rather to the ability to use the means at one's disposal so effectively that resistance seemed not merely futile but pathetic, without even the heroic element that traditionally informs last stands and forlorn hopes in Western military mythology. Prisoners usually look frightened and shabby compared to their captors—one reason why the current laws of war forbid showing their pictures. Even over a half-century's distance, prisoners of blitzkrieg appear shocked out of their higher cognitive abilities. Their conquerors seem from another dimension, unmarked physically and psychologically—"overmen" in the original sense of Friedrich Nietzsche.

The disaster that overtook the western allies in May and June of 1940 has been ascribed to the erosion of national will and morale during the interwar years. It has been presented as the fruit of strategic and tactical doctrines inadequate to meet the German challenge. It has been described as reflecting shortcomings of organization, training, and intelligence. In the same context the German victory is presented as a faute de mieux improvisation: a combination of unpredictable chance, Allied mistakes, and the behavior of a few hard-driving panzer generals who presented their own high command with a series of faits accomplis. Far from prefiguring a new way of war, the successes of 1940 arguably led Germany down a dead-end road of operative hubris, emphasizing combat at the expense of strategy. In an age of industrialized mass war, lightning victories would prove a temporary and fatal anachronism.

Blitzkrieg's real victor in 1940 was National Socialism. Hitler celebrated the successes of May and June in Nazi terms: as a triumph of will, informed by a consciousness of martial superiority that in turn depended on the racial superiority evoked and refined by the Third Reich. In that context, blitzkrieg played a central, arguably essential role in the "exterminatory warfare" that was Nazi Germany's true contribution to modern war making. Some forewarning was given by the treatment of the West African troops the French deployed in large numbers during the campaign's second half. The atrocities had historical roots: fear and resentment generated by French use of African "savages" in 1870 and 1914–18. The kind of close-quarters fighting in streets and woods characterizing many initial breakthroughs is not usually conducive to taking prisoners, and German soldiers were conditioned to be ruthless in combat. They arguably entertained as well a generalized sense that the war was, for practical purposes over, and regarded continued resistance as immoral because it was futile.

Neither direct orders nor wink-and-a nudge tolerance at higher levels sanctioned abuses that, rather than being systematic, tended to be situational by perpetrators, places, and times. After all allowances are made there is nevertheless no question that German soldiers, including men from the mobile divisions, disproportionately refused quarter to black combatants, disproportionately singled out black prisoners for brutal treatment including large-scale executions in non-combat situations, and justified themselves on racial grounds. Only the degenerate French would put subhumans into uniform, call them soldiers, and give them license to mutilate German wounded. It was an evil portent.

Another portent existed for those with wit or will to see. It is a familiar paradox that history's greatest war was directed and controlled by civilians: Franklin D. Roosevelt, Winston Churchill, Josef Stalin—and Adolf Hitler. Their styles ranged from Roosevelt's Olympian position as ultimate decision maker and arbiter to Churchill's hands-on interventionist approach. None eventually exercised more comprehensive control of their nation's war effort than did Hitler. It is a downplayed irony that he achieved that position in the face of a military establishment that, since the eighteenth century, had been widely considered the driving wheel of a Prussia/Germany that was "an army with its own country."

Whatever his motives, in front of Dunkirk, Adolf Hitler faced down the High Command on a military issue that was clearly in the operational sphere with no real elements of policy or politics. That had made him the first ever ruler of Prussia/Germany, king or kaiser, chancellor or president, to exercise direct control of the generals on their own ground. Hitler, convinced of his own military genius, determined to assert his authority at any price, saw the halt order as the capstone of a campaign he had shaped, in a war he had sought and initiated. It was the first step in what became a pattern of exercising direct command based on remarkable memory for details, adamant refusal to accept inconsistencies or discrepancies, and unshakable belief that decisions were best made spontaneously, with instinct processing data and will inspiring results. Well before the Reich's downfall, micromanagement would become an analgesic—not only for Hitler, but for his generals as well.

Prognostication was eclipsed by reconfiguration. The expansion of Germany's mobile forces initiated in the autumn of 1940 is generally and legitimately connected with Hitler's parallel decision to invade the Soviet Union. The reorganization, however, had an army taproot as well. The 1940 campaign left no serious doubt that large-scale mobile operations were the wave of the future, and that foot-marching infantry and horse-drawn artillery belonged to a rapidly vanishing past. Manstein, who did not entirely waste his time as commander of an infantry corps, voiced a consensus in reporting that existing infantry divisions lacked the firepower to break through defenses and the mobility to exploit success. That rendered them dependent on the panzers, and created the risk of a two-tier army. Certainly as well any prospective adversary would imitate the Germans by massing tanks, motorizing infantry, and using air power in ground combat. A smaller army would be able to upgrade its standard divisions by increasing their motorization and adding assault guns, self-propelled antitank guns, and antiaircraft guns to the orders of battle.

That perspective shaped the army's initial reaction to Hitler's decision, announced as early as May 15, to shift military production to the Luftwaffe and the navy while reducing the army to 120 divisions. Twenty of these, the Führer declared, would be armored, and ten more motorized. On June 18 the General Staff agreed to create ten new panzer divisions despite the continued shortage of armored and unarmored vehicles of all kinds. Six weeks later, on July 31, Hitler held a conference on strategic priorities. There he announced his intention to invade Russia early in 1941—before then, if possible. The result was another shift in the army's institutional emphasis: creating as many as possible combat-ready formations of any kind, in order to meet the mission's geographic demands as well as its operational ones.

The configuration of the army being created for the invasion of Russia exacerbated the difference between the panzers and the rest. Most of the new panzer and motorized divisions were created by converting and expanding 14 of the 36 active infantry divisions created after 1933. That meant well over half the original peacetime army, the hard core of Germany's ground forces, was now part of a technology-based elite that, for practical purposes after the invasion of Russia, would be increased only by the incorporation of the Waffen SS. The remaining active divisions that still marched to fight lost effectiveness by being heavily milked to stiffen the no fewer than sixteen "waves" of infantry divisions organized by summer 1941. Those toward the bottom of the list were scraping the barrel for cadres, weapons, and equipment, with much of the latter two coming from conquered and occupied countries. It was correspondingly obvious that the panzer and motorized divisions would have to do the serious work.

That would require a capacity for both assault and exploitation, and an improved level of sustainability. The most significant feature of the panzer arm's reorganization was the shift in the balance of tanks and infantry in a panzer division. The panzer brigade was reduced to a single regiment, usually of two battalions and around 150 tanks. The motorized brigade, however, was increased to two two-battalion regiments and a motorcycle battalion, with one of the rifle battalions riding half tracks. This 50 percent reduction in armored strength was subsequently excoriated by theorists like B. H. Liddell-Hart and field soldiers like Guderian for increasing rear echelons at the expense of fighting power, and privileging wheels over treads. It is frequently attributed to Hitler's fetishistic emphasis on numbers at the expense of everything else. In fact, the rebalancing had been considered after the Polish campaign, and confirmed in 1940. The motorcyclists had been effective as a swing force, able both to fight afoot and add punch to the reconnaissance battalion. There never seemed to be enough infantry, however, to cope with the near-simultaneous demands of breaking through defense lines, mopping up bypassed positions, securing exposed flanks, and consolidating captured ground in the face of counterattacks accompanying the armor.

It was certainly possible to increase the panzer division's infantry and keep its tanks at the same number: fewer divisions but more powerful ones. Massed tanks, however, had been shown to pose problems of control that limited their effectiveness against reasonably well-defended positions, Gembloux being the prime example. The large numbers of rear-echelon vehicles required by a two-tank-regiment division had regularly led to traffic problems significantly hampering operations. Radios had their limits. So did the talents of commanders. The German way of war depended on a high average rather than erratic genius. The commander of a panzer division had to be more than "a good ordinary general," but it flew in the face of experience to expect too many of them to be gifted battle captains in the mode of a Rommel. For the same reason of effective control, motorized divisions were kept at their existing strength: two three-battalion regiments with neither tanks nor half-tracks.

Fighting the French had also indicated that in armored war, quality was at least as important a force multiplier as numbers. Survivability was important both to sustainability and morale. The vulnerable Panzer Is and IIs were being replaced with the more formidable Panzer III coming off the Reich's production lines. The repeatedly demonstrated shortcomings of the 37mm gun as a main armament led to its replacement in the G version by a 50mm gun whose 42-caliber barrel made it a rough counterpart of the 75mm gun mounted on the early versions of the US Sherman—that is to say, a general-purpose weapon useful in supporting infantry, effective against tanks, but not a real tank-killer.

About 450 of this version were produced by February 1941, alongside 300 of an up-armored Model H. A number of older Panzer IIIs were also rearmed with the 50mm gun—a tribute to the generous design of the turret ring. The Panzer IV had been satisfactory overall; its E and F versions were distinguished primarily by increased side and frontal armor.

While scales of equipment varied a good deal in practice, a well-outfitted tank battalion of 1941 with German material had two or three light companies of 17 Panzer IIIs and 5 Panzer IIs, and one medium company of 10 Panzer IVs and 5 Panzer IIs. The Panzer IIs were filler, to be used and used up for reconnaissance and other secondary missions until enough IIIs and IVs became available. The tables reflected production figures that trailed far behind unit requirements. Hitler initially asked for as many as a thousand tanks a month. Minister for Armament and War Production Fritz Todt responded that it would cost two billion marks, require a hundred thousand skilled workers, and disrupt submarine and aircraft deliveries originally secured by cutting back the construction of new munitions plants.

The High Command received a similarly discouraging answer when it pressed for an increase in tank production from the 200 or so a month that remained standard. Goals of delivering 2,800 Panzer IIIs and IVs by April 1941 remained chimerical. In May 1941, plans were developed for a major production program: more than 34,000 vehicles to complete equipping the mobile divisions. The target date was 1944. Meanwhile, actual tank production reached a low of 120 in September 1940. One new panzer regiment was built around Panzer IIs originally adapted for underwater movement as part of the aborted preparations for invading Britain. As a point of comparison, as late as April 1941, material shortages and production problems meant that seven million rounds for the standard 105mm howitzer existed only as empty shell casings—no propellant, no explosive. By comparison the panzers were well off.

The numbers gap was filled in part by the factories of Bohemia. They continued the steady manufacture of enough 38(t)s to equip five divisions with three battalions, more than a hundred each, and keep 6th

Panzer Division's 35(t)s up to strength as well. But that 30 percent of its ground-force cutting edge went into battle in obsolescent tanks looted from a second-rate power is a clear sign that Wehrmacht planning agencies put more energy into preparing for the exploitation of Soviet resources than into providing the tools for their conquest.

One consequence was the inability to provide three battalions of up-to-date tanks for more than three of the reconfigured divisions that went to war against the USSR. Three battalions provided organizational flexibility. Three battalions might sustain effectiveness by consolidating. Two were far more likely to reach a tipping point, especially in fast-paced offensive action without regular pauses for maintenance and regular replacement of losses. A second loser in the armaments sweepstakes was the assault gun force. Four of the first six batteries served in France. Their low silhouettes and high firepower proved their worth from the beginning of the campaign. Regiment Grossdeutschland had nothing but praise for its six organic *Sturmgeschütz* (StuGs) at Stonne for working hand in hand with the riflemen in street fighting, demolishing barricades, and carrying heavy weapons and ammunition. The gun's limited traverse was not a problem in a direct-support role, while the vehicle's presence alone gave a valuable boost to the foot soldiers' morale.

The artillery, whose role in the West had been significantly limited compared to the Great War, was fully convinced and began training the first battalions (three six-gun batteries) in the summer of 1940. Service with the StuGs has been described as popular because it was the quickest way to decoration and promotion. The assault artillery did win more than 150 Knight's Crosses, with lesser medals in proportion. But they were won the hard way, and throughout the war the guns were manned by volunteers.

Men were easier to find than equipment. Despite the support of two powerful branches of service, assault gun production remained limited—around 30 per month and not exceeding 50 until June 1941. As a result only two battalions every three months, later three every two months, joined the pre-Barbarossa order of battle. Instead of being assigned to divisions, as originally intended, they were held as army troops, sent where need was greatest—another reinforcement of armor's elite, almost separate, status even when its crews wore artillery colors.

The emerging differentiation between the armored force and the rest of the army was further exacerbated by the absence of progress developing self-propelled antitank guns. The concept was simple enough: attach a gun to the chassis of an obsolescent tank, of which the army had an ample supply. Nevertheless by June 1941 the inventory of such vehicles amounted to about 150 of the 47mm Czech guns on Panzer I bodies mentioned in Chapter 3. Doing the same thing with captured French equipment does not seem to have even been considered at higher levels, though two tank regiments were eventually organized with French vehicles.

Antitank defense in general had a low practical priority in the run-up to Barbarossa. The near-useless 37mm towed gun was in the process of being more or less replaced by an excellent 50mm/62-caliber piece. Its early production runs were so small that they were issued to the infantry by two-gun sections. Infantry companies were issued small-bore antitank rifles: more sophisticated and less dangerous to their users than their World War I forebears, but effective only against the kind of light tanks that everywhere were being phased out of service. And doctrine expressly forbade using already scarce assault guns in an antitank role. The Landser in Russia would spend too long depending on well-placed hand grenades and overloads of nerve—or desperation.

In near-absolute contrast to its behavior after the Polish campaign, the German army in 1940–41 not merely accepted but enabled two massive disconnects: between a motorized/mechanized elite and everything else, and within that elite, between structure and equipment. Both cognitive dissonances were subsumed beneath a euphoria that exceeded even the "victory disease" that infected the Imperial Japanese Navy in the months between Pearl Harbor and Midway. Robert M. Citino describes a "literature of exaltation" that reflected the National Socialist intellectual structure of heroism and sacrifice. The Nazis' crude racism was also not without its appeal; soldiers in all places at all times seek as many credible grounds as possible to assert superiority over their enemies.

To interpret the army's mentality to a double penetration by National Socialist culture and Nazified personnel is nevertheless to overlook its roots in professional pride. The high-tech, low-cost victories of 1939–40 lifted the German generals' morale in ways incomprehensible to those who had not experienced the Western Front a quarter-century earlier. Places whose names had symbolized a generation's sacrifice and a generation's failure—Verdun, Ypres, Amiens—had fallen like beads pulled from a string, rating scarcely a line in official reports. The invasion of Britain had been a nonstarter, but that was easily rationalized by claiming special circumstances.

Citino accurately presents this pride in terms of satisfaction at what seemed the definitive culmination of decades and centuries of thought and effort: not merely a German way of war but a new paradigm of war itself. There was, however, another factor. The combination of mobility, firepower, and electronic communications developed and applied by the panzers was seen as merely the matrix, epitomizing and amplifying the warrior spirit of the new German soldier. Boldness, decisiveness, "necessary hardness"—these were the mainsprings of an unmatched triumph, facilitated perhaps by National Socialism but structured and inspired by the traditional bearer of German values: the army.

The exact balance of the developing synergy between Nazis and soldiers, the exact balance between values recently acquired and values long entertained, may legitimately be debated. The result, however, is clear: a level of hubris defying and denying the more balanced legacies of Frederick the Great, Moltke the Elder, and Hans von Seeckt. These men understood that Destiny is no man's drudge and Bellona no man's trull. It was a lesson their successors had yet to learn. The means of their instruction would be an army fundamentally flawed relative to its missions and flawed by design.

II

BARBAROSSA WAS AT bottom a strategic second choice, reflecting the Wehrmacht's inability to knock Britain out of the war in the summer

and fall of 1940. "Hot pursuit" by an improvised, airborne-tipped invasion immediately after Dunkirk was rejected as too risky. The army's
later invasion plans were too elaborate. Planned on a scale rivaling
D-Day yet depending on an amphibious fleet improvised from fishing
boats and barges, with thousands of horses included even in the first
wave, Operation Sea Lion's only military hope was a degree of naval and
air superiority neither the Kriegsmarine nor the Luftwaffe were able to
achieve.

Britain held on, and then counterattacked. By autumn 1940, British
mobile forces were running rings around Hitler's Italian ally in Africa.
By spring 1941, British fighters were mounting sweeps over northern
France. For Hitler, "smiting Britain's continental sword from her hand"
by overthrowing the Soviet Union became an increasingly attractive
option.

The invasion of Russia was also a product of geopolitics. Even before
1939, Nazi Germany and Soviet Russia had sparred for advantage in
east central Europe. Since the fall of Poland in 1939 the struggle had
approached Cold War intensity. At stake was the oil of Romania, the
wheat of Hungary, and strategic position for a conflict few in either
Moscow or Berlin believed could be postponed indefinitely by the
increasingly threadbare non-aggression pact the totalitarian rivals had
concluded in 1939.

Ideology added a third element to the compound. Since its inception in the depths of Hitler's psyche, National Socialism had rested on
two principles: annihilating the Jews and securing "living space" for the
German people. The annihilation of Soviet Russia was a step in both
directions. Hitler—and many other Germans—saw the Communist
government of the Soviet Union as having been created and sustained
by Jews. And since at least the nineteenth century, German imperialism
had been strongly attracted to a Russia perceived as a cornucopia of natural and human resources the "natives" would never be able to develop
properly. All that seemed necessary, in Hitler's words, was to "kick down
the door," and the whole rotten edifice would collapse.

A fourth contributor to Barbarossa was confidence. An air/ground
assault on the Soviet Union was what the Wehrmacht knew it knew

how to do. From the day when Hitler first summoned his senior officers to consider an invasion of the USSR, the operation's feasibility was never seriously questioned. Halder spoke for his colleagues when he noted to himself, "What operational objectives could be secured? What strength do we have available?" It was just another day's work.

Arguments periodically emerge that Barbarossa was a preventive operation, that Stalin had begun concentrating his armies forward in preparation either for a direct attack on Germany, or in order to take advantage of the collapse of capitalism he believed inevitable if war between Britain and Germany continued. Red Army Chief of Staff Georgi Zukhov did in fact urge Stalin to launch a preemptive strike in a memorandum submitted on May 15, 1941, but the Soviet dictator had no intention of taking such a risk. Aside from the impact of the 1930s purges on its officer corps and its self confidence, the Red Army was suffering the effects of rapid expansion—Stalin had created more than 100 new divisions since January 1939 alone—and a crash rearmament program that seriously destabilized an economy already oriented to military production. From Stalin's perspective it made the sense of desperation to maintain an armed truce with Hitler as long as possible.

Whatever might be the Reich's advantages on the levels of policy and strategy, the approximately 130 German infantry divisions in Barbarossa's order of battle carried weapons looted from a half dozen armies. There were five divisions of Waffen SS, with greater reputations for ferocity than fighting power. Client states—Romania, Finland, Slovakia—provided between 20 and 30 more divisions of limited operational value. Occupied Europe was stripped of everything with four wheels and an engine to provide logistic support for this mixed bag. Trucks were purchased from Switzerland. Other trucks were requisitioned from French North Africa. And in the final analysis, sustaining the invasion still depended heavily on captured railroads whose track gauge had to be altered to fit Western rolling stock.

Traditional logistics were just the tip of an iceberg of improvisation. The army expected to sustain itself directly from the campaign's beginning by utilizing captured Red Army resources and systematically exploiting the civil population. Whatever the military merits of this

approach for foot-marching, horse-powered formations, its applicability
to the mechanized troops was marginal. To cite only the most obvious
example, German tanks had gasoline engines. In the West they had been
able to refuel from local filling stations. In Russia such facilities were
limited, and Russian gas was of sufficiently lower octane to be a positive risk for already overworked motors. If anything at all went wrong,
solutions would have to be improvised. Meanwhile, the theater-level
planning for Barbarossa virtually guaranteed problems.

Hitler based Operation Barbarossa on the assumption that success
depended on shattering the USSR in one blow. His directive of December 18, 1940, could not have been plainer: the bulk of Russian forces in
the west was to be destroyed in a series of bold operations. The generals concurred. They never proposed to match the Russians face-to-face,
gun-for-gun, and tank-for-tank. Mechanized war depended on timing:
a dozen tanks on the spot were preferable to 50 an hour later. Mechanized war depended on disruption: confusion produced entropy while
discouraging resistance. And mechanized war depended on hardness.
An enemy could not merely drop his weapon and raise his hands. He
needed to feel defeat in his ductless glands—and in his soul. The close
synergy between Nazi principles and military behavior demonstrated
from the beginning of the Russo-German War was not entirely a consequence of shared racist values. It reflected as well the "way of war" the
German army had been developing since at least 1918.

How best then to break the enemy comprehensively? The first operational study began in July 1940. It projected a dual strike, one directly
on Moscow, the other on Kiev. This should be enough to destroy the
Red Army and disrupt the Soviet state. The ultimate objective was a
line: Rostov-Gorki-Archangel; anything to the east would remain
"Indian country" until further notice. A parallel study projected three
simultaneous assaults, toward Leningrad, Moscow, and Kiev. From the
beginning, in other words, long before Hitler's direct involvement, the
army's plans incorporated dispersion of the army's striking power.

This was not a manifestation of ignorance, willful or otherwise.
German planners were fully aware of the size of the Soviet Union. They

had reasonable ideas of the kinds of changes it might impose on an operational approach designed for application against small countries. Attaché reports and clandestine reconnaissance flights provided information both negative (on such issues as the lack of roads appropriate for rapid movement) and positive (indicating significant recent buildup of industrial capacity on both sides of the Urals). A series of map exercises in early December 1940 indicated significant problems of overstretch, producing results much like those of a similar exercise in 1913: German forces hung up in the middle of Russia as the enemy massed for a general counteroffensive. The conclusion was that German forces were barely sufficient for the assigned mission. And that was at the beginning.

Germany's overall mobilization might have been incomplete, but by the summer of 1941, 85 percent of men between 20 and 30 were serving in the Wehrmacht. The remainder were considered indispensable to the war economy. In May, Halder informed the Replacement Army that the initial battles would cost 275,000 casualties, with another 200,000 expected in September. The available replacement pool for the army was 385,000. Simple arithmetic indicated that the pool would be empty before autumn even given Halder's optimistic time frame.

Shortfalls were certain in another crucial area. The success of mobile war as practiced in Germany depended heavily on air support in a context of air superiority. The planes need not always be present, but they had to be available. The Luftwaffe had exponentially more experience than the Red Air Force, along with significantly superior aircraft and tactics. The Luftwaffe was also fighting in the West and the Mediterranean, suffering steady attrition of planes and crews. It would be covering a far greater geographic area than in 1940, with corresponding extension of technical and logistical demands. Even in a short campaign, the ground forces were correspondingly likely to be depending on their own skills and resources a higher proportion of the time than ever before.

Planning for Barbarossa rolled on, moving from conceptions into details without a bump. Private reservations, expressed in such passive-aggressive ways as buying and reading Baron Caulaincourt's memoirs of Napoleon's disastrous 1812 campaign, did not prevent participation of the middle-ranking officers who would be the field commanders. What emerged, significantly independent of Hitler's direct involvement, was a sophisticated version of what was essentially a military steeple-chase: three army groups lined up on the frontier, and at the starter's barrage, going as fast as possible in three extrinsic directions. Instead of the single clenched fist of Frederick the Great, or the elder Moltke's "moving separately and fighting together," the projected operation resembled a martial artist spreading his fingers as he struck what was intended as a killing blow. Instead of being structured into a decisive point, soldiers, cities, and resources shifted priorities in an ever-changing kaleidoscope. The closest thing to prioritization was Hitler's emendation of the army's original plan to provide for Leningrad's capture before mounting a decisive attack on Moscow. And all this was to be achieved on a campaign of four or five months' duration.

Scholars and soldiers increasingly, one might say overwhelmingly, describe Barbarossa as fundamentally flawed, a program for defeat even in a narrow military context. But while its dysfunctional genesis may have been in the fever swamps of hubris and racism, a steel thread linked Barbarossa to the real world: the panzers. The Führer and his generals were convinced that the army of the Third Reich had developed a style of war not merely countering the historic Russian strengths of mass, space, and determination, but rendering them irrelevant: a heavyweight boxer confronting a sawed-off shotgun. In his December directive Hitler emphasized "bold armored thrusts." The army's map exercises concluded that mobile units would decide the campaign and the war. At every turn the structure of Barbarossa was an inverted pyramid, with the panzers at the tip. *Va banque*, all or nothing—the Reich's fate rode with the tanks.

III

CONCENTRATION OF FORCE and effort were not dominant characteristics of Hitler's Reich. The Führer had initially reacted to Italy's debacle in

North Africa and its frustrated invasion of Greece with the amused malice the Germans call Schadenfreude. His interests in the Mediterranean involved encouraging support for Germany's Atlantic ambitions on the part of Vichy France and Falangist Spain, and attracting Balkan support for the developing attack on the Soviet Union. Neither end was best served by Italian-initiated upheavals that challenged the status quo by open-ended claims to enlarged spheres of influence. They were served even worse, however, by open-ended military catastrophe.

The Italian defeat in Greece created opportunities for Britain to negotiate a Balkan front of its own, supporting it by stationing planes on Greek bases. The oil fields of Romania were only the most obvious potential target. If the Italians were driven from North Africa, the stresses on British shipping would be reduced by the reopening of the Mediterranean. The French North African colonies might reconsider their allegiance to Vichy. An Italy subject to air and naval strikes would face the consequences of a loss of prestige that could potentially lead to the collapse of the Fascist system itself.

Hitler grew correspondingly determined to take action. As early as July 1940, the High Command had suggested dispatching a panzer division to North Africa. Spanish veteran Wilhelm von Thoma, sent to evaluate the situation, reported any serious mobile operations would require at least four divisions for an indefinite basis. In the run-up to Barbarossa, that proposal had no chance. As the Italian situation continued to deteriorate, the commitment of ground forces in the Mediterranean basin nevertheless seemed necessary.

The General Staff responded by projecting a large-scale mechanized offensive in the Balkans, to be mounted in the spring of 1941—quick in, quick out. Hitler entertained hopes that its threat would be sufficient: that the Greek government would reject British support and Yugoslavia would align itself with the Axis. Hitler sweetened the latter prospect by offering to exchange Yugoslavia's copper, zinc, and lead for modern weapons. The former prospect grew increasingly remote, particularly as Greece observed the steady movement of German planning missions and combat aircraft—specifically the ground-support specialists of VIII

Air Corps—into Bulgaria and Romania. When Romania, Hungary, and Yugoslavia formally joined the Axis in November 1940, allowing German troops transit rights across their territory, the question regarding war became not *if* but *when*. Even then it was not until the first arrival of British ground troops in Greece on March 7 that the German redeployment began in earnest.

From the beginning, the Balkan operation had been planned around the panzers. This flew in the face of Great War experience, of unpromising terrain, limited road networks, undeveloped infrastructures, and just about every other common-sense reservation that prudent staff officers could conceive. In another context, however, the projected force structure reflected, more clearly than at any time since the occupation of Austria, Hitler's conception of the ideal relationship between diplomacy and force. He sought to expand the basis for war in the eastern Mediterranean, to secure the southern flank of his forthcoming attack on the USSR, and to sequester Balkan economic resources for German use. None of those ends was best achieved by the use of force as a first option, and Hitler was correspondingly willing to keep talking. But time was an enemy when wasted. Even at the last minute, the panzer divisions could be turned loose to crush both local opposition and the burgeoning British presence in Greece—immediately and unmistakably, not least to discourage intervention by the Soviet Union, perhaps Turkey as well.

The actual deployment underwent a series of changes that both illustrated German skill in operational planning and reinforced confidence in the skill's applicability to the wider Russian stage. The final dispositions put a worked-in command and staff team on the Greek frontier: List's 12th Army and Kleist's renamed Panzer Group 1. With three panzer divisions and two motorized ones plus Grossdeutschland and two similarly configured claimants to elite status, the SS Leibstandarte and the Luftwaffe's Hermann Göring Brigade, Kleist was expected to overrun Greece from a standing start.

On March 27 the situation changed utterly. A coup deposed the Yugoslav government. Hitler responded with Operation Punishment: the destruction of Yugoslavia with "merciless harshness." Kleist swung his group 90 degrees and, beginning on April 8 as the Luftwaffe eviscerated Belgrade, drove into Yugoslavia's side with the force of a knife thrust. Breaking through initially stubborn resistance and scattering two Yugoslav armies, the group drove north as another panzer corps came south from Hungary into Croatia. Belgrade was the objective. What remained of it capitulated on April 12. The Yugoslav army, its morale shaken by recent political events, divided along ethnic lines. Lacking modern equipment, it never had much of a chance. In a week the panzers had shattered its fighting spirit and its fighting power alike by speed and shock, in terrain regarded as less suitable even than the Ardennes for mobile warfare, and without breaking a military sweat. The major challenge to the rear echelons was coping with the thousands of Yugoslavs trying to surrender. On April 14 the Yugoslav government called for terms.

A country was dismembered; a stage was set for more than a half century of civil war; and the panzers were responsible. Kleist's divisions were pulled into reserve as quickly as possible for redeployment to the Russian frontier, with a collective sense of a job well done that suggested favorable prospects for the future. The new divisions and the new commanders had performed well compared to the standards of 1940. A continuing tendency to outrun the infantry had no significant tactical consequences; the tanks alone spread demoralization wherever they went. Logistics posed occasional problems, but the fighting ended before they metastasized. Total German casualties were 150 dead, 400 wounded, and 15 missing. Nothing emerging from Yugoslavia, in short, inspired any last-minute second thoughts about another operation against a Slavic army and culture.

Kleist's turn to Yugoslavia left a suddenly diminished 12th Army the task of dealing with Greece. The initial German commitment to a Balkan blitz is indicated by an order of battle that even without the panzer group included a motorized corps headquarters, the first-rate 2nd and 9th Panzer Divisions, and the Leibstandarte motorized brigade of the Waffen SS—with Richthofen's Stukas flying close support. The Viennese tankers overran a Greek motorized division, seized Salonika, and took 60,000 prisoners, all in four days. The 9th Panzer Division, the

Leibstandarte, and the Stukas on the Germans' other flank scattered an entire Yugoslav army, and then turned south into the plains of Thessaly. It took until April 12 to break through Greek, Australian, and New Zealand resistance and the British 1st Armored Brigade and cut off the strong Greek forces reluctant to retreat from Albania. But yet again, once through the forward defenses, the panzers set the pace. Never outfought, the Greek army was increasingly overmatched. On April 21 the British decided to evacuate.

From the perspective of the Anzacs and the tankers, the rest of the campaign was a long fighting retreat, enduring constant air attack and bloodying the Germans where they could. For the panzers it was more of a mop-up, with the lead role played by 5th Panzer Division. Transferred from Kleist's group after the fall of Yugoslavia, it was bloodied at Thermopylae where a rear guard knocked out 20 of its tanks as they moved through the still-narrow pass. Recovering, the division pursued the British south, crossed the Isthmus of Corinth, and took more than 7,000 prisoners on the beaches of Kalamata, men left behind when the ships were withdrawn.

IV

THE BALKAN OPERATION also laid the groundwork for a legend. On February 12, 1941, Erwin Rommel was appointed commander in chief of German troops in Libya. It was a fancy title for a force composing only one of the new panzer divisions, the still-organizing 15th, a scratch brigade grandiloquently titled 5th Light Division (later upgraded as the 21st Panzer Division), and another mixed bag that became the 90th Light Division. Renamed the German Africa Corps (Deutsches Afrika Korps) it would make two years of history.

Hitler seems initially to have made his choice of commander as much on grounds of Rommel's availability as from any intuitive sense that he was giving a wider stage to a budding genius. German intervention in North Africa was originally intended as a minimum-scale holding operation. No senior panzer general suggested Rommel might be more useful against Russia; no one requested him as a corps commander in a mobile force needing a half dozen new ones. Instead he was dispatched to a sideshow that he would move to history's center stage by a spectacular succession of battlefield victories—the first of them enabled by the drawdown of British forces in the desert in favor of the campaign in Greece.

There are fashions in generalship as there are in clothing. For a quarter century after World War II, Rommel was considered a paragon of mobile war at the tactical and operational levels. In the next quarter century, military historians and professional soldiers have judged him with a sharper pencil. Nevertheless there remains an Erwin Rommel for every military writer's taste. There is the muddy-boots general leading from the front, inspiring his men by sharing their hardships as he led them to victory. There is the brilliant opportunist, master of forcing mistakes and exploiting them, dancing rings around British generals with courage and character but no imagination. There is the master of war on a shoestring, using Germany's military leftovers to frustrate and challenge the major land effort of a global empire. There is the soldier, making war by the rules, upholding the army's honor albeit serving a criminal regime. And there is the maverick, defying his superiors, his allies, and the Führer himself to fight and win his way.

In Britain these images ameliorate two years of humiliation. In the United States they play into idealized concepts of what a real general should be. There is, however, another side to the scale. That one depicts a general whose leadership style generated as much confusion as success. It presents a commander consistently overreaching his operational capacities, and correspondingly indifferent to issues of logistics and sustainability. It highlights an extensive, long-term network of connections between Rommel and Hitler—not least a publicity machine that critics describe as creating a myth from lucky breaks and obliging enemies. What emerges is a good corps commander, challenged beyond his talent by the problems of war-making at higher levels.

The desert war's principal contribution to the panzer mystique is its status, affirmed alike by Rommel's critics and supporters, as a "clean" war. Explanations include the absence of civilians and the relative absence of

Nazis; the nature of the environment, which conveyed a "moral simplicity and transparency"; and command exercised on both sides by prewar professionals, encouraging a British tendency to depict war in the imagery of a game and a corresponding German pattern of seeing it as a test of skill and a proof of virtue.

The nature of the fighting also diminished the close-quarter actions that are primary nurturers of mutual bitterness. Last stands, as opposed to stubborn defenses, were uncommon. Usually a successful German attack ended with a compound breakthrough. With tanks seeming to appear everywhere on the position, with no effective means of close defense, capitulation was an acceptable option. The large numbers of troops usually involved also inhibited both on-the-spot killings and post-action massacres. Hard war did not necessarily mean cold murder. Surrender offered and accepted correspondingly became part of the common law of the desert.

Creating preconditions for surrender was another problem. The two-year seesaw conflict across North Africa has been so often described in so much detail that it is easy to exaggerate its actual impact on Hitler's panzers. The campaign involved only three mobile divisions and never more than around 300 tanks at any one time. Technically the Germans maintained a consistent, though not overwhelming, superiority—reflecting as much the flaws in British tank design as the qualities of the German vehicles. The Panzer III, especially the L version with the 50mm/62-caliber gun, was the backbone of Rommel's armor, admirably complemented by the Panzer IV, whose 75mm shells were highly effective against both unarmored "soft-skinned" vehicles and unsupported infantry, even when dug in.

Not until the arrival in autumn 1942 of the US M3 medium did the balance begin to shift. With a 37mm high-velocity gun in its turret and a sponson-mounted 75mm, the M3 was a poor man's Char B without the armor of its French counterpart, with a high silhouette that made it difficult to conceal, and with a gasoline engine that caught fire easily. But there were a lot of them, and their reinforcement in time for El Alamein by more than 300 Shermans definitely tipped the armor balance in Allied favor. The Sherman's mid-velocity 75mm gun, able to fire both armor piercing and high-explosive rounds, made it the best tank in North Africa—except possibly for the later marks of Panzer IV, who brought their even higher velocity 75mm gun on line in numbers too small—never more than three dozen—to make a difference.

Nor was the Afrika Korps a chosen force, the best of the best. Its medical preparation consisted of cholera and typhus inoculations. Its equipment was Wehrmacht standard, with the addition of a few hundred sun helmets—most of them soon discarded in favor of field caps— and a few thousand gallons of camouflage paint in varying shades of brown. But the Germans had confidence in themselves and their officers, in their training and in their doctrine. Their divisions were teams of specialist experts trained to fight together, combining and recombining as the situation changed. Assembling them was like working with a child's set of Legos: individual pieces, once fastened together, would hold even if the construction seemed awkward.

That flexibility proved vital. German doctrine based on avoiding tank-on-tank combat meant that when it occurred it was likely to be a close-quarters melee. German gunnery training after the 1940 campaign stressed snap shooting and rapid fire—not least because of the limited effect of single hits on French armor plate. The British for their part during much of the campaign remained committed to destroying German armor by direct action, and their tanks were usually fast enough to counter the tactical maneuvering effective in 1940.

Rommel and his subordinates in consequence recast the section of the panzer-war handbook that addressed antitank operations. In their developed and ideal form, German positions were structured by interlocking antitank-gun positions supported by infantry, the panzers deployed behind them. Contrary to belief at the time, which eventually acquired the status of myth, the 88mm gun was not a standard element of German antitank defense in the desert. Its high silhouette made it vulnerable; its limited numbers made it an emergency alternative. The backbone of German defenses was the 50mm gun, able to knock out any British tank that could move well enough to survive in desert conditions.

By 1942 these were being supplemented and replaced in turn by 75mm pieces, heavy and difficult to move but effective even against the new American Grants and Shermans. Eventually the 90th Light Division would be configured as a virtual antitank formation, with 75mm Pak 40s assigned at rifle company level.

British tanks repeatedly and obligingly impaled themselves on the German guns. Robert Crisp, a South African–born officer serving with the Royal Tank Regiment, observed that British tank design and British tactical doctrines reflected a mentality that wanted to make a tank that was as much like a horse as possible, then use it as horses had been used in the Charge of the Light Brigade. As Rommel once asked a captured British officer, "What does it matter if you have two tanks to my one, when you spread them out and let me smash them in detail?"

British armor enmeshed and worn down by the antitank guns was disproportionately vulnerable to counterattacks from flank and rear by panzer forces numerically inferior but with the advantage of surprise—an advantage enhanced by the ubiquitous clouds of dust obscuring desert battlefields as powder smoke had done in eighteenth- and nineteenth-century Europe. Superior numbers were unnecessary. Properly timed, a single hard tap could shatter an already-confused British armored brigade like glass. Success depended on timing, and for that the excellent German radios were important. But even more important were situational awareness, initiative, and mutual confidence—the infantrymen and antitank crews knowing they were not being sacrificed; the artillery concentrated to provide fire support; the tankers confident the screening forces would hold while they moved into position. Time and again, from Operation Battleaxe in 1941 through Operation Crusader in November 1941 to the Battle of Gazala in May–June 1942, the technique worked—and set up the attacks that became Rommel's signature.

The panzers' offensive tactics in the desert followed and extended patterns established in Europe. Speed, shock, and flexibility repeatedly proved devastating against a British opponent whose reaction times were sluggish, whose tactics were uninspired, and whose coordination was so limited that desert humor described it as existing only when the commanding officers involved had slept with each others' wives before the war—a significant handicap, one might think, to multiunit operations.

Encirclement was, however, likely to prove chimerical. There were no obvious terrain features or cultural sites with deep meaning to encourage last stands. Even Cairo was not Verdun. The wide-open terrain and the Germans' always limited "desert sense" facilitated breakouts, the most familiar examples being the French at Bir Hacheim and 201 Guards Brigade at Knightsbridge. The British were even more completely motorized than the Germans, and correspondingly able to outrun them. The "Gazala gallop" of May 1942 may not have been heroic, but it did preserve much of 8th Army to fight again at El Alamein.

British defense systems were also far more formidable than anything encountered even in France during Case Red. The often-derided "boxes" developed as fixed position at mid-campaign usually featured elaborate minefields to disable vehicles, complex barbed wire systems to frustrate infantry, and defenders ready to fight to the limit, like 5th South African Brigade at Sidi Rezegh and 150th Brigade's stand in the Cauldron during Gazala. Losses in both men and vehicles incurred while overrunning these positions were likely to be high and, given the theater's low priority for replacements, permanent.

If the Afrika Korps did not want to conquer itself to death, an alternate approach must be developed. Rommel would respond by taking flexible movement to the operational level. His first major offensive, in April 1941, was undertaken despite a direct order to the contrary. Once the vulnerability of the thinly manned British positions was exposed, the battle became an exercise in deep penetration on a level not seen even in France. Columns became lost in broken, poorly mapped terrain, or were deceived by mirages. Engines overheated in 120-degree temperatures. Sandstorms slowed rates of march. But the German tanks, artillery, antitank guns, and motorized infantry wove tactical tapestries that baffled their counterparts.

Rommel seemed to appear everywhere he was needed, driving and inspiring. Benghazi fell on April 3. With the British reeling backward and the fortress of Tobruk besieged, Rommel set the next objective as the Suez Canal. His spearheads reached the Egyptian frontier. When the massive counterattack of Operation Crusader rolled the Germans back in turn, Rommel checked the drive, and then swung completely behind the British. This "dash to the wire" overextended his forces so badly that his own staff called it off while Rommel was out of touch at the front.

This time the pendulum swung all the way back to Rommel's original starting point around El Agheila. Two weeks later he counterattacked, taking the British by surprise and forcing them back 350 miles to the partially prepared Gazala line. Both sides reinforced as best they could, but again it was Rommel who struck first. On May 26, 1942 his last great offensive began. A month later the port of Tobruk and its 30,000 man garrison were in German hands. Eighth Army, what was left of it, had retreated to the El Alamein line. In Cairo, rear-echelon commandos were burning documents. In London, Churchill faced—albeit briefly—a vote of no confidence on the House of Commons.

Gazala was by any standards a striking victory. But by most standards the Axis troops were fought out. Men and equipment were worn to breaking points, depending on captured fuel and supplies for momentum. Down to fifty tanks at the sharp end, Luftwaffe support left behind in the wake of the ground advance, Rommel was nevertheless convinced that only by attacking could his force sustain the initiative. To halt was to be attacked by massively superior forces, and another backward swing of the desert pendulum might well be the final one. Better to try ending the process altogether: roll the dice, take the British off balance, and regroup in Cairo.

"Attack" had worked for Rommel in North Africa as it had in France. It had been the armored force's mantra since the beginning. It was a keystone of the German approach to war-making. This time under a new commander, Bernard Law Montgomery, 8th Army held. At Ruweisat Ridge on July 1, the panzers broke in. For the first time in the desert, they failed to break through. An end run was stopped cold at Alam Halfa by a mixture the Germans had patented: combined-arms tactics in a context of air supremacy. By this time Rommel's health had declined sufficiently that he returned to Germany, partly to recover and partly to lobby for more of everything. Rommel informed his doctor, "Either the army in Russia succeeds in getting through ... and we in Africa manage to reach the Suez Canal, or ..." He accompanied his unfinished sentence with a dismissive gesture suggesting defeat.

The stalemate at El Alamein is frequently described as the final, fatal consequence of either Rommel's fundamental ignorance of logistics or his culpable carelessness in supervising them. He thus epitomizes a senior officer corps whose tactical and operational proficiency manifested tunnel vision, with caste pride, misunderstood professionalism, or exaggerated vitalism relegating administration to those unsuited to command troops in combat.

When Halder asked Rommel what he would need to conquer Egypt and the Suez Canal, Rommel replied that another two panzer corps should do. When Halder asked how Rommel proposed to supply that force, Rommel replied that was Halder's problem. Rommel was being neither arrogant nor insouciant. He was expressing the mentality of the German army as reorganized after 1933. Even Halder declared after the war that quartermasters must never hamper the operational concept. Rapid expansion encouraged a more pragmatic, hands-on ethic than had been the case prior to the Great War. The pace Hitler demanded encouraged focusing on the operational level of war. Planning in turn revolved more than ever around operational considerations; the logisticians were called in afterward.

Rommel saw as well as anyone on either side of the war that victory in the desert depended on supply. He also understood that he had relatively little control of his logistics. Germany was a guest in the Mediterranean, depending on Italian goodwill and Italian abilities to sustain a small expeditionary force. From his arrival, Rommel successfully cultivated Italian senior officers and gained the confidence of Italian fighting formations. The Ariete Armored Division was close enough in effectiveness to its German stablemates to be virtually the Afrika Korps' third panzer division for much of the campaign. Italian infantry, artillery, and engineers time and again were the fulcrum on which the lever of Rommel's mobile operations depended.

The Italian army was not as retrograde in its understanding of mobile war in tactical and operational contexts as is frequently assumed. By 1940, Italian theorists had studied German successes in Poland and France and developed a doctrine of *guerra di rapido corso* (fast-moving war). Strategically, however, their generals considered Rommel's focus on Cairo and the Suez Canal as culpable overextension. The Wehrmacht High Command understood the Mediterranean theater's strategic function was to cover the German southern flank during the decisive struggle in Russia. North Africa was an outpost, best secured by a flexible defense.

On the other hand, Hitler had been reappraising Germany's strategic prospects ever since Pearl Harbor. The German navy was calling for systematic cooperation with Japan in a campaign designed to produce a junction in the Indian Ocean that would bring about the final collapse of the British Empire. For Hitler, the war's globalization only confirmed his decision for a 1942 campaign against the Caucasian oil fields. Hitler saw the Japanese conquests in Asia as weakening Britain's imperial position sufficiently that the presence of Axis troops in the southern foothills of the Caucasus would convince Britain to negotiate, and leave Russia to be finished off before the industrial potential of the United States, which Hitler admitted he had no idea how to defeat, could be developed and deployed.

If America's entry into the war threatened the Reich with grand-strategic encirclement, the military situation provided a window of opportunity—six to eight months, perhaps—for consolidating Germany's position in a continental redoubt of the kind depicted by geopoliticians like Halford Mackinder and Karl Haushofer. Mastery of what they called the "Heartland"—the Eurasian landmass—would set the stage for eventual mastery of the world.

Rommel had a complementary strategic vision. He believed, especially given the growing imbalance in material resources between Germany and its opponents, the best approach in North Africa involved maintaining the offensive at operational levels, taking advantage of German leadership and fighting power to demoralize the British, keep them off balance, and eventually create the opportunity for a decisive blow. That was a common mind-set among Germany's panzer generals as the war reached its middle stages. Rommel, though anything but an "educated soldier" in the traditions of the German General Staff, took the concept one level higher. He realized British strength would continue to be renewed as long as North Africa remained the primary theater where Britain could deploy modern ground forces. Yet he was also convinced that through operational art he could conquer Egypt and eventually move northeast toward the Caucasus, providing the southern pincer of a strategic double envelopment that would secure the oil fields of south Russia and drive across Iraq and Persia, breaking permanently Britain's power in the Middle East.

The prospect of Rommel at the head of a full-blooded Axis drive into the Middle East continues to engage counterfactual historians. It is a staple chapter in the alternative histories that show Germany winning World War II. But a crucial prerequisite for large-scale offensive operations in the Middle East was Axis maritime superiority in the Mediterranean. The Germans could make no significant contributions. The Italian navy had suffered heavy losses that its construction and repair facilities could not replace. Air power was no less vital, and here too the burden would have fallen on an Italian air force whose effectiveness was steadily declining. Obsolescent aircraft, lack of fuel, and indifference at senior levels proved a fatal trifecta. As for the Luftwaffe, those human and material resources not deployed to Russia were increasingly being reassigned to home defense.

Any Middle East offensive mounted from the Mediterranean would require a port. Alexandria, even if captured relatively undamaged, would be no more than the starting point for an increasingly long line of communication over terrain even more formidable, and less developed, than Russia. The survivability of German and Italian trucks in the mountains of Syria and the deserts of Iraq was likely to be less than on the Rollbahns of the Soviet Union. The Middle East lacked anything like a comprehensive, developed railway network. The problem of securing a thousand miles and more of natural guerilla/bandit country would have daunted the most brutal Nazi specialists in genocide.

The final damping factor of a Middle East campaign was its dependence on a successful drive through southern Russia to the Caucasus.

Should Rommel's panzer strength be doubled, without regard for the demands of the Russian front, or for how the additional tanks and trucks would be supplied, the offensive through Egypt would nevertheless remain a secondary operation. If German tanks did not appear in the southern passages of the Caucasus by early winter, any successes Rommel might achieve were likely to prove all too ephemeral. And yet the question remains: What might Rommel have achieved with a couple of additional panzer divisions, a little more gasoline . . . ?

V

THE BARRAGE OPENED with Teutonic precision at 3:30 AM on June 22, 1941. A half hour earlier, Luftwaffe bombers had crossed into Russia to strike major air bases. Earlier still, special operations detachments had infiltrated Russian territory, setting ambushes and seizing bridges. As dawn broke, three million men crashed forward under an umbrella of more than a thousand planes.

The Russians were taken completely by surprise at all levels. A train carrying Russian goods had crossed into Germany shortly after midnight. One unit of the Red Army reported it was under attack only to receive the response, "You must be insane!" Stalin suffered a nervous collapse. Foreign minister Vyacheslav Molotov confronted the German ambassador: "Surely we have not deserved this!"

Martin van Creveld's careful calculations have long since discredited the long-standing argument that the Balkan operation delayed Barbarossa by a significant amount of time—enough, perhaps, to set up the Germans' eventual defeat by "General Winter." Instead the unexpectedly rapid collapse of Yugoslavia made it possible to transfer and refit the mobile divisions ahead of the originally projected schedule. The reason their transport was not expedited was the slow arrival of the motor vehicles for the panzers' rear echelons. There was no point in rushing movements from the Balkans when trucks and related equipment were still arriving at what Halder called the last moment: the end of May and early June. Drivers and unit mechanics had scant time to get acquainted with their vehicles' quirks even had they nothing else to do—an unlikely circumstance in the context of the great invasion.

Spring also came late to western Russia in 1941. Thaws were heavy; streams and rivers overflowed; ground was soft. Here was a case when losing time in the short run meant saving it in the long run—especially given the ramshackle nature of the mobile divisions' supply columns.

The scale of Barbarossa and the subsequent operations of the Russo-German War preclude continuing at the level of detail presented earlier in the text. It is correspondingly useful to begin with a scorecard. Wilhelm Ritter von Leeb's Army Group North included Panzer Group 4. Erich Hoepner had three panzer and three motorized divisions, with two corps headquarters. One was commanded by Erich von Manstein. Restored to favor, in the coming weeks Manstein would emerge as a rising star of the armored force. Bock's Army Group Center had two panzer groups. Number 3, under Hermann Hoth, had three panzer and three motorized divisions. Panzer Group 2 was Heinz Guderian's: five panzer and three motorized divisions, plus Grossdeutschland. Guderian was also assigned the army's only horse cavalry division—an apparent contradiction in technological terms that reflected the potential threat from the waterlogged Pripet Marshes on his flank. Rundstedt commanded Army Group South, with five panzer and three motorized divisions along with the Leibstandarte, all under Kleist's Panzer Group 1.

As in France, the command relationships between panzer groups and field armies were left ambiguous—a situation that would contribute significantly to friction and ill-will as Barbarossa developed. In contrast to 1940, however, each group was assigned a number of infantry divisions: two for Hoepner, three for Hoth, no fewer than six each for Guderian and Kleist. As early as February, Hoth protested that the infantry would slow his advance and block the roads for the panzers' rear echelons. Bock and Guderian were unhappy for similar reasons. Bock's comment that his superiors did not seem to know what they wanted reflected Halder's ongoing concern about the mobile formations getting too far

ahead of the marching masses. But in 1941, Guderian commanded more
infantry than panzer divisions, and had fewer tanks than in the previous
year. In 1940 his corps frontages rarely exceeded 15 miles; in Russia, the
norm for his group would be 80 and more. Precisely how the infantry
was supposed to cope remained unaddressed.

The generally accepted rule of thumb is that an attack needs a local
advantage of three to one in combat power to break through at a specific
point—assuming rough equality in "fighting power." On June 22, tactical surprise produced a degree of operational shock denying conventional wisdom. The Red Air Force lost almost 4,000 planes in the war's
first five days—most of them destroyed on the ground. Other material
losses were proportional. Command and control at all levels seemed
to disintegrate. The Germans were nevertheless encountering not an
obliging enemy, but one caught between two stools. The impact of Stalin's purges on the officer corps has recently been called into question on
the basis of statistics indicating that fewer than 10 percent were actually
removed. The focus on numbers overlooks the ripple effects, in particular the diminishing of the mutual rapport and confidence so important
in the kind of war the Germans brought with them.

At the same time, in response to substandard performances in
Poland and Finland, the Red Army had restored a spectrum of behaviors and institutions abolished after the revolution of 1917, designed col-
lectively to introduce more conventional discipline and reestablish the
authority of officers and senior NCOs. These changes did not sit well
with a rank and file appropriately described as "reluctant soldiers." Nor
did they fit well on officers who were themselves profoundly uncertain
of their positions in the wake of the purges..

One result was a significant decline in training standards that were
already mediocre. Western images are largely shaped by German myths
describing the Russian as a "natural fighter," whose instincts and way of
life made him one with nature and inured him to hardship in ways foreign to "civilized" men. The Red Army soldier did come from a society
and a system whose hardness and brutality prefigured and replicated
military life. Stalin's Soviet Union was a society organized for violence,

with a steady erosion of distinctions and barriers between military and civilian spheres. If armed struggle never became the end in itself that it was for fascism, Soviet culture was nevertheless comprehensively militarized in preparation for a future revolutionary apocalypse. Soviet political language was structured around military phrasing. Absolute political control and comprehensive iron discipline, often gruesomely enforced, helped bridge the still-inevitable gaps between peace and war.

The winter campaign in Finland during 1939–40 had shown that Russian soldiers adapted to terrain and weather, remained committed to winning the war even in defeat, and maintained discipline at unit levels under extreme stress. But a combination of institutional disruptions and prewar expansion left too many of them ignorant of minor tactics and fire discipline—all the things the German system inculcated in its conscripts from the beginning. The Rotarmisten, the Red soldiers, would fight—but too often did not know how to fight the Germans.

The quality of Soviet tanks in the summer of 1941 has often been misrepresented. The Red Army fielded about 24,000 of them on June 22, 1941. More than 20,000 dated from the mid-1930s. The major types were the T-26 infantry tank, 9.5 tons with either a 37mm or a 45mm antitank gun; and the BT-7 "fast tank," a 14-ton Christie model with a 45mm gun whose road speed of 45 miles per hour had been bought at the expense of armor protection. Frequently and legitimately described as obsolescent, these tanks were nevertheless a reasonable match for anything in the German inventory, one for one, on anything like a level field.

The Red Army's institutional behavior prior to Barbarossa could not have been less suited to providing that level field had it been designed by the Wehrmacht. Since the 1920s the USSR had been developing sophisticated concepts of mobile armored warfare, and using the full resources of a command economy to produce appropriate equipment. By 1938 the Soviet order of battle included four tank corps and a large number of tank brigades whose use in war was structured by a comprehensive doctrine of "deep battle" that included using "shock armies" to break through on narrow fronts and air-supported mobile groups taking the fight into the enemy's rear at a rate of 25 or 30 miles a day. But in November 1939 these formations were disbanded, replaced by motorized divisions and tank brigades designed essentially for close infantry support.

One reason for this measure—the public one—was that the Spanish Civil War had shown the relative vulnerability of tanks, while large armored formations had proved difficult to control both against the Japanese in Mongolia and during the occupation of eastern Poland. Reinforcing operational experience were purges that focused heavily on the armored forces as a potential domestic threat. Not only were the top-level advocates of mobile war eliminated, including men like Mikhail Tukhachevsky; all but one commander at brigade level and 80 percent of the battalion commanders were replaced—and many of those they had replaced had succeeded men purged earlier.

German successes in 1940 combined with the running down of the purges to encourage reappraisal already inspired by the Red Army's dubious performance in Finland. Beginning in 1940 the People's Commissariat of Defense began authorizing what became a total of 29 mechanized corps, each with two tank divisions and a motorized division: 36,000 men and 1,000 tanks each, plus 20 more brigades of 300 T-26s for infantry support! The numbers are mind-boggling even by subsequent standards. Given the Soviets' intention to equip the new corps with state-of-the-art T-34s and KV-1s, the prospect is even more impressive. Reality was tempered, however, by the limited number of the new tanks in service—1,500 in June 1941—and tempered even further by maintenance statistics showing that 30 percent of the tanks actually assigned to units required major overhauls, while no fewer than 44 percent needed complete rebuilding.

That left a total of around 7,000 "runners" to face the panzer onslaught. It might have been enough except for, ironically, a command decision that played directly into the Soviet armored force's major weaknesses. Recently available archival evidence shows that, far from collapsing in disorganized panic, from Barbarossa's beginning the Red Army conducted a spectrum of counterattacks in a coherent attempt to implement prewar plans for an active defense ending in a decisive counteroffensive. The problem was that the mechanized corps central to these operations were too cumbersome to be handled effectively by inexperienced commanders, especially given their barely adequate communication systems. Their efforts were too often so poorly coordinated that the Germans processed and described them as the random thrashings of a disintegrating army. Most of the prewar Soviet armored force, and more than 10,000 tanks, were destroyed in less than six weeks.

Yet even in these early stages the panzers were bleeding. War diaries and letters home described "tough, devious, and deceitful" Russians fighting hard and holding on to the death. What amounted to a partisan war waged by regular soldiers was erupting behind a front line at best poorly defined. Forests and grain fields provided favorable opportunities for ambushes. Isolated tanks could do damage before they were themselves destroyed. Casualties among junior officers, the ones responsible for resolving tactical emergencies, mounted as the Germans found themselves waging a 360-degree war.

In Poland and France, terrain and climate had favored the panzers. From Barbarossa's beginnings they were on the other side. Russian road conditions were universally described as "catastrophic" and "impossible." Not only impressed civilian vehicles but army trucks sacrificed suspensions, transmissions, and oil pans in going so makeshift that armored cars balanced precariously on the deep ruts. Russian dust, especially the fine dust of sandy Byelorussia, clogged air filters and increased oil consumption until overworked engines gave in and seized up. Personal weapons required such constant cleaning that Soviet hardware, especially the jam-defying submachine guns, unofficially began replacing Mausers and Schmeissers in the rifle companies.

The earlier major campaigns had lines of communication short enough to return seriously damaged tanks to Germany. Divisions needed to undertake no more than field repairs. Russian conditions demanded more, and maintenance units proved unequal to the task. Not only was heavy equipment for moving disabled vehicles unavailable; workshops began running short on replacement parts almost immediately. Too often the result was a tank cannibalized for spares, or blown up before being abandoned.

Then conditions worsened. By early July episodic storms became heavy rains that turned dirt roads to bottomless mud and made apparently open fields impassable morasses. A first wave of vehicles might get through, but attempts at systematic follow-up usually resulted in traffic jams regularly described in words like "colossal." Dust and mud combined to make fuel consumption exponentially higher than standard rates of usage. Empty fuel tanks as well as breakdowns began immobilizing the panzers. Though figures vary widely, the histories and records of the panzer divisions in Army Groups South and Center present rates of attrition eroding combat-effective strengths to levels as low as 30 or 40 percent. Even small-scale Russian successes—three tanks knocked out here, a half dozen there; one searing encounter that left 3rd Panzer Division 22 tanks weaker in just a few minutes—had disproportionate effects on diminishing numbers.

Vehicle losses were only part of the panzers' problem, and arguably the lesser part. Effectiveness decreased as men grew tired and made the mistakes of fatigue, ranging from not checking an engine filter to not noticing a potential ambush site. Infantrymen constrained to leave their trucks to make corduroy roads from tree trunks, motorcyclists choked with dust that defied kerchiefs soaked with suddenly scarce water, and tankers trying to extract their vehicles from mudholes that seemed to appear from nowhere were a long way from blitzkrieg's glory days. There were still plenty of volunteers for high-risk missions. But by its third week Barbarossa had already cost more lives than the entire campaign in the West. And Moscow was a long way off.

With supply columns increasingly vulnerable to ambushes and concentrating on bringing up material, the panzer troopers helped themselves to what was available. Stress and fatigue synergized with ideologically structured racism to underpin behavior that from the beginning caused levels of bitterness noticed even in German official reports. It usually began by "requisitioning" food: portable items like chickens, eggs, fruit, and milk; stores of grain; cattle and hogs for impromptu butchering. Looting was regularly accompanied by destruction, and the effect on the victims was compounded by personalized meanness: smashing dishes, ripping up clothes and bedding, using boots and rifle butts in place of words and gestures.

The Germans as well found themselves facing "colossal" tanks against which German panzers and antitank guns seemed to have no effect. The T-34 disputes the title of the war's best tank only with the German Panther. Its design, featuring sloped armor, a dual-purpose 76mm gun, and a diesel engine and Christie-type suspension allowing speeds up to 35 miles per hour, set standards in the three essentials of protection, firepower, and mobility. Germans sometimes confused the T-34 with the BT-7. Few made that mistake a second time. Distributed in small numbers and manned by poorly trained crews, from Barbarossa's beginnings not only did the T-34 prove impervious to German armor-piercing rounds at fifty feet and less; it ran rings around Panzer IIIs and IVs used to dominating in speed and maneuverability.

More frightening, because it could not be mistaken for anything else, was the KV-I. At 43 tons, it was undergunned with a 76mm piece. It was mechanically troublesome and not particularly maneuverable. But with armor up to four inches thick, the KV did not have to move very often. Panzer Group 4 initially found the dense northern forest a greater obstacle than the Russian army. Manstein's new LXVI Panzer Corps covered almost 100 miles in four days, crossing Lithuania in a knife-thrust that carried it into Daugavpils and across the vital Dvina River bridges. The course for Leningrad seemed well set. Then the KVs made an appearance. The 37mm guns were useless. Mark IV rounds made no impression from front or sides. Six-inch howitzer shells burst harmlessly on the plating. One KV rolled right over a bogged-down 35(t), crushing it like a tin can. Another, in an often-told vignette, held up the entire 6th Panzer Division of Georg-Hans Reinhardt's XLIV Panzer Corps for two days, blocking a key crossroads, defying even 88mm rounds until, in an attack coordinated by a full colonel, pioneers were able to shove grenades into the turret.

Initially Leeb gave Hoepner a free hand. His group remained unattached to either of the armies and was allowed to make its own way forward. But more and more KVs appeared in the van of Soviet counterattacks. Sixth Panzer Division's 35(t)s engaged them at 30 yards. They overran the 114th Motorized Regiment, leaving in their wake a trail of crushed and mutilated bodies that sparked and fueled stories of unprovoked massacre. First Panzer Division's command post was caught so badly by surprise that the staff and commander used their pistols. The roads, few, narrow, and unpaved, had a way of disappearing entirely. Closely flanked by forests and swamps, they channeled and constrained German movement and were ambush magnets even for demoralized stragglers. Tanks, trucks, and half-tracks lurched from village to village as bemused officers discarded useless maps and sought directions from local civilians who offered only blank stares and shrugged shoulders.

Nor could towns be bypassed readily. Clearing them took time and lives. As the panzers approached Pskov their purportedly supporting infantry was mopping up in Daugavpils, 60 miles to the rear. Leeb's repeated reaction was to halt the armor despite vehement objections from Hoepner and his corps commanders that operations were being sacrificed to tactics. And Leningrad seemed ever farther away.

In contrast to Leeb's sector, Army Group South had ample open ground in front of it. Rundstedt used his infantry to make the initial breakthrough on a 50-mile front, and by the morning of June 23 the Landser were past the frontier positions. Breakout was another matter. The commander of the Southwestern Front (the Soviet counterpart of a German army group), Colonel General M. P. Kirponos, had four infantry armies and six mechanized corps under his hand, and understood how to use them. Panzer Group 1 met resistance featuring large-scale counterattacks better organized, and fighting withdrawals more timely, than those facing its counterparts. Not until early July would the panzer spearheads crack Soviet defenses and erode Soviet command and control to a point where one can speak of systematic maneuver operations beginning. Even then Soviet attacks regularly threw the Germans off balance.

Army Group Center's sector is usually referenced as the site of Barbarossa's greatest initial success. Panzer Groups 2 and 3 drove so deeply into the Soviet rear on each side of the fortress of Bialystok that on Day 2 of the offensive, Halder spoke of achieving complete operational freedom. On June 28, Hoth's and Guderian's spearheads linked up at Minsk in history's greatest battle of encirclement. The Germans claimed 5,000 tanks and 10,000 guns destroyed or captured. A third of a million Russians were dead or wounded; another third of a million were on their way to German POW camps.

Seen from the sharp end, the situation was less spectacular and less tidy. The mobile forces so far outpaced the marching divisions that the "pocket" was in many places no more than a line on a headquarters map. Red Army units might have been cut off but they neither surrendered nor dissolved. "Worse than Verdun," grimly noted one infantry colonel. Russian soldiers filtered through and broke through the purported encirclement in numbers that set German generals quarreling. Guderian and Gunther von Kluge, commanding 4th Army in Guderian's wake, reprised the earlier debate in France by disagreeing over whether it was best advised to seal the Minsk pocket tightly or continue driving along the high road to Moscow. Bock and Halder could see the advantages of both prospects too clearly to decide on either.

The High Command's decision to make another army headquarters responsible for clearing the pocket and put Kluge temporarily in command of both panzer groups (and confusingly retitled his command 4th Panzer Army for that period) has been interpreted as simplifying the command structure, and as braking the overaggressive panzers. Both were Band-Aids that did nothing to resolve the fundamental issue of overstretch. What they did was signal a level of indecision that encouraged Hitler to extend his direct involvement with operational issues.

To a degree the generals' behavior in these critical weeks reflected the ambiguities of the matrix established 70 years earlier by Helmuth von Moltke. While he stressed the importance of realizing that "no plan survives first contact with the enemy," he also asserted that the original plan needed to be good enough to allow improvisations within its overall framework. What held this dialectic together were the nineteenth century's limitations on mobility and shock. Subordinate formations—armies and corps—lacked the fighting power to achieve decisions

separately, but could not usually move far enough away from each other
to create real risks—at least when properly commanded.

The internal combustion engine and the radio had changed those
parameters—but to what degree? When exactly did the "artistic" daring
and initiative postulated by the "German way of war" cross the line into
chaotic solipsism? Or had that question lost its relevance to war-making
through what would later be called a paradigm shift?

The bones of contention, or perhaps the pawns on the board, were
the panzer and motorized divisions, consistently and haphazardly
shifted among higher commands, now as fire brigades cleaning up the
rear, now as spearheads restoring momentum at the front—and always
eroding their fighting power. But the panzer generals understood better
than their more conventional superiors that the battles of the frontier
were no more an end in themselves than their predecessors in 1914 had
been. They understood as well, albeit more viscerally than cerebrally, the
volcano's rim on which the campaign was dancing. No matter the initial
victories' costs and successes, they were the first stages of a campaign
whose outcome depended on the armored force maintaining its cohesion, its mobility, and its focus. Intelligence was reporting new Soviet
forces occupying positions on the road to Moscow. The schoolboy wisdom of running faster to restore balance after stumbling seemed all too
applicable.

Before the officially sanctioned date of July 3, Hoth and Guderian
sent their tanks toward the next geographic objective: the Dvina-Dnieper
line—more than 300 miles distant. By this time it was clear to everyone
involved that the gaps between panzer groups and infantry armies could
only grow wider. The Soviet forces still active behind the panzers' axes
of advance could only grow larger. In a sense Panzer Groups 2 and 3
were replicating Rommel's behavior in the desert. Just as logistics was
a rear-echelon problem, so was cleaning up whatever the armor left
behind.

From the beginning of this phase the panzers encountered resistance stronger than expected. Stalin had assigned Marshal Semyon
Timoshenko to organize the defense, concentrate reserves, and, above

all, counterattack at every opportunity. Timoshenko was no master of mobility but he was a hard man even by Soviet standards. His tanks and riflemen made the Germans pay for their tactical victories. A battalion of the 35th Panzer Regiment occupied the town of Staryi Bychoff on the Dnieper, only to be pinned down by a defense that cost 33 men and nine tanks—the regiment's heaviest losses in a single day since the start of the war. Its report describes the Russians as "hard-fighting, very brave soldiers." The Red Air Force reappeared in strength, and with new material. Nine Il-2 Sturmoviks, a formidably armored ground attack plane, gave Rommel's old division a taste of its French medicine on July 5, delaying the advance most of a day. One Il-2 took more than 200 ground-fire hits and made it home. Rain and terrain slowed the Germans as well. On one 50-mile stretch of road in Hoth's sector, 100 bridges in succession failed to take the strain of tanks and trucks. The often-overlooked pioneers were correspondingly vital for both panzer groups: bridging flooded rivers, repeating the job when the bridges collapsed, and all the time keeping watch for die-hard Soviet stragglers.

The Germans were winning on an increasingly frayed shoestring. Third Panzer Division was down to a third of its authorized tank strength. Fourth Panzer Division sent a staff officer all the way back to Germany in search of spare parts. A single tank battalion of 7th Panzer Division reported no fewer than five lieutenants killed in a few days— shot through the head by snipers who had a free hand because the riflemen's trucks could not keep up with the tanks. The motorized artillery as well was having increasing difficulty keeping pace, especially the heavy corps and army battalions so valuable for taking out Soviet prepared defenses. The result was increasing reliance on the Luftwaffe, and the air crews gave their best. Richthofen's VIII Air Corps, its Stukas using an early version of the cluster bomb, climaxed three weeks of constant effort by taking two of Hoth's divisions across the Dvina on July 8. The medium bombers of Air Fleet 2 hammered roads and rail junctions and interdicted troop movements—but against increasing fighter opposition that drew more and more German fighters into the air battle.

The tank and the airplane might be the Wehrmacht's concept of an ideal couple. But like most couples, stress brought out the worst sides of both partners. The ground units' war diaries contain an increasing litany of complaints about Russian aircraft being "masters of the skies," about the damage to tankers' morale from repeated attacks by low-flying Soviet aircraft, about Stuka strikes promised but never delivered. The Luftwaffe responded by describing the soldiers as "outrageously spoiled" by direct air support, and too quick to halt or even retreat in the face of opposition if German planes were not overhead. Richthofen himself upbraided his ground-pounding opposite numbers for refusing to recognize that in order to be effective, air power must be concentrated and could not be distributed piecemeal.

These arguments have been common in the air-ground relations of all armed forces, from North Africa through Korea and Vietnam, down to Desert Storm. Nevertheless they highlight the growing erosion of the German mobile forces, to the point where maneuver would become their only viable option.

And yet the panzers kept advancing—as far as 100 miles a day for some units. When movement stalled, group, corps, and division commanders probed for weak spots. When none existed, the colonels, captains, and sergeants created them. As Hoth smashed the Russian right, Guderian crossed the Dnieper south of Mogilev, and the panzers sought once more to create a giant pocket by meeting at Smolensk. With Soviet defenses in shreds and Soviet mobile formations scattered, the first German troops entered Smolensk late on July 15.

Eleven days later the German High Command declared the Smolensk pocket closed. The call was premature, but German skills showed to particular advantage against the major counterattacks mounted beginning in late July. German tank companies took advantage of Soviet inexperience to knock out two or three dozen T-34s at a time. On August 5, Bock announced the end of the fighting, the capture of another 300,000 prisoners, and the destruction of more than 3,000 tanks and almost as many guns.

It was the climax of a series of virtuoso performances that combine to make a case that the relative tactical and operational superiority of the panzers over their opponents was never greater than in the first half of July 1941, on the high road to Moscow. Guderian spoke of attacks going in like training exercises. Guderian's senior subordinates in turn praised his common sense and goodwill, the Fingerspitzengefühl, and not least the unflagging energy that marked him a master of mechanized war at the operational level. If Hoth lacked his stablemate's flair (and his gift for securing headlines), his handling of Panzer Group 3 produced results at the same level.

These successes were, however, the point of the spear—or better said, the tip of an iceberg. Army Group Center's mobile forces had by now outrun their logistics to a degree impossible for even the most operationally minded generals to overlook. Losses in tanks continued to mount. Rifle companies were shrinking to the strength of platoons. As a result, for the first time in the campaign, the panzers lacked the strength to force the pace of engagements. Instead they were increasingly constrained to wear down Soviet attacks and throw them off balance before counterattacking themselves. That pattern would become characteristic of German tactics and operations in the second half of the Russo-German War. Its systematic appearance at this early stage was another of Barbarossa's many warning signs.

VI

LIKE THE GIANT Antaeus of classical mythology or the Green Knight of medieval English lore, the Red Army seemed to derive strength from being knocked down. Initial estimates had allowed for around 200 Soviet divisions. By the end of the Smolensk operation, more than 300 had appeared on German charts. The USSR outproduced Germany in tanks during 1941. But in six weeks, the best Soviet commanders had been discredited, the best Soviet formations had been eviscerated, thousands of tanks, guns, and aircraft had been destroyed, and tens of thousands of square miles overrun. Was it entirely wishful thinking that sustained the German belief that one more strike would finish the job? And was that viewpoint underpinned by an unacknowledged but growing sense of the panzers as an ultimately wasting asset, best employed to their limits while they could still shape the campaign?

As early as July 8, Hitler had informed the Chief of Staff of his intention to divert mobile forces north and south with open options: to reinforce the attack on Leningrad, to cooperate with Army Group South in capturing Kiev, and to regroup for a drive on Moscow. Depending on the operational situation, this represented a flat denial of the concept of the decisive point. It also represented the downplaying of the moral importance of Moscow. The city's loss would be a prestige victory and an ideological triumph for National Socialism—a double body blow to the Soviet Union.

A fable with many versions in many languages describes a donkey starving to death because he is unable to choose among a half dozen full mangers. Franz Halder was no folklorist, but on July 23 he informed Hitler that the Russians had been decisively weakened—not decisively defeated. Every new operation had to begin by breaking enemy resistance, but overall infantry strength was down by 20 percent, and the panzer divisions averaged 50 percent short of establishment.

On the other hand, Kiev was the transportation and communications hub for the great industrial centers of southwest Russia. Leningrad, Lenin's city, was arguably more the USSR's moral center than was the official capital. Its capture would give Germany control of the Baltic Sea, create a united political and military front with Finland, and free Panzer Group 4 for employment against Moscow.

And if the enemy's army was considered the primary objective, as opposed to resources and territory, the pickings were likely to be easier on the wings than by continuing headlong into a sector the Soviets must defend at all costs, and where their counterattacks indicated they were doing just that. The pace of Army Group Center's advance was slowing perceptively enough to cause concern. At the same time, that advance was creating an increasingly exposed salient. Securing its flanks, especially the southern one, was a defensible response, especially in the context of those suddenly emerging reserves Wehrmacht intelligence had asserted the Red Army did not possess.

Rundstedt, whose army group could expect to benefit massively from a southern option, argued in public for the importance of continuing the drive on Moscow. He and Leeb, however, also had a particular sense of what they were on the verge of accomplishing with just a few of the right kinds of resources. Reduced to its essentials, the revised plan projected sending elements of Panzer Group 2 south with the mission of enveloping and destroying the Soviet forces engaging Rundstedt's left. Hoth's Group would turn north to assist in capturing Leningrad, then swing toward the Volga in cooperation with Panzer Group 4. Army Group Center would continue advancing on Moscow with infantry and sort out its rear areas and logistics until the mobile divisions returned.

When the Army High Command asked whether the campaign now sought economic objectives or destruction of Soviet military forces, the answer was "both." It would be oversimplified hindsight to describe Hitler as playing his senior generals against each other. It would be an equal oversimplification to describe the generals as blindly obsessed with their respective places in the history of war. Both factors were undeniably present—and it must be particularly emphasized that generals without high levels of alpha ambition are likely to be liabilities in senior command. What is significant about the decisions made as the Smolensk pocket closed is the underlying consensus that affirmed them: a conviction that the panzers could still move fast enough and strike hard enough to make ultimate choices unnecessary. Barbarossa's second stage would be predicated on what might be called a postmodern construction: a "flexible Schwerpunkt."

Depending on perspective, that placed the panzers in the role of either a chameleon placed on a plaid shirt, or a cartoon character running through a china shop shattering one glass after another by flicking his finger. In a month, XLI Panzer Corps had fought its way across 650 miles of forest and swamp to within 100 miles of Leningrad. Air supply sustained the final stage of an advance that by July 14 had thrown two bridges across the Luga River, the last major natural barrier before a city that was only two days' march away—on the maps. But Leeb was a cautious general; the Soviet defense was desperate; and Reinhardt's depleted divisions lacked the fighting power to overrun a city with two and a half million inhabitants. For armored forces, getting into a city was far less a problem than getting out of it—especially given the constrained time frame in which the attack on Leningrad was conceptualized.

Had Manstein's corps been directly involved, the story might have played out differently. Instead Leeb and Hoepner had turned Manstein southeast toward Novgorod and the Moscow-Leningrad railroad. It was the kind of maneuver operation basic to panzer doctrine, in which Manstein possessed unusual skill—and which the Soviets were determined to frustrate. A well-executed counterattack cut off 8th Panzer Division and took out half of its 150 tanks in the four days Manstein required to break the 8th free. Pushing slowly forward, the corps eventually also bogged down along the Luga River.

As for the projected reinforcement by Panzer Group 3, not until August 16 was Army Group Center formally ordered to transfer four of its mobile divisions to Army Group North—a consequence of increasingly forceful debates between and among Hitler and the relevant generals. The new arrivals proved just enough to encourage Leeb and Hoepner and not enough to turn the tide in their sector. With both of Hoepner's corps immobilized on the Luga, when Hoth's divisions finally arrived, Leeb committed them to strengthen his thinly manned front as opposed to reinforcing one of Hoepner's corps as a striking force. On September 8, Hoepner nevertheless renewed his group's attack.

Schlisselburg, widely regarded as a keystone of the defense, fell after heavy and expensive fighting. The Russians threw in everything they had. First Panzer Division engaged tanks literally fresh from factory assembly lines. But the city held—and the Army High Command grew increasingly insistent on transferring Panzer Group 4 south for the drive against Moscow. Sixth Panzer Division was ordered south on August 18. By the twenty-fifth the front had "stabilized" in a blockade that plunged Leningrad into three years of horror as Hitler ordered the starving of the city his tanks failed to conquer.

Army Group North's series of tactical victories between June and September neither camouflage nor compensate for unhandiness at the operational level. Leeb has come under especially heavy criticism for repeatedly halting or slowing the armored spearheads to allow the infantry to close up: a fits-and-starts process that gave the Soviets time to improvise Leningrad's defense. The dispersion of Hoepner's panzers in the first half of July further diminished blitzkrieg's prospects in the northern sector. Wilhelm Ritter von Leeb, in short, will never go down as a master, or even an apprentice, of mobile war.

In Leeb's defense, arguably even more than in Barbarossa's other sectors, logistics and rear security controlled the pace and nature of operations in the north. The first phase of the German advance had been through the relatively developed territory of the Baltic states: Latvia, Estonia, and Lithuania, which had been occupied by the Red Army in 1940 and were as yet relatively spared the blessings of Marxism-Leninism. The Germans benefited from overrunning large amounts of stockpiled Red Army supplies, and from capturing a number of major bridges and rail connections undamaged. Crossing into the USSR proper meant entering a literal wilderness, historically left undeveloped to provide a glacis for Russia's northern capital. The near-literal absence of infrastructure made exploiting local resources nearly impossible: there were no surpluses, however meager, to requisition, confiscate, or steal.

That put a rapid, unexpected burden on a supply system stretched to move its own bases forward into the northern wasteland. It was not mere reflex caution that led Leeb to insist repeatedly on the necessity for bringing the infantry forward as the price of the next advance. Guerilla activity in Army Group North's rear grew so serious that beginning on August 5, the entire 8th Panzer Division was withdrawn from the front and assigned to anti-partisan duties on the line of communications.

Developments in Army Group South followed a different pattern. Kleist shook off the initial Russian counterattacks, broke through an improvised "Stalin Line" on July 5, and started his tanks toward Kiev. In their wake marched the infantry of 6th Army, who were intended to do the heavy work of actually capturing the city. Fighting through strong resistance, especially by units officially overrun and reported as scattered, Panzer Group 1 had its first sight of Kiev's skyline on July 10.

With the infantry and heavy artillery a hundred miles to the rear, III Panzer Corps commander Eberhard von Mackensen nevertheless considered storming the city with the two panzer divisions and one motorized division coming on line. Sixth Army CO Walther von Reichenau, anything but battle-shy, compared the prospect of fighting house-to-house in Kiev to Verdun—not least because of the constant losses his infantry were already taking from persistent air and ground attack. It was Hitler, however, who pulled the plug, forbidding a direct attack on Kiev for the present and freeing Mackensen's corps for what seemed a far more promising mission.

The other two mobile corps of Panzer Group 1 had turned south of Kiev toward Uman. Red Army counterattacks, heavy air strikes, and poor weather slowed and disrupted the operation. Mutual envelopment operations at times left troops uncertain who was encircling whom. Nevertheless between July 16 and August 3, Kleist's group created and sustained a pocket that, when cleared, yielded more than 100,000 prisoners—no mean bag even by the standards of Minsk and Smolensk. Large numbers of Russians managed to escape a trap that, like the others in Barbarossa, never fully closed. They did so at the expense of their organization and much of their equipment as the Red Army began a full-scale retreat from Bessarabia and the western Ukraine, abandoning the Dnieper River line. An enraged Stalin ordered the dismissal of some generals, and the execution of others.

Uman was no more than second prize in the blitzkrieg lottery. Halder and Rundstedt originally projected an even bigger encirclement in the area of Kirovograd, one cutting off the entire Soviet force west of the Dnieper. That had exceeded the panzers' capacity. But with most of the Soviet front in apparent disintegration, with the Romanians advancing on Odessa and the Black Sea coast, the military prospects of a "southern strategy" began to match Hitler's original economic visions—particularly when the major alternative involved a direct assault on Moscow in the best traditions of the Great War. Blitzkrieg was about creating opportunities and seizing them. Panzer Group 1 had begun Barbarossa with the lowest force-to-space ratio of the four. The increasing development of the southern front had increased the distances among possible objectives. But Rundstedt, Kleist, and the mobile corps commanders had done well—better than well—playing cape-and-sword with the Red Army. Suitably reinforced, they could finish the job.

Orders might be given, but mobile war German style depended on informed consent. The pivotal figure in the developing shift of operational focus was Heinz Guderian. He was considered firmly in the Moscow camp—so firmly that on August 23 he flew to Hitler's Rastenburg headquarters with the intention of protesting in person against the projected reassignment of his group. By his own account at least he made a compelling presentation. Hitler then responded with his reasons for the Kiev option. Guderian's self-described reluctance to make a scene in the face of a firm decision need not be taken at face value. But nor should his critics' descriptions of careerism overriding principle be accepted without modification.

Guderian was at best a medium-sized fish in what had suddenly become a very big pond. His focus since June 21 had been to his front: operational and tactical. During the discussion Hitler had asked him a question: Did Guderian's men have one more great effort in them? Guderian answered yes—if given an objective whose importance was self-evident. Kiev was not Moscow. But keep Panzer Group 2 together, give its commander a free hand, and there was a solid chance of completing the operation before the autumn rains shut down southern Russia entirely. Hitler conceded the point, and Halder flew into an enduring rage at what he called Guderian's capitulation.

In Guderian's terms, that was just another sign that the Chief of Staff might talk the talk of mobile war, but could never walk the walk. When matters grew dark, it was time to step on the gas. It is always ill-advised to throw spitballs at an adversary armed with rocks. Guderian began his move south minus one of his corps, transferred at Halder's orders. But with massive Luftwaffe support, Panzer Group 2 broke the Soviet front within days. Third Panzer Division's commander Walther Model was one of a rising new breed of hard-charging risk-takers willing to make bricks without straw and mobile war with only a few tanks. In a tactical tour de force, a battle group of the 3rd Panzer Divsion captured a key bridge over the Desna River on August 26, motorcyclists and half-tracks shooting their way across as German and Soviet pioneers dueled under the roadbed for control of the demolition apparatus.

The panzers drove south, shrugging off poorly coordinated flank attacks. As he had done in France, Guderian chivied subordinates mercilessly. Soviet commanders at all levels were bewildered by the speed of the German advance and the ability of the Germans to be where they were not expected. By September 7, Panzer Group 2 had opened a twenty-mile operational gap between the Southwestern Front and its right-flank neighbor the Bryansk Front.

Meanwhile, Panzer Group 1 struck for the Dnieper. The first permanent bridgehead came at Kremenchug. Then, on August 25, the 13th Panzer Division captured an intact bridge at Dnepropetrovsk, opening a way into the Soviet rear. Semyon Budenny, commanding the Southwestern Front, was an old-line horse cavalryman, an anachronism in the internal-combustion era. But he knew well enough what mobile troops could achieve in empty space. He requested permission to retreat—and was promptly replaced. Stalin's determination to hold the line in part reflected the ongoing battle for Kiev, which fully justified Reichenau's grim prediction. It was street by street and house by house, with the Germans making little progress. Stalin ordered Kiev held and threw in reinforcements, as the Germans began turning two breakthroughs into one envelopment.

Facing massive counterattacks around Dnepropetrovsk, Kleist feinted north and drove through Kremenchug. The starring role went to one of the new formations: 16th Panzer Division, under another newcomer, Hans Hube. Crossing the Dnieper on September 11, by the thirteenth the division was 20 miles into the Soviet rear with two more divisions in close support. Again Stalin ordered Kiev held: no retreat without his authorization. Panzer Group 1 was down to half strength and less in tanks, but on the cusp of the kind of objective Guderian had described to Hitler. Hube led from the front as his tanks overran an army headquarters whose commander was constrained to escape through a window. The Luftwaffe, with V Air Corps supporting Kleist

and II Air Corps supporting Guderian, pounced on every Soviet effort
to establish blocking points and scoured the sky clean of Soviet aircraft.
On the evening of September 16—at 1820, to be exact—3rd and 16th
Panzer Divisions met to close the Kiev pocket at Lokhvitsa, more than
120 miles behind the city itself.

Kiev was the third of Barbarossa's major pocket battles, and the
greatest. Serious resistance ended around September 24; mopping up
took ten days longer. German official figures give more than 800 tanks
and almost 3,500 guns captured, along with more than 650,000 prisoners. Salvaging the equipment and transferring the men took weeks. Kiev
was also the smoothest of the envelopments. Leakage was minimal—
only around 15,000 Soviet soldiers managed to escape across the steppe.
Panzer Group 1 was worn thin, like a long-used knife blade. Winter was
close enough for Rundstedt to recommend suspending operations. On
October 1, Kleist's men, renamed the 1st Panzer Army, instead turned
south first to the Sea of Azov, then toward Rostov and the oil fields of
the Caucasus, 180 degrees *away* from the revitalized attack on Moscow
the High Command was calling Operation Typhoon.

The upgrading of Panzer Group 1, and eventually all the rest, to army
status was more than cosmetic retitling. On one hand it was positive: a
recognition that the mobile forces' effectiveness depended heavily on the
kind of autonomy denied when they were subordinated to army commanders rather than reporting directly to the army groups. In particular
the tension between Guderian and Hoth and their nominal superior
von Kluge had contributed significantly to a level of friction and delay
clearly unaffordable in the circumstances of the Russo-German War.
On the other side of the coin, establishing the higher panzer headquarters as armies downgraded their specialist function. Increasingly they
would be used in the same way as other armies, commanding mixed
bags of mobile and marching divisions, occupying sectors as often as
conducting mobile operations—in short, following the patterns developing in Army Group North but on a larger scale.

Kiev remains a subject of controversy among scholars and soldiers.
One school argues that the operation was a digression. It did not end the
war; the USSR did not collapse. Instead, Kiev (and Leningrad) further

strained an already overextended panzer force. Kiev arguably delayed the attack on Moscow by a month, giving the Red Army and General Winter time that could not have been bought in battle. But Kiev also destroyed or neutralized massive Soviet forces that would have been available against the right flank of the Moscow offensive. Nor could Stalin and his generals overlook the near-free strategic hand Kiev gave Rundstedt in southern Ukraine: diversion of strength and attention is usually a two-way process. And as Robert M. Citino dryly puts it, "Can any battle that nets 665,000 prisoners be considered a mistake?" Even the USSR's deployable resources, human and material, were not infinitely renewable.

Kiev was a crucial benchmark in another, no less decisive way. On September 24, a series of explosions shook the city. Preset, remote-controlled demolitions started fires that destroyed much of what remained intact after the fighting. Hitler ordered retribution. The army enthusiastically cooperated not for the first time in such exercises, but in a visible, spectacular way that made its position on the Jewish question unmistakable. Its culmination was the shooting of more than 30,000 Jews at Babi Yar—an operation that would have been impossible without army-supplied transport, administration, and area security.

Events in Kiev reinforced the growing awareness among Russians who had worked and sacrificed to build a Soviet future that the Germans were no less committed to destroying that future. The Soviet people did not become overnight the united and determined force of Communist myth. Panic, looting, wildcat strikes—a general breakdown of law and order prevailed in Moscow during the fighting. Well before then, however, it was increasingly obvious that whatever might be wrong with the USSR, it was nothing the Germans could fix—or wanted to.

Stalin's obscene treatment of his own people had created a significant opportunity the Germans failed to utilize. Stalin himself acknowledged the possibility in a speech of May 1945. Prospects for extending individual and local cooperation with occupation into a call for a joint war against Soviet tyranny nevertheless foundered from the beginning on Nazi-structured racism. Hitler forbade any consideration of Slavs as allies. Independently of Hitler, atrocities became a rear-area norm. Soldiers took snapshots of mass hangings and mass shootings, often sending them home to their families. Such messages as "1,153 Jewish looters shot," or "2,200 Jews shot," grew into boasts of 20,000, 30,000 shootings and more.

These body counts had little to do with actually fighting partisans. The vast, consistent discrepancy between the numbers of weapons seized and people executed make that point eloquently. The perpetrators submitted detailed reports to Berlin in codes so simple that British intelligence had been reading them since 1939. The information went unpublicized because the British government believed its release would jeopardize other code-breaking operations deemed vital to the war effort—especially the decryption of German raidio messages by the ULTRA operation.

Nor was the work confined to Nazi organizations. Einsatzgruppen, Waffen SS, and army "field-grays" came together in a common cause across occupied Russia. While generals like Leeb and Bock offered token protests, Reichenau called for "severe and just retribution against subhuman Jewry" and for a campaign of terror against all Russians. Hoth issued a more extreme version. Guderian declared he "made the order his own." Manstein, promoted to army command in the Crimea, took up his new post by demanding the eradication of partisans and "Jewish Bolsheviks."

Arguably more crucial to the war's metastasizing brutalization were the junior officers. In 1939 about half still came from more or less traditional sources: the educated middle classes broadly defined. With the outbreak of war, combat experience became the dominant criterion. There was less and less time to provide more than basic instruction to officer candidates who saw their survival to date as prima facie proof of skill and luck, and who tended to regard training courses in the Fatherland as an opportunity for unauthorized rest and recreation. After the fall of 1942, any German over sixteen could become an army officer if he served acceptably at the front, demonstrated the proper character, believed in the Nazi cause, and was racially pure. The Waffen

SS was more overtly egalitarian, but its basic criteria were essentially the same.

This relative democratization in good part reflected the growing synergy between National Socialist ideology and the demands of the front. Hitler wanted young men "as tough as leather, as fleet as greyhounds, and as hard as Krupp steel," correspondingly unburdened by reflection or imagination. The Red Army at its best did not offer sophisticated tactical opposition. What division and regimental commanders wanted in subordinates was tough men physically and morally, those willing to lead from the front and publicly confident in even the most desperate situations. One might speculate, indeed, that a steady supply of twentysomething lieutenants with wound badges and attitudes helped older, wiser, and more tired majors and colonels to suppress their own doubts about Hitler and his war. And men with such conditioning were more likely to encourage than restrain aggressive behavior against "others" and "outsiders."

VII

IN OTHER WARS Kiev was a victory for the ballad-makers. In this one it was no more than the first step to what the General Staff regarded as the campaign's finale: a drive for Moscow that Halder expected to force Russia out of the war on any terms Germany chose to impose. Hitler, who had been considering the prospect of continuing operations into 1942, found no difficulty accepting an audacity that matched, perhaps even exceeded, his own. A new directive of September 6 acknowledged Moscow as the focal point of the campaign's next stage.

The blitzkrieg team was frayed. The Luftwaffe's operational losses had been compounded by the problems of maintenance at improvised forward air strips, and crew fatigue the system refused to recognize. The 2nd Air Fleet, Army Group Center's opposite number, had approximately 170 single-engine fighters, about the same number of bombers, and 120 ground attack planes. The artillery's material losses had been limited, but its horses were dying, its vehicles were breaking down, and its ammunition reserves were limited. The infantry was tired. Average divisional strengths had been reduced by a quarter—more in the rifle companies. Morale was still high; and to some degree the shortage of men was compensated by material. Increasing numbers of 50mm anti-tank guns, effective against T-34s, were coming on line. Army Group Center had 14 battalions of the assault guns that had demonstrated their worth over and over again in all sectors. In the final analysis, however, the attack on Moscow would go as far as the panzers could carry it.

The code name was Typhoon, and reality approached rhetoric. The initial intention had been to redeploy 4th Panzer Group on Hoth's left and launch a two-pronged attack. The rapid victory at Kiev enabled Guderian's group to be brought up on the right. When the number was finalized, Bock had fourteen panzer and eight motorized divisions, more than 1,000 tanks on a 500-mile front. The panzers were not what they had been on June 21. Casualties had been heavy and replacements inadequate. But they remained the cream of the army: tempered but not yet brittle, respecting their enemy but still convinced they had the Soviets' measure.

Guderian's panzer divisions were still at about half their assigned tank strength. The situation in Groups 3 and 4 was better. Two of Hoepner's divisions had even enjoyed full, albeit brief, refits in France. The problem was sustainability. Shifting Panzer Groups 2 and 4 quickly and smoothly showcased the quality of German staff planning and traffic management, but it came with a price in wear and tear. Hitler had ordered engine production allocated to new vehicles, and the army group had received only 350 replacements. The shortage of other vehicles exceeded 20 percent. Fuel consumption was outstripping the Reich's production capacity. Existing supplies remained difficult to move forward due to the still-inadequate rail system.

The main German offensive was scheduled to begin October 2. Panzer Group 4 would follow the secondary road Roslavl-Moscow, then pivot left toward the Smolensk-Moscow highway. Panzer Group 3 would break through in the north and swing right. The two groups would meet at Vyazma in another by-now standard encirclement. The sting in Typhoon's tail, with apologies for the mixed metaphor, would be provided by Guderian. Panzer Group 2 would jump off two days earlier, break through to the northeast toward Orel-Bryansk, and create a second pocket. The one-two punch would shatter the Soviet central front and open for a second time the road to Moscow. Whether the city would be enveloped or captured by a knife-thrust up the middle was left to contingency. It would be a race against the weather, against Soviet ability to reinforce, and against the Germans' growing spectrum of losses and shortages. Success depended—again—on speed and shock. *Also—Panzer voran!*

The Germans' opponents were a mixture of worn-down veterans and grass-green conscripts. Most divisions were at half strength in men, less in equipment. All but a few of the tanks were old models, the same ones the Germans had already destroyed by hundreds. Higher headquarters lacked trained staff officers and mutual confidence. The Red Army did not expect the Germans to mount another all-out drive so close to the coming of the autumn rains. When air reconnaissance reported a massive German armored column advancing from Smolensk, the NKVD sought the crews' arrest for inciting panic.

The Germans did well enough on that score by themselves. Panzer Group 2 started 17th and 18th Panzer Divisions northwest toward Bryansk. Fourth Panzer Division advanced 80 miles northeast toward Orel in 24 hours, covered 150 miles in four days, and took the city's defenses so completely by surprise on October 3 that streetcars were still running when the tanks interrupted service. Casualties were fewer than 200 men. Bryansk fell on October 7, and 17th Panzer Division trumped 4th by overrunning an entire Front headquarters.

Hoepner's group in Typhoon's center was able to concentrate 560 tanks in two corps on a mere 50-mile front. The Soviets were simply pushed out of the way, and by October 5, Hoepner was ready to commit his reserve of two panzer and two motorized divisions: the third corps he had not had at Leningrad. Hoth's group had fewer and less powerful tanks than Hoepner. Its supply problems were greater due to inferior roads. Constant counterattacks slowed its pace. Nevertheless Panzer Group 3's spearheads found the junction between two Soviet armies, drove a wedge between them, and captured intact a number of major bridges over the Dnieper. Hoth's promotion to army command under Rundstedt on October 5 had no effect on the well-worked-in staff that welcomed Reinhardt from XLI Panzer Corps. Dependable rather than spectacular, he had raised and shaped 4th Panzer Division, led his corps through France and Russia, and was part of the panzer family.

The Red Air Force responded to Typhoon in force, the Sturmoviks doing particular damage to tank formations. Guderian recorded personally dodging a series of attacks by low-flying bombers. The panzer groups' initial successes nevertheless owed much to Richthofen's Stukas, and to the bombers who interdicted road junctions and rail lines, harassed troop columns, and disrupted communications to the point where the Soviets failed to grasp what was happening to them as it happened. The tanks were used up in small-scale counterattacks. The artillery was overrun in position; the infantry held its ground until cut off.

Infantry-armor cooperation was closer in the initial stages of Typhoon than at any previous time during Barbarossa. The foot-marchers secured the panzers' flanks by pinning Soviet frontline divisions in place, then crushing them with set-piece attacks that cost lives but inhibited orderly withdrawal even after Stalin was persuaded to authorize retreat late on October 5. The next evening, Group 3's 7th Panzer Division cut the Moscow highway at Vyazma from the north. At midmorning on the seventh, Hoepner's 10th Panzer entered the city from the south, closing a pocket containing 30 Soviet divisions from five armies. Elements of three more armies were enveloped when the infantry divisions of the German 2nd Army linked up with Guderian's panzers at Bryansk on the seventh and eighth.

The trapped Russians fought with by-now predictable desperation. The Germans were no less determined, and this time the infantry was close behind the tanks. Fighting continued until the end of October. When final accounts were tallied, the booty included 6,000 guns and mortars, 1,300 tanks, and almost 700,000 men. Another 300,000 Soviet soldiers died anonymously or just disappeared. A 300-mile gap had been torn in the Soviet line, and no reserves were available to throw in.

They had been sent to oppose Army Group South—an overlooked consequence of the battle for Kiev. Zukhov described the situation bluntly: The panzers' way was wide open; nothing could guarantee against their sudden appearance before Moscow.

The High Command and Adolf Hitler agreed. And then the same generals who had for weeks been focused on Moscow with laserlike intensity decided that the time had come to end the war on the flanks. Third Panzer Group, now 3rd Panzer Army, was sent northeast to cut the Moscow-Leningrad railway. Guderian's rechristened 2nd Panzer Army was ordered to send a corps southeast toward Kursk. The rest of it would join Hoepner and take Moscow—when, that is, the mobile divisions were no longer needed to secure the pockets, and once they could refuel.

Fourth Panzer Division lost two days in Orel with dry tanks and had to "borrow" 3rd Panzer's fuel allotment to push a weak battle group up the Tula highway. The tactical sun was shining on October 6 when 34th Motorcycle Battalion pulled off another of the *Husaresstücke* (hussar stunts) by now routine for the panzer bikers by seizing an undemolished bridge. When the tanks crossed, the situation changed. An ambush of T-34s knocked out ten of 35th Panzer Regiment's tanks and drove the Germans back across the bridge.

The advance resumed the next day, but the Germans were unable to reinforce and develop their success despite unusually strong air and artillery support. Fuel remained in short supply. The year's first snowfalls began on October 7. And 4th Panzer faced a different kind of opposition. The Red Army had begun awarding the title "Guards" to formations that distinguished themselves in combat. The 1st Guards Rifle Corps was not what Guards would become. But it put stones in the Germans' road for four days—time enough to construct a defensive line that held up the panzers for two more weeks.

In Hoepner's sector the only division initially available to take the Moscow road was Das Reich, the 2nd SS Motorized. This was the first time the panzer arm entrusted a Waffen SS division with a vital mission, but the men in black were stopped by a roadblock backed by a couple dozen T-34s and 30 BT-7s. Not until October 13 did the advance resume. By that time Zukhov had brought up enough troops to form the Mozhaisk Line near the 1812 battlefield of Borodino. Rain and snow, thaws and freezes, were turning the ground to mud and transforming the overall logistic situation from precarious to desperate. Breaking the Mozhaisk Line took two weeks, first to last. When it was done, five panzer divisions were 80 miles from Moscow as the crow flies. For two weeks more they got no farther.

Had it been available, 3rd Panzer Army might well have been too much for the hard-tried Ivans. But instead of enveloping the Mozhaisk Line's nearly open left flank, its divisions were advancing through the mud in the wrong direction. The veteran 1st Panzer Division covered 50 miles in five days to take Kalinin on October 14—but it was moving extrinsically, away from Moscow, as ordered.

Guderian's 2nd Panzer Army managed to scrounge enough fuel and ammunition to send XXIV Panzer Corps toward Tula on October 29. In fact the spearhead was a battle group formed from the 35th Panzer Regiment, brought up to 80 tanks by giving it most of the corps's runners, a rifle company in half-tracks attached from 3rd Panzer Division, and several truck-mounted companies of the Grossdeutschland Regiment. Commanding the mixed bag was Colonel Heinrich Eberbach, a scar-faced veteran of World War I and among the best of the third-generation panzer leaders emerging from Barbarossa. The one available road to Tula began disintegrating immediately, with maximum speed falling to ten or twelve miles per hour: low-gear driving that was itself an extra strain on overworked trucks. The Russians had blown the bridges and laid minefields everywhere. Eberbach's task force nevertheless advanced 50 miles in five days, and on October 30 he sought to take Tula by storm. The garrison, a mixture of local militia and NKVD troops, threw the Germans out and back in desperate fighting and bought time for reinforcements to pin 2nd Panzer Army in place outside the city till mid-November.

The battle for Tula highlighted the frontline consequences of long-term overextension throughout Army Group Center. It was not merely a matter of wrestling more supplies forward. The mobile units were declining in effective, deployable strength to a point where commanders were not merely halting units but cannibalizing them. It was common practice to strip out men and vehicles to form ever-weaker spearheads that might still be able to move but found it increasingly difficult to fight, even against the kind of amateur opposition initially faced in Tula. The shock, it might be said, was too small to create awe— and the confusion on which the panzers had depended since 1939.

The Germans had two choices. One was to go into what amounted to winter quarters, comprehensively refit, and prepare for another offensive in 1942. Kluge was already implementing that approach on his own initiative, tightening the 4th Army's lines and shifting de facto to the defensive. The alternative was to make one last, absolutely final try for Moscow before winter began in earnest. The distance was so close. The army had come so far. Von Bock urged pushing on. The High Command concurred—and convinced a more or less dubious Hitler.

The mind-set can be ascribed to ambition. Halder, Bock, Guderian, and their subordinates were concerned, not to say obsessed, with their personal places in history. Linked to that, though not as often noted, were stress and fatigue. Living conditions had been primitive even in headquarters. Leading from the front meant taking risks. Guderian was not the only senior officer who had faced Soviet fire, and it impugns no one's courage to say that experience is never shrugged off. The operational environment, in short, was anything but conducive to balanced judgment and cold reason in the pattern of the elder Moltke.

The senior staff officers' conference held at Orsha on November 13 declared the situation extremely serious and criticized the notion of another large-scale offensive. Halder's response that it was necessary to trust to "soldier's luck," and his later statement that "these battles are less a question of strategic command than a question of energy" seem, in hindsight, at best a desk general's heroic vitalism, and at worst, hubris in the classical Greek sense. But Halder was no fool. The Russians had repeatedly conjured armies from resources just as repeatedly described as exhausted by German intelligence. What might they achieve given even four uninterrupted months?

Experience and myth alike, moreover, taught what a Russian winter meant for soldiers—especially a winter spent in the open. Neither the military nor the political leadership had concerned itself with providing winter clothes and equipment for a campaign expected to be finished by autumn. Now coats, gloves, and scarves were collected haphazardly— many extorted from Europe's Jews—and piled up at railheads, taking priority behind fuel and ammunition. Eventually the survivors of the winter of 1941–42 would receive a medal. Its wearers dubbed it the *Gefrierfleischorden*: the frozen meat medal.

When the ground began freezing, there was a certain rejoicing from generals to privates. "Now [we] can afford to take risks," Bock declared. Instead the panzers lurched forward, measuring progress as much by the onset of winter as by desperate Soviet resistance. Tank crews lit fires under engines in the morning to thaw them enough to turn over. More and more vehicles already held together with spit and tape gave up the ghost. Aircraft had been withdrawn to Reich and the Mediterranean; all that remained was VIII Air Corps with fewer than 100 fighters and 200 strike aircraft—paper strengths heavily eroded by fuel shortages and frozen engines.

Reinhardt swung south, captured Klin, and reached the Moscow-Volga Canal on November 27, but was promptly ejected from the small bridgehead. The panzer army went over to the defense on November 30, supplies, men, and equipment exhausted by determined Soviet defenders. Guderian made a final attempt to envelop Tula, and on December 2 also shifted to the defense under heavy Soviet pressure and recurring blizzards. Hoepner's attack ground to a halt within sight and sound of Moscow. Its frontline units had no food, no gasoline, no ammunition, and almost no one left in the ranks able to pull a trigger. On the evening of December 1, a reconnaissance patrol reached the train station at Khimki—twelve and a half miles from Moscow: the closest the Germans would get. It might as well have been a hundred and twelve.

On December 5, with the temperature at 25 degrees below zero, the Red Army counterattacked. Its rear echelons disintegrating, Army Group Center fell back. Panzer Army 3 fought itself to near destruction covering Bock's left. Sixth Panzer Division expended the last of its 35(t)s and most of its other vehicles, converted its transport to local farm wagons, and reorganized what remained of its panzer regiment as a provisional infantry battalion.

Hitler's immediate responses were to issue a general "no retreat" order, and declare war against the US. The latter decision was the least debated; Hitler had to ask where Pearl Harbor was. The former decision reflected Hitler's fear that the army might unravel completely if subjected to the strain of a long retreat. Guderian responded by flying to Hitler's East Prussian headquarters. Met with a "hard, unfriendly" stare, for five hours he made the case for local withdrawals and a flexible defense. Hitler recommended using heavy artillery to blast foxholes into the frozen ground. Guderian described the likely result as so many washtubs. The conversation declined from there. On December 26, Guderian was relieved of command.

Hoepner was next among the senior panzer officers to feel the axe. On January 8 he ordered what was left of a hard-pressed infantry corps to pull back while the option remained. Hitler screamed of an idiotic decision, of criminal betrayal, of cowardice in the face of the enemy. Hoepner was relieved of command, denied a pension, and refused authorization to wear his uniform in public. In farewell, he announced that his behavior was based on responsibility to God and duty to his army and his people.

This was the same general who in May 1941 spoke of defending against "Jewish Bolshevism" as justifying a "battle for existence" against the Soviet Union. Panzer Group 4 had not merely implemented Hitler's order to shoot political commissars out of hand. Hoepner's command had been highly praised by the commander of Einsatzgruppe 4 for its close cooperation in "special missions." Comment might seem superfluous— except that Erich Hoepner became active in the military opposition to Hitler, and was executed on August 8, 1944. He died hard, at the end of a strangling rope in Plötzensee prison.

Other senior generals were dismissed at the same time, including all three army group commanders. They provided the scapegoats deemed necessary to focus blame away from the Führer, "the greatest warlord of all time." In fact the Red Army was years away from possessing the capacity to mount a sustained, coordinated offensive at any season, much less the depths of winter. The Germans gave ground under pressure, but were able to hold the roads and control the supply centers. By the end of February, they had more or less restored local stability along the front. On both sides, staff officers returned to their drawing boards. First sergeants counted the dead. Neither was underemployed.

CHAPTER FIVE

DEATH RIDE

WERE THE GERMANS defeated in Operation Barbarossa and the Battle for Moscow, or were the Russians victorious? The best answer to both is yes. The Soviet Union and the Red Army fought back from the beginning, mobilizing resources and developing skills to save their capital, frustrate the invasion, capture the initiative, demonstrate blitzkrieg's limits, and begin the still-continuing process of discrediting the myth of an inherently superior German way of war. That is no mean list of accomplishments in six months against any opponent, much less the Wehrmacht.

I

THE LONG LIST of specific German mistakes can be conveniently grouped under two headings: comprehensive overextension and comprehensive underestimation. Both reflected the general sense of emergency that had informed Hitler's Reich from the first days of its existence. Time was always Adolf Hitler's chief enemy. He was convinced that only he could create the Thousand-Year Reich of his visions, and to that end was willing to run the most extreme risks.

Hitler's generals, especially the panzer generals, shared that risk-taking mind-set and accepted the apocalyptic visions accompanying it. That congruence shaped Barbarossa's racist, genocidal nature.

From the campaign's beginning, terror and murder followed in the wake of the panzers. That was worse than a crime. It was a mistake antagonizing broad spectrums of a population that could have been mobilized to work for and with the conquerors, and in some cases act against the Soviet system. To behave differently would have required Nazis to be something other than Nazis—and, perhaps, generals to be something other than generals, at least when confronting Slavic/Jewish Bolsheviks.

The army would have been constrained to recast its institutional mentality. However intense the antagonism between the Führer and his commanders may have become in later years, in 1941 they possessed a common vision in which choices and priorities were unnecessary. Germany's weaknesses in numbers, equipment, and logistics were sufficiently daunting that reasonably prudent military planners would have advised against the entire campaign to the point of resigning. But partly through their own history, and partly through years of exposure to National Socialism, Germany's soldiers had come to believe in the "Triumph of the Will."

It is an overlooked paradox that the failure to reach Moscow may have averted a German catastrophe. Stalin proposed to continue fighting even if Moscow fell, calling on resources from the Urals and Siberia. Aside from that, capturing the city with the resources available—if it could be done at all—would have involved heavy losses, losses that would fall disproportionately on the mobile troops who would be first in and expected to do much of the heavy work. Comparisons with Verdun once again circulated in the armored force. And should the swastika fly over the Kremlin, Army Group Center would be forward-loaded at the far end of a long salient vulnerable to systematic counterattacks, containing a tenuous supply line exposed to constant harassment from a developing partisan movement. Operation Typhoon's outcome preserved the cadres—or the skeletons—of the panzers to anchor the defense during the winter and prepare for another try in the spring.

They did both well. In January 1942, 18th Panzer Division used its last dozen tanks as the core of a 50-mile thrust into Soviet-occupied territory to rescue an infantry division that had been surrounded for a

month. In 6th Panzer Division, Erhard Raus pragmatically employed
a series of local counterattacks as tactical training exercises for replacements. Was this heroic professionalism or wishful thinking? Or more
like magical thinking, the kind of insanity defined as doing the same
thing the same way and expecting different results? In 1807 and again
in 1918 the Prussian/German army had responded to defeat with comprehensive self-examination. In 1939 Hitler's army had responded to
victory by an internally initiated tune-up. Nothing remotely similar happened during the winter of 1941–42. Especially for the panzers, whatever
energy remained after replacing losses was devoted to improving existing systems.

That situation invites explanation in terms of desperation. As late
as the end of February, total tank strength was down to around 150—
for the entire Eastern Front. It was not a figure encouraging detached
speculation on better ways of war. But even at this relatively early stage,
a process of selection was taking place in the regiments and divisions.
Eighth Panzer Division's CO Erich Brandenberger was an old gunner,
as calm in demeanor as he was quick to react to emergencies. Heinrich
Eberbach took over 4th Panzer—no surprise after his success in making the most of small numbers on the road to Tula. Hans Hube's loss of
an arm in the Great War had not kept him from rising to command of
the 16th Motorized Division, staying with it when it was converted to
tanks, and building a reputation as a brilliant tactician. Hermann Balck,
marked as a comer for his work in France, had been on staff duty during
Barbarossa, but would make his mark beginning in May commanding
11th Panzer Division.

One cannot speak of a common personality type in officers who
came from everywhere in the prewar army. Some were religious; some
were skeptics; some were casually Gottglaubig—the Nazi term for
nondenominational. Some were deliberately muddy-boots; others took
conscious pains with their grooming. What these officers and their contemporaries similarly marked out for high command was pragmatism.
They were hands-on problem-solvers who maximized the material they
were given and did their best in the situations they confronted. "I'll

try, sir" was not an acceptable response in the panzer force that emerged from the rubble of Barbarossa. There was no try—only do, or do not.

Another thing the new generation of panzer leaders had in common was a level of bravery and charisma not seen among senior Prussian/German officers since the Napoleonic Wars. Omer Bartov has made a strong case for the increasing "demodernization" of the German army in the Soviet Union. Its simplified version describes a situation in which material and numerical inferiority, and the resulting high casualties, led to the erosion of primary-group identification and an emphasis on National Socialist ideology as a primary element of morale and fighting power. One might suggest that a tank crew is an automatically self-renewing primary group, as is to a lesser degree the men riding in the same half-track or truck. In the panzers, however, regiment and division commanders to a significant extent also facilitated primary groups by personal leadership.

Post-Barbarossa, an infantry colonel appearing in the front line was likely to generate a reaction similar to the one made famous by American cartoonist Bill Mauldin: "Sir, do ya hafta draw fire while you're inspirin' us?" His panzer counterpart, in a radio-equipped tank or half-track, usually with one or two more as escort, could have a decisive effect on events at the sharp end—and had a solid chance of surviving till next time. Such behavior had little to do with ideology, and not much more with "warrior spirit," but had much to do with mutual expectations. It was what one did when it had to be done. Even for generals it was often a matter of leading as though one's life depended on it—as it often did literally. And there are few greater boosters of combat morale than the effective presence at a hot spot of someone who seems to know what he is doing and what to do next. In 6th Panzer Division, a familiar catchphrase was *"Raus zieht heraus"*—"Raus'll get us out of this." Hans Hube's nickname was simply "the man"—not "the old man" but "the man."

The ethos had serious drawbacks. It led to a focus on "hitting the next target," a privileging of action at the expense of reflection at all levels and in all aspects of war-making. That pattern was, if not always

exacerbated, too often not balanced by the staffs. The abolition of the
Great General Staff by the Versailles Treaty combined with the rapid
expansion of the army under Hitler conspired to create a chronic
shortage of qualified staff officers, and encouraged the development
of new ones to meet staff requirements of the new formations. What
was important was solving the immediate problems of organizing and
training new divisions, and providing equipment and doctrine for new
branches—like the panzers.

It is not necessary to reference Nazi anti-intellectualism to understand that considering ramifications and implications was not a quality
particularly valued in the post-Barbarossa armored force. It is ironic to
think that Versailles, so often excoriated for failing to sustain German
rearmament, may have had a decisive "stealth success" in removing a
potentially significant counterpoint to the army's tunnel vision.

The panzer spirit also spread through promotion. Guderian's advocacy of a flexible, mobile defense against the Soviet winter offensive
might be sound in principle, but arguably lay outside the panzers' current capacities. His successor was corps commander Rudolf Schmidt,
whose nickname "Panzerschmidt" suggests determination rather than
finesse. Schmidt based his tactics on strong points established in villages that were magnets for Russians no less cold than their opponents,
and defended until relieved by battle groups built around whatever was
available and could be scrounged. Walther Model commanded a corps
during Typhoon, and in January 1942 brought his uncompromising
mind-set and a belief in the defensive potential of small armored battle
groups to 9th Army. Many other panzer generals would follow the same
path.

Reconfiguring the panzers' command profile would have meant
little if the armored force was not restored materially. That was the main
challenge during the winter and early spring of 1942. Overall losses during Barbarossa amounted to more than 1,100,000 men, and there was no
way they could be entirely replaced before resumed operations enlarged
the gap. Halder calculated the resulting loss of combat effectiveness as
from half to two-thirds in the infantry. The mobile divisions were better off in personnel terms, but not by much, especially given the loss in

specialists incurred by such measures as using dismounted tankers as infantry during the desperate winter months. More than 4,200 tanks had been destroyed or damaged during Barbarossa. There was no way an overextended industrial network and an overburdened repair system could compensate. As late as March, the gap between tables of organization and tanks in unit service was more than 2,000. The corresponding shortfall in trucks was 35,000. A quarter-million horses were dead, a loss no less serious to an army still largely muscle-powered and likely to remain so given an increasingly untenable gap between the Reich's oil resources and the Wehrmacht's needs.

Hitler had planned on using new production to expand the army to 30 panzer divisions. The best the overstrained factories and replacement systems could deliver was four: three built around existing army regiments and one formed by converting the 1st Cavalry Division. Grossdeutschland was upgraded to a motorized division, with selected recruits and a guarantee of the latest equipment as it became available. Authorizing tank battalions for the four SS motorized divisions absorbed still more production. Some effort was made to replace quantity by quality. The two light companies of each tank battalion were authorized 17 J or L versions of the Panzer IIIs with the long-barreled 50mm gun. An increasing number of the medium company's 17 Mark IVs were Fs and Gs, with a 75mm high-velocity gun that was the first clear match for the T-34 to appear in the armored force. These up-gunned tanks were issued to replace losses, so throughout 1942 panzer battalions would operate with mixed establishments of shorts and longs.

Most panzer and motorized divisions were assigned an antiaircraft battalion with eight 88mm towed guns and a couple dozen 20mms. In recognition of the Red Air Force's exponentially improving ground-attack capacity, the new addition was also a welcome upgrade of the divisions' antitank capability. The motorized divisions received an even larger direct force multiplier: an organic tank battalion. That gave them a ratio of six to one in infantry and armor, compared to the panzer divisions' four to two. Given the high casualties the motorized infantry had suffered in 1941, and given the Reich's limited ability to replace tank losses, the upgrading was more or less a distinction without a difference.

It was also a way of increasing the number of tank-equipped divisions without the problems inevitably accompanying new organizations.

The revamped structure of the motorized divisions was also a recognition that the hard-hammered marching infantry—some divisions were two-thirds short of authorized strength as late as May—were going to require mobile backup, "corset stays," even in what passed for quiet sectors. The status of the motorized infantry was acknowledged when, in October 1942, they were redesignated as grenadiers. In March 1943 they became panzer grenadiers. In June the motorized divisions were retitled panzer grenadiers as well.

The honorifics would gladly have been exchanged for a few dozen more half-tracks: a battalion's worth of those valuable vehicles was the best most mobile divisions could expect. Firepower was nevertheless increased, with the commander's track in each platoon sporting a 37mm gun, which was still useful in many ways. Other half-tracks carried a variety of increasingly heavy guns and mortars on improvised mounts. The 50mm antitank gun became a battalion weapon, and panzer grenadier battalions also had as many as eight infantry guns for direct support—substituting for towed field artillery too often bogged down, out of contact, or out of range.

The resulting amalgam of weapons and vehicles continues to delight war-gamers and order-of-battle hobbyists. In fact, the plethora of crew-served heavy weapons reflected the continuing shortage—or better said, *absence*—of tanks and assault guns. Another indication of the patchwork nature of the armored force's reconstruction is that the tank battalions for the motorized/panzer grenadier divisions were transferred from the panzer divisions: another institutionalized dispersion of a scarce and wasting asset.

The battle group system remained basic to the employment of the mobile troops, but experience produced modifications. Regiments evolved toward task force headquarters, with battalions becoming increasingly autonomous, transferred among them as needed for building blocks. In the offense or for counterattacks, battle groups were usually built around the tank battalions, the half-tracked rifle battalion, and the reconnaissance battalion. On the defensive the panzer grenadier regiments did the heavy work with the tanks in reserve—if they were available—for gap-plugging and counterattacks. Improvements in forward fire control in principle allowed the panzers' artillery to be centralized at divisional level, its fire allocated where most needed or most promising. In fact, battalions were often attached to battle groups for the sake of quick reaction.

The Eastern Front's major contribution to tactics was added emphasis on speed. The ability to form, commit, and restructure battle groups to match changing situations was often the major German force multiplier against a materially and numerically superior enemy that, even as its flexibility improved, was still structured around orders from above. The success of these formations, time and again, against all odds and obstacles, in turn fostered a sense of operational superiority that inevitably manifested itself in racial as well as military contexts. The results could range from triumph to disaster—but at division level and below the disasters, tended to be dismissed as the chance of war rather than signs of a fundamental shift in the balance of fighting power.

The developed battle group system was also a tactical response to a Soviet strategy that during the winter of 1941–42 sought to decide the war by breaking the German defenses along the entire front. Stalin and his key military advisors agreed that it was best done by hammering as hard as possible in as many sectors as possible, on the principle that something had to give somewhere. The plan had a political dimension as well: to restore domestic morale still far too labile for Stalin's peace of mind by providing at least small-scale victories.

A more prudent approach might have involved structuring military objectives to buy time: time for promised American assistance to arrive; time to restabilize an industrial base physically transferred east of the Urals; and above all, time to shake down a still-rebuilding Red Army as yet unable to translate strategic planning into operational and tactical success. Instead, recovered from the shocks of December, the Germans proved well able to parry, block, and then halt a series of ambitious offensives from Leningrad to Rzhev-Vyazma and south to Orel and Kursk.

Those successes were primarily achieved by the well-applied

economy-of-force tactics indicated above: mutually supporting strong points backed by relatively small armored battle groups. They validated infantry officers' assertions that with minimal direct infusions of the right kind of support, they could take care of both themselves and the Russians. Beginning in 1942, the Army Weapons Office began mounting captured Soviet 76mm and German 75mm high-velocity guns on Panzer II chassis. These 10.5-ton Marder tank destroyers, though open-topped and lightly armored, were potent killers of T-34s. They went first to the infantry. So did most of the increasing number of independent assault-gun battalions formed during 1942 whose low-slung Sturmgeschütz IIIs were armed with short and long 75mm guns in combinations depending on availability. A mobile division lucky enough to have one of these battalions attached for a time usually employed it with the panzer grenadiers, where its flexible firepower was no less welcome than among ordinary Landser.

The Red Army was not the only one able to restore itself under emergency conditions. With winter turning to spring, the Germans in Russia emerged as a combination of an ideologically motivated citizen army and a seasoned professional fighting force. The months in Russia had pitilessly exposed weak human and material links. New weapons still existed mostly on drawing boards, but officers and men knew how to use what they had to best advantage. A counterattack in late April relieved 100,000 men cut off in the Demyansk Pocket since January. Infantry, artillery, and pioneers, with substantial support from the Romanians, began the final attack on the Crimean peninsula on May 8. Most of the mobile divisions had been refitted. Some especially hard-tried ones like the 6th and 7th Panzer Divisions were sent all the way to France. The rest remained in Russia but out of the line for a few weeks. They would be ready by the time the *rasputitsa*, the spring thaw, ended.

II

ON APRIL 5, 1942, Hitler issued Directive 41, outlining the operational plan for the summer of 1942. Its focus would be in the south: a major drive toward the Caucasus to destroy Soviet forces in the region and seize the oil fields vital to both Soviet and German war-making. A secondary objective was Stalingrad—not for its own sake, but to cut the Volga River, isolate the Russians south of the industrial city, and cover the main assault's flank.

Compared to Barbarossa, the offensive's scale was reduced but its aims were no less ambitious. It would be launched on a 500-mile front. If it gained the set objectives it would create a salient of more than 1,300 miles—something like the distance from New York City to the middle of Kansas. Road and rail networks would grow thinner as the Germans advanced. Scheduling the main attack for the end of June left at best four or five months before rain and snow put an end to major mobile operations. Even if the offensive succeeded there was no guarantee that the Soviet Union would collapse or cease fighting de facto. It had other domestic sources of oil. It also had the support of the US and Britain, who were committed to keeping Russia in the war at all costs.

In grand-strategic terms the operation nevertheless made more sense to Hitler—and to his senior commanders—than any other option. It offered the opportunity to consolidate the Reich's military and economic position against the establishment of a second front in Europe—something Hitler considered possible in 1943. It projected extending the land war into Asia Minor and beyond, where the immediate pickings and possibilities seemed somewhat easier. And it offered a second chance for the reinvigorated German army to do what it so far had done best: win a mobile campaign in a limited time. That meant using the panzers. Again they would be at the apex of an inverted pyramid—this time one with direct global implications.

Operation Blue, in sharp contrast to Barbarossa, was designed as not a single entity, but a series of interlocking, mutually supporting attacks succeeding each other in a tightly structured timetable. In part that reflected the need to shift limited air assets from one sector to another as a force multiplier. It reflected as well the changing dynamics of the ground forces' order of battle. The winter campaign indicated that however much the infantry might recover from its December nadir, it could not expect to secure even shut-down fronts with its own resources. No fewer than ten panzer divisions were assigned to Army Groups North and Center. That left only nine panzer divisions available for Operation Blue. The order of battle also included a half dozen motorized divisions, but behind them the picture grew darker. Two-thirds of the infantry divisions projected for the offensive were either newly reconstructed or still in the process. They had time neither to rest the old hands nor to integrate their replacements, thousands of whom would be fresh from basic training. Their projected effectiveness was substantially less than their forebears of 1941.

The slack must be taken up by the panzers. In December 1941, a newly organized two-battalion Panzer Regiment 201, had been sent to the Leningrad sector. Its hundred-odd Panzer IIIs and IVs achieved the kind of disproportionate successes that reminded the generals why massed armor was a good idea. In February, each panzer division assigned to Blue was ordered to be reinforced with a third tank battalion. By May, however, it was clear the only way that was possible was by transferring them from other divisions. The same was true for the motorized divisions' tank battalions. When the shuffling and redesignating was finished, seven of the ten divisions in the "inactive" sectors had only a single tank battalion. In other words they were battle groups in all but name. Even more than Barbarossa, Blue was all or nothing—especially for the panzers.

One report submitted in May gave the offensive six months to seize the oil fields, otherwise, not only must offensive operations cease; the Eastern Front itself could not be sustained. Such prognostications left little room at command levels for public questioning. A good many two-o'-clock-in-the-morning doubts were nevertheless resolved when, on May 12, the Soviet Southwestern Front launched a spoiling offensive around Kharkov. Intended to disrupt German plans and regain the initiative, the attack's 650,000 men and 1,200 tanks were stopped within a week. By May 28 a counterattack built around 1st Panzer Army accounted for 240,000 prisoners, more than 1,200 tanks, and 2,000 guns. To Hitler and the High Command it seemed just like old times. Ivan was still Ivan. Closer to the front, perspectives were different. Eberhard von Mackensen had impeccable military bloodlines. His father was August von Mackensen, one of the more successful German field commanders of World War I. He had commanded III Panzer Corps since the invasion, and had made a reputation as the best horse in 1st Panzer Army's stable: quick-thinking and hard-driving. The Russians, he reported, had grown "more fanatical, more ruthless, and more solid." Victory had been won only by an all-out effort—plus a fair bit of luck. A corps commander's observations changed no one's mind.

On June 28, Army Group South tore the front wide open. Its CO was Fedor von Bock, getting a second chance by accident. Reichenau had replaced Rundstedt in Deceember 1941 and died from a heart attack six weeks later. Command in Russia involved unprecedented levels of physical, intellectual, and emotional strain. Bock suffered from stomach trouble—hardly surprising under the circumstances—but a few weeks' down time restored him sufficiently to take over an appointment for which no other clearly more suitable candidate was available. Six months later he had 68 divisions, 750 tanks, and more than 1,200 aircraft including, predictably, VIII Air Corps, with its obsolescent but devastating Stukas and the ME 109s that covered them. But Bock's expectations rested with the one-two punch of Kleist's 1st Panzer Army and the widely traveled 4th Panzer Army, which had moved from Leningrad to Moscow and now to the south under Hoth, transferred from his anomalous infantry command.

Bock's order of battle included around two dozen divisions from the Reich's allies and clients. These were the fruit of a winter's diplomatic arm-twisting. Mostly Romanian and Italian, these formations were nowhere nearly as well equipped, trained, commanded, or motivated as their German counterparts. Hopes for significant material support from the Reich had proved futile. Their projected roles in Blue were correspondingly limited: flank guards, screening, and occupying low-risk sectors of the line. Their numerical role in the operation nevertheless highlighted the weakness of the German assault force relative to its mission—and implied trouble should things not work as programmed.

If Hitler's directive was ambitious, the High Command's plan was audacious to the point of recklessness. Reduced to its essentials— arguably oversimplified—Blue would begin in the north, with 4th

Panzer Army leading a thrust toward the Don River and the rail hub and industrial center of Voronezh, then turning south to trap and finish off the Rotarmisten driven east by 1st Panzer Army and its accompanying infantry. Meanwhile, the 6th Army would advance to the Volga and Stalingrad while the 1st Panzer Army struck down the Volga to Baku and the Caucasus.

As early as July it was clear that a single headquarters could not manage the force, time, and space factors. Army Group South became Army Group B on July 7, taking over 4th Panzer Army. A newly created Army Group A assumed responsibility for Kleist's panzers. In its initial stages, Operation Blue nevertheless bade fair to replicate the summer of 1941. German mechanized spearheads rolled across the steppes under an air umbrella the Red Air Force, still repairing its loss of trained pilots, could not penetrate. By July 4, Hoth's vanguards were across the Don and at the outskirts of Voronezh. The LX Panzer Corps, pulling the rest of 6th Army behind it, linked up from the left with 4th Panzer Army on July 2, trapping one more Soviet army in a pocket.

The Red Army was still a heavy, blunt instrument, but not the bludgeon of 1941. The tank brigades formed from the detritus of 1941 were being combined into corps with the approximate armored strength of a panzer division. Beginning in October, they would be joined by newly created mechanized corps: panzer grenadiers without the half-tracks. Stalin and the High Command responded to Blue by launching a series of offensives against Army Groups North and Center, and by committing a high proportion of their increasing reserve forces to successive offensives around Voronezh.

These were not mere counterattacks, but parts of a systematic effort to regain the strategic initiative secured in December. Bock urged taking the fight to the Russians where they stood. Hitler and the High Command instead ordered Hoth south. Führer Directive 45 dispatched it toward Rostov, to cooperate with Kleist in encircling Soviet forces in the region and opening the way to the Caucasus. The infantry divisions and Allied formations left to Army Group B were ordered to capture Stalingrad and secure Army Group A's flank and rear. Bock was summarily dismissed, this time permanently.

Directive 45 reflected the consensus of Hitler and the High Command that keeping to time justified overriding the judgment of the commander on the ground. Robert M. Citino correctly interprets this decision as a long step away from a Prussian/German tradition of validating subordinates' initiatives. On the other hand, a case could be made—and was widely debated between the wars—that the Battle of the Marne in 1914 had been lost because of the German High Command's unwillingness or inability to control the movements of the army's right wing. Then, communications and maneuverability were alike severely limited. Now, radios and aircraft enabled constant contact among headquarters. And on the ground, the panzers could implement any sequence of decisions—even when, like this one, the result was a military snipe hunt.

With losses rapidly mounting, especially in the best divisions, the Soviet High Command, the Stavka, insisted space must temporarily be exchanged for time. Stalin finally authorized retreat on July 6, and the Soviets in front of Army Group A gave ground. Rostov fell on July 24 in a virtuoso cape-and-sword tactical performance by Mackensen and III Panzer Corps, executed at an overall cost of fewer than 1,500 casualties. There was no pocket, no gigantic new bag of prisoners and weapons. The new string of defeats and the abandonment of more of the industrial facilities created at such high human cost nevertheless generated a crisis in public morale serious enough for Stalin to issue Order 227 on July 28. It called for an end to retreat and demanded that every foot of Soviet soil be defended. Penalties ranged from service in a penal battalion to summary execution: a quarter-million Red Army soldiers were sentenced to death for failure to obey

On July 19, Stalin put Stalingrad on a war footing; on July 21, Stavka established a Stalingrad Front. Its three armies were a mixture of green troops and formations already hard hammered. But Order 227 was a reminder that there was nowhere to go. Stalingrad's citizens responded not only by digging trenches and filling sandbags, but by reporting to work and finishing their shifts.

The German High Command responded by reassigning Hoth's army to Army Group B and ordering it to attack Stalingrad from the south. The back-and-forth odyssey of Panzer Army 4 resembled the Kiev maneuver of 1941 in wearing down men and tanks. It was also a sign that Stalingrad was beginning to loom larger in German thinking than originally intended. No less significant was the fact that Directive 45 gave the Caucasus operation a separate code name. Calling it Edelweiss meant that Army Groups A and B were in effect now pursuing two objectives simultaneously rather than sequentially, as in Blue's original conception. This was no simple manifestation of Hitler's unfocused, dilettantish interference in command decisions. The High Command as well as the Führer were in the process of convincing themselves that for the Caucasus to fall, Stalingrad must be captured, not merely blockaded and screened. Hitler's concept was based on pursuit; Halder was thinking in terms of a battle. The underlying gulf between the presumptions was bridged by the assumption that the panzers would make prioritizing—creating a Schwerpunkt—unnecessary.

Success in that unspoken mission would in good part depend on the kind of command initiative that had just cost Bock his job. Army Group A was under Field Marshal Wilhelm List. Not a tanker by experience or ascription, he had worked with the panzers in France, commanded an armor-heavy army in the Balkan campaign, and was a reasonable choice to oversee the drive for the Caucasus. Kleist was expected to do the heavy work with three panzer and two motorized divisions plus, for what it might prove worth, the "Fast Division" of the Slovak army: about the same numbers he took into Greece against far less formidable opposition. The Germans were reckoning heavily on being received as liberators by the Caucasian people, and reckoning even more heavily on intelligence estimates that described Soviet forces in the region as on the edge of collapse. Instead, during August, resistance stiffened all along the line of advance. The 1st Panzer Army took Maikop on August 9, but the progress was slowed by the Red Army, by temperatures regularly exceeding 100 degrees, and by roadless, trackless, mountainous terrain unlike anything the panzers had experienced.

"Jungle-like thicket with no visibility," reported Hitler's aide Army Major Gerhard Engel. Kitchens could not be moved forward; wounded could not be moved back. Even the mountain troops, the German army's other elite force, made slow progress. Hitler fired List on September 9 and began directing Army Group A himself—his greatest departure from procedure to date. By the end of September, Soviet resistance—in particular air attacks enabled by the increasing withdrawal of German fighters to Stalingrad—combined with dust, broken terrain, fuel shortages, and unreplaced losses in men and tanks, brought 1st Panzer Army to a halt well away from the oil fields of Grozny and Baku, the original objective of Operation Blue. In the rear, Maikop's refining facilities had been well demolished, and the bureaucratic inefficiency endemic in the Third Reich handicapped their reconstruction. Specifically the technical experts declared that the equipment designated for the Caucasus would be better employed in Romania—or even the Vienna region.

One possibility remained. In the nineteenth century the Russian government had constructed the Georgian and Ossetian military roads through the Caucasus: still solid highways and ideal axes of blitzkrieg. It took a month for Kleist to concentrate and redistribute what remained of his striking power—by now half-strength and less in men and tanks. On October 25 the 2nd Romanian Guard Division broke open the Soviet front. The next night, 13th and 23rd Panzer Divisions, Mackensen's III Panzer Corps, broke out and started south. Outrunning Soviets who had never experienced a real German lightning attack, 23rd Panzer closed the Ossetian Road on November 1. To the south, 13th Panzer Division was 10 miles away from the Georgian Road. The next day it cut that distance to five miles; by November 3 to a mile and a half. Soviet resistance centered on the city of Ordzhonikidze. The 13th Panzer Division's infantrymen attacked on foot, into the teeth of a network of trenches, bunkers, and pillboxes matching anything in Stalingrad itself. A temporarily attached assault-gun battery supporting the riflemen accounted for twenty T-34s. On October 20 the division had 130 tanks. A month later it was down to 27. Division and corps had nothing left to stop the Soviet attack on December 6 that tore into the 13th Division's flanks while a blizzard kept the Luftwaffe grounded. On December 9, what remained of 13th Panzer broke the encirclement and fought its way home. They took their wounded with them—in the first trucks out. They were not a broken gaggle of stragglers. They were the 13th Panzer Division, and Ivan knew it.

Robert M. Citino's image of "a hard-driving panzer corps stopped, but still churning its legs" cannot be bettered. This was as far as the Germans got in Russia, and no less than Rommel's contemporary position in North Africa. Does the question arise as to what Kleist and Mackensen might have done with another two or three divisions? The question is even more apt because Mackensen's 16th Motorized Division had been detached to screen the widening gap between Army Groups A and B. In an exercise in irrelevance spectacular even by German standards for the time and place, it drove eastward onto the Kalmuck Steppe at right angles to the rest of 1st Panzer Army, getting to within 20 miles of the Caspian Sea before reality in the form of the Soviet counteroffensive intervened.

One more worn-down division was unlikely to have carried III Panzer Corps through the Russians to the far side of the Caucasus and the Turkish frontier. Had 4th Panzer Army been deployed alongside Kleist instead of fed into the Stalingrad blowtorch, the panzers would probably have run out of fuel 300 miles earlier. Had the Caucasus offensive been given logistical priority, the chances for a massively decisive Soviet counterattack against the correspondingly weakened German positions around Stalingrad would have suddenly improved. But had the 16th Motorized been in its doctrinal place, directly supporting the 13th and 23rd Panzer Divisions . . . who knows?

III

SINCE BARBAROSSA'S INCEPTION, the panzers had been considered and used as facilitators, enablers: the military magic that rendered irrelevant historic considerations of prudence and feasibility. Previously the dissonances between mission and material were arguably bridgeable by skill, spirit, and soldier's luck. In the fall of 1942, Germany's mobile forces were set tasks that denied illusions. Had 4th Panzer Army been started for Stalingrad in the first place, instead of sent south, its chances for catching the Soviets off guard and getting into the city would have been solid. Sixth Army by itself was unable to move that fast—in good part due to constant fuel shortages. And by the time Hoth's panzers returned, Stalingrad was in the process of becoming a formidable fortress and a fulcrum for counterattacks that delayed 6th Army even more.

As Franz Halder confronted that fact in the second half of July, he seems to have confronted—finally—three more. Soviet forces had grown beyond Germany's capacity to destroy them, unless the Soviets repeated mistakes it was clear they were learning to avoid. Hitler's decision to pursue simultaneous operations in extrinsic directions had overstrained German forces beyond the capacity of any qualitative superiority to compensate. And both Hitler's confidence in his ability as an operational military leader and his contempt and loathing for a High Command and an officer corps he saw lacking vision and will had grown beyond Halder's capacity to sway them in any systematic or predictable fashion.

Halder may have decided that the war was lost, and provoked his dismissal in September as an attempt to avoid his share of responsibility. His successor, Kurt Zeitzler, was more in the model of a troop staff officer than a traditional *Generalstabler* (general staffer), and deliberately sought closer contact with Hitler to improve the synergies of policy, planning, and command.

For both Zeitzler and Hitler that meant, in practice, finishing off Stalingrad. Sixth Army had two panzer and two motorized divisions. It took until August 7 to top up their vehicle tanks and fuel trucks. The Fourth Panzer Army, even lower on the fuel chain, moved forward by battle groups. Both armies met determined resistance in terrain handicapping the small-unit maneuvers that gave the panzers an edge over their numerically and materially superior foes. The VIII Air Corps provided its usual effective support—but its aircraft were also responsible for covering 1st Panzer Army. Nevertheless the little flags in the headquarters of both sides kept moving in the same direction: eastward, toward the Volga and Stalingrad.

On August 21, German infantry crossed the Don. Two days later,

16th Panzer Division reached the Volga. On September 2, 4th Panzer Army made contact with 6th Army's 21st Panzer Division 10 miles west of the city. Mission accomplished—at least the mission indicated in the original version of Operation Blue. The Volga was subject to interdiction. The Fourth Panzer and 6th Armies had established a continuous front before Stalingrad. The Luftwaffe seemed on the way to demolishing the city from above. The Soviets had successfully withdrawn into Stalingrad, but Weichs and 6th Arrmy commander Friedrich von Paulus, who had replaced Reichenau after the latter's death, believed this was the beginning of the end of organized resistance. To Hitler and the High Command, finishing the job by continuing into the city was preferable to staying in place and resigning the initiative. The third possibility of enveloping the enemy, the option that had squared so many circles since September 1939, did not exist: there was no maneuvering room except across the Volga, and no way across the Volga except through Stalingrad. The operational choice was a stark either-or.

The panzer commanders were more concerned than their superiors about committing to a fight whose nature denied the combined arms coordination and freedom of movement that was the key to their way of war. Summary relief of one recalcitrant corps commander encouraged the rest. On September 14 the German drive to the Volga River began. The panzer and motorized divisions were in the first assault wave, taking increasing levels of responsibility as infantry divisions, already weakened, shrank even further. The nature of the fighting has been described too often to require summarizing here. Also familiar is Hitler's order on October 6 that made Stalingrad's complete occupation the primary mission of Army Group A.

That meant using the panzers to destruction. Fourteenth Panzer Division had five tanks left by mid-November; 16th Panzer had two dozen. Twenty-Fourth Panzer Division, the former cavalrymen, clawed its way to the Volga by the end of September and brought the Soviet landing stage under fire. It had 34 tanks on October 17. A month later, it was down to a dozen; at the end, it counted only a couple of tanks and a few hundred men.

One of the division's reports expressed outraged common sense. Using panzers in urban combat was an emergency measure: "House rubble, bomb craters, narrow streets, minefields, barriers, and barricades greatly reduce mobility and ability to see . . ." Not having the armor protection of assault guns, tanks were best used to support infantry attacks as opposed to leading them, and were kept as a local reserve in defense. Regiments and battalions were not suitable for employment in cities. Platoons or sections, five tanks or fewer, were the standard. Even then second thoughts were appropriate—especially about committing tanks to work with infantry untrained in cooperating with them.

IV

ON AUGUST 26, Stalin bit a bullet of his own and appointed Zukhov his deputy supreme commander. Zukhov typified a new generation of Red Army generals: as fearless as they were pitiless, ready to do anything to crush the Germans, and not inhibited by threats from either front or rear. He shared his superior's conviction that Stalingrad must be held—but in a strategic context. The summer of ripostes was over. Since September, Stavka, urged on by Zukhov, had been developing plans for a decisive winter campaign involving two major operations, each with two stages. Mars would be launched in mid-October against a seemingly vulnerable sector on the hitherto relatively quiet front of Army Group Center: a salient around the city of Rzhev. It would be followed in two or three weeks by Jupiter, an attack in the Bryansk sector to the south intended to link up with Mars and shatter Army Group Center. Uranus would begin in mid-November and involved committing large mobile forces north and south of Stalingrad, encircling and destroying enemy forces in the resulting pocket. Uranus was to be followed and extended by Saturn, a larger double envelopment that would finish off whatever remained of Army Group B and isolate Army Group A in the Caucasus.

Described for years in Soviet literature as no more than a diversion,

Mars was in fact a complement to Uranus, a double penetration intended to put the Red Army on the high road to Berlin. It was to say the least an ambitious strategy for an army still on the road back from the seismic shocks of Barbarossa and Blue. Its prospects depended entirely on the ability of Stalingrad's defenders to hold.

Hold the Soviets did, in an epic defense that reduced the city to a wilderness of rubble, smoke, and ash; a battle whose ferocity surpassed anything the Germans had ever experienced. As the mobile units were compelled to substitute courage for skill and lives for maneuver, colonels and majors led from the front, hoping inspiration would make up for lost mobility. Instead Stalingrad became the domain of the assault gun.

The modified Panzer IIIs had already proven their disproportionate worth time and again with Army Groups North and Center during the summer, in sectors that were "quiet" only by comparison. Volunteers cut off from a parent branch, whose guns were still horse- and tractor-drawn, shuffled as army troops from division to division, the Sturmgeschütz-Abteilungen developed a self-image as buccaneering adventurers, successors to the sixteenth century's Landsknechts. Colorful unit insignia and colorful nicknames—"Buffalo," "Greyhound," "Tiger," "Unicorn"—proclaimed an attitude that was eroding in other parts of the army. Their official uniform was standard field gray, but when on pass or furlough not a few of the gunners decked themselves out in panzer black. "L/24s or L/42s, shorthorns or longhorns, we were the fighting bulls!" reminisced one old-time assault gunner. "'An Iron Cross or a wooden cross,' we'd joke going into a fight," recalled another. Bravado? Perhaps. But with tanks in short supply, assets to be husbanded for major emergencies, the assault gunners restored many a position and turned back many an attack.

In the process they developed a new specialty as tank killers. The assault gun's low silhouette was a positive advantage against opponents still learning how to read terrain. Having to aim the gun by pointing the vehicle was less of a problem in defense when targets came to you, and in large numbers unsupported by infantry. In Stalingrad there remained plenty of standard assault work to do, helping the infantry forward as they ground into the massive factory and warehouse complexes along the Volga. The price was high. Four assault-gun battalions fought in Stalingrad. One had only two of its original officers left by September. Another was down to two guns when the encirclement was complete. A third had so few survivors that it was impossible to reconstruct the details of its fight and finish.

Weichs fed Paulus's calls for more of everything by replacing German troops north and south of Stalingrad with Romanians and Italians. That gamble might have been justified if the German-tipped spearhead had been able to regain the initiative. Instead the panzers in Stalingrad were "demodernizing," losing the ability to fight anything but the close-quarters battle of attrition they had been created to avert. Even then Vasily Chuikov, Soviet commander in Stalingrad and as matter-of-fact a man as ever wore a uniform, spoke of an inexplicable force driving the Germans. It was a last flash of the fighting power that had carried the panzers through Europe, across North Africa, and into the heart of Russia. In mid-November the tide turned.

Stavka had held its hand for a month, waiting for the rains to end and the ground to freeze. A million men, 1,000 modern tanks, 1,400 aircraft, 14,000 guns—all of it went undetected by a German intelligence blinded by Soviet deception measures and by its own belief that the Red Army was as locked into Stalingrad as the German. On November 19 two tank-headed sledgehammers struck the Romanian armies holding the flanks of the Stalingrad salient. On November 23, the Soviet spearheads met at Kalach, 50 miles west of Stalingrad, in a textbook encirclement.

Professionals at the time and armchair generals since have frequently argued that 6th Army should have withdrawn immediately, with orders or without them. But the Germans were locked in close combat with an opponent determined not to let go. The maneuver-war mentality in the headquarters of what was a foot-marching army had declined after two months of static operations. So had the resources— above all tanks and fuel—to support a fighting retreat against superior numbers in midwinter. And at the back of many minds was the question of the wounded. Evacuating them would encumber what had to be a fast-paced strike in order to have any chance of success. As for leaving them—after 18 months, awareness of German treatment of Soviet prisoners and civilians was sufficiently widespread to make the option a nonstarter for all but the most callous.

Hitler's proposal to relieve Stalingrad from outside thus merely reinforced an attitude widespread in 6th Army. If it could be done at all, the panzers would have to do it. Most general accounts focus on the relief operation and its failure. In fact the German mobile forces had a threefold challenge between November and January. One involved keeping Operation Uranus, and eventually Operation Mars, from eviscerating the entire German position in Russia. A second involved withdrawing from a Caucasus front that was clearly no longer sustainable. Should either of those operations fail, the third challenge, successfully relieving Stalingrad, would do no more than present both what remained of 6th Army and its would-be rescuers to the Russians on the serving-dish of an ever-lengthening salient.

Fourth Panzer Army had escaped being encircled, but most of its divisions had already been sent to 6th Army. Hoth nevertheless began organizing a relief force. It was an exercise in making bricks without straw. His 16th Motorized Division, returned from its Caspian excursion with a stray greyhound as a mascot and the appropriate nickname of "greyhound division," was more or less sustaining the link with Army Group A. In the Russian breakthrough's northern half, a German panzer corps controlled 1st Romanian Armored Division and 22nd Panzer Division. Both were used up plugging ephemeral holes, with the 22nd taking such heavy losses it was disbanded in January. Kleist had been given command of Army Group A on November 21, and the High Command hoped to bring back at least some of his panzers for the Stalingrad operation. Most of them were, however, far away at the toe of the Caucasian sock. They were also needed to cover a retreat, finally authorized by Hitler on December 28, that could not afford to be conducted too rapidly lest it collapse into a rout of the sorely tried Germans. Eventually Hoth would acquire Kleist's 23rd Panzer Division, with fewer than three dozen tanks and an overall effectiveness so reduced it was rated only "conditionally suitable" for attacks, even by the desperate standards of December 1942. After six months of fighting, that was all the southern front could provide for the most crucial offensive of the war to date.

Matters were little better in a general context. Erich von Manstein, who by now had an established reputation as the Eastern Front's specialist in difficult missions, had been transferred from the siege of Sevastopol to the siege of Leningrad. Now he was handed command of a new Army Group Don and ordered to relieve Stalingrad. Manstein had Hoth and 4th Panzer Army. He was promised eleven divisions by mid-December. Three of them, formed from transferred Luftwaffe personnel, were close to useless. That meant—what else—primary responsibility rested with the panzers: three newly arrived divisions plus the 23rd.

Army Group Center provided 17th Panzer Division. It had been on the line most of the year, and seen its strength eroded in constant small-scale fighting. It suffered from comprehensive wear and tear. Eleventh Panzer Division had been in reserve since September. It was up to tank strength, most of its Panzer IIIs with the L/42; Balck was almost worth another division by himself. But 11th Panzer Division was immediately sent north to replace the broken 22nd along the line of the Chir River. Between December 8 and 22, the division virtually annihilated the Soviet 5th Tank Army, stabilizing the sector single-handed. It was an example of staff work, willpower, and tactical skill still legitimately cited as among the greatest divisional-level battles ever fought.

It also left 6th Panzer Division in the spotlight when Operation Winter Storm began on December 12, 1942. The division had been in France since May. Fully reequipped with German tanks, with one of its four infantry battalions in half-tracks and a fully rested Raus, the 6th fought to within 20 miles of Stalingrad by December 19. It was another virtuoso performance by a first-class formation and a top-flight general. It was not a blitz breakthrough in the style of 1941. On a single day the division's panzer regiment did gain 40 miles. But the Russians were craftier, more sophisticated in defense. Raus husbanded his limited number of tanks, advancing by night, using dive bombers and artillery to blast the 6th forward, mounting a series of attacks by panzer grenadiers on foot, whose tactics evoked the storm troops of the First War more than the panzers of this one. When the Soviets counterattacked, the panzer grenadiers let them through, shot down their accompanying infantry, then took out the tanks with grenades and explosive charges: 1918 all over again. On December 19, 6th Panzer Division seized and held a bridgehead over the Mishkova River in the teeth of the 2nd Guards Army. Raus saw his way to Stalingrad open, paved by "iron will, coupled with bravery and a skilled conduct of operations."

He was looking through blinders. Air support was minimal and unpredictable. The Luftwaffe had been dispersed more comprehensively than even the panzers, with already-weak groups and wings transferred and then reassigned in near-random fashion. Flank security on the ground was in the hands of a 23rd Panzer Division barely able to take care of itself. By the time 17th Panzer Division came up, its single panzer battalion had 30 tanks of all types. So many of its wheeled vehicles were disabled that one company in each motorized battalion was following the division on foot. Soviet counterattacks were increasing in strength and effectiveness across Hoth's front. The 6th Panzer Division might in fact have retained enough fighting power to push a battle group forward to 6th Army's perimeter. Less likely things had happened and would happen again. As early as the nineteenth, however Manstein concluded that such a corridor could not be held long enough either to reinforce or to evacuate the pocket.

The debate as to the precise responsibility for holding 6th Army on the Volga remains lively and venomous. Whatever the actual prospects of some combination of breakthrough and breakout at this late date, neither Manstein nor Paulus gave the order. They showed a corresponding absence of the moral courage that is a requisite for high command in any military system. The issue, however, was rendered moot by events on the ground. On December 16 the Soviets launched Operation Little Saturn, a less ambitious version of the original. The Italian 8th Army bought three days, and then splintered. As Soviet tanks and cavalry ran wild in the virtually undefended German rear areas, 2nd Guards Army began an offensive that pushed 4th Panzer Army's slender spearhead back toward its start lines. The Germans' attention refocused from the fate of Stalingrad to the survival of the entire south Russian sector.

Manstein made the best of what he had. In a series of ripostes between January and March 1943, he confirmed his reputation as a battle captain and blunted a Soviet operation already compromised by Stalin's overreaching, pushing Little Saturn and its successors beyond an already overstretched Red Army's capacity to sustain them. These achievements would have been impossible without the High Command's cold-blooded write-off of Stalingrad. Now hopelessly isolated, the garrison was expected to tie down as many Soviet forces as possible, for as long as possible. The endgame dragged on until February 2.

Meanwhile Stavka planned a major offensive toward Rostov, part of a new Stalin-devised grand strategic plan to drive the Germans back across the entire Eastern Front while the winter held, establishing an intermediate stop line extending from Narva to the Black Sea. From the first days of that offensive in late January, the Germans received an unpleasant tactical surprise. The Red Army was no longer following its familiar pattern of engaging German strong points and exposing themselves to paralyzing local ripostes by the panzers. Instead, they were masking the "hedgehogs" and driving past them deep into the German rear. That only reinforced Manstein's conviction that to restore the German position in south Russia, it was necessary to restore operational maneuver. That in turn meant taking the risk of refusing to use mobile divisions as the core of ad hoc task forces to cope with what were becoming routine emergencies. It involved concentrating the panzers and the motorized divisions, using them in coordinated, multicorps operations focused on the Russians' weak spots and institutional weaknesses. Operational maneuver, in short, meant returning to the basics tested in 1940 and applied in the summer of 1941.

In the contexts of January 1943, operational warfare had two immediate prerequisites. One was administrative: a united command in the southern sector. The entropy into which Operation Blue had fallen led to tunnel vision—every senior officer emphasizing his own problems, and addressing them without regard for the big picture. The second prerequisite was doctrinal: trading space for time. That concept is so closely associated with the by-now canonical ex post facto criticism of Hitler's intransigent insistence on holding all ground at all costs that it is easy to overlook its relative absence in a practical sense from the "German way of war." Prussia had been too small, the Second Reich too isolated, to make the concept viable in operational or strategic contexts; there was no space to exchange. Even tactically, the flexible approach of giving ground and counterattacking had required two years of total war and an increasingly desperate situation on the Western Front to take hold.

It was Manstein who not only understood the theoretical concept, but recognized its applicability on an unprecedented scale. It was also Manstein who had the intellectual force and moral courage to convince Hitler that operational exigencies overrode the strategic and economic arguments Hitler presented against them. With Soviet pressure increasing across the front, Manstein withdrew into the Donets Basin, north of Rostov, shortening the arc of his operational semicircle and concentrating his still-rebuilding mobile formations. The Russians in turn were outrunning their supply and overextending their communications. Forward units were living off the resources they carried for up to two weeks at a time. Their commanders' contact with higher headquarters was increasingly tenuous—and initiative even at corps level was not a Red Army hallmark. But the prizes on the horizon encouraged Stavka to go a stage further. At the beginning of February, Operations Gallop and Star retook the city of Kursk and drove forward, toward the industrial center and transportation hub of Kharkov.

Manstein benefited when, on February 14, Army Groups B and Don were merged into the reborn Army Group South. That gave him two panzer armies with a near-ideal command mix. Hoth had the longest tenure in senior panzer command. Not merely seasoned, but marinated, he was wise in the ways of the Soviets and clear-eyed in evaluating the capacities of his own forces. Mackensen had taken over 1st Panzer Army on Kleist's promotion, and his force and flair were still undiluted. Reinforcements were arriving steadily: men and vehicles for the veteran outfits beginning to see, if not exactly light at the end of the tunnel, then a chance of getting payback. Relief also came from some of the remaining best of the mobile divisions, Grossdeutschland and 7th Panzer; and a new player in the East, one with some fundamental differences in skills, equipment—and baggage: the SS Panzer Corps under Paul Hausser.

The question remained how best to use these resources. Not only did the Führer risk a little of Stalingrad by giving Kharkov's defense top priority, some of Manstein's subordinates were unwilling to give ground on Manstein's proposed scale. Manstein in general receives correspondingly high marks for cool calculation in conceding the loss of Kharkov in order to lure the Soviets forward and into better position for the counterstroke he was preparing. His postwar memoirs are more sanguine than the contemporary mood at his headquarters. Manstein did not sacrifice the city in order to recapture it. He saw the loss instead as the unpleasant but acceptable consequence of the few days needed to convince a visiting Hitler of the advantages of concentrating real reserves for a real counterattack. The Führer was nevertheless considering installing a newer broom when a relatively lowly panzer corps commander disregarded a chain of orders and withdrew his men at the last minute from a situation he considered hopeless.

Kharkov's loss was a major defeat in itself. In the wake of Stalingrad it seemed to prefigure disaster. The city fell on February 16. But next day 4th Panzer Army struck. Kharkov was retaken on March 14; Hoth's spearheads were back on the Donets a few days later. Mackensen's 1st Panzer Army covered Hoth's right against the Soviet Southwest Front, cutting off and cutting up its overextended 5th Tank Army and reaching the Donets on February 28. Seventh and 11th Panzer Divisions proved a lucky combination, with Hans von Funck handling Rommel's division like a master and Balck enhancing an already formidable reputation for coup d'oeil. The Luftwaffe played a vital role, mounting as many as a thousand sorties a day while shifting its emphasis between the two panzer armies. The weather for once worked in the Germans' favor just as they reached the Donets, with the rasputitsa setting in and immobilizing Soviet reserves.

Otherwise the tactical and operational patterns of Manstein's riposte are surprisingly familiar on both sides. He described a tennis player's "backhand blow." By this time Germans and Russians alike were more like boxers in the late rounds of a bruising fight: exhausted, punch-drunk, working more from memory than inspiration. The final version of the front line strongly resembled its spring 1942 predecessor.

Strategic consequences were another, more complex story. Manstein's success in restoring and stabilizing the southern sector of the German front has inspired assertions that Hitler and the High Command should have continued the offensive instead of throttling back and preparing for a climactic battle at Kursk. The obvious counter is that despite Manstein's careful stewardship, the panzers were fought out by the end of March, needing rest and reinforcement before going anywhere. Stavka had responded by reinforcing the sector from other parts of the front, to a level that made continuing the attack an invitation to overextension.

To contextualize that sentence it is necessary to return in time and space to the other half of Operation Uranus. Mars had been delayed a month by heavy rains, giving the Germans time to prepare—and for once, intelligence accurately predicted something like the massive Soviet forces involved.

More useful for the Germans, paradoxically, was Mars's timing. The attack began on November 24. And with the Stalingrad front collapsing, Hitler and the High Command were quite willing to allow early commitment of local reserves and "adjustments" of local front lines. The command team on the spot was also well suited to its responsibilities. Von Kluge had replaced Bock as CO of Army Group Center the previous year, and he had long expected an attack on his front. The sector hit hardest was held by Model's 9th Army, and Model took justifiable pride in his defensive skills.

The Red Army's initial commitment to Mars matched that to Uranus: 37 rifle divisions, 45 tank and mechanized brigades, plus dozens of independent artillery regiments: guns, howitzers, and the truck-mounted rockets veterans of the Eastern Front regularly described as the most terrifying of all Soviet weapons. They hit the Rzhev salient on both sides of its base. In some sectors penal battalions were in the first wave: men sentenced for a variety of military and political offenses, with at least a chance of pardon if they survived. Initially German strong points held. German panzers took heavy toll on their Russian counterparts. But numbers and courage wore down the determined defenders. More and more panzer grenadiers were being committed in sectors where original infantry garrisons were worn down by what seemed endless bombardment and assault.

Had the Soviets been able to get out of their own way, the German front might have broken from the attack's sheer mass. Instead, traffic and supply problems slowed and constrained the Red Army columns just long enough. By November 28, 9th and 5th Panzer Divisions were in position not merely to hold the flanks of a narrow salient driven into 9th Army's eastern flank, but to cut off elements of two tank corps at its apex. In the western sector it was the 1st Panzer Division, overcoming mud that immobilized even its light reconnaissance vehicles, which hung on along with elements of Grossdeutschland Division, then shifted into a series of local counterattacks in battle group strength— meaning whatever could be scraped together in the face of the latest Russian assault.

Here too the German line bent but did not break. It is no disrespect to the infantry that did most of the fighting and bore the heaviest losses to say that the backbone and muscle of the Rzhev salient's initial defense was provided by the panzers—and not least by the two corps headquarters that controlled the battle: Hans-Jürgen von Arnim's XXXIX Panzer on the east and Josef Harpe's LXI Panzer on the west. Von Arnim's career would be truncated by his next assignment to a collapsing North African front. Harpe would rise—briefly—to army group command, and sustain a dual reputation as a master of the well-timed armored riposte and one of the panzer generals openly sympathetic to National Socialism.

With his reputation, perhaps his position, and possibly his neck at stake, Zukhov brought the offensive's senior commanders together on November 28 for counseling and admonition. The attack resumed with renewed vigor the next day, featuring everything from tank attacks to cavalry charges. The weather grew more bitter in the first days of December. This year the Germans were well supplied with winter clothing, and had learned how to use trees and drifts to keep from freezing. The Landser held. When they could no longer hold, they pulled back. One battle group broke out with fewer than 100 men and three tanks: the last of what had been a reinforced panzer grenadier battalion. Its parent, 5th Panzer Division, was down by more than 1,600 men and 30 tanks. In Harpe's western sector, T-34s with "tank marines" mounted on the vehicles brought 1st Panzer Division to the breaking point before 12th Panzer Division arrived from army reserve. First Panzer Division was one of the divisions stripped to a single tank battalion earlier in the year. One of its companies accounted for more than 40 Soviet tanks in four days. Only two of its Mark IIIs remained operable at the finish.

Men, tanks, and ammunition: the Soviets seemed to have limitless supplies of each, and committed them regardless of losses everywhere along the German reinforcements arrived in driblets. Most of the anti-aircraft guns were being used as ground support, and the Sturmoviks had a correspondingly free hand. By battery and battalion, sometimes singly, the assault guns were essential wherever the panzers were unavailable. StuGs were the rallying points for battle groups cobbled together from whatever rear echelon troops were at hand, around the survivors of an infantry or panzer grenadier battalion. In turn they formed the nuclei of counterattacks that kept the Russians off balance, unable to break through where they broke in.

With the salient beginning to stabilize, Zukhov prepared for another major effort on December 7 and 8—only to be forestalled by a German counterattack launched one day earlier. Elements of Grossdeutschland and 1st Panzer Division struck the Russian front in Harpe's sector. Nineteenth and 20th Panzer Divisions hit the flank from the south, from outside the salient. By December 9 they had succeeded in cutting off a mechanized corps and most of a rifle corps—between 40,000 and 50,000 men. It was an order of magnitude short of Minsk, Smolensk, or Kiev. Compared to what was happening around Stalingrad, it was a victory to be celebrated.

From close up, the differences between 1941 and 1942 were even more pronounced. The pocket's front was being held not by infantry, but by panzer and panzer grenadier battle groups forming small strong points around the perimeter, linking up where possible, and pushing forward in fighting that was slow enough and costly enough to repli-cate in the open what had earlier happened in Stalingrad. It was not a tankers' battle in the previously understood sense: 19th and 20th Panzer

Divisions were even under command of an infantry corps. On December 16, the Russians succeeded in breaking out as organized formations, albeit with losses exceeding 75 percent.

Harpe's effort to mount a major counterattack to the northeast was stopped by a Russian defense that wore down the battalion-strength battle groups that were all Grossdeutschland and the 1st, 12th, and 20th Panzer Divisions were able to muster after days of close-quarters attritional fighting. In the end, however, it was the Red Army that stood down. Soviet casualties were more than 200,000 men, half of them dead. More than 1,800 of the 2,000 tanks committed had been lost. Grimly, the Germans reported fewer than 5,000 prisoners: quarter was neither asked nor given in most times and places in the Rzhev Salient.

David Glantz correctly describes the original strategic plan for Mars as too ambitious and Zukhov as too stubbornly optimistic to modify it. Operationally and tactically, Rzhev was nevertheless a watershed. This was the last time in a major sector the Red Army made the adolescent mistakes characteristic of its post-Barbarossa reconstruction: poor tank-infantry-artillery cooperation; inflexibility at all command levels; a tendency to reinforce failure at the expense of exploiting success. In a comparative context Rzhev, seen from a Soviet perspective, resembles the French offensives of 1915 in the Champagne and the later stages of the Somme a year later: a study in learning curves, facing an instructor charging high tuition.

The German victory was also a product of the limited geographic scope of Operation Mars. The essential difference between Mars and Uranus, the reason the Soviets succeeded on one front and not the other, was that in the south the Red Army established in Uranus's opening stage a force-to-space ratio in both halves of the breakthrough that the panzers could counter in neither. The German mobile forces immediately available lacked the mass to give weight to their impulsion, and were correspondingly swamped. At Rzhev the panzers were able to do what they did because the Soviet generals were obliging enough to commit their formations in action in limited sectors, as one might push candles into blowtorches, in a force-to-space ratio the Germans were just able to match.

Model, his subordinates—especially Harpe—and the mobile division commanders excelled at assembling, shifting, and committing both organized and ad hoc battle groups at key places and times. The initially limited, steadily eroding strength of the armored forces made that technique dependent on a battlefield small enough for the fire brigades to reach critical spots before the fires burst out of control. At Rzhev, the Germans were correspondingly able to assume control of the battle—albeit at a cost so heavy that the salient was abandoned in March.

In tactical terms Rzhev was characterized by the increasing long-term employment of panzer troops in the front lines. The panzer grenadiers in particular were the shock troops of the defense, time after time taking the brunt of Soviet attacks that had exhausted the undermanned and underequipped infantry formations. With only a battalion's worth of tanks available, a panzer division's counterattacks depended heavily on surprise and finesse while lacking the force to have more than a temporary effect. As had been the case in World War I, the Germans could no longer exploit their tactical successes.

Both of these developments moved the panzers away from their original roles. Both foreshadowed major revisions in the Germans' theory and practice of armored war but, in the immediate context of events in the winter of 1942–43, Rzhev invited interpretation as the counterpoint to Manstein's more visible, more spectacular riposte in the Don Basin. The conditions were different; the point was the same. A bear hunted long enough might increase his strength and improve his cunning. Killing him might be more difficult. But a bear remained a bear: a trophy waiting to be collected.

V

A HUNTER EXPECTING to take his trophy and live to admire it could nevertheless ill afford to lag behind his prey. If the second half of 1942 proved anything about the Eastern Front at the operational level, it was that the panzers were more than ever not merely the army's core, but its hope. The Reich's manpower resources continued to erode, making it impossible to keep the infantry divisions at anything like authorized strength. A new generation of personal weapons was coming off the drawing boards. Light machine guns, assault rifles, and rocket launchers would enhance the infantry's firepower and fighting power alike beginning in 1943. But at unit level the new hardware would at best be able to balance the lost men. In a wider context the Reich's factories could not produce enough of it to replace existing weapons in anything but fits and starts. What had begun in the 1930s as a choice to enable forced-draft rearmament had become a necessity in the context of forced-draft war. The panzers must be the focal point of the army's post-Stalingrad reconstruction.

Seven panzer and three motorized divisions—four if the 90th Light Africa Division were counted—had gone under in Stalingrad or surrendered in Tunisia. More than half the rest had been battered back to near-cadre status at Rzhev, on the south Russian steppes, or from Leningrad to points south. Reorganizing and reequipping them took most of a year. Even more than their predecessors, the revised tables of organization and equipment tended, in practice, to be approximations depending on what was available. The tank regiment was returned to its authorized two-battalion strength, each with four companies of 22 tanks—Panzer IVs in theory; in practice a mix of IIIs and IVs, depending on what was available. The antitank battalion was up-gunned to three batteries of open-topped, self-propelled Marders carrying the 75mm PAK 40, the definitive German antitank gun in the second half of the war, which inflicted much of the damage credited to the 88. The artillery regiment converted one of its battalions to self-propelled, full-tracked mounts: twelve 105mm howitzers and six 150mms. Both equipments were excellent. The lighter Wespe (Wasp), based on the still-useful Panzer II chassis, was a rough counterpart of the US M7 Priest. The 150mm Hummel (Bumblebee), with a chassis purpose-built from Panzer III and IV components, outmatched anything any other army's self-propelled divisional artillery would see until well into the Cold War.

The panzer grenadier regiments received a company of 20mm antiaircraft guns on half-tracks, and a company with six 150mm infantry guns on 38(t) chassis. Despite open tops and relatively light armor, these were generally used as assault guns manqué, and were correspondingly welcome. While the number of half-tracks could still not be stretched beyond a single battalion, the available vehicles began sporting a bewildering variety of heavy weapons. Each of a mechanized battalion's three rifle companies now had two 81mm mortars, two light infantry guns, and two 251 half-tracks with short 75mm pieces removed or salvaged from old Panzer IVs—all in addition to the 37mm guns on the platoon commander's half-tracks. The fourth "heavy" company had a section of two towed light infantry guns—even on an armored battlefield these were still useful against obstacles and entrenchments, and usually better than nothing—a platoon of three towed 75mm antitank guns, and another platoon of six of the 75mm 251s.

That was a lot of large-caliber firepower for 800 men. Its increased hardware would, in the next year, increasingly move the panzer division's mechanized battalion tactically apart from its three truck-riding counterparts, whose armament remained essentially unchanged, and into the panzer regiment's orbit.

A related major change in that panzer divisions' order of battle involved its "fast units." The reconnaissance battalion was expected to scout for information as opposed to fighting for it. On the Russian front, however, the terrain, the weather, and the enemy made reconnaissance by armored cars difficult. The motorcycle battalions faced constant difficulties maintaining effective combat strength as their mounts proved vulnerable to mud, snow, and Russian fire. The panzer arm made two problems into a solution by amalgamating the organizations into a reconnaissance battalion: one company of armored cars and three rifle companies, sometimes on motorcycles, sometimes riding the Volkswagen counterparts of US jeeps, but whenever possible converted to the light SdKfz half-tracks, finally at the production and deployment stage.

Like their larger counterparts, these chassis were also fitted with heavy weapons. No fewer than 14 official variants of this useful light armored vehicle would be introduced in the course of the war, carrying everything from extra radio equipment to a 20mm cannon turret. The new-style reconnaissance battalion also had a support company including a pioneer platoon, three 75mm antitank guns and a couple of the ubiquitous light infantry guns, and—as they became available—no fewer than six of the 75mm L/24s originally mounted on Panzer IVs, now transferred to SdKfz 251 half-tracks. Small wonder that the new formation was increasingly considered—and used—as an additional panzer grenadier battalion, with scouting and screening capabilities.

The net result of the chopping and changing was to facilitate splitting the panzer division into armored/unarmored or tracked/wheeled categories. The tanks and half-tracks, the self-propelled artillery and antitank guns, and the pioneer company with SdKfz 251s could form a battle group that was able to operate independently of the motorized elements, kept up to strength by internal transfers, and available at short notice for the kinds of emergencies that were the norm at Rzhev and Stalingrad, or in the Don Basin. The corresponding risk involved enhanced entropy: further decentralization of the panzer arm in the face of steadily increasing Soviet fighting power.

The panzer grenadier divisions received little more during 1942 than their new titles. The infantry battalions had two 81mm mortars per rifle company, a heavy company with three 75mm antitank guns, and another with—eventually—four 120mm mortars. Copied from a particularly effective Soviet weapon, these were intended to provide organic close-support for panzer grenadier battalions that had done far more fighting in isolation than the original doctrine for motorized infantry had expected. The reconnaissance battalion was upgraded to panzer division standards, though with lower priority for the light half-tracks. The antitank battalion usually had two self-propelled batteries. All of the remaining artillery and heavy weapons were moved by truck, just as on September 1, 1939. Their independent offensive power, even with the tank battalion authorized the previous year, was not much greater—a fact highlighted by the introduction of the MG 42.

German rifle squads were, unlike their US counterparts, built around a light machine gun. The MG 42 was the best of its kind in World War II and set design standards for another half century. The MG 42 resembled in appearance its predecessor, the MG 34: shoulder-stocked, bipod-mounted, and belt-fed in its usual configuration.

What distinguished it was a uniquely high cyclic rate of fire—up to 1,500 rounds a minute. Even with a quick-change barrel (five or six seconds was the usual time frame), that was hardly normal usage. But in emergencies the "Hitler saw," as the gun was known, could lay down a near-impenetrable cone of fire.

Standard issue around the turn of the year was one MG 42 per squad; enterprising panzer grenadiers doubled it. The extra weight was not important in a truck or half-track, which could also readily carry enough spare barrels and extra ammunition belts to keep the guns in action. On every front after 1942 the characteristic tearing-silk *brrrrip* of an MG 42 drove the boldest infantryman down until he could make sure of the gun's position, and the likely locations of any other MG 42s waiting for a would-be hero. Panzer grenadiers, finding more and more of their employment on the defensive, increasingly depended on their MG 42s as they waited for the panzer counterattack that would restore the situation—if it materialized.

The status quo ante Stalingrad was not completely restored. Tenth Panzer Division was never reformed, while 15th Panzer was converted to panzer grenadiers. Grossdeutschland, though retaining the panzer grenadier title, was upgraded to de facto panzer status with two tank battalions and a half-track battalion in each panzer grenadier regiment. Sixtieth Motorized emerged from the post-Stalingrad reconstruction of 6th Army as the Feldherrnhalle Panzergrenadier Division, to commemorate Hitler's first strike for power in the 1923 Beer Hall Putsch.

The 14th and 36th Motorized, on the other hand, became standard infantry divisions—reflecting a growing shortage of vehicles, equipment, and cadres that stabilized the ceiling of the army's effective panzer forces for the rest of the war. The infusion of strength that carried the panzers through 1945 and sustained them as the army's backbone came from an external source: one the soldiers had long viewed askance but would come to welcome—at a price.

Replacing the panzers' material losses was not a simple one-for-one process. The workhorse Panzer III was increasingly outclassed by its Soviet opponents—less from any qualitative improvement than because the Russians were beginning to learn how best to take tactical advantage in particular of the T-34's powerful gun and high maneuverability. The Panzer III's chassis was too light, its turret ring too small, to be a useful transition to the next panzer generation. They were issued as stopgaps, and by mid-1943 appeared in no more than company strength.

The Panzer IV, in contrast, had a future. Improved muzzle braking enabled it to carry the 43-caliber Tank Gun M 40, and a more powerful 48-caliber version introduced in late 1942. More than 1,700 of these F and G models were produced or upgraded before they gave way in March 1943 to the definitive late-war Panzer IVH. Its armor was significantly increased: 80mm on the front and 50mm on the turret, 30mm on the sides and 20mm in the rear—the latter reflecting Red Army infantrymen and antitank crews' willingness to come to close quarters for a kill. The additional protection increased weight to 25 tons and reduced speed to 21 miles per hour, but the Model H could still move and maneuver well enough. Its 75mm, 48-caliber gun was roughly equivalent to the T-34's main armament, and effective against almost anything it could reach.

The Panzer IVH integrated a useful set of upgrades into a state-of-the-art light medium tank, intended to equip one battalion in each panzer division. More than 3,000 would be built in 1943, and more than 3,100 in the war's final 18 months. They were nevertheless regarded as stopgaps, holding the line for a new generation of exponentially more powerful armored fighting vehicles.

The signifier of that family of weapons systems was the Panzer VI, better known as the Tiger I. The Tiger lent its aura to the whole German armored force. Even experienced British and US troops were likely to see Tigers behind every hedgerow and leading every counterattack. A cursory search turns up at least a hundred books in English, French, and German devoted to the Tiger's origins and performance. The vehicle's genesis can be traced to a 1935 Army Weapons Office report describing a 30-ton vehicle with a 75mm main gun capable of piercing the armor of French heavy tanks. Redesignated "escort tank," "infantry tank," then "breakthrough vehicle," the concept sputtered along through the 1930s, reflecting a lack of consensus on how the tank should be armed and used, and the problems of designing a chassis able to support the projected weight and an engine able to move it.

The firm of Henschel and Sons made just enough progress to spark Hitler's interest. Following the Third Reich's common approach of pitting competitors directly against each other, in the fall of 1940 automobile engineer Dr. Ferdinand Porsche was commissioned to design a 45-ton tank. Krupp, fearing to be shut out of potentially lucrative contracts, offered Porsche a turret designed around an adaptation of its 88mm Flak as the main armament. Not until May 1941, however, did the project begin taking material form—and that reflected concern for the heavily armored British infantry tanks encountered in North Africa rather than anxiety about what might await in Russia.

Gun power was a key issue in the discussion. It was generally agreed that the new tank's main armament be able to penetrate around four inches of armor from a distance of a mile. This was a major leap forward, but the army was looking a long distance ahead. It projected the Henschel design to mount a completely new kind of weapon: a tapered-bore gun of around 75mm. Tapered-bore began as a German effort to increase the effect of small-caliber antitank weapons by squeezing the round as it traveled through the barrel, thus improving muzzle velocity and penetrating power without raising the gun's size and weight. That enabled a tank to carry more rounds—an important factor, given the proven difficulty of replenishing ammunition in the midst of a battle—and allowed for a lower weight, with corresponding advantages using roads and bridges.

Germany produced two major versions. The 28mm model, usually mounted on an armored car or half-track, was issued to the mobile troops to improve their firepower despite its still relatively limited effect against tanks. The 75mm tapered-bore closed its round down to 55mm. Its performance was well above its conventional counterpart, and correspondingly attractive to panzer technocrats. Though the guns were complex and expensive, the critical problem involved raw materials. The armor-piercing rounds required tungsten cores. Tungsten was also necessary for the armament industry's machine tools, and neither Germany nor its victims had any indigenous sources. Supplies had to be brought in by blockade runners—a small-scale and unpredictable process—or imported from Spain, which was not much easier given Allied pressure on Franco's government. Finding enough of the metal to produce and supply more than a token number of large-caliber, tapered-bore weapons was a corresponding impossibility. But it required Hitler's direct intervention to "convince" the army and the firm of Henschel that they were pursuing a dead end.

The tapered-bore issue merits discussion because of the familiar trope that Hitler was solely responsible for the technical dead ends that plagued the armored forces during the war's second half. The generals too suffered from technocratic grandiosity, and entertained visions whose implementation depended on final, total victory. When it came to the projected heavy tank, Hitler's principal technical criterion was relatively modest. He accepted pursuing the tapered-bore solution, but as a backup wanted the Krupp 88mm to be replaced by an 88mm whose effectiveness was equal to a more powerful Rheinmetall design. Krupp unsurprisingly replied that a direct switch to the Rheinmetall gun was technically impossible. Nor could Rheinmetall develop and produce a conventional 75mm gun to match either the theoretical tapered-bore weapon or the existing 88mm in time to meet production schedules. Krupp's gun and turret was therefore adopted for both the Porsche and Henschel designs as much by default as intention.

No more than its design parameters were the Tiger's production schedules developed on an emergency basis. Even the appearance of the KVs and T-34s during Barbarossa failed to concentrate German minds and efforts. Instead Porsche and Henschel were told to have a half dozen of their respective designs available—by the summer of 1942. After all, the Russians would be crushed before the new tanks could take the field, in any case.

The first Tiger was a birthday present for the Führer in April 1942. Its production runs were set modestly, at 15 a month by September. The Porsche and Henschel versions competed through the summer. In

October, the Henschel won the contract for what passed for mass production in the Reich—not especially surprising, given its insider position on the project.

The leading authorities on the Tiger agree that it was no purebred.
Its technical genesis was ad hoc, incorporating components from several firms and several design projects. Modifications continued on the
production lines, ranging from mud guards on the hull to a redesigned
turret. Though the vehicle's final size and weight—57 tons—enabled
it to absorb the changes with relative equanimity, it was always high
maintenance. That does not mean unreliable. "Tiger was not a lady,"
in the words of one old hand. "But she was like a good woman. If you
treated her right, she'd treat you right." Extending the metaphor, Tiger
was also no cheap date. Range on a full tank was only 125 miles. Speed
was on the low side of adequate by previous panzer standards: about 20
miles per hour on roads, half that and less cross-country. But with an
88mm gun behind more than 100mm of frontal armor, the Tiger could
outshoot anything on any battlefield. Through the rest of the war, for
most Allied tanks to have a chance at penetrating a Tiger's armor, they
had to maneuver within the killing range of its gun. No one ever sought
the experience a second time.

The Tiger was all muscle, a slab-sided beast as sophisticated as a
knee in the groin—and no less effective. Its cross-country mobility was
as good as most of its contemporaries. Far from being a semi-mobile
Möbelwagen (furniture van), it was intended for offensive operations—
not merely breakthrough but exploitation, if proper attention was paid
to refueling. The Tiger's technology nevertheless completely inverted
the army's existing armor doctrine. It was twice as heavy as anything else
in the inventory of a panzer arm that from its beginnings had emphasized speed and maneuverability. Its tactical doctrine, always flexible,
improvised, or random depending on perspective, developed into three
primary missions. Tigers were expected to lead armored attacks against
strong positions, to break through prepared defensive works and overcome enemy defenses generally, and to destroy heavy tanks and equivalent targets at long ranges.

The first two points are essentially identical with British practice in

World War I and French theory in the 1920s and '30s. The third, whose relative importance increased by the month, reflected material and numerical circumstances in Russia that offered an unusually target-rich environment. That is to say a Tiger company could expect to find ample numbers of poorly handled Soviet tanks within range of its guns.

There were things the Tiger could not do. The first three battalions had two companies each of nine Tigers and ten Panzer IIIs with the idea that the lighter tanks could perform screening and scouting missions more effectively and economically. The Tigers' usual employment, however, favored their concentration into "pure" companies of 14, three to a battalion, with the battalions deployed as army troops to cooperate with the panzers in the kind of decisive sectors where Panzer IIIs were little more than targets.

The Tigers benefited from a policy of allowing recruits to volunteer for Tiger duty; from having their own training facilities; and from building crews, whenever possible, from experienced men, be they casuals, recovered wounded, or transfers. They later benefited by converting existing tank formations. The resulting mix of still-enthusiastic seventeen- and eighteen-year-olds with still-crafty old hands proved as effective as it usually does in war. Success was enhanced as well by the Tiger's high survivability rate. Not only did displaced crews usually live to fight again; they were likely to regard the loss of their vehicle as an accident rather than a certainty waiting to happen. That sharp contrast to the men who took Shermans and Cromwells into action after D-Day did much to sustain morale and effectiveness in Tiger battalions throughout the war.

Like their British predecessors in 1916, the Tigers were initially fed into combat on small scales. One battalion went to Leningrad in August 1942 to shore up a front eroding under steady Russian pressure. A second was dispatched to Tunisia in November as a response to the Allied invasion. The third, Heavy Tank Battalion 503, was assigned to Army Group Don in December 1942. It made its bones in a series of rearguard actions and small-scale counterattacks that reduced it to two operating Tigers by the time it was withdrawn in late February. In two months, however, the 503rd accounted for more than 70 Soviet tanks

and 55 antitank guns for the combat loss of only three Tigers—a kill
ratio that more than compensated for maintenance problems resulting more from enemy fire than mechanical defects. As for mobility,
one company covered more than 65 miles in ten and a half hours with
no breakdowns—an impressive achievement for a complex vehicle with
limited field testing.

If the Tiger seemed immediately promising, the same could not be
said for its intended stablemate. As early as 1938, the Weapons Office
had begun considering replacements for the Panzer III and IV: something along the same lines, in the 20-ton category with improved armor,
armament, and chassis. A few prototypes were developed in leisurely
fashion through 1940. Its priority remained low in the early days of
Operation Barbarossa, when the Russian heavy tanks appeared sporadi-
cally. That began to change as the campaign progressed. In particular the
T-34 was impossible to ignore. Its gun could take out Panzer IIIs and
IVs at more than a thousand yards—ten times the effective range of the
German tanks against the T-34's comprehensively well-sloped armor.
The Soviet vehicle's mobility over mud, swamp, and dirt roads was no
less impressive.

On October 5, 1941, Guderian's 4th Panzer Division encountered a
brigade of T-34s. Not only were the Germans stopped cold; for the first
time in a head-to-head fight at even odds, their losses were significantly
greater. Well before that oft-cited day, however, it was clear in the panzers that besides upgrading and upgunning an entirely new weapons
system, it was necessary to sustain the synergy of technical and human
superiority on which their effectiveness depended. Continuing to rely
on crew expertise and command skill to compensate for inferior equipment created an ultimately unsustainable imbalance in a military/politi-
cal system structurally vulnerable to attrition and overextension.

Guderian had something his colleagues lacked: enough influence
to demand an inquiry. In late November 1941, a commission of officers and civilian designers toured the combat zone, examined derelict
T-34s, and evaluated the situation. Guderian recommended copying the
T-34—not literally through reverse engineering but by imitating the
essentials. The Weapons Office replied by citing the problem of produc-

ing diesel engines, and by making the point that copying what existed gave the Soviets an automatic lead for the next generation. On returning to Berlin, the commission issued contracts to Daimler-Benz and MAN for a 30-ton tank with a difference.

When the prototypes were completed Hitler favored a Daimler version resembling the T-34. The Weapons Office supported MAN, in good part because of a larger turret ring. The soldiers won politically and technically. Working on the Tiger, Rheinmetall had sought to balance the army's wish for a relatively light main armament and Hitler's insistence on maximum hitting power. The eventual result was a 75mm L/70 piece developed too late for the Tigers, but mounted on the MAN chassis just in time to give the Panther the most ballistically effective tank gun of World War II.

Preproduction was authorized in May 1942; the first of what were eventually designated Panther Model D reached the proving grounds in November. Apart from the predictable teething troubles, two fundamental issues emerged. One was protection. The Panther's well-sloped frontal armor was 80mm on the hull and 100mm on the turret. This was a substantial improvement over the Panzer III and IV, but would it suffice against the weapons likely to be introduced as a counter? That increase, moreover, was at the expense of side armor not much better than the Panzer IV. The Panther's other problem was the engine. The tank weighed 45 tons. Its Maybach 230 engine delivered a power-to-weight ratio of 15.5 horsepower per ton: lower than its panzer predecessors, lower than the T-34, and low enough to seriously strain the entire drive system.

One difficulty sustained the other. The Panther D's already overstrained engine could not take the additional strain of up-armoring. As a result the tanks were disproportionately vulnerable to a flank shot. On the other hand, the cadres and crews of a Panther battalion were expected to avert or solve that kind of tactical problem, especially since the new vehicles were expected to be assigned to existing, experienced battalions. "Not perfect, but good enough" was a verdict rendered in the developing crisis of the Eastern Front. Serial Panther production was authorized in November 1942, with a projected delivery of 250 delivered by May 1943 and a projected deployment of a battalion in each panzer division, replacing Panzer IVs.

As a stopgap measure pending the Panthers' design, production, and delivery, Guderian's commission had recommended upgrading the army's assault guns. About 120 of the Model IIIF with a 75mm L/43 had entered service in 1942, prefiguring the assault gun's development from an infantry support vehicle into a tank destroyer. As a rule of thumb, the longer a gun, the less effective its high-explosive round. From the infantry's perspective, however, the tradeoff was acceptable, and the Sturmgeschütz IIIG was even more welcome because of its 75mm L/48 main armament. The effective range of this adapted Pak 43 was more than 7,000 feet. It could penetrate almost 100mm of 30-degree sloped armor at half that distance. The IIIG took the original assault gun design to the peak of its development by retaining the low silhouette and improving frontal armor to 80mm by bolting on extra plates, all within a weight of less than 25 tons. The family was completed, ideally at least, with the addition of a 105mm howitzer version in one of the battalion's three ten-gun batteries to sustain the infantry support role.

The one-time redheaded stepchild of the armored force now had a place at the head table. There had been 19 independent assault gun battalions in May 1941. In 1943 that number would double. Constantly shifted among infantry commands, their loyalty was to no larger formation. Continuously in action, they developed a wealth of specialized battle experience that led infantry officers to follow the assault gunners' lead when it came to destroying tanks and mounting counterattacks. Assault guns cost less than tanks. Lacking complex revolving turrets, they were easier to manufacture, and correspondingly attractive in an armaments industry whose workforce skill and will were declining with the addition of more and more foreign and forced labor and the repeated combouts of Germans destined for the Wehrmacht.

Meanwhile, tank production was in the doldrums. The Panzer III was so clearly obsolete as a battle tank that its assembly lines had been converted to providing chassis for assault guns. By October 1942, production of the Panzer IV was down to 100 a month. The General Staff recommended a leap in the dark: canceling Panzer IVs and concentrating exclusively on Panthers and Tigers. Previous outsiders like Porsche, and a new generation of subcontractors turning out assault guns, were jostling and challenging established firms. But the German automotive industry, managers and engineers alike, had from its inception been labor-intensive and conservative in its approaches to production. As late as 1925 the US Ford Motor Company needed the equivalent of five and three-quarters days' labor by a single worker to produce a car. Daimler needed 1,750 worker days to construct one of its top-line models. When it came to design, focus was on the top end of the market and emphasis was on customizing as far as possible by multiplying variants. It was a far cry from Henry Ford's philosophy that customers could have any color they wanted as long as it was black.

For their part, the civilian tank designers were disproportionately intrigued by the technical challenges Panthers and Tigers offered. They took apparent delight in solving engineering problems in ways that in turn stretched unit mechanics to limits often developed originally in village blacksmith shops.

One might suggest that by 1942 a negative synergy was developing between an armored force and an automobile industry, each in its own way dedicated to an elite ethos and incorporating an elite self image. The designers were correspondingly susceptible to the dabblings of Adolf Hitler. Previously, his direct involvement in the issue had been limited, his demands negotiable, his recommendations and suggestions reasonable. The Hornet, for example, combined the Hummel's armored open-topped superstructure with the 88mm L/71 gun Hitler had wanted for the Tiger. The vehicle's bulky chassis made it too much of a target to render feasible stalking tanks in the fashion of the Marder and the assault guns. But its long-range, high-velocity gun was welcome to the half dozen independent heavy antitank battalions that absorbed most of the 500 Hornets first introduced in 1943.

The Ferdinand, later called the Elephant, was a waste-not/want-not response to the Porsche drives and hulls prepared in anticipation of the Tiger contract that went to Henschel. Hitler saw them as ideal mounts for a heavily armored tank destroyer mounting the same 88mm gun as the Hornet. Ninety were rushed into production in spring 1943 and organized into an independent panzer regiment. Without rotating turrets, at best they were Tigers manqué, with all the teething troubles and maintenance problems accompanying the type and no significant advantages. At 65 tons, any differences in height were immaterial. And the omission of close-defense machine guns as unnecessary would too often prove fatal for vehicles whose sheer size made them targets for every antitank weapon in the Red Army's substantial inventory when they were sent into action at Kursk.

The Hornet and the Elephant were mere preliminaries. Since adolescence the Führer had liked his architecture grandiose, his music *molto pomposo*, and his cars high-powered. In June 1942, he authorized Ferdinand Porsche to develop a super-heavy tank: the *Maus* ("Mouse"—and yes, the name was ironic). The vehicle carried almost ten inches of frontal armor, mounted a six-inch gun whose rounds weighed more than 150 pounds each, and weighed 188 tons. Its road speed was given as 12.5 miles per hour—presumably downhill with a tail wind. It took more than a year to complete two prototypes. To apply a famous line from the classic board game PanzerBlitz, "The only natural enemies of the Maus were small mammals that ate the eggs."

The complete worthlessness of the Maus as a fighting vehicle in the context of World War II needs no elaboration. Neither does the total waste of material resources and engineering skill devoted to the project. The Maus was nevertheless a signifier for Germany's panzer force during the rest of the war. Apart from its direct support by Hitler, the Maus opened the door to a comprehensive emphasis on technical virtuosity for its own sake, in near-abstraction from field requirements. The resulting increases in size at the expense of mobility and reliability were secondary consequences, reflecting the contemporary state of automotive, armor, and gun design. After 1943, German technicians turned from engineering to alchemy, searching for a philosopher's stone that would bring a technical solution to the armored force's operational problems. Hubris, idealism—or another example of the mixture of both that characterized so many aspects of the Third Reich's final years?

The Maus thread, however, takes the story a few months ahead of itself. Its antecedent combination of institutional infighting, production imbroglios, and declining combat power led an increasing number of Hitler's military entourage to urge the appointment of a plenipotentiary troubleshooter—specifically Heinz Guderian. Guderian describes meeting privately on February 20, 1943, with a chastened Führer who regretted their "numerous misunderstandings." Guderian set his terms. Hitler temporized. He was given the appointment of Inspector-General of Panzer Troops, reporting directly to Hitler; with inspection rights over armored units in the Luftwaffe and the Waffen SS, and control of organization, doctrine, training, and replacement. That was a lot of power in the hands of one officer.

There was also a back story. Guderian had spent most of 1942 restoring his stress-shaken health, which centered on heart problems, and looking for an estate suitable to his status, to be purchased with the cash grant of a million and a quarter marks Hitler awarded him in the spring of 1942. Norman Goda establishes in scathing detail that once Guderian became a landed gentleman on an estate stolen from its Polish owners, his reservations about Hitler as supreme warlord significantly diminished. Cash payments, often many times a salary and pension, were made to a broad spectrum of officers and civilians in the Third Reich—birthdays were a typical justification. Since August 1940, Guderian had been receiving, tax-free, 2,000 Reichsmarks a month—as much as his regular salary. Similar lavish gifts were so widely made to senior officers that Gerhard Weinberg cites simple bribery as a possible factor in sustaining the army's cohesion in the war's final stages.

The image of an evil regime's uniformed servants proclaiming their "soldierly honor" while simultaneously being bought and paid for is so compelling that attempting its nuancing invites charges of revisionism. Nevertheless there were contexts. A kept woman is not compensated in the same fashion as a streetwalker. Dotation, douceur, "golden parachute," hush money, conscience money, or bribe—direct financial recognitions of services rendered the Reich were too common to be exactly a state secret. Guderian and his military colleagues were more than sufficiently egoistic to rationalize the cash as earned income, as recognition of achievement and sacrifice in the way that milk and apples are necessary to the health of the pigs in George Orwell's *Animal Farm*.

The appointment Hitler signed on February 28, 1943, ostensibly gave Guderian what he requested. But lest any doubt might remain as to who was in charge, only the heavy assault guns, still in development stages, came under Guderian's command. The rest, whose importance was increasing by the week, remained with the artillery. It was a relatively small thing. But Guderian's complaint that "somebody" played a "trick" on him belies his own shrewd intelligence and low cunning. The desirability of trust between the head of state and the general in such a central position was overshadowed in Hitler's mind by Lenin's question: "Kto, kogo?" (Who, whom?): the question of who was to be master. Guderian had spent a year in the wilderness. Now he was back on top. Omitting the assault guns was a reminder that what had been given could be withdrawn at a chieftain's whim. It might well make even a principled man think twice before deciding and thrice before speaking. And Hitler's army was increasingly commanded by pragmatists.

From the Führer's perspective, Guderian's appointment was one of the heaviest blows he had struck against the High Command. The ground forces' key element, the panzers, were now under his personal authority—at one remove, to be sure, but Guderian was the kind of person whose ego and energy would focus him on the job at hand, and whose temperament was certain to lead to the same kinds of personal and jurisdictional clashes that had characterized his early career. Hitler would have all the opportunities he needed either to muddy the waters or to resolve controversies, as circumstances indicated.

VI

NINETEEN FORTY-TWO MARKED the end of Hitler's panzers as originally conceived and configured. For the rest of the war, the army's armored force plateaued, then declined—not only absolutely but relative to a counterpart and a rival, a battle companion and a partner in the Third Reich's crimes. The Waffen SS made its first appearance at stage center in the aftermath of Stalingrad. Previously its formations had served individually. Now it was an SS Panzer Corps that retook Kharkov in March, anchoring Manstein's counterattack to the Donets with a combination of maneuver engagements recalling Barbarossa at its best, and close-gripped street fighting suggesting Stalingrad in reverse. The campaign's price was almost 12,000 SS men killed or wounded. And if Russian prisoners and civilians were regularly shot out of hand, if several hundred wounded Red Army soldiers were murdered when the SS overran a Kharkov hospital—victory has its price, and Manstein was not especially squeamish.

An overjoyed Hitler declared the SS Panzer Corps to be worth 20 Italian divisions, and ordered that it be given priority in personnel and equipment—including the latest tanks. The discontent that last caused in the army was balanced by a sense, albeit sometimes grudging, that the men who wore the lightning runes had the right stuff for what the panzers knew was a coming showdown battle for control of the Eastern Front.

The Waffen SS has been described in terms ranging from "soldiers like the rest" to a criminal institution distinguished even in the Third Reich for ideologically based bestiality. It is unrivaled in the spectrum and intensity of the attention lavished on it. Not merely SS divisions but regiments and battalions have their own English-language histories. Waffen SS military reenactors exist in Britain and the US, carefully proclaiming their nonpolitical, non-revisionist ethos on websites whose constructions nevertheless often resemble—too closely for comfort—throwbacks to purported glory days on the Russian Front.

Simple anti-Communism has never contributed much to the enduring fascination with the Waffen SS. More relevant is the underlying and uncomfortable question whether criminality is a component of military effectiveness. Another element involves taboo-breaking. In a Western culture where traditional masculine values are increasingly downgraded when not denigrated, there can be a certain appeal in the men who—in mythic terms at least—lived large, accepting neither boundaries nor limitations, staking everything on the iron dice of battle for themselves and their comrades.

Those kinds of subtexts guarantee controversy. A historiography of the Waffen SS is a book by itself; a study of its images a second; and an analysis of its fascination a third. All three, however, begin at the same point: the focal point of this work. The identity of the Waffen SS is constructed around its panzer divisions. They established a legitimate reputation as some of the most formidable combat formations in the brief history of armored war. Waffen SS soldiers learned tactical and technical skills quickly. Waffen SS officers combined a charismatic fearlessness and an aggressive, opportunistic approach to command that together focused an esprit de corps able to overcome heavy odds and survive high casualties.

Waffen SS achievements involved more than iron discipline and battlefield ferocity, more than often-cited superior weaponry allegedly obtained at the army's expense. F. Scott Fitzgerald speaks of a whole-souled emotional equipment as necessary in modern war. The Waffen SS ethos was a blend of vitalism and racism—culturally, ideologically, and institutionally based—that nurtured and synergized conscious ruthlessness and conscious brutality, each an integral element of Waffen SS fighting power. That fighting power in turn manifested the inseparability of war and racism in Nazi Germay. One was the other, and the Waffen SS epitomized both.

The Waffen SS grew out of the Schutzstaffel (security force) created in 1925 to protect Nazi Party meetings and senior cadres. From its beginnings the SS was a party instrument rather than a paramilitary force of the kind otherwise familiar in Weimar Germany. Its loyalty was personal, to Hitler himself, and inspired his creation after the seizure of power in 1933 of the regiment-sized Leibstandarte (bodyguard). Its title suggests its function: to secure the regime against a coup. Created at the same time was a second armed element: the Totenkopf (Death's Head) units guarding the concentration camps. A year later a number of gun-carrying local leg-breakers called Political Emergency Readiness Formations were combined into three regiments of Verfügungstruppen (special service troops) equipped, like the Leibstandarte, as motorized infantry.

This was scarcely a promising matrix for expansion—especially given Hitler's simultaneous emphasis on the "Two Pillars Theory" hailing the Wehrmacht as the Third Reich's sole "bearer of arms." SS chief

Heinrich Himmler combined the zeal of an ideologue and the soul of a bureaucrat. His response, echoed by Hitler, usually spoke of the SS as National Socialism's ideological soldiers: a party force, limited in size and focused in purpose, which was nevertheless honored to serve alongside the army in the field.

The explanation was fairly transparent, especially when volunteer enlistment in any of the SS armed branches became an alternate form of military service. But there were not that many of them relative to a rapidly expanding army. Compromise seemed reasonable in the context of all the other compromises the soldiers were making with the New Order. Besides, four extra motorized regiments might prove a useful addition to a mobile force at best none too large for its projected mission.

Nothing, moreover, indicated that the effectiveness of the armed SS would transcend its numbers. Himmler's vision aspired to a new human type, able to serve as a model and an instrument for revitalizing the Nordic race. It was a vision readily marketable among the Hitler Youth and the Labor Service in the early years, when the Reich was still an empire of dreams, when the General SS attracted doctors, attorneys, and businessmen—and when the black uniform was still fresh and new. The Leibstandarte in particular looked elegant. Its close-order drill was unmatched even by Grossdeutschland. Its men were handsome: not a pair of glasses in the ranks, at least on parade.

But could these "asphalt soldiers" fight? The SS officer corps at this stage was a mixed bag of ideologues seeking to serve the Reich, opportunists seeking quick promotion, and second-tier transfers the army was not eager to retain. There were some exceptions. Paul Hausser was a retired army major general who justified his advancement in the SS by professional competence as a trainer and commander. Felix Steiner transferred in as a major because he admired SS ideas of training. But most of the men who rose from commanding companies and battalions to leading divisions and corps by 1945 did it in what came to be understood as the SS way: headlong energy and ruthless, never-say-die aggressiveness. SS doctrine emphasized speed and ferocity. SS training stressed physical toughness and incorporated risk to an extent surpassing the army.

From the beginning Himmler was determined to develop an officer corps fundamentally different from its army counterpart. Once the cadres of transfers were in place, Waffen SS officer candidates were required to spend time in the ranks—two years initially, less as the war progressed. Only after that enlisted service were they eligible for the Junkerschulen, the special officer training schools, the best known—or most notorious—being Bad Tölz. The curriculum, ironically, included extensive instruction in table etiquette and similar bourgeois social graces. This reflected the fact that a higher proportion of SS officers were from lower social strata than their army counterparts. It reflected as well Himmler's determination that his personal armed force would stand out in every particular.

Hausser, Steiner, and their senior-officer counterparts also stressed breaking down the hierarchic rank stuctures still considered characteristic of the army. Officers and noncommissioned officers were encouraged to get to know their men, to participate in team games. In the field, rations and facilities were essentially the same—at least at company and battalion levels. "Pulling rank" off-duty was strongly discouraged. In principle, any Waffen SS man could request of another, from corporal to general, to "speak with you as a comrade," and that request would be honored.

The army's collective reservations regarding SS military effectiveness nevertheless seemed justified by the Polish campaign. Exchanging SS black for army field gray, done on the outbreak of war, did not transform party activists to German soldiers. Lectures on Nordic racial superiority and the world mission of the Third Reich were no substitute for a sense of terrain. Heedless—and brainless—valor was a quick ticket to a mass grave. Employed by regiments under army command, the SS distinguished itself by disproportionately high casualties, by junior officers who knew how to lead but not command; and by majors and colonels baffled by situations that required solutions more sophisticated than a headlong assault. The High Command also found SS units prone to commit atrocities against Poles and Jews more systematically, more publicly, and on a larger scale than the army was willing to stomach—yet.

The SS response was standard military alibi: high-risk missions, inadequate equipment, misuse by unsympathetic generals. Supported by Hitler, Himmler took steps to bring the armed formations together as the Waffen SS, to form the three Verfügungs regiments into a motorized division, and to form another three-regiment motorized division around a cadre of concentration camp guards. The Totenkopf (Death's Head) Division was well named. Its commander, Theodor Eicke, was a protégé of Himmler's whose motto was "tolerance is weakness." He had been committed briefly to a mental hospital by a Party superior. He encouraged contempt for "military" virtues and behavior among the men he supervised as Inspector of Concentration Camps. But as a division commander Eicke had his points. He made his men obey superiors, focused their camp-conditioned viciousness with a spectacularly demanding training program, and used his connections to scrounge modern equipment for the collection of thugs and aspiring thugs who called him "Pop."

It must be noted that the often-cited distinction between the Waffen SS and the concentration camp system existed only in the minds of apologists. Throughout the war, exchanges took place between camp personnel and field units, usually on the basis of physical fitness.

From the Leibstandarte the Waffen SS drew an identity as the Führer's personal elite. The Verfügungstruppen contributed a willingness to learn soldiering from the professionals. Totenkopf emphasized ferocity for the fun of it. In the 1940 campaign the latter tendency predominated. Under orders, elements of Leibstandarte and Totenkopf carried out large-scale massacres of British POWs; in the Totenkopf, it was standard procedure to give no quarter to French black troops. Operational effectiveness was another matter. During the fight for Holland, Leibstandarte added a German general to its bag by severely wounding Kurt Student when some of its men opened fire on what turned out to be surrender negotiations. In a campaign otherwise characterized by low German casualties *Verfügungsdivision* was manhandled twice: by the British in front of Dunkirk and again at the Aire River on June 7 during the final attack on France.

Hitler nevertheless had no problems with expanding and upgrading the Party's army. Leibstandarte received enough new bells and whistles, including its own reconnaissance battalion and a full battalion of assault guns, to be redesignated a division. *Verfügungsdivision* got a new title: Das Reich. The major institutional development of the Waffen SS, however, was external. Volunteers for the Waffen SS were still ample, but the army controlled the supply through a regulation that no one registered for conscription could volunteer for any form of service until his local military district approved. With available manpower increasingly stretched between the Wehrmacht and industry, the kind of high-quality recruits demanded by the Waffen SS were an increasing source of friction well before preparations for Barbarossa got underway.

Gottlob Berger, in charge of SS recruitment since 1938, initially responded to the army's barriers by turning to the ethnic German communities still not called "home to the Reich." Several thousand volunteered, especially from Romania. Even before the overrunning of Western Europe, Berger proposed the enlistment of volunteers from racially suitable non-German sources. Himmler was not merely receptive but enthusiastic. He saw a future that would begin with a European crusade against Bolshevism and end with a Germania extending from the Atlantic to the Urals. The Waffen SS would be at the forefront of this effort, eventually developing into a multinational force that would not merely supplant the Wehrmacht but transcend it.

In the summer of 1940 the SS began soliciting volunteers from Germany's "Nordic" conquests: Norway, Denmark, the Netherlands, Belgian Flemings. In September, Hitler, despite reluctance to provoke an army that was also recruiting in the conquered territories, authorized a new SS division. Built around an experienced Verfügungs regiment, it would include a Regiment Westland drawn from Belgium and the Netherlands, and a Scandinavian Regiment Nordland. Hitler christened it the Viking Division and authorized its organization as a motorized division.

The Viking Division generated as many myths and legends as any German formation of the Second World War. Foremost is its enduring image as a body of blond, blue-eyed, six-foot Scandinavians: berserkers. In fact, Viking from its inception had more Germans than "Nordics" in its ranks—more than 90 percent. In January 1942, an SS survey listed the number of Finns, Norwegians, and Danes at around 5,500, not all of them serving in Viking. Yet its non-Germans gave Viking a particular ambience, one that endured when most of the originals were dead or in hospitals.

The Viking Division's motivations have been endlessly debated. It is reasonable to suggest that most recruits, like most human beings generally, were motivated by combinations of factors whose respective influence was constantly changing. Some were proto-Europeans and some anti-Communists. Some saw German Europe as a given and wished to make their way in the new world. Others were indigenous fascists, encouraged or pressured by local movements seeking to curry influence. More volunteers than might be expected were motivated by economic considerations exacerbated by conquest and occupation. And a good many are best described as adventurers. The Low Countries and Scandinavia had worked assiduously during the twentieth century to create societies congenial to slightly overweight men with briefcases. They offered little scope and less encouragement to the kind of large living suggested by the SS. Boredom can be as good a recruiting sergeant as hunger.

Whatever their motivations, the "Nordics" provided the seedbed of the division's professionalism. Unlike some of their counterparts in the German army's European "legions," Viking's men had generally enlisted as individuals. Even when ideologically based, the volunteers' motives seldom included the genocidal racism at the heart of the German SS. Their cadres, mostly from the *Verfügungsdivision*, were more concerned with making them battle-ready than with their ideological development. The Germans who filled out Viking's ranks in good part acculturated to the foreigners—not least, as one old hand reminisced, because their exotic aura helped pick up girls.

Its variant identity did not make Viking anything but an SS division. During service entirely on the Eastern Front, the men whose shoulder patch was a stylized longship acquired and preserved a reputation as not being freely given to the large-scale, gratuitous ferocity characteristic of their fellows. That of course did not avert shooting Jews on what admittedly by SS standards were limited numbers: a few hundred here and a few hundred somewhere else, usually justified as "reprisals" and underwritten by an internal order that Jew-killing was not a punishable offense.

Leibstandarte and Das Reich served in the Balkan campaign, enhancing the Waffen SS reputation for aggressiveness and arrogance. An officer of Das Reich at the head of a dozen men was able to bluff the mayor of Belgrade into suspending resistance until it was too late. When some men of the Leibstandarte hesitated to advance against a Greek position, their battalion commander, himself in the front line, got them moving by throwing a grenade at them. "It's not bragging when you back it up." And if the army as an institution still found the Waffen SS as a concept unpleasant to swallow, its four motorized divisions on the ground looked better and better as Barbarossa's orders of battle were finalized.

In June 1941, the Waffen SS remained firmly under the army's organizational thumb. Leibstandarte and Viking went with Army Group South, Das Reich with Center, and Totenkopf with North. Hoepner kept the Skulls in supporting roles. Mopping up stragglers and maintaining contact with Bock's left flank, the division took heavy casualties as it fought toward Leningrad through the forests and swamps.

Das Reich was initially not even allocated road space by Army Group Center, but when it found a way to the front it played a crucial role in the late July fighting around Yelna. One of its staff officers used the division's last reserve, its pioneer battalion, to stop a major Soviet breakthrough. The corps report singles out the SS riflemen for "fearlessness and bravery," swarming over heavy tanks to set them afire with gasoline when the antitank guns proved useless. And the casualty records show Das Reich took almost three times the losses of 10th Panzer Division, which fought alongside it.

That pattern persisted throughout the drive for Moscow. As part of Hoepner's Panzer Group 4, Das Reich fought to within sight of Moscow, then was caught in the Soviet counterattack and hammered so badly its effective remnants were organized into a battle group and the remaining survivors sent all the way to France for rest and refitting. Not for a year would it return to the east, and to a new emergency.

Leibstandarte was also held in the wings during Barbarossa's early stages. It was a week before it joined III Panzer Corps, then XLVII Panzer Corps, for the drive into the Ukraine. Leibstandarte had always been the best of the Waffen SS formations, and it sustained that reputation both in the attack and while fending off Soviet counterattacks. It got as far as the Black Sea before turning north in November 1941 and rejoining III Panzer Corps to play a key part in capturing the city of Rostov. A Leibstandarte rifle company set up the victory by capturing a vital railway bridge before it could be blown. Its quick-thinking CO ordered his men to shoot up a locomotive and stormed across under cover of the clouds of steam.

That was the kind of warrior performance that inspired Mackensen to inform Himmler that every unit wanted to have Leibstandarte on its flank in a tight spot. And if the "toughness" Mackensen praised manifested itself occasionally in the mass shooting of Soviet prisoners—as many as 4,000 in a single incident, according to one allegation—the usual explanation was that the shootings were reprisals for the murder and mutilation of captured SS men. It was a fig leaf, but it camouflaged what the army understood to be a negotiable trade for SS "discipline, eagerness, and enthusiasm."

Soviet counterattacks drove the Germans out of Rostov and inflicted heavy casualties. By the turn of the year, more than half Leibstandarte's originals were dead or wounded. The replacement pool was almost exhausted; Soviet counterattacks so reduced its fighting power that Leibstandarte was not considered for Operation Blue. Instead it was withdrawn to France in June for refitting—and assignment to the newly forming SS Panzer Corps.

Viking saw its first action fighting for Tarnopol in Galicia, then shifted south across the Dnieper and served alongside Leibstandarte in the capture and loss of Rostov. Viking also held the line in the Ukraine during a winter of counterattacks. Unlike Leibstandarte, Viking was not favored with reassignment to France. Instead, replenished and reequipped on the ground, it received its own tank battalion and proved a key to the successes of 1st Panzer Army during its drive into the Caucasus. Viking crossed the Kuban Steppe in hundred-degree temperatures, fought into Grozny as the oilfields burned, sent spearheads toward Astrakhan, and won consistent praise from the panzer corps to which it was assigned.

By no means was all of this flattery aimed at Himmler by uniformed politicians. Retitled "panzer grenadier" in October 1941, Viking increasingly assumed the role of a panzer division in a theater where armor was scarce and distances wide. Half its 50 tanks were Panzer IIIs, and its officers made up for the relative lack of armor with by-now predictable aggressive tactics that earned the grudging respect of the Soviets. Steiner proved a clear-eyed general as well as a hard-driving commander. As early as mid-September he reported to his SS superiors that Hitler's directive was impossible: the Caucasus could not be crossed before winter set in.

If Viking was at one end of the Waffen SS approach to war-making, Totenkopf set new standards at the other. The Skulls were one of the half dozen divisions and 100,000 men trapped in what came to be known as the Demyansk Pocket by the Soviet Northwest Front's massive offensive of February 1942. When terrain, weather, and command arteriosclerosis put an end to the operation, Demyansk remained, attacked repeatedly by a total of five Soviet armies, and kept minimally supplied by air. And by all accounts and admissions, Totenkopf was the backbone of the defense. Combining with army troops or fighting on their own, the SS men held nothing back. Eicke's pathological ferocity focused a spirit of "no quarter, no surrender" that rendered four-fifths of the division casualties by the time the pocket was relieved in April.

Not many of the original concentration camp guards remained when Totenkopf's remnants joined Leibstandarte and Das Reich in France. By this time the occupied zone was developing into a rest and refit area for divisions burned out in Russia. "To live like God in France" is a familiar German proverb, and the SS survivors took full advantages of the opportunities provided in a society still complaisant, if not enthusiastic, about its situation. It was not all down time. The SS divisions were reconfigured and upgraded to panzer grenadier status. The title was another fig leaf to keep the army quiet. While not officially renamed until October 1943, all three were full-fledged panzer divisions where it counted, with, thanks to the lobbying of Himmler and Hauser, two-battalion tank regiments, at least a battalion on infantry in half-tracks, and—eventually—a company of Tigers.

This upgrading was a major step in an anomaly. The Waffen SS was the only large-scale high-tech elite force fielded by any army during World War II. The special forces, rangers, raiders, and commandos, the paratroopers, even the US Marines, depended to varying degrees on the quality of their personnel to compensate for a lack of the hitting power sacrificed to mobility and flexibility. The Red Army's guards units were upgraded to recognize combat performance. Only the Waffen SS—and only its best divisions—combined physical, ideological, and material elements to the same degree.

With their generous allowances of supporting weapons, the divisions' authorized strengths grew to more than 20,000—a sharp contrast to the army, whose divisional strengths were being steadily reduced to cope with diminishing manpower. There were certain costs involved. The reinforcements' standards of training were generally described as low. For the first time, even Leibstandarte was constrained to accept men born outside the Reich but "German" by official standards of racial descent—which, in passing, grew increasingly flexible as the war continued. A living link with the worst aspects of the Waffen SS also returned to its ranks when Eicke, recovered from his wounds, resumed command of Totenkopf. Its men welcomed him like a returning father.

Hitler had first authorized an SS Panzer Corps in May 1942, strongly against army wishes. Its commander was Paul Hausser, recovered from a wound that cost him an eye, and supremely confident that his corps was just the instrument needed to restore the situation and turn the tide in the east. Redeployed east in January 1943, it played a crucial role in Manstein's offensive. Hausser, the "lowly corps commander" mentioned above, may well have averted a second Stalingrad by defying Hitler's initial order to hold Kharkov. His men paid for the city's recapture with more than 12,000 casualties. Leibstandarte's fighting strength was reduced by almost half, the city square was renamed in its honor, and its men were accused postwar of clearing a hospital by the simple expedient of shooting its 700 patients. Das Reich also took heavy losses in the city's industrial zone, and according to one of its captains, had the subsequent pleasure of showing the ladies "who the real men were" in Kharkov. The Skulls lost their CO when Eicke's light plane was shot down between the lines on February 23, 1943—and took more losses recovering the body. Manstein received the Oak Leaves to the Knight's Cross of the Iron Cross, and came away with a different attitude toward the men in black who had helped hang it around his neck. The Waffen SS would be front and center in the next German offensive.

CHAPTER SIX

ENDGAME

THE BATTLE OF Kursk established the conditions for the rest of the Russo-German War. It developed in the wider contexts of a war that the Reich's leadership, from Hitler downward, understood now hung in the balance. In the aftermath of El Alamein, Hitler had reinforced defeat in North Africa, committing two panzer divisions plus a number of Tiger tanks to Tunisia, creating a new panzer army headquarters to command them. The result was a few tactical victories, won against inexperienced troops, that proved operationally barren and strategically empty.

Rommel, worn down mentally and physically, halted one attack when the American artillerymen facing it had a fifteen-minute supply of ammunition remaining. He managed to concentrate three panzer divisions for an attack against 8th Army, which was advancing from the east—the largest armored attack the Germans made in the entire campaign. But ULTRA intercepts gave Montgomery an outline of his enemy's intention. Rommel ran headlong into a multilayered, prepared defense that tore the heart out of the panzers. "I have six hundred anti-tank guns, four hundred tanks, and good infantry holding strong pivots," Montgomery commented. "The man must be mad." After less than a day Rommel ordered a withdrawal from the battle that, by all accounts, ranks as his greatest embarrassment.

Were these events stumbling blocks or straws in the wind? Hopes for the U-boat campaign and faith in new weapons, from nerve gas to

super-long-range cannon to rocket bombs, were balanced against an
aerial offensive absorbing increasing amounts of the Reich's high-tech
capacities and the prospects of a cross-channel invasion sometime in
1943 by an alliance demonstrating an uncomfortably high learning
curve.

I

PARADOXICALLY, CIRCUMSTANCES SEEMED more promising in the East.
The victories at Stalingrad and in the Caucasus initially encouraged the
Soviet High Command to plan a major offensive on a front extending
from north of Smolensk to the Black Sea. But the price of success had
been high. The Germans, against expectations, had come back strong
and added a new high card to their order of battle in the SS Panzer
Corps. The second front long promised by the western Allies still consisted of promises and substitutes. Significant evidence indicates Stalin seriously considered the prospects of a separate peace with Hitler,
or with a successor government willing to respond. Tentative contacts,
most of them indirect, began in Sweden during the spring of 1943 and
continued for most of the year.

By any rational calculation, the Reich's short-term prospects of total
victory in Russia were close to zero. The concluding volume of *Das
Deutsche Reich und der Zweiten Weltkrieg* summarizes a project begun
thirty years ago by suggesting that without Hitler's iron determination,
Germany would probably have been ready to conclude peace in 1943.
But by that time the National Socialist Führer State had so far eroded
the principal institutions of state, Wehrmacht, and party, that neither
institutional nor personal forums for discussing the issue existed. No
one but Hitler was responsible for the whole. No one—above all no one
in the military—was willing to risk considering the whole and acting
on the results. Like many a plan before it, Operation Citadel would take
on a pseudolife of its own.

Postwar historians in general have followed the generals' memoirs in
blaming Kursk on Adolf Hitler. He is indicted, tried, and convicted first

for refusing to accept the professionals' recommendations and shift to an operational defensive, temporarily trading space for time while making good the losses of the winter campaign, allowing the Red Army to extend itself in a renewed offensive, then using the refitted panzer divisions to "backhand" it a second time. Once having accepted the concept of an offensive, Hitler is described as first delaying it while the Russians reinforced the sector, then abandoning it when, against the odds, the generals and the Landser were on the point of once more pulling the Reich's chestnuts from the fire.

Reality, as might be expected, is a good deal more complex. Hitler badly needed a major victory to impress his wavering allies—perhaps even to convince Turkey to join the war. And his argument that south Russia's resources were significant for sustaining Germany's war effort could not be simply dismissed. The army high command, moreover, was not precisely of one mind on the issue. Guderian, restored to power and favor, argued against any major offensive during 1943 in favor of rebuilding a panzer force stretched to the limits by the fighting at the turn of the year. Wait until 1944, he urged, then strike with full-strength panzer divisions built around Panthers and Tigers, with increased numbers of half-tracks and assault guns and a mobile reserve strong enough to hold any second front the British and Americans could open.

For his part, Manstein believed Guderian took no account of time. His often-cited advocacy of an elastic defense taking full advantage of German officers' mastery of mobile warfare and German soldiers' fighting power has gained credibility with hindsight. But the concept was barely articulated in early 1943. To the extent that it existed, it was Manstein's brain child, tested over no more than a few months, for practical purposes unfamiliar even in the panzer force. Experience would show that elastic defense was by no means a panacea. Its success depended on an obliging enemy—and the Red Army of 1943 was anything but obliging.

Manstein himself saw elastic defense in the existing strategic contest as essentially a temporary expedient, to wear down Soviet forces and prepare for a grander design. Manstein initially intended a combined general offensive by his Army Group South and Army Group Center against a hundred-mile bulge around the city of Kursk, driven into the German lines during the winter fighting. A double penetration would cut off Soviet forces in this Kursk salient, and draw Soviet reserves in that sector onto the German anvil in the fashion of 1941. With Kursk eliminated and the German front shortened by 150 miles, reserves could more readily be deployed for future operations against the Soviet flanks and rear.

Manstein described this ambitious operation as a "forehand stroke" that must be made quickly, while the Germans could take advantage of the dry season and before Soviet material power grew overwhelming and the Western allies could establish themselves on the continent. It was correspondingly disconcerting when Kluge's Army Group Center replied that it lacked the resources to participate in the kind of assault he projected. Paradoxically, that refusal made Manstein's commitment to the Kursk operation even firmer. He considered it a high-risk window of opportunity that must be seized even with limited resources.

Army Chief of Staff Kurt Zeitzler was also attracted by the prospects of eliminating the Kursk salient, albeit for less ambitious reasons than his subordinate. He considered weakening the Russians in the southern sector and shortening the front quite enough to be going on with.

By default the generals' debate kicked the decision upstairs, to Hitler. On March 9 his Operations Order No. 5 provided for a spring offensive with the purpose of denying the Russians the initiative. After a couple of false starts, it became the basis for Operation Citadel, whose scope was defined in an order of April 15. The opening paragraph of Operations Order No. 6 spoke of "decisive significance . . . a signal to all the world." In sharp contrast to the far-reaching objectives set in 1941 and 1942, however, the operational geography was so limited it requires a small-scale regional map to follow. That did not make Kursk a limited offensive. Success offered a chance to damage the Red Army sufficiently so as to at least stabilize the Eastern front and perhaps develop a temporary political solution to a militarily unwinnable war.

The operation was militarily promising. Strategically even a limited success would remove a major threat to German flanks in the sector and limit prospects for a Soviet breakout of the Dnieper. The experiences of Operations Barbarossa and Blue indicated that the Germans won their victories at the start of campaigns and ran down as they grew overextended. Citadel's relatively modest objectives seemed insurance against that risk. This time, forward units would not be ranging far beyond the front in a race to nowhere in particular. There were no economic temptations like in the Ukraine in 1941 or the Caucasus in 1942. Kursk would be a straightforward soldiers' battle. As for what would come next, sufficient unto the day was the evil thereof. It was a line of thinking—perhaps a line of feeling—uncomfortably reminiscent of Ludendorff's approach to the great offensive of March 1918: punch a hole and see what happens.

Kursk seemed to be the kind of prepared offensive that had frustrated the Soviets from division to theater levels for eighteen months. Geographically, the sector was small enough to enable concentrating overstretched Luftwaffe assets on scales unseen since 1941. Logistically, the objectives were well within reach. Operationally, the double envelopment of a salient was a textbook exercise. Tactically, from company to corps, the panzer commanders were skilled and confident. For the first time since Barbarossa they would have tanks to match Soviet quality.

But would there be enough of them—indeed, enough armor of any kind? As had been the case throughout the war, the tip of the upside-down pyramid was the panzer arm. By the end of the winter fighting, the eighteen panzer divisions on the Russian Front had a combined strength of only around 600 serviceable tanks. The shortages of trucks and other supporting vehicles were even greater. Refreshing the divisions in situ meant fresh demands on men already bone tired.

Friedrich von Mellenthin, widely accepted as a final authority on panzer operations, declared the "hardened and experienced" panzer divisions to be ready for another battle once the ground dried. But Mellenthin was a staff officer, a bit removed from the sharp end. Some divisions of his own XLVIII Panzer Corps were down to fewer than two dozen tanks apiece. Fourth Panzer Army's old pro Hermann Hoth informed Manstein on March 21 that men who had been fighting day and night for months now expected a chance to rest. Even hard-charging company and battalion commanders were reporting widespread apathy.

Operations Order No. 6 emphasized speed. But Army Group South reported that its panzers could not be ready for battle until the first half of May. Army Group Center complained that partisan attacks and air strikes were seriously delaying rail movements. Walther Model, whose 9th Army would carry the weight of the northern arm of the proposed pincers, insisted postponement was necessary. Perhaps even that aggressive general had lost faith in the operation's prospects. Certainly he was well aware of the overall weakness of Army Group Center's front. Shifting its resources southward invited a repetition of Rzhev, where the Soviets had come far too close to a victory under similar conditions.

Hitler was having his own second thoughts. He postponed the attack until May 9, partly with the intention of bringing as many Panthers and Tigers on line as possible. When the overworked assembly lines failed to deliver, Hitler postponed the attack again, then again, and finally set the date for July 5. The delay was later widely criticized among the soldiers. Some of this was reflex; "ask of me anything but time" was a military axiom long before Napoleon aphorized it. Some was second-guessing, typically expressed by Mellenthin's assertion that the Russian position at Kursk was vulnerable in May. It might indeed have been—to the kind of attack the Germans delivered in July. The postponements enabled doubling Citadel's strength, bringing the order of battle to a quarter million men and over 2,500 armored fighting vehicles for a 60-mile front. The postponements enabled refitting the panzer divisions, bringing them to near full strength of 150 or so tanks. Approximately 150 Tigers and 200 Panthers were included in the inventory—most of them concentrated in a few units.

The panzers would be sporting new coats. After over eighteen months, higher headquarters had become officially aware that the dark gray with which the armored force had gone to war was poor camouflage in the greens and browns of rural Russia. The new scheme authorized in January 1943 was a base color of dark yellow, with crews at liberty to apply olive green and red brown mottling to suit specific conditions. As spring broke out, would-be artists employed spray guns and brushes.

Eighteen hundred aircraft, two-thirds of the Luftwaffe strength in Russia, were available to support the operation—a number enhanced by the high quality of the air and ground crews compared to a Red Air Force still learning its craft. The now-legendary Stuka would make its last appearance in a dive-bomber role and its first as a tank-buster with two 37mm cannon mounted below the wings. The Stukas were joined by five ground-attack squadrons equipped with Fw 190s, and by five more squadrons of specialized antitank aircraft: the Henschel Hs 129, whose twin engines, heavy armor, and 30mm cannon made it the ancestor of the US Air Force's well-known A-10 Thunderbolt, and no less formidable in action.

Delaying the attack also gave the old hands in the panzer divisions the breathing space they so badly needed. It gave them time to welcome returned wounded, to integrate replacements, to learn the individual characteristics of the Panzer IIIs and IVs most of them were still riding. It gave them opportunity to experience a buildup like few had ever seen. Reactions, even among the old hands, oddly resembled those widespread in the BEF in the weeks before the Battle of the Somme in 1916. There was just too much of everything for anything to go seriously wrong.

The catch-22 was that the Red Army had been steadily countering the German buildup with one of its own—one whose scale escaped both German intelligence and German reconnaissance. Its strategic matrix, as mentioned above, was offensive. Its operational intention was to break the Germans and advance to the line of the Dnieper. And tactically it would begin on the defensive—by design. Intelligence sources, including Western-supplied ULTRA information, and common sense alike indicated the Germans would attack rather than wait to be overrun. And this time there was only one sector of the entire front offering anything like a favorable opportunity. The question was not "where" but "whether" the offensive could be stopped.

Preparation began in mid-April to make Kursk a fortress and a killing ground. The salient was configured as a combination of battalion defensive sectors, antitank strong points, barbed wire, and minefields. The forward belt alone included 350 battalion positions, each a network of mutually supporting trenches and bunkers. There were seven more of them, with a depth extending over 100 miles. Minefields averaged over 2,500 mines per mile. These active and passive defenses were structured to steer the panzers against antitank strong points largely built around combinations of antitank rifles and light 45mm guns. Both were long obsolescent and correspondingly expendable. Both were useful only at point-blank ranges. Both were proof of Stavka's commitment to replicating Stalingrad in the steppe.

Manning the fixed defenses were some of the best infantry of the revitalized Red Army, including a number of Guard divisions who had earned the honorific the hard way. Supporting them was a mass of artillery, heavy mortars, and rocket launchers—close to 20,000 barrels, many organized in complete divisions, working with calibrated ranges. Behind the salient, the sword to the shield was a striking force under Ivan Konev, who would finish the war second to none in the Red Army as a master of operational art. His Steppe Front included over 4,000 tanks commanded by some of the best of a new generation of Soviet armor generals: M. E. Katukov of 1st Tank Army, A. G. Rodin of 2nd, and a dozen others forgotten to history but familiar enough to the Germans.

Overall responsibility in the northern sector rested with Central Front's Konstantin Rokossovsky. Polish born, he had spent three years in the Gulag during the Great Purge. Released in 1940, his lost teeth replaced by the best Soviet metal, he showed his own mettle from Moscow to Stalingrad. Facing off against Manstein, Voronezh Front's N. F. Vatutin had demonstrated his capacity for high command since the start of the war. A leader from the front, respected by his subordinates and his soldiers, Vatutin was a risk-taker who appreciated staff work: an uncommon but welcome combination in the Red Army.

No less significant was the synergy between the geographic scale of Kursk and the Red Army's command and control methods and capacities. Since Barbarossa, those had developed in contexts of top-down battle management, reflecting both the Soviet principle that war is a science and the fact that Soviet commanders at all levels were essentially the product of experience. At this stage of the war, and arguably much later, senior Soviet officers resembled their counterparts in the armies of Napoleon: both lost effectiveness when operating independently. Previous German offensives had found no difficulty in getting inside Soviet decision loops, generating increasingly random responses that frequently collapsed into chaos. Kursk's small scale enabled timely response to German moves as the defense slowed the German pace. It also enabled a level of management absent in previous major battles, cresting in turn a confidence at all levels of headquarters that a culture of competence had replaced a culture of improvisation from desperation.

Those were significant force multipliers, in a situation arguably not needing them. It is a familiar axiom of modern war, expressed mathematically in something called the Lanchester equations, that an offensive requires three-to-one superiority. Soviet doctrine reduced that to 3:2, assuming superior planning, staff work, and fighting power. By the time the preparations for Kursk were complete, the Soviet defenders outnumbered the attackers in every category of men and equipment, in almost every sector. The average ratio was somewhere between 1:1.5 and 1:2.5. On paper the outcome seemed assured. But wars are won in the field, and the panzers had made a habit of defying odds.

Given the respective rates of buildup, it seems reasonable that an attack mounted by the forces available in April or May would have lacked the combat power to overcome the salient's defenses even in their early stages. The Germans' only chance was the steel-headed sledgehammer they eventually swung in July. And that highlights the essential paradox of Kursk. The factors that made the battle zone acceptable in operational terms also made it too small to allow for the application of the force multipliers the panzers had spent a decade cultivating. Geographically Kursk offered no opportunity for operational skill and little for tactical virtuosity. Militarily the strength of the defensive system meant the German offensive had to depend on momentum sustained by mass—which is another way to describe a battle of attrition, the one type of combat the German way of war was structured to avoid.

Hitler's panzers thus faced a second paradox. Not only were they the tip of an inverted strategic pyramid, operationally and tactically they were required to match the Red Army's strengths at the expense of their own. And once the fighting started, a third paradox developed. One of the tactical advantages initially considered in planning Kursk was that the limited geography would enable the infantry to remain close to the armor and assume responsibility for mopping up. But the Reich's systemic and increasing shortages of replacements favored giving priority to the panzers—army and SS alike. The advantage was often marginal: Leibstandarte's ranks were in part refilled by unceremoniously transferred Luftwaffe ground crews. But infantry divisions already chronically understaffed were in the process of being reduced to six battalions instead of the original nine.

The resulting formations were easier to handle. New weapons like the MG 42 enhanced their firepower. But they lacked staying power when pitted against defenses like those of Kursk. As a consequence the panzers were increasingly constrained to use their own resources—tanks as well as panzer grenadiers—to secure the ground they captured at the expense of sustaining offensive momentum.

On the right half of the German pincer, Army Group South deployed Hoth and 4th Panzer Army on its right. With six army panzer divisions and the SS Panzer Corps*, plus an independent regiment including all 200 available Panthers, this was the largest armored force ever previously put under a single commander. Its mission was correspondingly straightforward. Screened on his left by the three panzer divisions of Army Detachment Kempf's III Panzer Corps. Hoth was to break through and join forces with Army Group Center's 9th Army attacking from the north. Model had another six panzer divisions, one of panzer grenadiers, and seven infantry divisions which he proposed to use to open the way for his mobile forces. Sixty miles separated Model and Hoth. It would be the longest distance in the history of Hitler's panzers.

"It's time to write the last will and testament!" one SS trooper wrote in his diary while awaiting the order to advance. Across the line Soviet soldiers swapped their own grim jokes—like the one about the tanker who reported almost everyone in his unit had been killed that day. "I'm sorry," he concluded, "I'll make sure I burn tomorrow."

---

*It was officially renamed II SS Panzer Corps in June, but the original designation remained common usage during Kursk.

On the evening of July 4 1943, the Germans sent their men the infallible signal: a special ration of schnapps. An Alsatian serving in the SS promptly deserted—and convinced a high-status interrogation team, including a forty-nine-year-old political advisor named Nikita Khrushchev, that the German offensive would be under way before dawn on July 5. Soviet false alarm would be risky. But giving the Germans the advantage of tactical surprise might be fatal. The Red Army acted. In Model's sector a massive Soviet bombardment preempted the German barrage, which only opened an hour later. It was the start of a very long day for the German infantry, which took heavy losses against a nightmarish maze of trenches and strong points. The panzers made better local progress—up to five miles—thanks in good part to the Tigers. Ninth Army was nevertheless a long way from a breakthrough by nightfall.

Hoth and Kempf led with their tanks but had little better fortune. Hoth's XLVIII Panzer Corps included the Panther regiment, of which great things were expected. Instead it ran into a minefield, losing almost half the tanks to mines and mud, breakdowns, and inexperienced crews. At day's end the corps had done about a mile better than Model but remained a long way away from a breakthrough, much less a linkup.

When the Waffen SS crossed their start lines around 4 AM, they advanced in a modified version of the long-standard wedge. This time the Tigers were the point, with the AFVs on each side and the infantry, in half-tracks or on foot, in the middle: trucks were suicidal in these close quarters. The prewar idea of the wedge had been to throw antitank gunners off balance and off target. Here the Russians kept their heads and kept the Tigers under fire. As the mastodons shrugged off hit after hit, the panzer grenadiers, directly supported by tanks and assault guns, closed in under cover of waves of Stukas and ground-attack aircraft. The panzers took out machine-gun and antitank positions; the infantry cleared trenches with grenades and flamethrowers. In the close-quarters fighting, mercy was rarely asked or given. Leibstandarte counted only a little over a hundred prisoners for the day, most of those accidental.

By evening elements of the SS Panzers were as far as 15 miles into the Soviet defenses. They continued their drive the next day as a worried Soviet command shifted sector reserves, including an entire tank army, into their path. Here again the few available Tigers were decisive, picking off opposing T-34s at long range, shifting position to evade return fire, then finding new targets. By noon the panzer grenadiers had fought their way into the defenses sufficiently for tank and half-track battle groups to begin pushing forward against T-34s dug in to their turrets, pillbox fashion. This was Vatutin's idea, and Zukhov flew into a rage at what he called a senseless waste of armor. But Vatutin understood that his main task was to tie up the Germans until the strategic reserve could intervene. Even a Tiger engaging a dug-in tank from the front was vulnerable to others on its flanks, and the Red Army still had enough mobile tanks to mount counterattack after local counterattack.

Forty-eighth Panzer Corps and Kempf's divisions slowly closed up on the SS flanks despite having to weaken their spearheads by detaching ever more armored units for flank security; Soviet tank losses correspondingly mounted. By July 13, Army Group South would account for the defeat of over 1,200 tanks at a cost of only a hundred of its own AFVs. The ratio was a tribute to the German tank gunners and to the panzer grenadiers who, especially in the SS sector, accounted for a good share of the kills. No less did it reflect the high quality of German front-line maintenance and the high morale of crews willing to take their field-repaired vehicles back into combat. "We no longer flinched when a steel hand knocked," recorded one SS tanker. "Instead we wiped away paint flakes, loaded, aimed, fired." Easily written, and not so easily done, as British and US crews in similar circumstances would later affirm.

Fourth Panzer Army continued its advance through July 8—no spectacular breakthroughs, but relentless and remorseless enough that the Soviets were giving ground steadily. The heavy armor and long-range guns of the Tigers and the constant hammering from the air were taking human toll as well. More and more prisoners were shuffling rearward under token guard. Tank crews were abandoning their vehicles under Tiger guns. An entire tank corps was smashed when caught in the open by a flight of Henschel 129s: fifty T-34s were destroyed in an hour. Stavka responded by summoning reinforcements. Pavel Rotmistrov's 5th Guards Tank Army was to move his whole force 120 miles and be ready for action by July 9—around the village of Prokhorovka.

The German nickname for an officer like Hermann Hoth is *alter Hase*—"old hare." Unlike the English "old fox," who outwits danger, the hare stays alive by anticipating it. Well aware of the strong Soviet reserves in rear of the salient, Hoth was convinced from the beginning that they posed too great a risk to his right flank to ignore, or to trust to Kempf. He proposed to respond by having the SS swing northeast and draw the Soviets onto their guns on the high ground around the village of Prokhorovka. Once the threat was suppressed, 4th Panzer Army would resume its original axis of advance. A series of map exercises developed the concept; a series of discussions with Manstein convinced the Field Marshal to accept it. On July 9 Hoth pulled the trigger and set the stage for a legendary clash of armor.

His decision reflected in part Model's failure to match 4th Panzer Army's progress. The Russians had expected the main German effort in Central Front's sector. Rokossovsky had a two–to-one superiority over Model in artillery. He could call on an entire air army for support. And he was a battle captain. Part fireman, part chess player, he juggled and shifted his reserves to keep abreast of the attackers. German panzer wedges were blunted by the synergy of sophisticated defenses and T-34s employed in numbers too great for even the Tigers to suppress. On this front as well the Soviets had enough tanks to dig in large numbers of them as pillboxes. Panzers fell prey to everything from Sturmoviks to antitank rifles and Molotov cocktails. A dozen Tigers fell to antitank mines in a single day—repairable to be sure, but nevertheless out of action when badly needed.

Unable to develop a weak spot, Model decided to create one. He tried three times, first at the high ground around the village of Olkhovatka, then at the village of Ponyi on the Orel-Kursk railroad, then again at Olkhovatka. No one ever suggested Walther Model possessed more tactical sophistication than he needed. When a hammer failed, he sent for a bigger hammer. Olkhovatka earned the dubious sobriquets of "second Verdun" and "second Stalingrad." Ponyi became a "second

Douaumont." As tank losses mounted 9th Army's war diary spoke of a "rolling battle of material attrition." Infantry casualties were no less massive. And the Olkhovatka ridge still held out.

On July 10 Model broke off the attack, but he by no means accepted defeat. Most of the armor losses were temporary, with only a total of 63 write-offs by the 11th. Army Group Center was sending him two more panzer divisions. Model now proposed a relatively indirect approach flanking Olkhovatka from the right. The new attack was set for July 11. The same day the Red Army swung its own hammer.

The plans of the Soviet high command balanced the defensive at Kursk with a series of offensives. One was against the Orel salient in Army Group Center's sector: the other half of the monad formed by Kursk, and just as vulnerable geographically. It was authorized to begin when the German attack was stopped. On July 11 the first probes were launched. On the 12th large-scale attacks struck the salient's north flank and apex. The Germans had been preparing defenses for months, but the force and timing of the onslaught came as a surprise—a tribute to Soviet deception operations and another failure on the part of the German intelligence service. The blow fell on the by now ironically named 2nd Panzer Army. It consisted of 14 infantry divisions, with a single panzer division in reserve. Within hours Model was ordered to send four of his panzer divisions north, effectively ending any serious prospects of a serious offensive in his sector.

The southern half of Citadel was still functional. What was intended as pincers might become a hammer-and-anvil operation—if 4th Panzer Army could clear its front. That burden rested squarely on the Waffen SS. Its orders established three missions: break the Soviets to their immediate front, draw along with them the army panzers on their left, and open an alternate route to Kursk. Any one was a tall order. Hoth was not likely to admit it, even to himself, but Hausser's men were arguably better suited than the army formations—in terms of ideology, experience, and leadership—for the kind of head-down head-butting that lay ahead. And in another context they might well be considered expendable: party troops in what was at the sharp end still an army war.

Manstein underwrote Hoth by ordering Kempf's III Panzer Corps to strike Prokhorovka on the right flank of the SS. He also released two panzer divisions from army reserve to develop any success. Hausser spent a day repairing damaged tanks and moving the Skulls from their assignment of covering the corps right flank to a key assault role on the left. That latter was an overlooked successful exercise in traffic control that said a lot about the high level of the corps's staff work and administrative efficiency. Totenkopf responded by forcing two bridgeheads over the flooded Psel River on the tenth. By noon the next day the pioneers had finished a bridge strong enough to carry Tigers.

Totenkopf was in position to either swing left and support the army's panzers or swing right to help its sister divisions. The latter were taking longer than necessary with their advances against opposition that by now included an airborne division. Between them, Leibstandarte and Das Reich, again benefiting from pinpoint support by Luftwaffe Stukas, were able to crack the final defenses in front of Prokhorovka in a series of massive frontal attacks. No less seriously from a Soviet perspective, most of the positions selected for Rotmistrov's counterattack were lost. Planning had to begin again from scratch, and on-the-fly improvisation was never a Red Army strong point.

Rotmistrov's attack was only part of a major offensive inside the salient, the whole intended to coordinate with the attack on Army Group Center. On July 12, 1st Tank Army, with another five armored and mechanized corps, was scheduled to envelop and break through XLVIII Panzer Corps into the German rear and join Rotmistrov's spearheads around Prokhorovka in a Soviet Cannae, an armored version of Stalingrad.

Attacking into these preparations, XLVIII Panzer Corps made no significant progress. Its tank crews were tired enough to make expensive tactical mistakes. The panzer grenadiers had taken heavy casualties, especially among officers and NCOs. It was easier to repair tanks than replace men, and the past week had taught caution to the boldest.

Kempf's III Panzer Corps, in contrast, finally eroded its opposition and broke out into open country. Lieutenant General Hermann

Breith understood his craft, and two of his divisions, 6th and 7th Panzer, counted among the Wehrmacht's best. By nightfall the corps was well on its way to Prokhorovka. But the distance to be covered and the resistance to be expected were sufficient to make counting on its appearance the next day a risky proposition.

Hausser counted on no one but his own soldiers. Maintenance crews worked through the night to put over 300 tanks and assault guns on line, including 16 Tigers. Hausser's orders were as sophisticated as a kick to the groin: Leibstandarte straight ahead into Prokhorovka, with Totenkopf and Das Reich running interference on its flanks. Rotmistrov responded by placing three tank corps in his first line and a mechanized corps in reserve: over 800 AFVs, around 500 of them T-34s. By now it was clear at all levels that engaging the Germans at long range was playing with the other man's deck. "Close in" was the mantra. Get to within 1,500 feet at least, and then try to shorten the range further.

The German attack went in at 6:30 AM, July 12. The Soviets jumped off at about the same time. Rotmistrov left a colorful firsthand account of a close-quarters death grapple: tanks engaging at gun-barrel length, hulls exploding, turrets being flung randomly around the battlefield, and tanks burning like torches. He told of the difficulty of determining who was defending and who was attacking. His description set the tone for the reconstruction of a fight costing the Germans as many as 400 tanks, including dozens of Tigers, epitomizing the coming of age of Soviet armor and marking the beginning of the road to Berlin's Reichstag. Prokhorovka is commonly described as the greatest armored battle in history, the most important victory of the war, the graveyard of Hitler's panzers.

Prokhorovka's reality was a good bit less spectacular. Rotmistrov's attack went in as he described it, wave after wave at high speed. But initially it faced not a similar mass, but two companies, most of whose crews had been in an exhausted sleep as late as 5:30. It seemed a long-standing panzermann's nightmare come true: a steel avalanche impossible to stop by courage or skill. The Tigers opened fire at 1,800 yards, their optical sights enhancing the skill of their gunners. As the range closed, the Panzer IVs joined in. A good crew could deliver four or five rounds a minute, and the SS were very good. More and more Soviet tanks slewed aside, burst into flame, and exploded, strewing chunks of armor plate and whole turrets across the killing zone. Then, unexpectedly, the leading T-34s drove headlong into one of their own well-camouflaged anti-tank ditches. Fifteen feet deep, it upended tanks like they were children's toys. Across a three-mile sector the charge eroded into a maelstrom of small-scale combats. The Germans gave ground and counterattacked, and by the time the seesaw fighting ended in mutual exhaustion around mid-afternoon, who held the initiative in that sector was a matter of opinion and optimism.

The men who fought there interpreted Prokhorovka in mythic terms. Division Das Reich reported a panzer grenadier lieutenant carrying an incendiary grenade that was touched off by a Russian bullet. Divesting himself of trousers and underwear, the officer led his company on to its objective naked from the waist down and gave a new meaning to the concept of risking all for the Führer. A far more familiar Soviet account has two tankers restarting a disabled and burning T-34 to ram a Tiger and send both vehicles up in flames. The commander of the allegedly demolished Tiger reported that he had in fact dodged away at the last minute. The only Leibstandarte Tiger reported as a total loss for July 12 fell to gunfire. The legend nevertheless survives.

The best comparison of material losses, based on official records, lists well over 300 Soviet armored vehicles as having been destroyed, with most of their crews blown up or incinerated. The tank corps listed more dead and missing than wounded: 3,600 out of a strength of around 7,000. Stalin, famous for describing a million deaths as a statistic, was sufficiently enraged at these figures that he initially proposed to court-martial Rotmistrov. German casualties amounted to 522. Their recorded total loss of tanks in the sector was only three—another reflection of the effectiveness of German maintenance and the survivability of even the older models of tanks.

On the left, Totenkopf fought what amounted to a separate battle, holding its ground and then counterattacking successfully enough to lead Rotmistrov to shift some of his by now scarce reserves to stabilize the line. To Hausser's right, III Panzer Corps spent the day fighting the sound of the guns—and initially fighting panzer style for the only time in the entire Kursk operation. On his own initiative the CO of the 11th Panzer Regiment pushed a tank battalion and one of panzer grenadiers in half-tracks forward through unsuspecting Soviet positions during the night of July 11. With a captured T-34 in the lead, the Germans reached and crossed the Donets by morning—a little over 10 miles from Prokhorovka.

Two years earlier, perhaps even in the high summer of 1942, this might have been the beginning of something. In 1943 it was a dead end. The Russians had always known how to fight. They had learned how to move. And a series of counterattacks made what might once have become a spearhead into a long salient. Rotmistrov's reinforcements confirmed the result. Breith's corps spent the day fighting in three directions simultaneously. Its commander described an advance to Prokhorovka as out of the question.

Things in the Prokhorovka sector might well have been far worse, perhaps disastrous, for the Germans had Grossdeutschland and 3rd Panzer not been able to shift left and move south in time to blunt 1st Tank Army's thrust. Third Panzer Division was down to fewer than 40 tanks and Grossdeutschland was not much better off when, by evening, mutual exhaustion put an end to the fighting. No real hope remained for immediate coordination with the SS. Two divisions had nevertheless averted what was intended as a major breakthrough, and done so smoothly enough to treat the matter as near-routine in their reports.

On July 10 the British and Americans landed in Sicily. It was a long way from Kursk and a long way from Germany. It was also the "second front" not only Hitler but generations of German generals had feared. Almost by reflex the Führer determined it was necessary to reinforce the west with enough armor to cancel the invasion and underwrite Mussolini's tottering regime. On July 13 he summoned Manstein and Kluge to his Rastenburg headquarters and informed them of his decision to suspend Operation Citadel. Kluge, with his own sector exploding, insisted he needed 9th Army to restore the situation. Manstein, citing the destruction of as many as 1,800 Soviet tanks, insisted his army group could finish off the Russians in the salient if given Hitler's authorization to commit its three reserve panzer divisions.

Hitler compromised and temporized. Ninth Army was committed in the north. Model was also given command as well of 2nd Panzer Army; Schmidt's open and sulfurous criticism of the way the war was being run had recently led to his dismissal and an official recommendation that he be confined to a psychiatric hospital.

Army Group South was given a few days to continue its offensive. Breith's corps did succeed in establishing contact with the SS, but only on July 15, by which time most of the Russian forces in the sector escaped. Manstein remained convinced he could draw Soviet reserves into the kind of mobile battle which maximized the panzers' advantages and his own talents. In theory perhaps—but all along Manstein's front Soviet resistance showed no signs of weakening, much less collapsing. On July 17 Hitler ordered the SS Panzers off the line, effectively shutting down Citadel once and for all.

Manstein insisted that this decision threw away a victory. That case might be made in an operational context. But any gains on that level would almost certainly have been promptly swept away by the long-prepared, comprehensive Soviet counteroffensives that decisively shifted the balance of the Russo-German War. For Hitler's panzers the shining times were over. The next 18 months would see their role, and their nature, change essentially. But before considering that new order of things, it seems appropriate to cast up Citadel's accounts.

The balance of losses clearly favored the Germans. Far from the hundreds of armored vehicles described in Soviet sources, the total number of write-offs for Model and Manstein combined was around 250. Red Army losses in contrast were so large that they were released only after the collapse of the Soviet Union, and even now they remain difficult to calculate. The best low figure is around 1,600; the best maximum somewhere short of 2,000. The Germans suffered around 55,000 casualties, including 9,000 dead. Official Soviet losses are given at 177,000, with strong evidence indicating an actual figure of over 300,000.

The discrepancy between Soviet estimates of German armor losses and the actual figures can be ascribed to varying combinations of propaganda, adrenaline, and inexperience. The Soviet Union needed heroes from its ranks—needed them badly. The stress of combat encouraged tank crews to overestimate the effects of their gunnery, in much the same way American heavy bomber crews consistently exaggerated the number of fighters shot down. Inexperience led as well to underestimating the high survivability of German tanks, and their high reparability even after taking several hits.

On the German side, statistics invite comparison to air war in other contexts. As with fighter pilots, a relatively small number of crews scored a disproportionate number of kills. Promotion, decoration, and recognition increasingly accompanied high scores. Some old-timers have said they could not be bothered to notice their number of kills. But contemporary evidence strongly suggests that successful panzer crews kept as careful track as their fighter-pilot contemporaries—and that official records were kept with corresponding care whenever possible.

The statistics speak strongly against conventional arguments that Kursk broke the back of the German panzers. Instead the battle highlighted a shift in technical effectiveness that enhanced the tactical advantages the panzers still retained. The Tigers proved masters of the field wherever they went—at Prokhorovka alone, 15 of them accounted for eight times their number of T-34s. The crews of the often-denigrated Ferdinand described themselves as on the whole "very satisfied" with their vehicles. And the Panther's failures were generally understood as a mixture of teething troubles, inexperienced crews and commanders, and the fortunes of war. German soldiers were better trained; German combined-arms offensive tactics coped effectively with one of military history's most sophisticated defensive systems against superior numerical odds. And at seventh and last, the Germans held the field when the fighting ceased.

Why then can Kursk still be considered decisive? Karl-Heinz Frieser, whose research has done much to strip away the veils of legend, stresses the symbolic value of stopping in its tracks the greatest armored attack the Wehrmacht ever mounted—on level terms, without the advantage of weather or soft spots. Whatever remained of the myth of

German invincibility—for both sides—faded into the sun and dust and blood of the Kursk salient.

Kursk, however, was more than a psychological experience. The Red Army not only held its ground; the distinguishing features of its developing excellence were the hallmarks of its success: density, redundancy, management, movement. The Soviets concentrated and massed their forces alike on defense and offense. They planned and deployed in integrated layers, on scales the Germans could not hope to match except locally and under special circumstances. Instead of trying to outdo its enemy in flexibility and initiative, the Red Army was learning to master control—arguably a better practical response to the increasing scale and pace of mobile warfare than the German "mission approach," whose emphasis on individual initiative easily led to cross purposes against a competent enemy. Finally Soviet formations from regiments to field armies were learning to move—not to maneuver tactically, German-style, but to get from place to place expeditiously and in order, arriving ready to fight. Rotmistrov's Guardsmen offer the best examples, but Citadel as a whole provides no significant examples of Red Army units victimized by quicker German reaction time. Rotmistrov's narrative of events may be part propaganda device, part personal gasconade. But it's not bragging when it's backed up. At Kursk the Red Army earned and paid for the right to tell its war stories to anyone willing to listen.

II

Das Deutsche Reich und der Zweite Weltkrieg trenchantly describes the twelve months from the end of Kursk to the Red Army's summer offensive of 1944 as "the forgotten year." That period featured continuous fighting from Leningrad to the Black Sea, on scales surpassing those of 1941–42 and with losses far larger, especially on the Soviet side. The story of the panzers becomes correspondingly difficult to reconstruct as the divisions bloodied at Kursk were scattered to bolster resistance in a dozen sectors.

The German retreat from Leningrad and the successful, albeit temporary, stabilization of the northern front in the Baltic states owed little yet much to the army's panzers. They were stretched too thin elsewhere to provide major assistance to the hard-pressed Landser. But the Red Army in the north was still learning its craft. Three Tigers by themselves played a vital role in holding a reestablished defense line around Narva, Estonia. A panzer division that arrived with only three dozen tanks was the spearhead of a counterattack that plugged a critical gap between two German armies. And the buccaneering assault gunners kept appearing where they were most needed, shifting from sector to sector and division to division to shore up infantrymen as outgunned as they were outnumbered. By October one battalion recorded a thousand official kills.

Part of the panzer gap was filled by the Waffen SS. By the end of 1942 the army had essentially decided the small units of foreigners it had managed to raise were more trouble than they were worth. Heinrich Himmler, always on the lookout to enhance the scope of his ramshackle empire within an empire, took them in. In early 1943 he activated III (Germanic) Panzer Corps, to include the Vikings and a new division eventually designated the 11th SS Volunteer Panzer Grenadier Division (Northland).

Had Hitler not intervened its honorific might have been "Varangian," a reference to the Scandinavian guard troops of the medieval Byzantine empire and a reflection of Himmler's desire to base the division on Aryan volunteers. In fact Northland absorbed most of the remaining foreign legions—including, for a while, a 50-man British detachment—and made up its strength with "ethnic Germans" from outside the expanded state and "Reich Germans" from territories annexed during the war. Northland saw its first action and made its first bones in the no-quarter partisan fighting in Yugoslavia. In November the division and III SS Panzer Corps were sent to the Leningrad sector. When it proved impossible to withdraw Viking from the fighting in the south, the corps was fleshed out by the ostensibly Dutch SS Volunteer Panzer-Grenadier Brigade Nederland. Despite having only a single tank battalion plus some assault guns, it played an important role in the successful defense of Narva over the winter of 1943–44.

The III SS Panzer Corps is best understood in the context of the far more numerous unmechanized Waffen SS formations also thrown into what Reich propagandists described as "the battle of the European SS." Some were Belgian, with Flemings and Walloons carefully separated. Others were local: Latvians, Lithuanians, and Estonians. Interpreted by postwar apologists as participants in a crusade against Bolshevism, they wore SS runes but saw themselves fighting against Russia and for their homelands.

In the war's final months the Waffen SS would incorporate Bosnian Muslims, Croats, Italians, Frenchmen, and plain criminals into grandiosely styled "brigades" and "divisions" whose only German elements, in the words of one contemptuous Landser, were a few German shepherd watchdogs. Another thing these ragtag formations had in common was that they only saw German tanks by accident. The Waffen SS, in short, was subdividing into an elite fighting core, according to many accounts disproportionately favored in personnel and equipment; and a fringe of increasingly desperate men who, as they felt the ropes tighten around their necks, took little account of their behavior to prisoners and civilians.

Army Group Center's post-Kursk circumstances were arguably even more perilous than those of Army Group North. When the general Russian offensives began in that sector, 3rd Panzer Army on the far left had not a single armored vehicle under command. Its neighbor, 4th Army, began the battle with 66 assault guns against almost 1,500 Soviet AFVs. The Germans nevertheless executed a fighting retreat into White Russia despite the Red Army's desperate efforts. Companies were commanded by sergeants; local reserves were nonexistent, and replacements were a forlorn hope. As early as September 8, one army commander reported the total combat strength of his infantry was fewer than 7,000 men. A month later Kluge contacted Hitler directly and pulled no punches informing him that no general could command without men, weapons, and reserves. The Russians had all three.

Things might have become far worse had the Red Army in this sector not regressed to tactics making the Somme and Passchendaele appear sophisticated by comparison. Massed infantry, massed armor, and massed artillery hammered at the same points time after time, until nothing and no one remained to send forward or the Germans gave way.

The German plight was compounded by a well-coordinated partisan uprising in their rear. The army group had been preoccupied with holding its front since 1942. Now it faced an exponentially increasing number of strikes against communications systems and railroads. Security forces responded with large-scale, near-random executions and, as the front receded, scorched earth—when anything remained to scorch. This was no mere torching of villages and looting of houses. It involved the systematic destruction of militarily useful installations. In total war that meant anything. What was not burned was blown up. Thousands of civilians were "evacuated," a euphemism for being driven west with what they could carry, with the alternative of risking execution as partisans or being shot at random. Files named "Protests" and "Refusals" are conspicuously absent from otherwise well-kept German records. What was important to senior officers was that the devastation be carried out in order and under command. German soldiers were not mere brigands.

The fight of Army Group Center was largely a foot soldier's affair—with the by-now usual and welcome support of the near-ubiquitous assault guns. At the beginning of October the army group's order of battle included a single panzer division itself reduced to battle group strength, and two panzer grenadier divisions in no better shape. Those figures remained typical. Yet ironically the panzers' major contribution to the retreat played a large role in setting the scene for future debacle in the sector.

It began in March 1944 when the Red Army enveloped the city of Gomel and its patchwork garrison of 4,000 men. Gomel was a regional road and rail hub, as much as such existed in White Russia. Hitler declared it a fortress; the High Command supplied it from the air and ordered its immediate relief.

Initial efforts were thwarted by soft ground and the spring thaw. But after 10 days a battle group of SS Viking fought its way into the city.

It required 18 hours and cost over 50 percent casualties. The lieutenant commanding received the Knight's Cross. The hundred-odd surviving panzer grenadiers were welcome. The half-dozen Panthers were vital in holding off Soviet armor while LXVI Panzer Corps put together a relief force from an already worn-down 4th Panzer Division and a battle group built around what remained of Viking's Panthers. The combination broke the siege on April 5, though it was two weeks before the link to the main front was fully reestablished.

The defense of Gomel solidified Hitler's conviction that he had found a force multiplier. Gomel was on a small scale. But if larger "fortresses" could be established and garrisoned, under orders to hold to the last, the Soviets would be drawn into siege operations that would dissipate their offensive strength while the panzers and the Luftwaffe assembled enough strength to relieve the position. Army Group Center considered the idea good enough to be the best available alternative. The operational consequences of shifting to this fixed-defense approach would be demonstrated within months.

The southern sector of the eastern front saw far more armored action than the other two in the months following Kursk. The Red Army's performance was also exponentially better. Most of the best Soviet tank generals had been sent to that theater to see off the Kursk offensive and to prepare for the series of strikes expected to—finally—destroy German fighting power in south Russia.

It began on July 17. First Panzer Army and the re-created 6th Army initially held positions along the Mius River. Manstein planned a counterstrike, using Das Reich and Leibstandarte to stun the Soviets on 1st Panzer Army's front, then shifting them to 6th Army's sector to join Totenkopf and 3rd Panzer in a larger concentric attack. When Hitler forbade it, Manstein borrowed the words of General von Seydlitz from two centuries earlier: His head was at the Führer's disposal, but while he held command he must be allowed to use it.

Eventually, reinforced by a total of five panzer and panzer grenadier divisions, 1st Panzer Army did mount a tactically successful counterattack. But Manstein still faced over two and a half million men, 50,000

guns, 2,400 tanks, almost 3,000 aircraft. Purists sometimes suggest
that Stavka should have used this overwhelming superiority to generate battles of encirclement, panzer style. But Stalin remembered all too
clearly how Manstein had thwarted a similar approach after Stalingrad.
At front and army command levels there also seems to have been a
near-visceral desire to smash an enemy that had so often embarrassed
them, and to do it with strength the Germans could not hope to match.
Even airborne forces were thrown into the operation.

Ninth Army, 4th Panzer Army, and Detachment Kempf, rechristened 8th Army but with the same resources, paid the bill. Model
secured Hitler's permission for a fighting retreat from the Orel salient
as part of the general withdrawal of Army Group Center. Fourth Panzer
Army was split into three parts by the Soviet onslaught, each fighting its own desperate battle. Useful reinforcements were few—the 8th
Panzer Division arrived with no tanks. A staff officer at Army High
Command confided—but only to his diary—that the end might come
before the new year. Manstein had to fight Hitler almost as fiercely as
the Russians to secure permission to do anything but "hold, hold, hold!"
Guderian cattily observed that Manstein was inappropriately tentative
in the Führer's presence. In fact Army Group South's commander not
only insisted that disaster awaited were he not allowed to fall back to
the line of the Dnieper River, but on September 14 he declared that he
would issue the orders the next day on his own responsibility. Hitler
conceded defeat.

The success of the retreat depended on the panzers. Materially
Manstein was playing a handful of threes. In contrast to Kursk, there
were few chances to recover and repair damaged tanks. Casualty evacuation was random. Units constantly on the move meant stragglers were
usually lost for good. It took two weeks to reach the Dnieper. By that
time Army Group South counted fewer than 300 serviceable tanks
and assault guns. The average infantry division's frontline strength was
around a thousand men. Its average front was twelve to thirteen miles.

Even Tigers felt the strain. In the course of the campaign, Army
Group South's single battalion of Panzer VIs was increased to four. But

their commanders complained the Tigers were victimized by their reputation: thrown in piecemeal, shuttled from sector to sector, denied time
to maintain the complex and sensitive vehicle. Too often they were used
as mobile pillboxes. Too often their infantry support was nonexistent or
ineffective.

The tankers ascribed that last to poor training and low morale. From
the infantry's perspective, it was often common sense. The Tiger was
essentially different from the familiar assault guns, whose low silhouettes and maneuverability enabled them to seek ambush positions and
use cover—almost like a Landser on treads. The Tigers were big. They
drew fire like magnets and attracted Soviet tanks like flies to manure.
Any smart rifleman—and slow thinkers had short life spans in the
autumn of 1943—was likely to avoid them rather than take the risk of
providing close-in protection.

As they fell back, the Germans scorched the earth. That is a polite
military euphemism for a swath of devastation covering hundreds of
square miles, sparing nothing and no one except by accident. "They are
burning the bread," Vatutin admonished his men. Few Soviet soldiers
did not know what hunger felt like. Small wonder the Russians succeeded in throwing bridgeheads across the river. Small wonder that the
Germans' best chance of holding was to destroy them before they could
metastasize. And small wonder that they failed.

On November 3 the 1st Ukrainian Front began crossing the Dnieper
in force around Kiev, on Manstein's northern flank. Fourth Panzer
Army's few remaining AFVs foundered in the Soviet tide. The 25th Panzer Division, sent to restore the situation, had spent most of its existence
in the peaceful surroundings of Norway. Botched transportation schedules temporarily made it a panzer division with no tracked vehicles at
all. Yet the division managed, somehow, to halt an entire tank army and
set the stage for another of Manstein's signature counterattacks.

This one would be made without Hoth, summarily dismissed by
Hitler for his failure to hold the river line. His replacement represented
no loss in ability. Erhard Raus had been tempered in the front lines
from Leningrad to Kursk. Tactical command of the counterattack was

in the arguably even more capable hands of Hermann Balck, now commanding XLVIII Panzer Corps. Even the weather obliged, freezing the mud to stability by the time Balck went in.

Hitler had rejected Manstein and Guderian's proposals to concentrate every tank in the southern sector for a short, massive blow. Forty-Eighth Panzer Corps counted only 200 tanks and assault guns, but they were manned by some of the Wehrmacht's best, divisions like 1st Panzer, 7th Panzer, and Leibstandarte. For three weeks they ran rings around the baffled Rotarmisten. Balck's corps was on the point of executing a 1941-style encirclement when a captured map showed the intended pocket contained no fewer than seven Soviet corps. Even for the intrepid Balck, that was a bit much. And despite virtuoso German performances from corps headquarters to tank crews, the Soviet bridgehead was still intact.

Further south, 1st Panzer Army and Army Group A, whose sector had been relatively quiet since the withdrawal from the Caucasus, came under increasing pressure in mid-August. Initially it was possible to plug gaps and secure flanks by using available AFVs as emergency relief. But when an eagerly awaited panzer division turned out to consist of seven tanks and an under strength panzer grenadier regiment, operational reality had an unpleasant way of unmistakably asserting itself. The situation was worsened in 1st Panzer Army's sector, where Hitler had ordered an already dangerously deep salient where the Dnieper bent west at Zaporozhye to be expanded to a bridgehead—not for military reasons but to protect a dam producing electricity described as vital for the industry of occupied Ukraine, a dam that was also widely understood to symbolize Soviet achievement.

The extended deployment required to sustain this propaganda illusion drove Manstein to near-wordless fury. It took only four days for the Red Army to overrun the bridgehead in mid-October. The resources it had absorbed were unavailable to resist a far larger attack against 6th Army on 1st Panzer's right: over a half-million men and 800 tanks against a fifth of the number of armored vehicles, in wide-open country. By the beginning of November the Crimea was isolated and Army Group A cut in half.

The Russians were learning how to keep moving tactically and operationally, and figuring out how to coordinate their movements on a theater level. On October 15 another sledgehammer shattered 1st Panzer Army's left wing, and in 10 days covered the 100 miles to Krivoi Rog. On October 24 a second front-level offensive broke out of another Dnieper bridgehead a few miles south of the first. Mackensen, anything but an alarmist, reported the gap could not be closed, that his exhausted men had no more left in them. Hitler responded by giving Manstein control of 1st Panzer Army and a temporary free hand.

This time Manstein planned a movement. A panzer corps headquarters rotated from his army group through 1st Panzer Army's rear zone into position on its left flank. It took command of Totenkopf, of 24th Panzer Division, in Italy since its reformation after Stalingrad, and of 14th Panzer Division, another Stalingrad revival currently shaking down in France. On August 28 this hastily assembled force drove southeast, into the Soviet rear toward Krivoi Rog. Mackensen's LVII Panzer Corps attacked in the opposite direction two days later. Both operations took the Russians by surprise and succeeded in linking up to cut off the Soviet spearheads and restabilize the sector.

It was another neat local victory, and Mackensen's last fight in Russia. On November 4 he was transferred to Italy, replaced by a no less capable man. Hans Hube had lost an arm in World War I, led a panzer corps with sufficient distinction to be flown out of Stalingrad, and done well against the British and Americans in Sicily. He had a reputation for willpower and energy. He would need both in the face of still another coordinated Soviet offensive in what again seemed overwhelming force.

The Soviet Union had paid for its successes against Army Group South with over 1.5 million casualties, a quarter of them dead or missing. The German front still held—barely—but its defenders were so tired and apathetic that in the words of one report, they no longer cared whether they were shot by the Russians or their own officers. And this was the elite Grossdeutschland Division, which enjoyed its own personal battalion of Tigers.

On December 24 the Red Army struck again: four fronts, 2.25 million men, 2,600 tanks. Fourth Panzer Army was again hammered into fragments, each making its own way west as best it could. Manstein almost by reflex saw the best response as shortening the front and concentrating his armor for a counterattack, as he had done after Stalingrad. When Hitler refused, Manstein, on his own responsibility, pulled 1st Panzer Army out of the line and redeployed it on 4th Panzer's right. Hube had his own III Panzer Corps, XLVI Panzer Corps transferred in haste from France, and a provisional heavy tank regiment with a battalion each of Tigers and Panthers, plus some attached infantry and armored artillery. His counterattack cost the Russians a few tens of thousands of men and around 700 tanks. It was a victory—but only in the most limited tactical sense.

The experiences of Mackensen and Hube showed clearly that even in reasonable strength the panzers could do no more than restore local situations. Both counterattacks, moreover, had depended for half their striking power on divisions transferred from the west. How long would it be before Allied initiatives made that impossible?

Any doubts that the balance in armored war had definitively shifted should have been dispelled by the Battle of the Cherkassy Pocket. The Germans still held a 100-mile stretch of the Dnieper north of that city. Hitler projected its use as a springboard for a proposed spring offensive and forbade withdrawal. On January 24, two Soviet fronts hit the sector with a third of a million men, artillery, tanks, and aircraft in proportion. Inside of a week a half dozen divisions, including what was left of Viking, were cut off in the city of Korsun: around 60,000 men. Their armor support totaled two dozen tanks and half as many assault guns.

Hitler, remembering Demyansk, ordered the pocket to hold and promised supply from the air. Those melodies were too familiar. Manstein, well aware of the morale-sapping fear throughout his army group that the pocket would become another Stalingrad, planned a major relief operation using no fewer than nine panzer divisions. Initially every one of the divisions he proposed to use was already engaged elsewhere in Russia, and one was literally stuck fast trying to move through early spring mud. The four divisions finally assembled under 8th Army's XLVII Panzer Corps had a combined total of 3,800 men in their eight panzer grenadier regiments. Their progress was predictably limited.

That left it up to Hube. His strike force for the unusually domestically named Operation Wanda—III Panzer Corps—included 1st, 16th, and 17th Panzer Divisions, Leibstandarte, and the heavy regiment. But the Panzer IV's Tigers and Panthers bogged tread-deep in mud the wide-tracked T-34s traversed with relative ease. Fuel consumption spiraled; breakdowns multiplied; supply vehicles were immobilized. By February 15 it was clear that the pocket could not be relieved. Instead Manstein ordered a breakout in the direction of the mired III Panzer Corps, code word "Freedom."

Orders were to leave anyone unable to march. For one of the few times in Wehrmacht history, something like a mutiny took place. Wounded who could be moved were loaded onto every available vehicle. With its seven tanks and three assault guns, Viking took the point and carried the retreat through the first Russian defenses. But III Panzer Corps was unable to fight its way to the designated meeting point and unable to contact the pocket by radio. Command and control were eroding even before the Germans entered a Russian combined-arms killing zone around dawn on February 16. For over four hours Russian tanks and cavalrymen chased fugitives through the ravines and across open ground. This was one of the few verifiable occasions where T-34s systematically ran over fleeing men. And the killing was likely both payback and pleasure.

Around 36,000 men, including 7,500 wounded, eventually reached III Panzer Corps's lines. Eighty-three hundred of them belonged to Viking and the Walloon SS brigade attached to it. Total casualties in the pocket amounted to around 20,000: no bagatelle, but a long way from Stalingrad. First Panzer Army's loss of over 150 AFVs reflected its inability to move immobilized tanks and repair breakdowns, rather than any sudden forward leap in the effectiveness of Soviet armor. Nevertheless, though Goebbels's propaganda machine described a great victory, the battle for the Cherkassy Pocket highlighted the continuing decline of Hitler's panzers from a strategic and operational force to a tactical instrument.

To maintain and restore even temporarily Army Group South's sector of the Eastern Front in the months after Kursk had required the commitment of most of the army's combat-ready armor. That commitment, moreover, was increasingly ad hoc. A "panzer division" in the German order of battle was increasingly likely to be on the ground with as many tanks as could be made operational combined in a single battalion; the mechanized panzer grenadier battalion and the reconnaissance battalion, both brought to something like table of organization strength by transfers from the remaining panzer grenadiers; the half-tracked pioneer company; and a few self-propelled guns. These remnants were repeatedly thrown in against odds of ten to one or higher without time to absorb replacements and work in new officers. They might bear famous names and numbers. They were not what they once were. But then the same could be said about an entire Reich approaching the point of unraveling.

The tipping point on the Eastern Front was even more clearly indicated in March 1944. The Korsun-Cherkassy breakout enraged Stalin, but was not even a speed bump to the continuing Russian offensive. Zukhov had taken over, and his hands drove the spearheads that tore 50-mile gaps in the front, left 1st Panzer Army facing in the wrong direction, and created within days a pocket containing over 200,000 men, fighting soldiers, their rear echelons, and the detritus of an occupation. Twenty-two divisions were represented. One had only 600 men and not a single antitank gun, and that was all too typical. The isolated Germans counted 50 assault guns and 43 tanks, some of them unable to move for lack of fuel.

One veteran spoke of "clean undershirt time," when one looked for anything white enough to make a surrender flag. Hitler insisted on "holding what there is to hold." Manstein informed Hitler that he intended to order a breakout on his own responsibility. Hitler temporized to show who was in charge, then agreed.

Manstein's plan was by now almost conventional: reinforcements from France, this time the refreshed II SS Panzer Corps, to attack from the outside; 1st Panzer Army to drive west toward the SS spearheads. Radio interceptions—midlevel Red Army communications security had not progressed too far since 1914—helped Manstein time the breakout.

Hube brought another idea to the table. His experience at Stalingrad and Cherkassy had convinced him of the risks involved in depending on a relief force. If one appeared and made contact, all was well and good. If necessary, however, Hube was prepared to fight his own way through in a "traveling pocket."

Hube's plan and its execution are still studied in war colleges. He had four corps headquarters, three of them panzer. He had elements of 10 panzer divisions—all the command elements he needed. The problem was how best to organize the operation. Given overall Russian superiority in the sector, conventional wisdom suggested a strong armored spearhead. The problem was that the tankers might move ahead too fast and too far, leaving the rest of the army to fend for itself—a polite euphemism for being overrun and destroyed. Instead Hube did the opposite. He organized the breakout in two parallel columns. Each had a vanguard of infantry supported by assault guns. The panzers formed the rear guard, in a position to move forward and support the advance forces when necessary.

Hube commanded the breakout in person. He had kept his men active in the days of preparation, sublimating feelings of despair and panic. Straggling and desertion were minimal. Zukhov's threat to shoot every third prisoner if the pocket did not capitulate by April 2 was not generally known, but would have surprised few. That the Soviet marshal later restricted proposed victims to senior officers was limited comfort to anyone aware of the concession.

Hube originally wanted to break out to the south and head for Romania. Manstein insisted on a western direction despite the longer distance and the numerous river crossings it entailed. He had the senior rank and the final word. On March 27, 1st Panzer Army started west. It had the advantages of surprise; sluggish enemy reaction enabled the rear guard to close up to the main columns relatively unmolested. Hube kept his men closed up and moving. Improvised airstrips enabled the Luftwaffe to bring in fuel and ammunition and evacuate wounded—a major continuing boost to morale and a tribute to "Aunt Ju," the Ju-52 transports that could land and take off from ground that was unusable by even the American Dakotas. On April 6, 1st Panzer's spearheads made contact with elements of II SS Panzer Corps. A few days later its divisions were in action on a new defense line that held this time. Hube, awarded the Knight's Cross with Diamonds, was killed in an air crash on his way to receive it.

His death was at once irony and paradigm. Hans Hube had conducted an epic, indeed heroic operation—but in the wrong direction. First Panzer Army brought out its tanks and its wounded at a cost of 6,000 dead and missing. Its anabasis bought time, but to what purpose? "For slow exhaustion and grim retreat/For a wasted hope and a sure defeat." The words of an American captured on Bataan in 1942 might well serve as an epigram—or an epitaph—for the saga of Army Group South in the endgame months of the Russo-German War.

III

ALBERT SPEER'S APPOINTMENT as Minister of Armaments in February 1942 brought no immediate, revolutionary change to Germany's war industry. But Speer had Hitler's confidence, as much as anyone could ever possess it. He was an optimist at a time when that was a declining quality at high Reich levels. He concentrated on short-term fixes: rationalizing administration, improving use of material, addressing immediate crises. And he faced a major one in tank production.

In September 1942 Hitler called for the manufacture of 800 tanks, 600 assault guns, and 600 self-propelled guns a month by the spring of 1944. In April 1944 the army's panzer divisions had fewer than 1,700 of their total authorized strength of 4,600 main battle tanks: Panthers and Panzer IVs. That gap could not be bridged by admonitions to take better care of equipment and report losses more accurately. The long obsolete Panzer II was upgraded into a state-of-the-art tracked reconnaissance vehicle. But a glamorous renaming as Luchs, or Lynx, could not camouflage an operational value so limited that production was canceled after the first hundred. Other resources were also diverted to the development of a family of tracked and half-tracked logistics vehicles and increased

numbers of armored recovery vehicles, both in their own ways necessary under Russian conditions. The growing effectiveness of the Soviet
air force led to the conversion or rebuilding of an increasing number of
chassis into antiaircraft tanks with small-caliber armaments. The continued manufacture of early designs—again necessary to maintain even
limited frontline strength—further impeded production. Between May
and December 1942, tank production actually declined despite constant
encouragement and repeated threats from the Reich's highest quarters.

One positive result of the slowdown was the ability to address the
Panther's shortcomings. The original Model D received improved track
and wheel systems. Das Reich received a battalion of them in August,
23rd Panzer Division in October, and 16th Panzer in December. All
played crucial roles in Army Group South's fight for survival. The D's
successor, the Model A, had a new turret with quicker rotation time
and a commander's cupola. Both were important in the target-rich but
high-risk environment of the Eastern Front. Engine reliability remained
a problem, in part because of quality control difficulties in the homeland,
and in part defined by the tank's low power-to-weight ratio. Improvements to the transmission and gear systems nevertheless reduced the
number of engine breakdowns. Modifications to the cooling system cut
back on the number of engine fires.

Soft ground, deep mud, and heavy snow continued to put a premium
on driving skill. One Panther battalion reported having to blow up 28
tanks it was unable to evacuate. Fifty-six more were in various stages
of repair. Eleven remained operational. But during the same period
Leibstandarte's Panther battalion reported only seven combat losses—
all from hits to the sides and rear. Of the 54 mechanical breakdowns,
almost half could be ready within a week. On the whole the improved
Panther was regarded as excellent: consistently able to hit, survive hits,
and bring its crews back.

Toward the end of 1943 the High Command began rotating battalions officially equipped with Panzer IIIs—the old workhorse was still
pulling its load—back to Germany for retraining on Panther Model As.
The reorganized battalions were impressive on paper: 4 companies each
of 22 or 17 tanks, plus 8 more in battalion headquarters. First Panzer

Division welcomed its new vehicles in November. Others followed, army and SS, the order depending on which division could best spare a battalion cadre. By the end of January 1944 about 900 Panther As had reached the Russian front, in complete battalions or as individual replacements.

As good as they were, the Panthers were a drop in the bucket compared to the mass of Soviet armor facing them. As compensation the High Command began considering a Panther II. Beginning as an up-armored Model D, during 1943 the concept metamorphosed—or better said, metastasized—into a lighter version of the Tiger. Weighing in at over 50 tons, it was originally scheduled to enter service in September 1943, but was put on permanent hold in favor of its less impressive, more reliable forebear.

The same might have been better applied to another armored mammoth. The Panzer VIB, the "King Tiger" or "Royal Tiger," could trace its conceptual roots all the way to the spring of 1941. Prototypes emerged in 1943; the first production models appeared in January 1944. The VIB was best distinguished by a redesigned turret with a rounded front and a cupola for the commander. Its second characteristic feature was an 88mm L/71 gun (that translates as 19 feet long!) that could take out any allied tank at extreme ranges. Its frontal armor, more than seven inches in places, was never confirmed as having been penetrated by any tank or antitank gun. Its Maybach 700 horsepower engine gave it a reasonable road speed of 24 miles per hour. But if the King was dipped in the River Styx for strength, it was also left with an Achilles heel. Its weight was immobilizing. Only major road bridges could support it. The tonnage increased fuel consumption when fuel supplies were a growing problem, and also overstrained the drive system to a point where breakdowns were the norm.

The point was initially moot, since only five VIBs were in service by March 1944. But the situation was replicated in other end-of-the-war designs. The Jagdtiger was a tank destroyer version of the VIB carrying a 128mm gun—not only the heaviest weapon mounted on a German AFV, but an excellent design in its own right. At over 70 tons, however, and with only 20 degrees traverse for its main armament, the vehicle was only dangerous to anything unfortunate enough to pass directly in front of it.

The Panther's tank destroyer spin-off was far more promising. Indeed the Jagdpanther is widely and legitimately considered the best vehicle of its kind during World War II. An 88mm L/71 gun, well-sloped armor, and solid cross-country capacity on a 45-ton chassis made the Jagdpanther a dominant chess piece wherever it appeared. Predictably, preproduction difficulties and declining production capacity kept its numbers limited.

For all the print devoted to the Panthers, the Tigers, and their variants, the backbone of the armored force through 1945 remained the Panzer IV. Its final versions had little enough in common with the "cigar butts" of 1940. The Model H officially became the main production version in March 1942. Its armor protection included side panels and grew to a maximum of 3.2 inches in front, at the price of increased weight (25 tons) that cut the road speed to a bit over 20 miles per hour. A later J version incorporated such minor modifications as wider tracks and wire-mesh side skirts just as effective as armor plate in deflecting infantry-fired antitank rockets.

Guderian in particular considered the new version of a well-tried system a practical response to the chronic frontline shortfalls in tank strength in the East. The Panzer IV was relatively easy to maintain —and relatively easy to evacuate when damaged. Over 3,000 of them would be produced in 1943, and standard equipment of the army panzer divisions was set at a battalion each of Panthers and Panzer IVs.

Guderian's opposition to the assault gun had eroded with experience. Not only was its frontline utility indisputable, it could be manufactured faster and in larger numbers by less experienced enterprises than the more complex turreted tanks. Guderian correspondingly advocated restoring the panzer regiments' third battalions and giving them assault guns as a working compromise.

The vehicles he intended were significantly different from the original assault guns and their underlying concept. The mission of supporting infantry attacks had become secondary at best. What was now vital was holding off Soviet armor. The self-propelled Marders, with their light armor and open tops, were well into the zone of dangerous obsolescence. In 1943 the Weapons Office ordered the development of a smaller vehicle mounting a scaled-down 75mm gun on the chassis of the old reliable 38(t). The 16-ton Hetzer (Baiter) was useful and economical, and continues to delight armor buffs and modelers. It was, however, intended for the infantry's antitank battalions, and did not appear in combat until 1944—one more example of diffused effort that characterized the Reich's war effort.

On the other hand, the Sturmgeschütz IIIG, with its 75mm L/48 gun, seemed highly suited to tank destruction and was readily available—until Allied bombing intervened. The factory manufacturing the bulk of IIIGs was heavily damaged in late 1943. To compensate, Hitler ordered the available hulls to be fitted to Panzer IV chassis. The result proved practical enough to encourage the production of over 1700 Jagdpanzer IVs by November 1944, despite Guderian's protest at the corresponding fallout of turreted tanks. The new name of "tank destroyer" suited the vehicles' new purpose, though their predecessors continued in service under the original title, creating confusion during and after the war that remains exacerbated by the vehicles' close resemblance.

The Jagdpanzer IVs were intended for the panzer divisions and the assault gun battalions, whose number grew to over three dozen during 1943. A slightly heavier version with a 75mm L/70 gun like the Panther's and the unflattering nickname of "Guderian's Duck" began entering service in August 1944. It proved first-rate against armor in Russia and the West; almost a thousand were produced during the war. The "Duck's" long gun made it uncomfortably nose-heavy (the source of its sobriquet), but by then that was among the least of the panzers' problems.

Apart from a few emergency variations churned out in the war's final months, the technical lineup of Hitler's panzers was complete. As a footnote the design staffs, after years of work, finally developed the war's best armored car. The SdKfz 234/2 Puma had it all: high speed, a low silhouette, and a 50mm L39 still effective against tanks in an emergency.

Unfortunately, by the time the Puma and its variants entered production, the panzers' need for a long-range reconnaissance vehicle was itself long past. Now their enemies all too often found them.

IV

FOR THE FIRST half of 1944, German strategic and operational attention remained focused on Russia—specifically on a southern sector whose vulnerability had been repeatedly tested and too often confirmed. Guderian spoke for the panzers in a report of March 27, 1944. He bluntly informed Hitler that the war in the east could never be won by static defense. Whenever the panzers' mobility was disregarded, whenever they were engaged piecemeal, catastrophe followed. The situation demanded the formation of a strong operational reserve to be used in a mobile defense, Manstein-style.

Hitler dismissed Guderian's urging as nonsense. He described it as criminal to give up anything bought with German blood without another bloody fight to hold it. To make his point, on March 30 the Führer removed Kleist from command of Army Group A and dismissed Manstein as well. The time for operations, he declared, was over. Now was the time for stubborn defense. Any doubt of how that should be defined was also removed when Hitler appointed Ferdinand Schörner commander of the renamed Army Group South Ukraine. Schörner during the war had devolved from an unimaginative field leader to a less imaginative thug with a penchant for ordering drumhead executions.

Manstein's rechristened Army Group North Ukraine went to Model. His perceived status as "Hitler's favorite general," combined with an abrasive personality and a no-excuses approach to command, have combined to reduce his stature as a capable general. He also had some of the best of the new generation of panzer officers: Raus at 4th Panzer Army, Josef Harpe succeeding Hube at 1st, and Breith and Balck commanding corps. Even before Model's arrival, these men were coming to a consensus, based on their post-Barbarossa, post-Stalingrad experiences, that the army could no longer execute sweeping maneuvers in the

Manstein style. The discrepancy in armored forces was too overwhelming. Tactical success was all even the best-executed counterstrokes could achieve, and even those were questionable except under strongly favorable conditions.

Manstein's approach had another weakness. It reduced the infantry to little more than pawns. Soviet attacks were based on mass and planning. Artillery broke down the defenses; infantry overwhelmed them; tanks drove into the rear zones. Failure at any stage meant repeating the sequence; as many as 30 consecutive attacks in the same local sector had been verified. The increasingly frequent result was the overrunning and dislocation of the defending German infantry divisions. That in turn meant the sacrifice of their antitank capacity. Two-thirds of the infantry division's guns were towed 75mm pieces too heavy to move in a hurry. The remainder were thinly armored, open-topped mounts vulnerable to almost any heavy weapon.

Infantry without antitank guns were like oysters without shells. Personal weapons, an upscale copy of the US bazooka and the fire-and-forget Panzerfaust rocket, were coming into service and would prove highly effective. Their short ranges, however, made them almost suicidal to use in open country or against tanks massed on Soviet scales. The best the foot soldiers could do was get as far out of the way as possible. And by the time the panzer reserves intervened, they found themselves fighting off the back foot, reacting to superior force as best they could.

As Raus dryly noted, the Soviet system was foolproof as long as the Germans did not interfere. Instead Army Group South's command team favored a "battle-zone defense" that could be as much as 25 miles deep. The infantry manning the front lines would fall back to prepared positions a mile or so in the rear just before the Soviet hammer fell. The artillery would simultaneously switch to prepared alternate firing positions. Extensive minefields covered by antitank guns would channel the Red Army onto killing grounds. Panzer battle groups reinforced by antitank and assault guns would be available for immediate intervention to choke off local breakthroughs and mount local counterattacks, enmeshing the Soviets in a modern version of the Roman arena's retiarius-secutor gladiatorial combats.

What Model and his principal subordinates had in mind was a long way from Hitler's primitive concept of defense. Both nevertheless dated to the Great War. The Führer had been imprinted by his experiences in 1914–15, under a doctrine that stressed holding and retaking ground at all costs. By 1917 a more flexible approach had developed, much along the lines of thinking in Army Group South, with armor added to the counterattack punch. It would require excellent communications and careful timing. But a combined-arms zone defense in earlier versions had worked for Model at Rzhev and against him at Kursk. At least it gave the Landser a fighting chance. On the other side of the war zone, Erwin Rommel was simultaneously advocating a similar approach based on similar reasoning to resisting Allied landings whose success would also depend heavily on mass and firepower.

Panzer purists in East and West objected vehemently. Balck in particular held his ground so stubbornly that Model unusually gave up the argument and resolved the issue by transferring all of Balck's panzer divisions to other commands. The deeper significance of the issue, however, lies in the armored force's growing institutional acceptance of a strategic, operational, and tactical environment mandating a fundamentally defensive focus.

Armies are not infinitely, or even significantly, malleable institutions. They tend to finish much as they began; learning curves seldom imply paradigm shifts. The German army of World War II was unusually successful in reconfiguring itself in the middle of a conflict. Nevertheless, seen from a bit of distance and with a bit of irony, the zone defense concept amounted to the inversion of the approach that the panzers had so effectively employed in 1940, though restoring the all-arms cooperation significantly disrupted by the exigencies of the last 18 months in Russia.

The new order's prospects in the East were, however, limited in view of the storm brewing on the Russian side of the battle line. For mid-1944 Stavka planned a series of mutually reinforcing strategic offensives along several axes. The initial operation proposed for 1944 was a drive into Romania: a follow-up of the winter's successes in the Ukraine intended militarily to open the way to the Balkans, politically to force Romania out of the war, and economically to deprive Germany of Romanian oil. Simultaneously, pressure in the Leningrad sector and Byelorussia would be renewed, eroding German resources and pinning their forces in place. The offensives on the flanks would be followed by Operation Bagration: a massive blow against Army Group Center with the intention of annihilating the forces in that sector and compelling the Germans in the north and south to retreat or risk envelopment. If success reinforced success, as Stavka expected, the entire German front might well dissolve, opening the way to Berlin and Western Europe before the British and Americans did more than gain a foothold on the continent.

This was the broad-front Grand Design Stalin had sought from the beginning. The program was ambitious, but the Red Army of 1944 had the material strength to implement, and the operational sophistication to plan, the largest, most geographically extensive, coordinated strategic offensive in the history of war. Technically, its armored forces in particular had also moved to an advanced stage.

In 1942 and early 1943 the Red Army's crucial problem had been maintaining inventory. Design innovation had been suspended. Production increases combined with the advent of the Panthers and Tigers to encourage new developments. In April 1944 the T-34/85, armed with an 85mm gun in a three-man turret, began entering service. Arguably a cut below the Panther technically, the T-34/85 was a battlefield match for both the big German cats—and it could be manufactured in far larger numbers. The KV was replaced on Soviet assembly lines by the JS, named for Josef Stalin. Its definitive World War II version, the JS II was armed with a 122mm gun: the largest caliber used in any numbers by any army. Its low velocity compared to the Panther and Tiger was balanced by the 55-pound weight of its shell: enough to crack open any armor at battle ranges. At 46 tons, its 600 horsepower engine gave the JS a road speed of around 23 miles per hour, and its well-sloped turret armor conferred solid protection from glancing hits. It took the field at the same time as the T-34/85, and was an even less pleasant surprise to German tank crews and panzer commanders.

A new generation of assault guns emerged as well, including one of the war's signature AFVs. In early 1943 the roomy hulls of obsolescent KV tanks had been used to mount a 152mm howitzer adapted from an artillery piece. Any shortcomings in range and muzzle velocity were balanced by a shell weighing almost 100 pounds. First used at Kursk, the SU 152s were promptly nicknamed *zvierboi*, "animal hunters," and supported every Soviet offensive in 1943 before being supplanted by the JS 152 and its variant JS 122, mounting the tank's 122mm gun in a fixed hull mount.

In contrast to the Panthers and Tigers, optimized for armored combat, the new Soviet AFVs were designed for breakthrough and exploitation. Compared to their German counterparts, their guns had better high-explosive capacity, enhancing their use against unarmored targets. Their range was longer; their reliability greater. Generally, for the rest of the war the JS heavies, organized by battalions, were the backbone of break-ins and breakthroughs. The T34s, both 76s and 85s, were deployed by brigades in the tank and mechanized corps for the breakout and exploitation stages.

The Red Army's summer offensive began when 4th Ukrainian Front isolated the Crimean peninsula in April and overran the garrison a month later. But 2nd and 3rd Ukrainian Fronts were not merely checked but defeated in their efforts to break through into Romania in April and May. The Soviets threw several bridgeheads across the Dniester but were unable to develop them. Initial Soviet casualties were heavy. The spring thaw slowed their tanks as impartially as it had German ones in other wet seasons. The Germans again scorched the earth partly in preparing their defenses, partly under orders, and partly from choice, leaving a swath of devastation that impeded already overextended lines of communication. The Red Army nevertheless did not bog down. It was checked by a defensive system that succeeded in neutralizing a discrepancy in men, tanks, guns, and aircraft that was about two-to-one across the board.

Again the panzers played a key role. Three divisions with different provenances: Totenkopf, Grossdeutschland, and 24th Panzer—which still preserved its horse-cavalry panache—illustrated time and again

Raus's metaphor of the fencer who interrupts his opponent's sequence of moves just when he exposes himself to strike. The 2nd Ukrainian Front described German defensive belts supported by small armored forces operating from ambush, slowing and stopping advances thrown into confusion by their sudden appearance. Recurrent phrases like "poor target identification" and "unobserved artillery fire" suggest that Soviet troops were still on the down side of critical learning curves involving situational awareness and situational response at tactical levels.

The conclusion reached by Hitler and the High Command that the summer's main assault would be in the Ukraine has been widely criticized and frequently described as a result of Soviet *maskirovka* or "deception"; a failure of German intelligence and reconnaissance; a willful overlooking of the geographic vulnerability of Army Group Center's sector. The frequently overlooked late-spring offensive discussed above also contributed to German decision making. The Russians had been hammering at the Ukraine for 10 months and had gained enough to make following up on successes a solid option. The Germans understood very well the political and economic consequences of further losses in that region. They were aware as well that increasing sectors of the front were in the hands of Romanian and Hungarian troops whose morale was even shakier and whose fighting power was even less than in the weeks before Stalingrad.

Despite a year's worth of evidence both that the USSR possessed the resources to mount simultaneous large-scale offensives and that Stavka did not share the German concept of a Schwerpunkt, High Command planners projected the consequences of a Soviet breakthrough in the south in militarily ethnocentric terms. They forecast either a full-strength drive into Romania and the Balkans or a replay of the panzers' 1940 left hook, aimed toward the Baltic. Should the latter be the case, Army Group Center had done well and fought well the previous year. Its longtime commander, Gunther von Kluge, had been hospitalized by a traffic accident. But his replacement, Ernst Busch, had a reputation as a steady if unspectacular tactician with a good record in defensive operations of the kind he was expected to face.

That logic indicated the mobile divisions' deployment. As of May

31, Army Group South Ukraine had Grossdeutschland, seven panzer, and one panzer grenadier divisions. Army Group North Ukraine counted seven panzer and two panzer grenadier divisions, plus no fewer than four full-strength battalions of Tigers. Army Group North, an armored-force stepchild since 1941, possessed one panzer and one panzer grenadier division and a Tiger battalion. Army Group Center had two panzer divisions, a panzer grenadier division, and a lone battalion of Tigers.

Those ratios remained essentially unchanged over the next month. For the first time in its brief history, the Eastern Front was becoming something of a stepchild. Its strategic reserve lay 1,500 miles away, preparing to throw the Allies into the English Channel as invasion loomed in the long-neglected West. Its operational reserve did not exist—not least because too many of the East's mobile divisions were in no condition to be redeployed casually from sector to sector. Neither replacements nor reinforcements were prominent in their pipelines. As late as May, only five panzer divisions had a Panther battalion. Third Panzer Division listed 12 operational Panzer IVs; 12th Panzer only three. This was thin protection against a looming storm.

The run-up to Operation Bagration also offers an opportunity to address a subject that almost disappears from view after 1941: panzers and partisans. In the proliferating body of literature analyzing German anti-partisan operations in the context of a war of extermination implemented by ordinary soldiers against ordinary victims, panzer units are conspicuous by a marginal presence. That reflects three facts. Neither the Reich nor the Wehrmacht was interested in winning hearts and minds. Once the Eastern front stabilized in 1942, the limited strength of German rear security forces relative to the burgeoning partisan movement encouraged near-random violence as a deterrent. And when additional force was needed to ratchet up the terror, infantry divisions were more likely to be deployed than panzers always in demand at the front and ill-equipped for fighting in swamps and forests.

Those points made, there is no evidence that when panzer formations were employed behind the lines in Russia, they systematically behaved any differently from any other units. In March 1944, Army

Group Center's 9th Army established camps in its rear zone. They were meant to contain all civilians unable to work—whether due to age, gender, or sickness—to keep them from aiding the partisans. The victims, as many as 50,000, were confined in barbed-wire enclosures without shelter, clean water, or sanitary facilities. A few loaves of bread thrown over a fence caused panic and riots. Fires were forbidden at night though the ground froze hard. After a week, hunger, cold, and disease had turned the swamp into a cemetery. As many as 13,000 Russians died.

The units involved in this roundup included 5th and 20th Panzer Divisions—as normal a pair of formations as the Wehrmacht offered. Twentieth Panzer did distinguish itself by bringing in 7,000 more civilians than the trains could accommodate. Otherwise it was a routine exercise. There was nothing spectacular: no mass shootings, no more than occasional brutality—just indifference; just another day's work on the Russian Front.

V

OPERATION BAGRATION BEGAN on June 22, 1944—three years to the day after the German invasion. The Red Army struck in the initial phase alone with 1.25 million men, more than 4,000 tanks and assault guns, more than 23,000 guns, mortars, and Katyushas, and almost 6,500 aircraft. Army Group Center simply disappeared so completely that it required years and decades to begin piecing together a coherent narrative of events in the first hours and days.

With only a single panzer division immediately available, any notion of a zone defense was illusory. The three panzer divisions transferred in were committed by battalions to stabilize critical situations, if only for a few hours. The army group's assault guns desperately shifted from sector to sector, fighting by batteries and single vehicles to cover retreats and open escape corridors. Model relieved Busch on June 28. The best he could propose was to construct a new front around Minsk, stabilizing it with new divisions from Germany. But Hitler continued to insist on holding ground, hanging on to "strong points" existing in little more than name, and counterattacking at every opportunity. Some units tried to obey; others dismissed the directives as Soviet deception. At least one division commander committed suicide.

On June 30, Zeitzler, turning at the last like a stepped-on worm, refused to take responsibility for Hitler's order to hold on in the Baltic despite what was happening to Army Group Center. By his own account at least, Zeitzler concluded by insisting the war was militarily lost and it was time to make an end. In the aftermath of the confrontation he collapsed. Whether from a heart attack or a nervous breakdown, the result was the same: an exacerbation of order-counterorder-disorder. Both the Führer and the High Command believed the "real" Soviet offensive in the Ukraine was yet to come. The fighting in Normandy was absorbing more and more of the Western theater's mobile forces. Army Group Center was on its own.

Minsk went under on July 3 as the 5th Panzer Division and a Tiger battalion sought vainly to keep open the way west. By July 8, 5th Panzer was down to 18 operational tanks. Vilna's garrison was authorized to break out only when Adolf Heusinger, who had temporarily replaced Zeitzler, urged Hitler to allow the surrounded men to choose how they wished to die. For two and a half years 3rd Panzer Army had been an armored army virtually without tanks. Now Reinhardt, last of the original panzer chieftains, remembered he had led a division before he became a colonel general. Taking command of elements of 6th Panzer Division, just arrived from reconstitution in Germany, he rode with the leading tanks, cut a 20-mile corridor through the Red Army to Vitebsk and brought out 3,000 survivors.

It was another fine piece of panzer soldiering—in a minor key. The Red Army did even better armored work on a decisive scale. On July 18, 1st Byelorussian Front drove two spearheads deep into Army Group Center's southern sector, trapped most of 2nd Army, and headed for the Vistula. Driving into a near-vacuum, the Front's vanguards reached the river on July 25; the first permanent bridgehead was established four days later.

If the frontline emergency was not enough, Heusinger was among those injured in the unsuccessful July 20 attempt on Hitler's life. His successor as Chief of Staff (officially Acting Chief) was Heinz Guderian. He seems to have been at least aware of the assassination plot, and probably indirectly approved. Certainly Guderian authorized temporarily delaying the movement from Berlin to the Eastern Front of some armored units the conspirators intended to use to take control of the capital after Hitler's death. On July 20 he took pains to be absolutely elsewhere: hunting by himself on his new estate in East Prussia. Though Guderian was able to sidestep the suspicion that fell on him, there seems to be little doubt that he would have served a new government with the same competence with which he continued to serve Hitler: a combination of ambition, opportunism, and patriotism, marinated in an increasing level of fatalism.

For the record Guderian referred to his appointment as a burden he felt compelled to accept. He briefly underwrote Hitler's perspective by denouncing proposals for withdrawal as defeatism and pessimism. Whether that behavior reflected opportunistic gratitude for his promotion or lack of information on what was really happening in Russia remains unknown—perhaps even to Guderian himself.

The events of July 20 further complicated responding to a disaster reaching such dimensions that Hitler overlooked Model's policy of breaking out encircled troops where possible and establishing a new, firm defensive line along the Vistula. Here again the panzers bore the weight of the action. Viking and Totenkopf Divisions were returning from brief stints in the rear after having been taken off the line in the Ukraine. The Skulls were Himmler's pets because of their concentration camp origins, and he saw to it that the division received a full battalion of Panthers. Viking had no similar patron, but on August 1 it managed to field 64 tanks, two-thirds of them Panthers. Fourth Panzer Division, fresh from a long spell in France and Germany, was one of the only two fully equipped panzer divisions in Russia, with 80 Panzer IVs and the same number of Panthers. The newcomers' battle groups managed to clear a path for 2nd Army's more or less orderly retreat. They sustained enough fighting power to play vital roles as well in the second half of Model's operational plan, a riposte aimed at the Red Army formations drawing up to the Vistula.

Soviet losses had been heavy; Soviet organizations had been disrupted by victory; Soviet logistics had been overextended by distance. These are usually cited as the operational reasons the Red Army slowed and stopped east of Warsaw. On the political side it is frequently asserted—and sometimes held as an article of faith—that Stalin ordered the halt in order to leave the Germans free to destroy the Polish Home Army, which rose on August 1 expecting Soviet support, and thereby facilitate Poland's "liberation" as a Soviet satellite.

Hitler's panzers also had a good deal to do with that course of events. Taking a chapter from Manstein's book in the winter of 1942–43, Model pulled three panzer divisions out of the line, sacrificing ground to concentrate force. He added the newly arrived Parachute Panzer Division "Hermann Göring" to the blend, and hit the 2nd Tank Army from four sides at once in the open ground east of the Vistula with about 300 AFVs against 800. Clogged roads and disrupted rail schedules were almost a relief to staff planners able to turn their attention away from the dismal overall prospects. The result was a reduced version of another classic envelopment executed 60 miles north in 1914: the Battle of Tannenberg which destroyed an entire Russian army. Now SS, army, and Luftwaffe tankers fought side by side in a three-day battle that cost 2nd Tank Army two-thirds of its strength and perhaps threw Stavka and Stalin off at least part of their game.

The tragic events in Warsaw, the Wehrmacht's savage suppression of the rising and the destruction of the city on Hitler's orders, have understandably overshadowed this event. Soviet accounts are, equally understandably, silent on the subject. German records were lost or scattered. An outstanding piece of archival investigation, one of many by the Militärgeschichtliches Forschungsamt's Karl-Heinz Frieser, makes the case against categorizing the event as just another rear-guard fight, another meaningless tactical victory for the panzers. In its aftermath, Soviet planning for the central sector shifted, returning to the proven pattern of coordinated frontal attacks.

This was done against Zukhov's vehement urging to maintain the strategic/operational initiative by driving past Warsaw, toward the Baltic through East Prussia—not least in order to bring the war home to what Russia had long understood as Germany's heartland. This bold stroke just might have finished the war in the east six months earlier. As it was, 30 German divisions were gone: 400,000 men—over 250,000 of those simply listed as "missing." Army Group Center had time to stabilize its front—but that front now lay in Poland. And this comprehensive disaster invited others. Army Group North had been not merely outflanked but virtually isolated. Hitler insisted on holding a "Baltic Fortress" under attack by elements of four Soviet fronts, including numbers of new JS-IIs.

Army Group North had a veteran Tiger battalion, the 502nd. Its 30 tanks wreaked company-scale havoc wherever they appeared. In one fight, the first-ever encounter of Tigers and Stalins, the 2nd Company accounted for fifty JS-IIIs and T-34s without a single loss. On another occasion, three Tigers knocked out 18 Soviet AFVs in one long summer evening. But the 502nd could not be everywhere at once. The army group's 200 assault guns were needed to shore up the infantry. Demodernization had progressed so far that in some sectors, Landser took the chance of letting tanks roll over them in order to use satchel charges against their sides and decks—"poor man's war" with a vengeance.

The result was predictable. On July 31, Red Army vanguards reached the Baltic Sea, the first stage of what became a 75-mile gap between Army Groups North and Center. The German response was also predictable: turn to the panzers. Third Panzer Army received an armored transfusion. Reinhardt had taken over the army group on August 16 when Model was transferred to the Western Front. Reinhardt's replacement was Raus, no less capable a panzer general. Instead of bits and pieces, he had six divisions, including Grossdeutschland, newly arrived from Romania, plus an improvised task force with 60 tanks. Each one would be needed: as at Stalingrad, Army Group North was too overextended to do more than hold its ground as opposed to participating in a breakout.

What Raus did not possess was a viable plan. Hoping to catch the Russians off balance, the High Command sent in the panzers on such a broad front that mutual support was impossible. Raus and his staff officers were unable to drive forward an advance that opened no more than a narrow, fragile corridor to the trapped army group before grinding to a halt. Then instead of using the hard-won passageway as an escape hatch, Hitler funneled reinforcements through it—including a panzer division whose forlorn-hope assignment demonstrated Hitler's determination to hold the Baltic to the end. And 3rd Panzer Army's headquarters was eventually established in Willkischken, just on the Prussian side of the 1939 border with Poland. The Reich was steadily and inexorably receding.

Guderian and the High Command insisted Army Group North be authorized to break out and rejoin Army Group Center. The distance was still short enough, and the terrain sufficiently broken, that lack of armor was less of a handicap than had been the case elsewhere in such operations. As further incentive, a high proportion of the Army Group's units and men came from the Reich's eastern provinces and would be fighting for their homes and families. Hitler vetoed every proposal. In September, 15 Soviet armies, 1.5 million men and over 3,000 tanks and assault guns, struck Army Group North all along its line. Schörner, transferred in July to the Baltic and initially committed personally to holding on, nevertheless knew a lost hand when dealt one. He flew to Hitler's headquarters and in an eloquent quarter of an hour convinced Hitler to allow a retreat. Abandoning Estonia, the army group pulled back into Courland.

On October 5, seven Soviet armies rolled over a 3rd Panzer Army again reduced to one of its titular divisions, driving its remnants westward and reaching the Baltic coast four days later. A series of frontal attacks in the next few weeks drove Army Group North inextricably into the Courland peninsula. They also forced using the available armor in detachments, dooming any unauthorized breakthrough before it started. The eventually renamed Army Group Courland had the 12th and 14th Panzer Divisions and enough assault guns and tank destroyers to field initially around 250 AFVs on a good maintenance day. By November 1, 14th Panzer Division was down to 21 runners. Twelfth Panzer reported 19. A half million soldiers and civilians were trapped against the Baltic

Sea. They had no real hope of rescue, even should Hitler change his position that where the German soldier planted his boots, there he remained. Alive or dead made no difference.

Of no less consequence, the panzer divisions vainly expended in the north were unavailable to reinforce a southern sector whose long-expected turn finally came on July 13. Harpe had taken over from Model in command of Army Group North Ukraine. Since Army Group Center's collapse, seven of his panzer divisions had been ordered north. There remained 1st, 8th, 16th, and 17th Panzer, 20th Panzer Grenadier, and SS Viking: three each in reserve of 1st and 4th Panzer Armies as a counterattack force with a total of around 500 deployable AFVs. First Ukrainian Front, the immediate opposition, had 1,000,000 men, over 2,200 tanks and assault guns, and enough artillery to deploy 400 pieces per mile in the sectors chosen for the initial breakthrough.

The massive discrepancies in force and fighting power negated the concept of a zone defense. Harpe's armored reserves disappeared in days, absorbed before the full Russian strength developed. Over 40,000 Germans were cut off around Brody. This time there were no miracle escapes. The German commanders on the ground reacted slowly; only fragments were able to fight their way through to panzer battle groups barely able to hold the line, much less counterattack with any effect. By July 18, 4th Panzer Army was down to 20 tanks and around 160 assault guns—the latter, as in the northern sector, fully absorbed in keeping the hard-pressed infantry formations from being entirely scattered by what seemed endless numbers of T-34s. The battalions had been renamed brigades, but initially without any increase in strength.* Batteries and individual crews ran up their scores into three figures. But the front kept moving back.

Even against determined resistance, the Russians moved fast. Lublin fell on July 24 after a breakthrough attempt by 17th Panzer Division failed—though nobody in authority seemed to ask what the prospects

---

* Eventually some "Army Assault Artillery Brigades" would have 45 guns plus an "escort battery" of riflemen and pioneers. That upgrading, however, was in the future and too often on paper.

for success were in the first place for a worn-down division pitted against an entire army. Against Hitler's orders, Harpe ordered a general retreat to the Vistula. The key regional transport and communications center of Lvov fell on July 27. On July 29, a Soviet tank army crossed the Vistula in force at Sandomierz. By the end of the month the Army Group's front was over 120 miles farther west, into Galicia and the Carpathian foothills. Its losses approached 100,000, but its line was intact, the worst of the gaps plugged, and Harpe expressed a hope of hanging on until reinforcements arrived from somewhere—anywhere.

Instead the High Command ordered a full-scale counterattack against the Sandomierz bridgehead. The job was given to Balck, who took over 4th Panzer Army on August 5 for an attack that began on August 10—another example of what had become a pattern of expecting senior panzer officers to substitute energy and willpower for the careful planning required of the weaker party. The III Panzer Corps achieved initial success through surprise, but was stopped within a few days. A second local counterattack by four panzer divisions on August 28 was canceled after three days; a third was called off when Balck and his staff failed to bring the exhausted panzers on line in time.

The Red Army no longer buckled when faced with the unexpected—particularly on the defensive. Flexibility was still not a major characteristic of Soviet armored formations, but solidity is also a military virtue. The Soviet tankers who held their ground around Sandomierz were motivated by more than fear of NKVD firing squads. They knew that support was on hand, and that support would arrive in a force the Germans could no longer match.

At company and battalion levels, Red Army tankers were taking the measure of their German opponents. The 501st Heavy Tank Battalion was the first to take Tiger Bs into action on August 11. In three days, 14 of 30 were lost to an approximately equal number of T-34s and JS-IIs. The Soviets shifted quickly from attack formations to ambush positions, taking full advantage of the Stalins' cross-country capacity to strike the Tigers' vulnerable sides and rears. The 122mm guns cracked open the Tiger B like a coconut. And when they evaluated the three undamaged tanks they captured, Red Army experts were unimpressed by its technology.

By the end of August, North Ukraine's front was relatively quiet—less from anything Harpe and his commanders did than because of the Soviet decision to reinforce a more spectacular victory to the south. Schörner had used the time after the abortive Russian spring offensive and before his transfer to replace equipment and train men. Army Group South Ukraine's divisions were at full operational strength; its front was stable. The army group's chief of staff even boasted that troops could be made available to other fronts if necessary.

In the first three weeks of July, South Ukraine paid an initial installment on the bluster with five panzer divisions and two battalions of assault guns. The Romanian government and high command, already badly shaken, was anything but reassured. Nor was Schörner's replacement a particularly inspired—or inspiring—choice. At best, Johannes Friessner was what Napoleon called "a good ordinary general," with no experience of the kind of war waged in the open ground of the southeast. The first thing he learned was that his staff considered the available reserves—two panzer and a panzer grenadier division—insufficient to block a Soviet offensive. The second thing he learned was that Hitler would allow no front adjustments. The third was that his staff was right.

Second and 3rd Ukrainian Fronts were commanded by two of the best Russian wartime marshals: Rodion Malinovsky and Fyodor Tolbukhin. Stavka had rebuilt their combined force to over 900,000 men and 1,400 AFVs. Eighteen hundred planes guaranteed near-supremacy in the air. The hammer fell on August 20 in the Pruth valley. The sector was held by a mix of German infantry and Romanians already looking over their shoulders. Successful local counterattacks by panzer battle groups could do nothing to restore a situation that, by August 24, saw Russian spearheads meet near Leovo and cut off the German 6th Army. A Bagration-scale disaster was in sight, and Friessner was not the man to convince the Romanians otherwise. On August 23, Romanian King Michael dismissed Prime Minister Ion Antonescu. Within days the new government took Romania out of the war, then in again—against Hungary and Germany. Bulgaria, which had supported the Axis without declaring war on the USSR, declared war on Germany three days after Tolbukhin's tankers crossed its border on August 5.

For a while everybody was shooting at everybody else. The Luftwaffe bombed Bucharest. The Romanians took about 50,000 German prisoners. The Russians finished off 6th Army for the second time during the war and drove toward Hungary and the Balkans. Not only did 600,000 men and 26 divisions suddenly find themselves on enemy territory; as Red Army spearheads entered Yugoslavia, the entire German force in the southern Balkans was threatened with envelopment.

The transformation of occupied Yugoslavia from a strategic backwater to the key to the Eastern Front's right half, the successful evacuation of Greece and Albania, and the stabilization—again temporary—of what remained of the Reich's Balkan sector, is a story of its own. It has little to do with the panzers. Apart from a few pawn pieces like the self-propelled antitank guns organic to some infantry divisions and a few of the ubiquitous assault guns, a vital sector fought a vital campaign on a technical level little advanced from that of 1918. The 2nd Panzer Army, sent south in August 1943 and commanded eventually by an artilleryman, spent most of its time disarming Italians and fighting partisans with no tanks at all under command. It was a far cry from the days of 1940–41 for those of Guderian's former staff officers who remained at their posts.

Romania's change of sides left Army Group South Ukraine no option but to save what could be saved and fall back on the Carpathians. The new line was formed by divisions officially designated as "remnants." They included 13th and 20th Panzer, who covered the retreat until they had almost nothing left. By August 29, 20th Panzer Division was down to 1,300 men and no tanks: a "panzer battle group" by designation and courtesy. A similar fate overtook most of the assault gun battalions: guns lost, vehicles destroyed, survivors escaping on foot in small groups.

Favorable terrain, Soviet overextension, and increased commitment by a Hungarian army fighting on its doorstep with German guns at its back, enabled the establishment of something like a stable front covering

Budapest and the oil fields of Lake Balaton, which were now more vital than ever with their Romanian counterparts gone. Initially it seemed more of a speed bump than a battle line. On October 6, Malinovsky broke through a Hungarian sector on a 60-mile front around Debrecen. That was only 130 miles from Budapest, most of it open ground: the only question apparently was which of the front's elements would arrive first.

The Germans had stationed large forces in Hungary since March. When Regent Miklós Horthy attempted negotiations with Stalin, he was deposed on October 16 and replaced by a fascist puppet government. In the aftermath of the coup, the German High Command had been moving reserves into Hungary for a counterattack of its own. Operation Gypsy Baron, a nice reference to the Strauss operetta, was ambitiously expected to recover the Carpathian passes. Instead its forces were thrown in to block the Red Army: 227 tanks and assault guns, German and Hungarian, against almost 800. In a near-classic encounter battle, the 1st, 13th, and 23rd Panzer Divisions up and encircled part of the Soviet vanguard. But taking a page from their enemies' playbook, the Russians managed to break out despite losing over half their armor.

Malinovsky proposed to regroup and rebuild his tired front. Stalin ordered him forward. The offensive resumed on October 29. When it stalled, Stavka authorized heavy reinforcements, including 200 tanks, and ordered Tolbukhin to close up on Malinovsky's right. Through November and into December, the Russians fought their way forward on both sides of Budapest, cutting the rail line to Vienna on December 23 and beginning the siege of a city neither German nor Hungarian generals believed could be defended.

The panzers' direct role in this process was limited. They had shot their bolt at Debrecen. Battle groups of a thousand men and a few dozen AFVs were merely drops of water on a hot stove. The men and the tanks that could have made up some of the autumn's losses had instead been sent west to the Ardennes. In the face of Hitler's insistence that Budapest be held to a finish, panzer commanders on the spot risked no more than minor movements.

VI

THERE WAS A sidebar to the campaigns of 1944. On September 10 the 1st Byelorussian Front, resupplied and reinforced, mounted a major offensive north of Warsaw, aimed northwest at the Narew River. It was stopped by Viking and Totenkopf, who thereby played a crucial role in the Warsaw Uprising's defeat; but on October 10 it resumed, extended on the left by the 3rd Byelorussian Front. By October 21, the Red Army had captured an undamaged bridge across the Angerapp River, in the heart of East Prussia. Nothing seemed to stand in the way of the T-34s until Friedrich Hossbach was given most of the armor in the sector and ordered to counterattack.

This was the same Hossbach who, as Hitler's adjutant in 1937, kept the records that became the Hossbach Memorandum. An infantryman by branch, he had commanded 4th Army since mid-July. Now he had a worn-down 5th Panzer Division, the similarly attenuated Hermann Göring, and the newly organized Führer Grenadier Brigade. Together they amounted to around 100 tanks and assault guns. Not much seems to have been expected, but Hossbach was able to hit both flanks of the breakthrough simultaneously. Fifth Panzer went in from the north on October 21 with 22 tanks. Two days later they made contact with the Führer Grenadiers advancing from the south. The Soviets panicked, abandoning tanks and equipment in a rush to the rear the Germans lacked the strength to stop. Third Byelorussian Front, shut down for the winter. So did the campaign against East Prussia. But the future prospects of Army Group Center, were inescapably grim.

Just how grim was suggested at the East Prussian village of Nemmersdorf—the site of the Angerapp crossing of October 21. Elements of the 2nd Guards Tank Corps held the bridgehead against counterattacks for about four hours, then withdrew. When German troops entered two days later, they found a scene that German propaganda described as a massacre, with hundreds of civilians raped, shot, and butchered. The actual events remain subjects of debate, with allegations of photos doctored, corpses brought in from elsewhere, numbers exaggerated. One recent scholarly investigation reports fewer than 30 verifiable murders, with lesser atrocities on the same limited scale.

These numbers have in turn been challenged. What is certain is that Goebbels and East Prussian Gauleiter Eric Koch used Nemmersdorf to inspire a spirit of resistance locally and nationally. What is also certain is that the Landser, foot-marchers or panzermen, had a winter to think about the story—and perhaps to remember other villages at other times, when the situation had been reversed. The victory rings on a Tiger's gun barrel might move steadily toward the muzzle. An assault gun battalion might note its thousandth confirmed kill. But when Ivan came again, the fight would be to the finish.

CHAPTER SEVEN

FINALE

As Hitler's vision of kicking in Russia's front door drowned in blood on the Eastern Front, France increasingly became a rest-and-recuperation zone for burned-out frontline units. Even the West's supreme commander as of March 1942, Field Marshal Gerd von Rundstedt, had received his appointment after being removed from his army group in Russia. A few weeks in France to absorb equipment and replacements, to forget the war as much as possible, was a dream that ran a close third to a long furlough or a million-mark wound. Simultaneously the "hero-thieves" of the replacement service staged comb-out after comb-out in the formations that watched the coasts. In 1942 and 1943, just about anyone who wanted to fight, who was able to fight, or who could conceivably be made to fight, was transferred eastward. Their replacements were the lame and the halt, the elderly and the invalid, whole battalions recruited from Russia's Asian communities or from prisoners of war.

I

In those contexts, might the US-initiated projects for a full-scale landing in the spring of 1943 have caught the Wehrmacht at its lowest ebb? For a good part of 1943, High Command West had fewer combat-ready divisions than it possessed in 1942. It was absorbed in implementing Hitler's September 1942 order to increase the coastal defenses by no fewer than 15,000 strong points. The archives include far more correspondence on details of the Führer's blockhouse projects than on proposals for repelling a full-scale cross-channel invasion. The Allies' Mediterranean initiatives drew attention southward. During 1943, the Germans in the West had so many immediate priorities that concern for a D-Day-type operation moved toward the bottom of the list by default.

But it did not disappear. The case for a 1943 invasion of northeastern Europe appears plausible only because of distractions themselves largely the product of Anglo-American initiatives in the Mediterranean. Almost from its creation, High Command West was convinced the Allies would eventually strike northwestern Europe in force. The only question was when and where the blow would fall. Without Operation Torch and its aftermaths, the Germans would have been free to concentrate on preparing for a major landing mounted from Britain. And D-Day was an operation that could only be undertaken once.

Britain's moral and material capital was nearly exhausted, its fighting manpower so limited that the army sent to Northwestern Europe had to cannibalize itself, breaking up entire divisions to keep the rest operational. Failure, to say nothing of disaster, would have had incalculably negative consequences for the war effort of the island kingdom. The US was powerful enough to bear and recover from the material consequences of defeat on Europe's beaches. The psychological impact was a different story entirely. June 1944 in England invites comparison in US military history with July 1863 in Pennsylvania. Both occasions generated a sense of participation in something Hegel might have called a world-historical event. Seen in this light, the cross-channel invasion was more than a military operation—too much more to risk its launching in anything but the most favorable circumstances possible.

As High Command West coped with the challenges generated by the Russian and Mediterranean theaters, the Atlantic Wall began taking on a life of its own. By mid-1943, particularly around the major ports, the Wall looked authentic, with trenches, ditches, and minefields, machine-gun nests, concrete strong points, and heavy artillery emplaced in what even to men who knew better seemed impregnable bunkers. The commanders on the spot, however, were not exactly sure what to do with it.

The defense of Western Europe had, by late 1943, become an army responsibility. The Kriegsmarine, defeated in the U-boat campaign, its remaining surface vessels penned in harbor, could do little more than conduct coast-defense operations with a mixed bag of small craft. The Luftwaffe's attention had shifted to the Eastern Front and to the Reich itself. Staff and operational assignments to Air Fleet 3, responsible for Western Europe, were viewed as either dead ends or rest cures.

On October 25, 1943, Rundstedt submitted a comprehensive memorandum describing the challenges and requirements of a sector that in the next year could expect to become a major theater of operations. He sarcastically noted that he would be very glad if Hitler read this report despite his busy schedule. Otherwise the Führer might accuse his generals of failing to keep him informed should things go wrong, as he had done in December 1941. And there was a great deal to go wrong in the sectors allotted to High Command West.

Rundstedt argued from a paradox. The Atlantic Wall, conceived and ordered by Hitler as the main battle line, lacked the depth to hold by itself. On the other hand, abandoning the coast without a fight would sacrifice the advantage of the Channel as a moat. It would mean the loss of a heavy investment in fortifications. Above all, it would require staking the campaign on a mobile battle in northeastern France against an enemy whose strong point was a capacity for mobile warfare. Therefore, Rundstedt argued, the coastline must be defended to the last.

Rundstedt expected an invasion not much later than spring, 1944. He believed the Allies would land first in the Pas de Calais, then in Normandy and Brittany: sites offering the easiest passages, the shortest supply lines, and the closest locations to Germany's frontiers. The Allies enjoyed air and naval supremacy. They already had as many divisions available for such an operation as Rundstedt could muster in his entire expanded theater. Most were first-class assault troops, young, sound of wind and limb, and equipped with the best American and British industry could provide.

Experience in both world wars showed that landings made in sufficient force would succeed. But a combination of local counterattacks to disrupt initial successes, supplemented once the Allied Schwerpunkt became apparent by the concentrated blows of a massed reserve, provided the window of an opportunity for defeating the invasion, or at least so bloodying the Anglo-Americans' noses that they might reconsider their military and political options.

Success once more depended on the panzers. A Führer Directive of November 3 accepted most of Rundstedt's basic propositions. For two and a half years, Hitler declared, the Reich's energies had been directed against Asiatic Bolshevism. Now an even greater danger had emerged: the Anglo-Saxon invasion. In the east, space could be traded for time. Not so in the west. An Allied breakout from a successful landing would have prompt and incalculable consequences for the Reich. No longer could the west be stripped for the sake of other theaters. Instead its defenses must be strengthened by every means possible—above all its mobile defenses.

In October 1943, the Western theater had only around 250 armored vehicles—no more than a token against the thousands available to the Western Allies. Its half dozen mobile divisions were skeletons or embryos. The General Staff and the armored force were instructed to provide Panzer IV tanks and assault guns for the reestablished, replenished, and newly created armored formations ultimately responsible for defending northeast Europe.

Was Rundstedt, a man of advanced years and fixed opinions, the general to throw the Allies into the sea? In November 1943 the Führer sent Rommel, restored to health and underemployed commanding a shadow Army Group B, to prepare plans and suggestions for the best ways of meeting an Allied invasion. The appointment arguably reflected Hitler's long-standing practice of establishing parallel systems for solving difficult problems. Rundstedt was familiar with that process, and pleased enough with the Führer's newfound interest in the west, that he offered the newcomer full cooperation. Rommel recognized the awkwardness of his position and took pains to avoid stepping on his senior's toes. But the army's senior and junior field marshals were like oil and water. Rundstedt tended to let situations develop before he acted, all the while commenting on those developments with an irony that could alternately inspire admiration or fury in his associates. Rommel was a driver, accustomed to seeing every situation as an emergency, making snap decisions, and making those decisions work.

Rundstedt broke the fast-developing ice. On December 30 he made a formal proposal to make Army Group B responsible for the region most exposed to invasion: the Netherlands, Pas de Calais, and Normandy. Rommel applied his famous energy to the Atlantic Wall with good effect. The heart of his thinking, however, involved deploying the panzer formations so close to the coast that they could engage as the enemy crossed the beaches. Without the immediate help of mechanized reserves, the Field Marshal insisted, their air and naval supremacy meant the Allies were certain to get ashore somewhere. Undisturbed for any length of time, they would flank the defenders out of their fixed defenses and roll up the Atlantic Wall like a rug.

Rommel's approach offered the advantage of employing the panzer divisions in ways grown familiar to their officers in Russia: counterpunching a tactically vulnerable enemy, with dash and tactical skill compensating for inferior numbers. It offered as well a closer link between the mechanized formations and the semi-mobile infantry divisions manning the Wall. As was the case with Model and Raus, Rommel's plan made it less likely that the former would regard themselves as pawns for sacrifice. One of the reasons for the German infantry's Homeric combat record on the Eastern Front was the widespread knowledge that surrendering to Ivan involved high levels of immediate risk and complete certainty of subsequent discomfort. Conditions of British or American captivity were so favorably mythologized that not a few prisoners taken during the D-Day campaign seemed surprised when their first meal did not include steak.

Rommel thought in wider terms as well. Repulsing the landings at the shoreline would buy military time that might be exploited politically. A decisive victory presented to the Führer by his favorite marshal might well prove an entering wedge for a negotiated peace. If not, there was always the German Resistance, whose plans and hopes for direct action against "history's greatest warlord" were increasingly open secrets among those in the know at High Command West. Best evidence indicates Rommel was not directly involved in any conspiracies. He was, however, tactician enough to profit from any opportunities created by Hitler's removal.

Rommel's principal critic was Leo Geyr von Schweppenburg. His prewar career combined wide experience as a staff officer and attaché with early involvement in developing the armored force. He took 3rd Panzer Division through Poland and led panzer corps in Russia under Guderian in 1941 and Kleist during Operation Blue before his appointment as commander of Panzer Troops West in July 1943. Geyr was no admirer of the battle group tactics that had emerged in Russia as a response to a chronic shortage of tanks. These small formations, he argued, would be disproportionately vulnerable to Allied firepower. What was needed were large-scale counterattacks against the invasion beaches: counterattacks in divisional strength or more. Geyr's response to the threats from sea and air was to keep German armor well clear of the coast, in camouflaged positions out of range of naval guns. Admittedly, to reach the operational zones the mechanized forces would have to move by night. Properly trained troops under competent officers could nevertheless expect to arrive in good time to throw the invaders back into the Channel.

Rommel expected the invasion to have higher levels of air support than anything previously seen in history. The northern French roads suitable for major troop movements led across rivers and through cities: inviting targets for Allied bombers. It was unreasonable, Rommel argued, to expect divisions positioned according to Geyr's proposals to reach the battle zone, reorganize, and refit, in less than ten days or two weeks. That was all the time and more the invaders would need to establish a bridgehead impregnable to anything High Command West was likely to bring against it.

The debate played out against a background of evidence that the British and Americans from Africa to Anzio had not demonstrated any particular skill in armored war. The end game in Tunisia had been a triumph of mass against overextension. In Sicily the Italians had collapsed; the Luftwaffe was conspicuous in its absence. But the hastily rebuilt Hermann Göring and 15th Panzer Grenadier Divisions, fighting in dispersed battle groups, kept the Allies off balance and bought time for a reverse Dunkirk across the Straits of Messina. Nor were German panzer specialists impressed by what they considered George Patton's military excursion to Palermo and along the north coast.

The Italian campaign only highlighted the Allies' limitations not merely in using armor, but in thinking about its use. In some of Europe's most broken terrain the Americans committed a full armored division and the British no fewer than five (though only three at any one time), plus a large number of smaller independent units. Periodically, so many tanks were deployed for a particular operation that they got in their own and everyone else's way—the Liri Valley comes to mind operationally, and tactically the New Zealand armored brigade at Cassino.

On the other hand, the 16th Panzer Division came close to defeating the Salerno landing single-handedly. At Anzio the panzers played a central role in transforming Winston Churchill's hoped-for wildcat into a "stranded whale." Those achievements, and a score of lesser ones, had depended on a substantial armored presence, usually from three to five panzer and panzer grenadier divisions. The defense of northwest Europe would require proportionally stronger mobile forces. Where were they to come from in the existing context of compound overstretch?

Adolf Hitler was no Cadmus. Nevertheless the Third Reich had sown at least some of the dragon's teeth that provided the legendary founder of Thebes with his army—with almost as much internal conflict as that among Cadmus's dragon-blooded warriors. On December 31, 1942, Hitler authorized the formation of two new Waffen SS divisions, the 9th Hohenstaufen and the 10th Frundsberg. The 9th took its name from the rulers of the medieval Holy Roman Empire, the 10th from a famous commander of mercenary Landsknechts. For most of their careers they served in tandem beginning with their training in France and their brief introduction to combat on the Eastern Front in early 1944.

Beginning in 1942 the Waffen SS found its sources of volunteers, German, ethnic German, and foreign, falling far short of replacement requirements. Increasing numbers of Germanics were being assigned to the ethnic SS divisions springing up throughout occupied Eastern Europe. Hohenstaufen initially received a number of Hungarian Germans. From 1943, however, the ranks of the Waffen SS panzers were in general filled by men from the draft pool, supplemented by periodic infusions of compulsory transfers from the Luftwaffe and the navy.

Standards were upheld by the instructors. More than an army already stretched to its limits, the Waffen SS provided strong, experienced, and motivated cadres to its new armored formations. "*Meine Ehre heist Treue*," "loyalty is my honor," was the SS motto. For the Waffen SS it meant above all fidelity to the principles of National Socialism and the Führer who embodied them. It also meant unconditional trust among comrades. Discipline remained rigid, but "character development" emphasized initiative, aggression, and self-reliance in a context of teamwork. By 1943 parade-ground drill had been abandoned in favor of weapons proficiency, terrain orientation, and camouflage instruction.

Contradictions among these concepts were downplayed as training periods grew shorter. Compliance was an increasingly acceptable substitute for belief. And should compliance fail, sterner methods might be applied. An SS prisoner, himself an Alsatian, described a Waffen SS officer in Normandy ordering an Alsatian deserter beaten to death by his own company.

A third Waffen SS armored division authorized in 1943 is perhaps the most familiar. The 12th SS Panzer's antecedents went back to May 1942. In that month, three weeks of pre-military training was ordered for all boys between sixteen and eighteen, under the auspices of the Hitler Youth. The army and the SS competed vigorously to provide cadres, many from the panzers. Old-style drill sergeants had little place in a system staffed by combat veterans often only a few years older than their charges. The military emphasis was on skill, will, and initiative in an environment of comradeship. The ideological elements, as a rule directly provided by Hitler Youth officials, synergized with the war stories to foster an ethos of struggle and sacrifice for Volk and Reich.

The next step, at seventeen, was eligibility for at least three months of compulsory labor service. Now under Wehrmacht control, like its peacetime predecessor the Arbeitsdienst emphasized hard work under

hard conditions as opposed to focused military or ideological instruction. After 1942 every German drafted into the Wehrmacht at eighteen
had passed through these programs, at least in principle. Back to back,
they were a natural pipeline to military service and a natural recruiting
agent for Hitler's panzers, army or SS.

When the 12th SS Panzer Division opened its ranks to volunteers
under the official draft age, sixteen- and seventeen-year-olds lined up
in a fashion reminiscent—albeit on a smaller scale—of the "war volunteers" of August 1914. With a cadre drawn primarily from the Leibstandarte and supplemented by army officers with Hitler Youth experience,
with chocolate replacing cigarettes in the rations—smoking was officially bad for one's health in the Reich—the division began training in
the summer of 1943.

The instructors took their military responsibilities seriously and
found willing students in the teenagers who filled the ranks and set the
tone in the combat units even as older men were assigned to the support
and technical services. As for ideological conditioning, the volunteers
had by then largely indoctrinated themselves. German adolescents were
less creatures of propaganda and illusion than many postwar accounts
depict. Certainly after 1942 they had a reasonable idea of what was waiting for them "out there," and reasonable grounds for believing that the
skills and attitudes acquired in a Waffen SS uniform were eminently
transferable to the Russian Front as survival instruments and coping
mechanisms. If one had to board the train, why not travel first class? Or
in the cruder language of young men among themselves, if you were in
the bucket at least it should be full of—euphemistically—fertilizer.

The Waffen SS also formed three new panzer grenadier divisions:
the 16th and 17th in October 1943, the 18th in January 1944. The 16th
drew its cadres largely from the Skulls. The 18th was built around an SS
brigade initially formed from Totenkopf formations, with a three-year
record of stomach-churning atrocities in Russia—mostly behind the
lines. Both were predictably most dangerous to civilians, the 16th in
Italy and the 18th in Russia. The 17th was forced to show its mettle in
northwest Europe, against an enemy that fought back.

The Waffen SS also formed another corps. After the recapture of

Kharkov in 1943 Leibstandarte's commander Sepp Dietrich was recalled to Germany to command I SS Panzer Corps, intended to include his old division and the Hitler Jugend once it was ready for operations. Dietrich, who had fought in the embryonic tank force during World War I and remained a noncommissioned officer in spirit and perspective, was respected for his courage and for caring about his men. Though it took a while, Dietrich also developed a sense of his limitations. He commanded and allowed—better said, encouraged—his staff officers to do the thinking. Many of these were army transfers, and Dietrich as a corps commander was consistently willing to cooperate with army generals after D-Day.

The army's principal contribution to preparing for the invasion involved reconstructing and reequipping divisions battered to pieces in Russia. In addition, the 16th Panzer Grenadier Division was upgraded to the 116th Panzer Division in spring 1944. A number of panzer grenadier formations emerged: a Führer Escort Brigade and a Führer Grenadier Brigade, both expanded to divisions in early 1945; a Feldherrnhalle Division based on the old 60th Motorized and drawing some manpower from the original storm troops of the SA; and a Brandenburg Division built around the army's special operations units.

In December 1943 the instruction and demonstration units of the panzer schools were stripped to form the Panzer Lehr Division. An elite force with an initial strength of almost 200 Panzer IVs, Panthers, and Tigers, its creation nevertheless indicated the panzers' desperate straits. Their principal advantage had always been quality. Quality depended on training—more so as the casualty lists increased. Now, like a peasant family in a hard winter, the army was eating its seed grain.

During the war's final months a number of ephemeral panzer formations appeared and disappeared. Some had high numbers: 232nd and 233rd. Others had inspiring titles: Clausewitz, Holstein, Müncheberg. What they had in common were cadres provided by training schools and replacement depots; equipment provided ad hoc; and ranks filled by stragglers from broken units, completed from hospitals and convalescent homes and by locally raised recruits, often obtained practically at gunpoint. Few of them lasted long enough to do more than swell Allied tallies of prisoners.

From Hitler who authorized them to the senior officers who created and committed them, these cobbled-together armored formations challenge any notion of a professionally informed "genius for war." They highlight as well an operational situation, desperate through 1943, that erupted into full-blown crisis in 1944. The panzers, the core of Germany's war effort, had been ruthlessly expended and marginally nurtured. As the army's combined-arms capacities diminished, the panzers had evolved—or derogated—from a spearhead to a fire brigade to a firewall, expected not merely to restore emergencies but to avert them. As for personnel, "by 1944," recalled one army tank driver whose war began at Sedan and ended in the Bulge, "we were like bad soup: old bones and green vegetables."

The Third Reich's ultimate vanity formation, however, owed its existence to Hermann Göring. The Luftwaffe chief controlled the Reich's antiaircraft and airborne forces, but wanted his own ground combat unit as well. The Hermann Göring Division began in 1933 as a 400-man police unit. It grew to be a regiment, then a brigade. In late 1942 it became a division, then a panzer division brought to strength by transfers from the Luftwaffe and the paratroops, and brought to effectiveness by combat-experienced army tankers. Lost in Tunisia, it reformed in Sicily, fought there, in Italy, and then—as noted in Chapter 6—was transferred to Russia in September 1944. Administered by the Luftwaffe, it was operationally subordinated to the army, which facilitated its acceptance by the soldiers almost as much as did its acknowledged fighting power.

The division had a predictable and cultivated reputation for "hardness." In Italy and Warsaw, elements were involved in large-scale shootings of "partisans." A table of standings for indictable war crimes by panzer divisions would probably put it roughly between the Waffen SS and the army. But Göring saw to it that the division was kept well up to strength and on the A list for equipment. Like the Hitler Jugend Division, it attracted a good number of teenage volunteers. Its training facilities—army-provided—kept Hermann Göring's combat effectiveness at a level that made it a welcome presence in any sector—and also facilitated overlooking such regularly alleged peccadilloes as using civilians for human shields.

II

RUNDSTEDT'S REFUSAL TO decide between Rommel and Geyr led both to seek the Führer's ear. As the jockeying intensified, the Field Marshal found himself in the position of a poker player who antes but refuses to bet: his stack of military/political chips was steadily diminishing. In February 1944, with more and more armored divisions arriving in France, Rommel's Army Group B was given the right to command any formations of Panzer Group West in its operational area. Rommel also received the right to recommend sector assignments and command appointments for the mobile formations directly to Rundstedt, thus bypassing Geyr.

In May Hitler created a new army group headquarters under Rundstedt to control southern France, and assigned it three panzer divisions: 9th, 11th, and 2nd SS. Rommel's Army Group B also received three panzer divisions: the 2nd, 21st, and 116th. The cream of the panzers—1st and 12th SS Panzer, 17th SS Panzer Grenadier, and Panzer Lehr—remained under control of Panzer Group West, but not exactly under Rundstedt's command. Instead the Panzer Group was now designated part of the Wehrmacht High Command reserve, which, in practice, placed it under Hitler's direct authority.

The reorganization invites dismissal as no more than another example of Hitler's meddling in matters outside his competence. Rundstedt's sarcastic comment that Hitler's decision left him only the authority to move the sentries in his headquarters is nevertheless at best a half-truth. The field marshal had forgotten a fundamental military axiom: the first duty of a commander is to command; specifically, to decide the organization of his theater. War abhors vacuums. Adolf Hitler filled the one created by Gerd von Rundstedt.

Assigning three mechanized divisions to southern France left seven available for the decisive sector. Either massed as a central reserve or posted within close range of the prospective beaches, they represented a force strong enough to shape, if not decide, the coming battle—not a chess queen, but properly used, perhaps a pair of knights. Their dispersion not only created the obvious possibility of being too weak everywhere. It generated a subtler risk of making everyone just strong enough to generate a false sense of security.

On June 6, 1944, Normandy was a network of isolated, thinly garrisoned strong points. Its armored reserve, the 21st Panzer Division, was still partly equipped with French tanks captured in 1940. Even in those contexts the roots of German defeat ran deeper than a single day's fighting. Hitler's alleged late arising on that morning was less important than his continued uncertainty as to whether the Normandy landings were only a diversion. That uncertainty was shared throughout High Command West, however much it was denied later. Committing the armored reserves meant that the die was indisputably cast, and for all their alleged battlefield virtuosity, the generals were no less reluctant than their Führer to throw the final switch.

Uncertainty rendered moot the question of whether Rommel or Geyr was right about the panzers. Might Rommel's presence at his headquarters, instead of en route to Germany to plead for more tanks farther forward, have made a difference? Rommel could not repeal the laws of space and time. The 21st Panzer Division, which was closest to the invasion zone, played a critical role in frustrating the British attempt to capture the city of Caen but was unable to mount any counterattacks until afternoon. Panzer Lehr and Hitler Jugend were on their way to the invasion site by the evening of June 6. Rundstedt's headquarters was planning a corps-strength panzer counterattack for as early as the seventh. They believed it might after all be possible to contain, perhaps even defeat, the long-feared invasion. One SS officer dismissed doubt by describing the enemy as "little fish. We'll throw them into the sea in the morning."

The Allied beachheads held, though the British and Canadians were hard pressed at some points, especially by Hitler Jugend. Initial defeat left the panzers the fulcrum of later hopes and plans. The Germans' intention was to withdraw mechanized units presently committed, to bring in others from quiet sectors and the Reich (in particular 9th and 10th SS Panzer, currently deployed in Hungary), and to hit the Allies before they could convert a buildup to a breakthrough. That was frustrated in good part by a massive campaign against roads and railroads by Allied aircraft and the French Resistance. The 9th and 10th SS Panzer Divisions took longer to cross France than to move from Hungary. Tigers, which were difficult to transport safely by rail, used up engine life and track mileage in extended road marches. Second SS Panzer Division, Das Reich, responded to Resistance harassment during its move toward the beachhead with an escalating series of atrocities, culminating in the massacre of over 600 civilians at Oradour-sur-Glane on June 10.

Oradour, a crossroads town, was doomed for no better reason than convenience. There was some talk of excess and of courts-martial, but the death in combat of the senior officer who was directly responsible put an end to such sentimentality. Nor was Oradour an isolated incident. On June 22, 11th Panzer Division, responding to the Franco-American invasion of southern France, recorded killing 125 "resistance fighters" at a cost of 4 wounded. Following the custom of the Eastern Front no prisoners were reported.

Air power was proving even more decisive than expected. Allied tactical air forces were close to their peak strength on D-Day, and the force-ratios they could apply to the still-constricted beachhead were exponentially higher than during the rest of the campaign. In the British sector especially, fighter-bombers cruised the battlefield looking for targets of opportunity: "cab ranks," the tankers and infantrymen called them.

The direct effectiveness of air attacks against the German tanks has been accurately called into question. The impact of constant bombing and strafing on crew morale and crew effectiveness was beyond doubt even in the best divisions. The Soviet Sturmoviks' normal attack formation was a circle, rotating over a target until ammunition was exhausted. Units of antiaircraft like the Flakpanzer coming into service had some chance to disrupt the strike, maybe bring down a few of their tormentors. The fighter-bombers struck by twos and fours, seemingly out of nowhere, then were gone before even a good gun crew could find their range.

Staff cars, traveling alone or with small escorts, made even more tempting targets. Casualties mounted among senior officers trying, in the German tradition, to keep touch with their forward units. Rommel was only the most prominent victim. On June 10 the headquarters of Panzer Group West was crippled by a hundred-plane strike that wiped out most of the the senior staff. Geyr was "only" wounded, but his was the kind of narrow escape that left brave men shaken, their judgments clouded and their perspectives skewed. Fritz Bayerlein, hardly the exemplar of a timid man, assigned "broom commandos" to sweep away tire tracks left in roads and fields by the vehicles of his Panzer Lehr Division.

From the Germans' perspective the Schwerpunkt of the Allied offensive was in the British/Canadian sector where Montgomery, initially in overall command of ground operations, mounted a series of attacks, the major ones named after famous British races. Their purpose, whether to open the way into France or to engage and wear down the German armor reserves, has been intensively debated. Their image is of a series of ham-handed, head-down disappointments that generated casualty rates comparing with the worst weeks of the Somme and enhanced an already-pervasive caution at all levels of command.

Photos of burned-out British tanks littering such battlefields as Epsom and Goodwood are matched by the stories of their burned-out crews. SS First Lieutenant Michael Wittmann's single-panzer destruction of two dozen armored vehicles in 15 minutes at Villers-Bocage has earned him his own website, the designation "badass of the week" on another, and a commemorative T-shirt available through the Internet. Less well known but no less worthy of recognition is the ramming of a King Tiger by Lieutenant John Gorman's Sherman. Though Gorman belonged to the Irish Guards, his action reflected less Emerald Isle panache than desperation caused by a jammed gun. Both crews abandoned their disabled tanks, briefly confronted each other, and then ran for their own sides with the war story of a lifetime.

British armor in Normandy had significant shortcomings. Divisions trained as instruments of exploitation made heavy weather of assignment as breakthrough forces. Interarm cooperation was poor, within the armored divisions and between the infantry divisions and the independent tank formations supporting them. The heterogeneous origins of the armored forces, ranging from war-raised infantry battalions converted to tanks, through cavalry regiments that were still riding horses in 1941, to the Foot Guards themselves, facilitated operational entropy that could not be entirely overcome by transfers and replacements.

Orthodox criticisms of the tankers have nevertheless been recently and successfully challenged by a common-sense observation: British concepts of armor employment did not replicate German ones. Twenty-first Army Group intended to make the Germans fight its kind of battle. That involved making carefully prepared set-piece attacks supported by heavy firepower in narrow sectors. It involved exploiting success without taking excessive risks. It was a concept based on technology and material, setting steel to do the work of flesh: in June and July alone, British tank losses totaled around 1,300.

The British way in Normandy combined the "colossal cracks" that were Montgomery's specialty with the "bite and hold" approach developed in World War I and identified with trench-warfare generals like Plumer and Rawlinson. Normandy added something new to the mix. By 1944 the German practice of responding to enemy tactical success by an immediate, often improvised, armor-tipped counterattack, was common knowledge. The obvious response was to defeat the counterattack. That involved consolidating ground gained, bringing up towed and self-propelled antitank guns, and "seeing off" the panzers. An outstanding example was offered by 1st Tyneside Scottish on July 1 at Rauray. This typical infantry battalion, supported by a company of Shermans, stopped five separate attacks by battle groups of Hohenstaufen and Das Reich in a 14-hour fight that accounted for the destruction of around 35 tanks and assault guns. Ten of those were claimed by the Tynesiders' antitank platoon, whose six-pounders had little chance against a Panther except in close-quarters fighting.

Like Frederick the Great's oblique attack order two centuries earlier, the panzer counterattack lost mystique and effectiveness as its predictability increased. The Allies of 1944 were not the French of 1940 or the Russians of 1941–42. Getting inside their decision cycles might still be possible. Throwing them significantly off balance was likely to be a serious and expensive proposition. In Rommel's words, "a soldier . . . must have sufficient intelligence to get the most out of his fighting machine. And that these people can do. . . ."

The Germans' tactical problem was exacerbated by Hitler's insistence on holding forward positions as opposed to sanctioning the flexible defense sought by the panzer commanders. This policy offered some advantage, as it kept the fighting in the Normandy bocage, among the best defensive terrain in northwest Europe. But it also exposed an infantry whose declining quality often led to heavy, morale-sapping losses. By mid-July German casualties approached 100,000. Fewer than 6,000 replacements had arrived.

The panzer divisions High Command West and Army Group B originally intended for a major counterattack were being drawn one by one into frontline killing grounds. They not only had to replace now-lacking infantrymen, but provide fire support to compensate for a nonexistent Luftwaffe and artillery whose strength rapidly declined under Allied bombs and shells. One panzer grenadier battalion came off a bitterly contested hill with fewer than 50 men still standing. The Hitler Jugend division was eviscerated in a month, losing 17,000 men and its commander—but not before murdering enough Canadian prisoners to initiate a mercifully brief episode of mutual reprisals.

Generals were easier to find than soldiers. The commander of 7th Army, facing the Americans, committed suicide on June 27, and was replaced by Paul Hausser—the first time an SS general was assigned an army command. Geyer drew up a searing critique of the first month's fighting that attracted Hitler's attention. On July 6 he was also relieved, his command renamed 5th Panzer Army and assigned to Heinrich Eberbach, whose solid Eastern Front credentials and reputation as an enthusiastic Nazi was in Hitler's eyes a winning combination.

Meanwhile, the Americans, under Omar Bradley, chewed through the bocage with more determination than finesse. Moving into the

Cotentin peninsula, 1st US Army captured a devastated Cherbourg on June 26, but made slow progress toward St. Lo and the open country beyond it. The Germans in this sector multiplied its natural defensive potential by the flexible tactical system dating from World War I and modified in Russia: holding front lines thinly, determining the American tactical Schwerpunkt, then counterattacking. But Normandy was kept short of troops in favor of the northern sector. On July 24, 14 divisions, half of them mechanized, were concentrated around Caen. The Americans faced nine, only three mechanized and one of them just rotated south for a rest cure after being badly mauled by the British while supporting the worn-out infantry. Panzer Lehr Division, for example, was virtually semi-mobile, using its tanks to patrol gaps between strong points manned by panzer grenadiers whose half-tracks had been left behind as useless in the bocage.

On July 25 Allied bombers and American artillery blew open the German front and blew up most of Panzer Lehr. As a combination of shock and exploitation, Operation Cobra succeeded brilliantly. German reserves were exhausted. German commanders who had spent six weeks responding to local, specific threats were unable to readjust their thinking to the changed scale of events. German resistance eroded, then crumbled, then collapsed. A single Panther of Das Reich held up an armored column for most of a morning. But on July 31, 4th Armored Division captured the key road junction of Avranches. On August 1 George Patton's 3rd Army became operational and began transforming the breakthrough to a breakout.

Von Kluge, recovered from his accident, had replaced Rundstedt on July 7. Ten days later, he assumed command of Army Group B as well when Rommel was wounded in an air attack. He described the situation in blunt terms as a *Riesensauerei* (ratfuck), with the Americans on the verge of being able to do what they wanted, where they wanted.

Matters grew worse after Montgomery launched his own offensive on July 30. Operation Bluecoat was no blitzkrieg, but it made steady progress against a series of armored counterattacks characterized by tactical skill at the expense of coordination and shock power. Tigers, King Tigers, and Jagdpanthers appeared here and there, by twos and threes, to create temporary shock, awe, and havoc before breaking down or being disabled. Hohenstaufen was down to 34 AFVs on August 4, after only two days' serious fighting.

Kluge recommended retreat across the Seine. Hitler ordered instead a counterattack toward Avranches and eventually the coast, to be mounted by no fewer than eight of the mechanized divisions currently deployed in France. Kluge, who was significantly involved in the July 20 plot against Hitler, was in no position to temporize, much less protest. Nor was the counterattack's concept exactly an example of an amateur making war with maps. Indeed, had Kluge consulted a map he might have concluded that the serpentine, narrow Seine was unlikely to be more than an inconvenience to the motorized Allies. Once Normandy was lost the next viable long-term defensive position was the West-wall, on the borders of the Reich itself. Throwing the Allies into the sea might by now be a chimera. But using what remained of the panzers to throw the Americans back into the bocage was a reasonable alternative to seeing the armor ground down day by day or enveloped by an Allied breakout.

Hitler's admonition to attack at full strength was also theoretically sensible. Kluge, however, was in no position to concentrate the divisions that were holding together his rapidly collapsing front. He managed to assemble 2nd and 116th Panzer, Das Reich, and elements of the Leib-standarte in XLVII Panzer Corps under Hans von Funck—about 300 tanks and assault guns. Funck was a first-rate tank man who had commanded 7th Panzer Division from 1941 to 1943 and XLVII Panzer Corps since March. Speed was his best force multiplier, and the panzers had not forgotten how to hit fast and hard. Going in on the night of August 6, Das Reich captured Mortain and opened the road to Avranches. On its right, the army's 2nd Panzer drove through one American regiment and almost encircled another.

"Almost," however, was the operative word. Funck and Kluge lacked the reserves to exploit initial successes. The Americans rallied instead of breaking. Artillery fire called in by a battalion surrounded on high ground outside Mortain took toll of Das Reich's columns; antitank guns blocked the division's armor. The 30th Infantry Division and elements of 3rd Armored halted and then counterattacked 2nd Panzer and Leib-standarte. Omnipresent fighter-bombers—American Thunderbolts and British Typhoons—savaged the unarmored vehicles backed up on every road in the sector. Orders to shift to the defensive were garbled or mis-understood, risking both the operation and the troops involved.

Kluge reported the attack no longer feasible. Hitler ordered it con-tinued, sent Eberbach south to command the strike force in place of Funck, and told him to jump off on August 11. Eberbach, whose Nazi sympathy was mostly situational, reported the state of his troops was such that he could not attack before August 20. It took almost two days for him, Hausser, and Kluge, working together, to change Hitler's mind.

Meanwhile 3rd Army took Le Mans on August 8, and II Canadian Corps mounted Operation Totalize against German positions south of Caen now weakened by the withdrawal of their panzer elements for the Mortain offensive. On the night of August 7–8 two infantry divisions, each led by three battle groups of a tank company or battalion and an infantry battalion mounted in improvised full-tracked armored person-nel carriers, bit deeply into the German defenses. But the two armored divisions, one Canadian and one Polish, which were expected to com-plete the operation by opening the way to the Falaise road junction, were both green. They faced, moreover, a Hitler Jugend Division that moved into the gap with its ranks refilled, its tanks replaced, and a new commander, Kurt Meyer.

Cocky beyond the point of arrogance at 34, Meyer kept in touch with his forward elements by motorcycle, and had 18 broken bones to prove it. His involvement in the murder of Canadian prisoners, which earned him a sentence as a war criminal, was arguably a resume-enhancer in his particular subculture. In his first outing as a divisional commander, Meyer also proved a master of flexible defense. Supported by a Tiger battalion and by 88mm flak guns firing over open sights, Meyer's Pan-thers and Panzer IVs bent, snapped back, and held. By August 10 the division was down to 35 tanks. But Falaise was still 13 miles in its rear.

By August 13 it was reasonably clear on both sides of the line that the German armies in Normandy were on the ragged edge of being surrounded. No more than a 30-mile gap remained between the Allied pin-cers; whatever happened on the ground, the Jabos, the fighter-bombers, would be waiting. Kluge, fighting with a piano wire around his neck, had his command convoy shot out from under him on August 14 and spent the day out of contact. On August 15 he finally prepared an order for a general retreat and informed Hitler and the High Command that withdrawal was necessary. Hitler authorized the withdrawal and simul-taneously replaced Kluge with Model.

Kluge committed suicide; Model was in no position to do more than implement Kluge's orders. At this stage the Germans' situation was desperate but not hopeless. The Canadians were making heavy weather of the final advance on Falaise, owing in good part to Hitler Jugend, which for the second time in ten weeks fought its frontline units to near destruction. Eberbach's panzers were still holding on along the southern flank. German staffs also knew how to organize retreats; one might say they were becoming specialists in the subject.

The problem lay in implementation. The long-standing postwar debate among British, Canadian, and US soldiers and scholars over exactly who failed to close the Falaise pocket, and why, has tended to obscure the actual results of withdrawing through a steadily shrinking bottleneck. The full strength of Allied tactical air power came into play. Artillery, even tank guns, joined in to create a gauntlet of fire defying all efforts to break through it. Second and 9th SS Panzer Divisions bought time and space on August 19–20 against an isolated 1st Polish Armored Division. But when the tallies were cast, 10,000 Germans were dead, 50,000 were prisoners, and the Normandy campaign was over.

The question now was whether the Germans could retreat faster than the Allies could pursue them. Continuous air strikes combined with a suddenly burgeoning French and Belgian Resistance to inflict constant nagging losses. The panzers, army and SS, had salvaged a surprising number of men, but their AFV strengths were frequently counted in single digits. By early September Army Group B was down to 100 tanks—2,200 had been lost. Not only damaged tanks, but most of the field repair facilities as well had been abandoned.

The resulting decision was to withdraw the bulk of the panzers behind the Westwall, into Germany, for reequipment. German armor nevertheless fought two sharp rear-guard actions in the autumn of 1944. The most familiar was a coincidence: the dropping of the British 1st Airborne Division onto II SS Panzer Corps and its 9th and 10th Divisions around Arnhem. Two bodies cannot occupy the same space. Whatever the strategic possibilities of Operation Market-Garden, its execution reflected a combination of groupthink and hubris at all command levels, particularly culpable in discounting intelligence reports of a mechanized German presence.

The "bridge too far" is better understood in British paratrooper John Frost's words as "a drop too many." A World War II airborne division had no chance in a close-quarters, stand-up fight with two armored divisions, even in the midst of refitting, unless it confronted an extremely obliging enemy. German corps commander Wilhelm Bittrich, in the Waffen SS since 1934, had led Das Reich, then Hohenstaufen capably. His division COs, Walter Harzer and Heinz Harmel, were both in their thirties, both "fast-burners" who had proven themselves in Normandy. Taken fully by surprise, the SS panzers reacted promptly and with deadly effect. Arguably more remarkable was their punctilious concern for red crosses, white flags, and soldierly honor.

Farther south the Lorraine campaign pitted George Patton against a reconfigured 5th Panzer Army, and both of them against weather and terrain. The Lorraine plateau, surrounded by natural barriers, with its rivers running north-south, and with successive lines of high ground that had shaped tactics in earlier wars, did not lend itself to sweeping mobile operations even apart from the overlapping networks of man-made fortifications that crisscrossed the region. Constant rain turned fields into glutinous mud. "I can imagine no greater burden," wrote a frustrated Patton, "than to be the owner of this nasty country where it rains every day and where the whole wealth of the people consists in assorted manure piles."

The Americans were short of fuel and replacements. The Germans were short of everything except experience—and some of that experience was questionable. Fifth Panzer Army was led by Hasso von Manteuffel. He had commanded a battalion, a regiment, and a brigade of panzer grenadiers in Russia, a division in North Africa, and finally 7th Panzer Division and Grossdeutschland in the east. Like most of his contemporaries he led from the front, and was enough of a Hitler favorite to be promoted directly to army command despite the impeccably aristocratic background that gave him the nickname "panzer baron."

Half his armor strength was in divisions that had been shot to pieces since June 6; the other half consisted of four newly organized panzer brigades. Ideally including a battalion each of Panthers and Panzer IVs and a fully mechanized panzer grenadier battalion, these brigades were originally intended as mobile reserves to counter enemy breakthroughs before they could become breakouts. Their commanders and cadres were largely Eastern Front veterans. However, they lacked the staying power to cope with the levels of artillery and air support available through US communications systems. They lacked the experience and training to counter small-unit tactics far more flexible than anything encountered in Russia. Not least, they often lacked a maintenance element to repair damaged tanks and salvage broken-down ones. That meant rapid, permanent declines in armored strength.

The brigades were also the only reinforcements available for the Lorraine counterattack. In preliminary operations, the 106th under Franz Bake, among the best of the panzers' regimental-level COs, took the 90th Infantry Division by surprise before dawn on August 8. By late afternoon, three-quarters of Bake's men were down and only nine of his original 47 AFVs were still operational. On September 13, a French armored battle group encircled and annihilated the 112th Panzer Brigade: a fight at even odds that prefigured the fate of the general offensive launched five days later.

Fifth Panzer Army's attack was structured along the lines of the ripostes at which the Germans had become so expert in Russia. This was the first time Patton's army had faced one of these sophisticated, multiple-axis strokes on a large scale. In some of the heaviest armored fighting since Normandy, 4th Armored Division took advantage of fog to come to close quarters with the Panzers at Arracourt on September 19, claiming a kill ratio of ten to one and showing comprehensive battalion-level superiority over German units that made such un-German mistakes as reading maps incorrectly. Manteuffel was ordered to push on even as losses increased beyond prospect of immediate replacement. On September 29 his superiors finally ordered him to stand down. Of more than 600 tanks and assault guns initially committed, almost 500 had been lost for no advantage in particular.

III

THE SLOWDOWN OF the armored war in the West offers an opportunity to address the campaign's major technical subtext: the quality of Allied armor. For practical purposes that means the Sherman tank. Three major variations of the M4 tank fought in Northwest Europe: the original M4, the M4a3 with a 76mm high-velocity gun, and the Firefly, a British variant mounting their 17-pounder antitank gun. Shermans were the principal equipment of the American, Canadian, French, and Polish armored formations, plus two of the three British armored divisions and four of their seven three-battalion independent brigades. For good and ill, it was a Sherman war.*

The image of victory in the West achieved by throwing thousands of tanks against the enemy's hundreds remains one of the major tropes in the historiography of World War II. An anecdote that developed in many versions during the final months of World War II describes a German officer boasting to his American captors of the superiority of German weaponry. When asked why, if his hardware was so good, he was the one in the POW cage, the answer was, "I had a battery of 88s. The Americans kept sending tanks down the road. We kept knocking them out. We ran out of ammunition. You didn't run out of tanks."

The other side of that story is the Germans' grim nickname for the Sherman as the "tommy cooker," recognition of the Sherman's propensity for bursting into flame before the crew could get out. Allied

---

* The "Sherman factor" is even larger if the Cromwell, which equipped a half-dozen British armored battalions, is understood as a Sherman counterpart, with higher speed but the same kind of medium-velocity 75mm gun and similar protection.

equivalents—the polite ones—were "Zippo" and "Ronson." A continually growing body of technically and tactically oriented works concedes the mechanical reliability of US tanks but emphasizes shortcomings in armor protection and firepower by comparison not only to the German Panzer IVs, Panthers, and Tigers, but the Soviet Union's T-34s and the KV/JS family of heavy tanks.

Underlying the discussion is the assumption that American industry could have manufactured and distributed armored fighting vehicles of any kind desired and in any numbers requested. Between 1942 and 1945, the United States manufactured almost 50,000 Shermans. To this figure can be added over 6,000 Grants and Lees, with their sponson-mounted 75mm cannon, and another 7,000 plus of the M3/M5 family of light tanks. Common sense correspondingly indicates that the technical shortcomings of US tanks vis-à-vis their principal opponents reflected policy decisions rather than production capacities.

American tank development between the wars was structured by a consistent commitment to mobility and reliability over gun-power and armor protection. In that sense the Germans and Americans had more in common than is generally understood—and for many of the same reasons. The Armored Force created in 1940 took most of its immediate cues from the Germans' experience in France. Those successes were understood—legitimately—as greatest and most cost-effective when achieved by maneuver as opposed to combat. US tanks were similarly projected for use in masses, by divisions and corps, as instruments of penetration and exploitation as opposed to breakthrough. Those missions were perceived as demanding above all speed and reliability. In 1940 those qualities were technologically easier to incorporate in a light tank—especially for a country with no significant experience in tank design and manufacture.

Fast, reliable light tanks were by no means an end in themselves. Mediums would be necessary to break resistance too heavy for the light tanks and to serve as a counterattack force when necessary. Tables of organization for armored divisions initially called for a ratio of one medium regiment to two light ones. After the Tunisian campaign that proportion was reversed. The Sherman's gun proved effective at up to

2,500 yards firing armor-piercing ammunition. Its high-explosive shells were devastating not only to infantry positions (a major original purpose of the medium tank) but against dug-in antitank guns as well.

Responsibility for creating the conditions for armor to operate belonged to the infantry divisions. They were not expected to operate alone. American know-how and productive capacity would deliver any number of armored fighting vehicles a fully mobilized army might require. Mobilization plans provided for independent tank battalions to support and cooperate with them on a more or less one-to-one basis, similar to the original German concept of the assault gun.

The US Army had another expected ace in the hole. In 1940 none of Europe's armies, even the Soviet Union, intended to pit tanks against tanks as a matter of course. Given the vehicles' relative scarcity, such tactics made no more sense than a chess player seeking to exchange queens as an opening gambit. The preferred counter was the towed antitank gun. America developed an alternative: high-velocity guns on self-propelled carriages. The definitive initial Tank Destroyer—a literal, conscious translation of the German Panzerjaeger—was the M-10: a three-inch-high velocity gun in a lightly armored, open-topped turret on a modified Sherman chassis, relying on surprise, speed, and shock against its better-protected adversaries.

The tank destroyer concept has been so sharply and systematically criticized that its genesis is often overlooked. The motto of "seek, strike, destroy" was meant to be applied against the kind of tanks operational in the early 1940s. The M-10's three-inch gun was at the time of its adoption as good as any armor-piercing weapon on tracks, even the 76mm gun of the Russian T-34. Doctrine called for using tank destroyers in masses—at peak strength there were over a hundred battalions—to stop massive, high-speed, flexible attacks of the kind that took the Germans to the gates of Moscow.

Tank destroyers were, in short, not a bad idea at the time. Ironically they were intended to counter just the kind of operation the overstrained panzers were never able to mount against American forces that were consistently on the offensive. And on the offensive, tank destroyers were enough out of their element to be without a role—particularly as the nature of German tanks changed. With their thin armor and relatively high silhouettes, M10s "stalking" Panthers or Tigers resembled nothing so much as ants attacking an armadillo.

The Shermans were left on their own. Were they good enough? In North Africa, then in Sicily and Italy, American tankers regularly encountered up-gunned Panzer IVs, Panthers, and Tigers. On the whole the Shermans coped—not perfectly, but they coped. To supplement the medium-velocity gun, the US introduced a 76mm design based on the M-10s three-inch. Intended primarily to engage tanks with armor-piercing rounds, the gun was something of an afterthought in the contexts of doctrine that still discounted tank-versus-tank combat, and of experience that asserted the importance of tanks in direct support of infantry. It was correspondingly unpopular among senior officers who preferred the more versatile medium-velocity 75. The proportion of 76mm Shermans in the armored divisions reached an average of a third only at the end of 1944. For the independent battalions, it stabilized at a little over a fourth.

The British took a different tack, mounting their 17-pounder anti-tank gun—ballistically a rough equivalent of the German 88—in one out of four of their Shermans. In the weeks after D-Day, none of the alternatives proved optional. The 75mm gun was ineffective against German frontal armor at any but near-suicidal ranges. American crews quickly learned that the 76mm was second-rate. To make it better fit a Sherman turret, the Ordnance Department reduced the barrel by over a foot, correspondingly reducing muzzle velocity, ballistic effectiveness, and armor penetration. The Firefly was an excellent tank killer, but its long barrel stood out from the Sherman shorthorns, making it a distinctive and favorite target.

Bocage restricted maneuver. Enough German tanks were present to provide far closer mutual support than had been common in North Africa and Italy. Crew losses mounted; crew morale declined. Awkward questions were raised in Parliament, thanks in good part to the Establishment connections of the Guardsmen riding tanks. Eisenhower contacted Chief of Staff George Marshall demanding that AFVs with 90mm guns be made available as soon as possible. Allied heavy bombers even devoted some effort to knocking out the Reich's tank factories.

US armored divisions were reorganized prior to D-Day, and the number of by-now nearly useless light tanks reduced to a fourth of their strength. The reconfigured divisions, with three battalions each of tanks, infantry in half-tracks, and self-propelled light howitzers, were significantly more mobile than their German and Soviet counterparts. But with only slightly more than 10,000 men, their shock and staying powers were so limited that after the war, a board recommended adding three infantry battalions and virtually doubling the division's size.

The new organization reflected the updated field manual released in January 1944, which addressed destroying enemy forces in combat more than did its predecessor, but continued to stress the armored division's primary role as offensive operations in enemy rear areas. This had worked well enough in Sicily, where George Patton kept the 2nd Armored Division concentrated and used it for exploitation, most notably in the 100-mile lunge to capture Palermo. Admittedly resistance was light, but US armored divisions had never been intended to engage their panzer counterparts directly. German and Soviet armor created opportunity; Americans developed it. Tank killing fell, albeit by default, to artillery and air power.

Nor were Soviet-style deep operations part of the Allied repertoire. Operational art was irrelevant to Britain's fundamentally maritime strategic paradigm. It required 40 years to develop in the US after World War II, and even then was presented with more enthusiasm than understanding. No specialized armored higher headquarters existed or evolved in either army. US armored divisions were usually allocated among standard corps in a ratio of one to two or three infantry divisions. That reflected both Eisenhower's broad-front strategy and America's policy of deploying the smallest possible army. The "90-division gamble" meant armored divisions had to be kept up front instead of being concentrated panzer-fashion.

That the British, after briefly testing the use of massed armor in Normandy, accepted a similar system reflected the fact that the Allied armies were fully motorized.* The race across France and Belgium showed infantry divisions could keep pace with the armor in a way neither the Germans nor the Soviets could match, while heavily concentrated armor tended to get in its own way. The riflemen were also supported by armor on a scale considered jaw-dropping by Landser standards. An American infantry division on the offensive could usually count on a battalion of fifty Shermans and another of three dozen tank destroyers able to serve as assault guns manqué or to tie into the radio network as supplementary fire support. Its British counterpart could call on up to a brigade of Shermans or Churchills, the latter roughly a better-protected, turreted counterpart of the Sturmgeschütz IIIF, plus a family of specialized armor: flame-throwing tanks, mine-clearing tanks, and tanks with turrets removed and converted to armored personnel carriers.

It nevertheless remains defensible to suggest that in terms of doctrine and material, Allied armor on D-Day was ideally configured to defeat the panzers of Operation Blue. Technical changes during the campaign were marginal. The M-18 Hellcat tank destroyer, introduced in late 1943, could make the incredible top speed of 55 miles per hour, but had almost no protection and carried the same 76mm gun as the new mark of Sherman. Although official tank destroyer doctrine still considered a heavy gun unnecessary, a 90mm gun on a modified M-10 chassis went into production in April 1944. By V-E Day, 22 battalions of them were on the ground in the European Theater of Operations. The M-26 tank, whose heavy armor, 90mm gun, and 48-ton weight made it a reasonable counter to the Panther, was not standardized until 1945; only around 200 were serving with the armored divisions when the war ended.

---

* British armored divisions in 1944 had a force ratio based on the "ideal" panzer division of 1941–42: three tank battalions, one mechanized and three truck-borne infantry battalions, and an "armored reconnaissance" battalion, also tank-equipped. Their initial employment in separate armored and infantry brigades proved too rigid and usually gave way in practice to a battle group system pairing tank and infantry battalions, two pairs to each brigade. An interesting organizational footnote is the British experiment in 1942 with "mixed divisions" of two infantry and one tank brigades—the same combination initially advocated for postwar US armored divisions. However, based on infantry divisions with an infantry ethos, the experiment proved a failure.

US design and procurement agencies did manage to develop and
introduce by late 1944 the definitive light tank of World War II. Weighing a bit over 18 tons, with a medium-velocity 75mm gun adapted from
an aircraft model and a top speed of 35 miles per hour, the M-24 was
ideal for 1941. In 1944 all it needed was a buggy whip.

On the British side the number of Fireflies was doubled. More
17-pounders were mounted on more Lend-Lease M-10s, and on obsolescent tank chassis, of which there were so many in Britain's inventory.
At best these were stopgaps. But British tank designers, who for much
of the war might as well have been working for the other side, finally
got it right with the Comet, a fast 35-ton Panther killer with a modified
17-pounder gun and a better all-round tank than the M-26. But only a
single armored division received the new vehicles during the war. The
even better Centurion set postwar standards of effectiveness for years,
but only began field trials in May 1945, reflecting a government decision to delay projects that could not enter service in 1944. The bureaucrats responsible did not have to clean human remains from burned-out
Sherman hulls.

With those points made, others can be offered as counterweights.
Stephen Zaloga appropriately observes that technical comparisons and
tank-on-tank duels are disproportionately interesting to battle buffs and
war gamers, particularly with the development of computerized visuals.
In fact, the number of tank-versus-tank battles fought during the European campaign was limited, and many of those were small scale, involving a half dozen on each side. Postwar research, moreover, indicated that
in those situations the most important factor was reaction time: seeing
first, firing first, and hitting first. Second came tactics: positioning and
movement. Technical comparisons were less significant.

An experienced crew, or a well-trained one, had a better chance in
a direct confrontation. On the other hand, a poor crew with an inferior tank in a hull-down position, or on the flank or rear, had at least a
first-strike edge over better men advancing in a state-of-the-art AFV.
That held true even for the much-vilified tank destroyers. British M-10s
manned by artillerymen successfully engaged Panzer IVs in Normandy;

M-18s showed well against attacking Panthers at Arrancourt and many another now-forgotten sites.

"Advancing," however, is the operative word. About half of all Allied tank losses in the European theater of operations came from high-velocity gunfire. British and Americans alike tended to describe any such round as an 88. Case studies suggest that as many as three-fourths were in fact 75mm. These could have come from Panthers or Panzer IVs, assault guns or open-topped tank destroyers—and not least from the towed antitank guns, whose crews contributed heavily to German defensive successes in Normandy. One or two well-positioned, well-camouflaged Pak 75s (and the Russian Front had made the Germans experts in concealment) could slow the boldest tankers until infantry could arrive to finish them off. And the gunners often had a good chance of getting clear to fight again before matters reached grenade range.

"Advancing" might also be cited as an adjective modifying the positive consequences of the Sherman's well-established mechanical reliability. While it is certainly preferable to have tanks on line rather than under repair, recently available German statistics for the Eastern Front make clear that the crucial variable in maintenance was ability to recover the vehicle. In the predominantly offensive campaign for Northwest Europe, where the Allies generally occupied the battlegrounds, would it have been any more difficult to salvage a less-reliable tank with higher survivability in combat?

Much clearer is the fact that missions shaped proficiency. By 1944, as the previous chapter indicates, the panzers were configured by equipment and experience to fight other mechanized forces, whether by holding a front or counterattacking. Most Allied tank engagements were combined-arms operations involving buildings and entrenchments, troops caught in the open and unarmored vehicles. A Sherman in an American armored division might carry as little as a third of its gun ammunition in armor-piercing rounds. Machine guns could be used more often than the main armament in "routine" situations: the .50-caliber on the turret of most Shermans chewed through earth and walls with devastating effect.

It is correspondingly reasonable to suggest that tank crews conditioned to that kind of fighting might lose a little of the type of situational awareness required for tank-on-tank action. But the panzers were always somewhere in the background. Any German tank encountered could take on the dimensions of a Panther or Tiger. Allied and Japanese airmen in the Pacific similarly reported destroyers as cruisers and cruisers as battleships. Stress and adrenaline were major factors; panzer crews in Russia were no less prone to upgrade their opposition for scoring purposes and bragging rights.

Armor revisionists are fond of stating—accurately—that only three Tiger battalions fought in Normandy, all in the British sector. It is no less true that in their greatest number, during the Battle of the Bulge, Panthers were only a quarter of the AFVs committed—even before they started breaking down. But in the middle distance on a cloudy day, the differences between a Panzer IVJ and a Tiger can be difficult to discern even without the distractions of combat. What stood out was their common feature: the long-barreled, high-velocity gun calculated to make instant believers of US Ordnance types more interested in engines and transmissions than in weapons design.

V

DURING THE AUTUMN of 1944, in the aftermath of the failed attempt on Hitler's life on July 20, and in the aftermath of the Red Army's colossal breakthroughs in the East, the Nazi regime and the German people mobilized their last reserves of ferocity and fanaticism. The propaganda vision of a people's community at arms and the free rein given to violence on both foreign and home fronts enhanced a pattern of exploitation and dehumanization already permeating German society from the factories to the countryside. Rationality gave way to passion and to fear as retribution loomed for a continent's worth of crimes.

The Wehrmacht went out fighting and it went down hard. Like the German people, it neither saw nor sought an alternative. The prospective fate implied in the Allies' demand for unconditional surrender could assume terrifying form to men who had seen—and participated in—the things done "in the name of the Third Reich and the German people." That meant reconstructing shattered divisions by placing officers at road junctions and impressing every man without a clear destination, even if cooks became tankers and sailors found themselves in the Waffen SS. It meant filling out ranks with teenage draftees and men combed out of the increasingly moribund navy and air force. It meant reequipment by an industrial system that continued to defy the best efforts of the Combined Bomber Offensive. It meant morale enforced by laws making a soldier's family liable for any derelictions of duty. It meant field courts-martial that seemed to impose only one sentence: death.

Combine Eisenhower's commitment to a continuous front with the relative weakness of Allied ground forces, and weak spots must inevitably emerge. The most obvious one was in the American sector: the Ardennes Forest, a static sector manned by a mix of green divisions and veteran outfits that had been burned out elsewhere. Hitler's intention, shared and underwritten by High Command West, was to replicate the success of 1940 by striking through the Ardennes for Antwerp. The port's capture would both create a logistical crisis for the Allies and divide the British from the Americans, opening the way to their defeat in detail and—just possibly—to a decisive falling-out between partners whose squabbling, egalitarian relationship was never really understood by German strategic planners who believed in client systems rather than alliances.

That the Allies still had absolute control of the air over the front, and that German fuel supplies were about enough to get their tanks halfway to Antwerp, did not concern the Führer. Nor were his generals excessively disturbed. The planners of High Command West preferred in principle a more limited operation: a double envelopment aimed at Liege. They were, however, never able to convince even themselves why Germany's last reserves should be used that way. What was to be gained, except a drawn-out endgame?

At least the West was geographically small enough to offer something like a legitimate strategic objective. The Eastern Front presented only the prospect of a second Kursk, with the last of the panzers feeding themselves into a Russian meat grinder somewhere east of the existing front line. Panzer Lehr's Fritz Bayerlein echoed many of his counterparts when he said he persuaded himself that the attack would succeed in order to give his orders credibility and sustain the aggressive spirit of his subordinates. If Operation Watch on the Rhine proved a Twilight of the Gods, then it would be a virtuoso performance as far as the army's professionals and the zealots of the SS could make it.

By mid-December a buildup overlooked or discounted by confident Allied commanders gave the Germans a three-to-one advantage in men and a two-to-one advantage in armored vehicles in their chosen sector of attack. A new 6th SS Panzer Army had been organized in September under Sepp Dietrich. By this time in the Western theater the distinctions and antagonisms between army and Waffen SS had diminished, especially in the panzer formations, where the consistently desperate situation and the relatively even numbers of divisions made close mutual support a necessary norm. In the projected offensive, 5th Panzer and 6th SS Panzer Armies would fight side by side with few questions asked.

Part of the army panzers' reconstruction involved reorganization. Both in Russia and in the West, the events of 1944 had resulted in serious losses of trained specialists and no less serious discrepancies between the numbers actually available in the combat units and those in the divisions' rear echelons. One response was pairing panzer divisions by twos in permanent corps that would assume service and training responsibilities. Five were organized and saw action, against the Russians in the final campaign. More significant was the introduction on August 11 of the Panzer Division Type 1944. This gave each panzer grenadier regiment an organic pioneer company and each tank battalion organic maintenance and supply companies. Both changes acknowledged the decentralization that had become the panzers' tactical and operational norm. Battalions consistently shifting rapidly from place to place and battle group to battle group would now be more self-sufficient. Divisions would now be better able to concentrate on planning and fighting—at least in principle.

The new panzer divisions were still authorized two tank battalions, each of as many as 88 tanks. Paper may be infinitely patient; reality is less

forgiving. In the autumn of 1944, Allied heavy bomber strikes repeatedly hit most of the big tank manufacturing complexes: Daimler-Benz,
MAN in Nuremberg, and the Henschel Tiger II plant in Kassel. Speer
was able to sustain production, but only around half of the 700 Panthers and Panzer IVs scheduled for delivery in December reached the
intended users.

The shortages also reflected decisions made in the Armaments
Ministry. Speer had kept up tank production by transferring resources
from the manufacture of other vehicles and by cutting back on spare
parts. The latter dropped from over a quarter of tank-related contracts
in 1943 to less than 10 percent in December 1944. Critical resources, like
the molybdenum that made armor tough as opposed to brittle, were
in critically short supply. Quality control slipped badly in everything
from optics to transmissions to welding. The continued willingness of
Germans to report for work despite the bombing is often cited. The
on-the-job efficiency of men and women deprived of everything from
their homes to a night's sleep has been less investigated.

The increasing use of slave labor in war plants had consequences
as well. Distracted, tired foremen and overseers were easier to evade.
Risks that seemed foolhardy in 1943 took on a different dimension as
the Reich seemed on the edge of implosion. Deliberate sabotage was
probably less significant than hostile carelessness. But increasing numbers of panzers were coming on line with screws poorly tightened, hoses
poorly connected—and an occasional handful of shop grit or steel filings
deposited where it might do some damage. That was no small matter in
contexts of frequently inexperienced crews and frequently nonexistent
maintenance vehicles.

The immediate response was to reduce the number of tanks in a
company to 14, and where necessary to replace those with assault guns of
varying types. Even with these makeshifts, 15 panzer divisions still had
only one tank battalion. Sometimes an independent battalion would be
attached—Leibstandarte, for example, benefited by receiving the Tigers
of the 501st SS as its de facto second battalion. Other divisions found
themselves with new battalions equipped with Jagdpanthers or Jagdpanzer IVs, trained for antitank missions rather than tank tactics, or in

the close cooperation with panzer grenadiers that remained the assault guns' mission in an offensive.

Training and equipment were general problems in divisions preparing for the Ardennes offensive. Panzer Lehr, the army's show horse, had its full complement of men, a third tank battalion equipped with assault guns, and one of the supplementary heavy antitank battalions. Das Reich, however, reported a large number of inexperienced recruits, and reported individual and unit training as at low standards. Leibstandarte described morale as excellent, but combat readiness above company level as inadequate. The 116th Panzer Division was short of armor, motor vehicles, and junior officers and NCOs. Second Panzer Division lacked a third of its vehicles: on December 14, one panzer grenadier battalion was riding bicycles. It was all a far cry from the spring of 1940.

In its final form, Watch on the Rhine* incorporated three armies deployed on a 100-mile front under Model, commanding Army Group B since Rundstedt had been restored, at least nominally, to his former position in September. The balance of forces at the cutting edge, and their missions, demonstrated the army's decline relative to the Waffen SS. Dietrich's 6th SS Panzer was the spearhead, with Leibstandarte, Das Reich, Hohenstaufen, and Hitler Jugend as its backbone, and five army infantry divisions as spear-carriers and mop-up troops. Fifth Panzer Army would cover Dietrich's left, and Manteuffel had the army's armored contribution: Panzer Lehr, 2nd and 116th Panzer Divisions, plus four infantry divisions. Protecting his left flank in turn was the responsibility of 7th Army, with four infantry divisions and no armor to speak of.

Watch on the Rhine's order of battle incorporated 200,000 men, 600 armored vehicles, almost 2,500 supporting aircraft—that number itself a triumph of concentration involving stripping the Reich's air defenses. Radio silence was draconically enforced. Camouflage was up to Eastern Front standards. Parachute drops and sabotage units were

---

* The name was changed to Autumn Mist (*Herbstnebel*) in December, but to avoid confusion the original is used throughout.

expected to confuse surprised defenders even further. The offensive seemed structured to maximize what the Germans—the panzer troops in particular—considered their main strength: sophisticated tactical and operational expertise.

Model could in principle call on another ten divisions, but only two were panzers; the offensive would rise or fall with its starting lineup. The operational plan was Sichelschnitt recycled. Dietrich, at the Schwerpunkt, was to break through around Monschau, cross the Meuse around Liege, and strike full tilt for Antwerp. Manteuffel would cross the Meuse at Dinant and aim for Brussels. The panzers were expected to be across the Meuse before the Allies could move armor sufficient to counter them.

As so often before, however, German focus devolved into tunnel vision. None of the specific plans addressed the subject of Allied air power. The responsible parties similarly avoided addressing directly the fuel question. By comparison to the Western campaign's early months, fuel supplies were impressive, but the Panthers and Tigers were always thirsty. Were the Americans likely to be so confused, so feckless, and so obliging as to leave their fuel dumps intact as refilling points? In the climate of December 1944, asking such a question suggested dangerous weakness of will and character.

Sepp Dietrich might be an unrefined, unimaginative, hard-core Nazi, but he did not lack common sense. All the Waffen SS had to do, he later said sarcastically, was "cross a river, capture Brussels, and then go on to take Antwerp ... through the Ardennes when the snow is waist-deep and there isn't room to deploy four tanks abreast let alone armored divisions. When it doesn't get light until eight and it's dark again at four—and at Christmas." Sixth SS Panzer Army had four days to reach the Meuse. Dietrich and his staff set the infantry divisions to breach US defenses on day one, December 16. When the hastily reconstituted army units faltered in the face of determined American resistance, the word was "panzers forward." But Kharkov and Kursk were a long way back. The Waffen SS had made its recent reputation in defensive fighting. Experience in offensive operations had been diluted by expansion. Officer casualties had been heavy. From battalion to division, 6th SS

Panzer Army correspondingly eschewed finesse in favor of head-down frontal attacks.

Tactical maneuver was further restricted by rain periodically freezing into snow as temperatures hovered in the low thirties. Fields already saturated by the heavy rains of early autumn turned into glutinous paste when the heavy German tanks tried to cross them. The alternative was straight down the roads and straight down the middle from village to village. Each attack was expected to put the finishing touches on an enemy that seemed on the ragged edge of breaking. Yet the "Amis" held on—and without the fighter-bombers grounded by the same weather that slowed the panzers.

For the sake of speed the SS neither used their reconnaissance battalions to probe for weak spots, nor their pioneers to assist the tanks. The tanks repeatedly pushed ahead and just as repeatedly lost contact with their infantry, only to run afoul of ambushed Shermans and M-10s, or bazooka teams taking advantage of relatively weak side armor. Even the 57mm popguns of the infantry's antitank units scored a few kills. The panzer grenadiers, many of them half-trained recruits or converted sailors and airmen, were at a surprising disadvantage against American regiments, some of which had been in action since Normandy.

The 12th SS Panzer Division, on the German right, lost most of its Panthers in the first two days and made no significant progress thereafter. Its neighbor, Leibstandarte, similarly held up, responded by sending forward an armor-heavy battle group. It included most of the division's striking power: a battalion each of Panthers, Panzer IVs, and Tiger Bs: together around 100 tanks, a mechanized panzer grenadier battalion, pioneers, and some self-propelled artillery. Its commander was Lieutenant-Colonel Jochen Peiper. He had been Himmler's adjutant from 1938 to 1941 and had enjoyed the Reichsführer's mentoring and patronage. He had developed into a hard-driving, charismatic risk-taker whose men followed him in good part because of his reputation as someone who led from the front and was the hardest man in any unit he led. Peiper was, in other words, an archetype of the kind of officer the Waffen SS nurtured in Russia and now turned loose in the West.

Peiper was also just the man to throw the dice for an entire panzer army. His mission was to reach the Meuse, capture the bridges before they were demolished, and hold until relieved. It was 100 miles over back-country roads that were little more than trails. Orders were to avoid combat when possible, and to tolerate no delays. The battle group's movements were a model tactical exercise—at first. The panzers bypassed confused American rear-echelon troops, slipped between elements of American convoys, and overran American supply dumps. With his fuel low, Peiper refilled his tanks with 50,000 gallons of US gas captured without firing a shot.

The panzers captured a key bridge at Stavelot on December 18, and pushed through to the Amblève River. All they had to do was cross, and the way to the Meuse would be open. But an American engineer battalion blew the bridges Peiper was expecting to rush—in one case literally under the gun of a Tiger VIB. American tanks and infantry, moving faster than expected, retook Stavelot and cut the panzers' line of communication. The sky was clearing, and the fighter-bombers returned to hammer Peiper's columns relentlessly. The battle group was down to three dozen tanks, as much from breakdowns as from combat loss. Its infantry, exposed to the weather day and night in their open-topped half-tracks, on cold rations and broken sleep, were numb with cold and fatigue. Peiper requested permission to withdraw. It was refused. Relief attempts were stopped almost in their tracks. As the Americans closed in, Peiper made his stand at a village called La Gleize. After two breakout efforts failed, with his tanks out of fuel and his ammunition exhausted, on Christmas he led out on foot the men he had left. Moving by night, 800 survivors of the 6,000 who began the strike a week earlier made it back to Leibstandarte's forward positions.

Peiper left behind about 100 of his own wounded and another 150 American POWs. The senior US officer later reported that the Germans had appropriately observed the rules of war. But from the operation's beginning, Kampfgruppe Peiper and the rest of Leibstandarte had left a trail of bodies in its wake: as many as 350 Americans and well over 100 Belgian civilians. The consequences were epitomized by the

GIs bringing in some prisoners from Peiper's battle group who asked an officer if he wanted to bother with them. He said yes. Not everyone did. For the rest of the war it was not exactly open season on Waffen SS prisoners, but they surrendered at a higher degree of immediate risk than their army counterparts.

Pieper was not necessarily a liar or a hypocrite when he not only insisted at La Gleize that he did not shoot prisoners, but seemed surprised by the allegation. He is best understood as resolving a specific form of the cognitive dissonance that increasingly possessed the Wehrmacht in particular and the Reich as a whole. The question of whether someone, Peiper or a superior, somehow either gave orders to take no prisoners or made it clear that "no delays" was a euphemism for "no prisoners" is misleading. Since Normandy, a pattern had developed in which both sides processed refusing quarter, shooting prisoners, and similar frontline atrocities, as mistakes, misunderstandings, or part of "the filth of war": fear, frustration, vengeance, the semi-erotic thrill of having an enemy completely at one's mercy.

Inexperienced troops are more prone to be trigger-happy, and there was ample inexperience on both sides of the line in June 1944. Even a thoroughly ideologized German was likely to see a difference between more or less Aryan "Anglo-Saxons" and despised, despicable Slavs. Nor was there much to gain by making things worse than they had to be. Within the same few days in Normandy, elements of the Hitler Jugend murdered Canadian prisoners in cold blood, and other troops of the division negotiated a local truce with a British battalion enabling both sides to bring their wounded to safety. Such agreements were not everyday occurrences, but they did happen. An officer of 9th Panzer Division describes one of his men bringing a wounded American back to his own lines and returning laden with chocolate and cigarettes as tokens of appreciation. A story improved in the telling? Perhaps. But nothing similar was plausible even as a rumor in the East. And one Russian Front was bad enough.

What did transplant from the East was a frontline culture that since 1941 had developed into something combining convenience and indifference, embedded in a matrix of hardness. Hardness was neither cruelty nor fanaticism. It is best understood in emotional and moral contexts, as will focused by intelligence for the purpose of accomplishing a mission. It was—and is—a mind-set particularly enabling the brutal expediency that is an enduring aspect of war.

In commenting on Kurt Meyer's trial and death sentence, a Canadian general asserted he did not know of a single general or colonel on the Allied side who had not said "this time we don't want any prisoners." In fact, there is a generally understood distinction, fine but significant, between not taking prisoners and killing them once they have surrendered. Recent general-audience works on the Canadians and Australians in World War I, for example, are remarkably open in acknowledging relatively frequent orders at battalion and company levels of "no prisoners" before an attack. Shooting or bayoneting unarmed men is another matter entirely. It might be called the difference between war and meanness.

James Weingartner highlights the discrepancy between the US Army's judging of war crimes by Americans and its response to comparable offenses involving Germans. That was not a simple double standard. For the Americans, as for the British and Canadians, expedience and necessity remained situational rather than normative, on the margin of legal and moral systems but not beyond them. On the German side of the line, hardness transmuted expediency into a norm and redefined it as a virtue. Impersonalization and depersonalization went hand in hand. Interfering civilians or inconvenient POWs might not be condignly and routinely disposed of—but they *could* be, with fewer and fewer questions asked externally or internally. The French government was shocked and embarrassed to find Alsatians represented among the perpetrators of Oradour. Defended in their home province as "forced volunteers," they were tried and convicted, but pardoned by Charles de Gaulle in 1953 for the sake of national unity.

The inability of the Waffen SS to break through on the north shoulder removed any possibility of success Watch on the Rhine might have had. Instead of exploiting victory, Das Reich and Hohenstaufen found themselves stymied by roads blocked for miles by abandoned vehicles out of fuel or broken down. While the SS ran in place, however,

Manteuffel had used his infantry skillfully to infiltrate, surround, and capture most of the green 106th Infantry Division's two forward regiments before sending his armor forward. The 116th Panzer made for Houffalize. Second Panzer and Panzer Lehr pushed through and over the 28th Infantry Division toward Bastogne, destroying an American armored combat command in the process.

The 101st Airborne Division got there first, dug in, and has been celebrated in story, if not song, ever since. The Germans originally hoped to take the town by a coup de main. When that proved impossible, Bayerlein argued that Bastogne was too important as a transportation center to be bypassed. Manteuffel was already concerned that his forward elements were too weak to sustain their progress; attacking Bastogne in force would only make that situation worse. He was also too old a panzer hand to risk tanks in a house-to-house fight against good troops. The Panzer Baron had begun his career in the horse cavalry, understood the importance of time for Watch on the Rhine, and decided to mask the town and continue his drive toward the Meuse.

That the choice had to be made highlighted the growing difficulty the panzers faced in being all things in every situation. In 1940, motorized divisions had been available for this kind of secondary collateral mission. In 1941, the marching infantry could be counted on to come up in time to free the panzers for their next spring forward. In 1944, 15th Panzer Grenadier Division did not arrive at Bastogne from army group reserve until December 24.

Fifth Panzer Army benefited from a cold front that set in on the night of December 22, freezing the ground enough for the Panthers to move cross-country. Soft ground, however, was the least of Manteuffel's problems. His spearheads knifed 60 miles deep into the American positions, along a 30-mile front. Second Panzer Division, generally regarded by the Americans as the best they faced, got to within five miles of the Meuse on December 24—ironically near Dinant, where 7th Panzer had staged its epic crossing in 1940. But its fuel was almost exhausted. Model responded by ordering the division to advance on foot. Brigadier General Meinrad von Lauchert had been commanding the division only since December 13. He had been a panzer officer since 1935, led everything from a company to a regiment in combat, and recognized bombast. But he was not a sorcerer, and could not conjure fuel where none existed. Second Panzer was at the far end of its operational tether.

By platoons and companies, Americans fought bitter defensive actions throughout the sector—in one case holding out in a castle. Thirty-two men would be awarded the Medal of Honor from first to last during the Battle of the Bulge, and determination increased as word spread that the Germans were not taking prisoners. To the north, what remained of the 106th, a regiment of the 28th, and combat commands of 7th and 9th Armored Divisions, held another key road junction— St. Vith—for five vital days against first infantry, then the elite panzers of the Führer Escort Brigade from Model's reserve. Not until 2nd SS Panzer Division advanced far enough to threaten the town from the north did the hard-hammered garrison withdraw.

In the process of working their way forward, elements of Dietrich's panzers seeking to evade the clogged roads in their sector began edging onto 5th Panzer Army's supply routes. Manteuffel ordered them kept off; the corps commander responded by establishing roadblocks whose men were authorized to use force to regulate traffic. There are no records of shots being fired, but army and SS columns remained entangled as tempers flared and cooperation eroded.

Model released some of his characteristic nervous energy by briefly directing traffic himself, while reassuring Hitler that the chances of victory remained great. But the overall supply situation was rapidly deteriorating. The clearing skies accompanying the cold front meant the return of allied planes en masse: an average of 3,000 sorties a day, disrupting operations and turning the movement of troops and vehicles to nighttime—including the vital fuel trucks.

Model had from the beginning recommended eschewing a drive to the Meuse in favor of a quick turn north to isolate and then encircle the dozen or so American divisions concentrated around Aachen. Dietrich's staff had been clandestinely working on a similar backup plan since December 8. Manteuffel underwrote their thinking on December 24, when he phoned the High Command and declared Antwerp was beyond his reach.

Any lingering optimism was dispelled on Christmas when 2nd Panzer was attacked by its literal counterpart, the 2nd US Armored Division. The Americans encircled the panzers' leading battle group, destroying it as artillery and RAF Typhoons frustrated relief efforts by the rest of the division supported by elements of the 9th Panzer, newly arrived from High Command reserve. Six hundred men escaped—walking and carrying no more than their personal weapons. It was getting to be a habit for the panzers. Two thousand more were dead or prisoners. Over 80 AFVs remained on the field, knocked out or with empty fuel tanks. The rest of the division fought on around the village of Humain, so fiercely that it took one of the new flame-throwing Shermans to burn out the last die-hards. On December 27, 2nd Panzer was withdrawn. On January 1, 1945, it reported exactly five serviceable tanks.

Panzer Lehr, on 2nd Panzer's left, had moved more slowly and less effectively—due in part perhaps to a bit of self-inflicted fog and friction. Bayerlein missed a possible chance to reach the Meuse when, on December 22, he halted to rest his men and allow them to celebrate Christmas with the extra rations sent forward for the occasion. According to some reliable accounts, Panzer Lehr's commander had also sacrificed a good part of December 19 flirting with a "young, blond, and beautiful" nurse in a captured American hospital.

The story invites comparison with the "yellow rose of Texas," whose dalliance with Santa Anna allegedly distracted the Mexican general in the crucial hours before the battle of San Jacinto. But a harem of nurses would have made no difference as Allied reinforcements continued to arrive in the northern sector and Patton's Third Army conducted a remarkable 90-degree turn north that took it into Bastogne on December 26.

Hitler was confronted with two choices: evacuate the salient and withdraw the panzers for future employment, or continue fighting to keep the Allies pinned down and draw them away from the industrial centers of the Ruhr and the Saar. Being Hitler, he decided on both. The infantry was left to hold the line, supported by what remained of the army's panzers and, temporarily, the Waffen SS, for whom Hitler had other plans.

The operational result was two weeks of head-down fighting as American tanks and infantry hammered into the same kind of farm-and-village strong points that had so hampered Watch on the Rhine. Now it was German antitank guns ambushing Shermans whose relatively narrow treads restricted their off-road mobility in the deepening snow. Not until January 16 did Patton's 11th Armored Division connect at Houffalize with elements of the 1st Army advancing from the north, forcing back Panzer Lehr despite its orders to hold the town "at all costs." For the next two weeks the Americans pushed eastward as the defense eroded under constant artillery fire and air strikes. It was not elegant but it was effective. The Bulge from first to last cost the Germans over 700 AFVs—almost half of the number committed. About half the Panthers still in German hands were downlined for repair.

VI

THE BATTLE OF the Bulge was the end of panzer operations in the West. Afterward it became, in Manteuffel's words, "a corporal's war—a multitude of piecemeal fights." It was not much of an exaggeration. Operation North Wind was originally intended to support the Ardennes offensive. Launched into Alsace in January, well after Watch on the Rhine had failed, North Wind burned out four more mechanized divisions to no purpose on any level, strategic, operational, or tactical. The American spearheads that pushed toward the Rhine in February and the British and Canadians that struggled through the Reichswald to their north encountered limited armored opposition, and most of that on company scale. As the Allies crossed the Rhine, encircled the Ruhr, and fanned out across a dying Reich, the scale diminished further.

At least so it appeared. Much of the time the Germans were shuffling the panzers from crisis point to crisis point in a near-random fashion defying close analysis. Regiments and divisions, reduced to cadres and skeletons, mounted counterattacks noted in their records and histories that had so little impact that they failed to make Allied war diaries except as last stands.

Panzer Lehr offers a good case study. After Houffalize it was withdrawn into reserve and rebuilt—numerically at least. The quality of the replacements was described as "bad": poor training, no experience. Vehicles were in short supply. Most of the tanks were under repair or lying by the side of the road somewhere. When new ones arrived they had not been adequately inspected and tested at the factories. They had not been "driven in" due to the lack of fuel. For the same reason the quality of the new drivers was low. Without time for checkups and overhauling at unit level, non-operational losses were an ongoing problem even when moving from skirmish to skirmish.

Panzer Lehr next saw action in February, committed to the Reichswald in support of the hard-pressed 116th Panzer. Its counterattacks were repeatedly stopped by tank and artillery fire of an intensity the division had never experienced. Mobile operations did not occur, grumbled one commenter, because the enemy refused to engage in them! From the Reichswald, Lehr was ordered south against the US 9th Army. It was "urgently awaited" locally—but as a mobile antitank defense against the fast-moving Americans. Hitler wanted a full-scale counterattack—a mission the panzer regiment's commander dismissed as "clearly unimaginable." Instead Lehr went into the line around Rheydt and Mönchengladbach and took heavy losses from air strikes and ground attacks. It fell back to Krefeld too weak to defend the city.

For what it was worth, Panzer Lehr's tank destroyers helped hold the Adolf Hitler Bridge across the Rhine until it could be blown. By then the division had only 20 serviceable tanks. Its panzer grenadier regiments had been reduced to battalion strength. Fuel shortages and breakdowns cost heavy vehicle losses. Communications equipment, a core element of the panzers' effectiveness throughout the war, was in short supply. Replacements were so scarce the division was impressing stragglers. When, on March 7, Panzer Lehr Division was finally authorized to retreat across the Rhine itself, infantry strength was down to a single battalion. Two tanks remained operational. "It would be superfluous," noted the commenters, "to describe the mood of the totally exhausted soldiers."

Two days later a battle group of fragments, built around 18 freshly repaired or newly arrived tanks, was ordered to the Remagen bridgehead. Along with bits and pieces of the 9th and 11th Panzer Divisions, grandiosely titled "Corps Group Bayerlein," it was expected to wipe out the bridgehead before the Americans could reinforce it. Bayerlein, Model—whose army group was responsible for the sector—and Hitler disagreed on the timing and direction of the attack. Albert Kesselring, who replaced Rundstedt as High Commander West on March 11, added his voice to the mix.

Hitler had convincingly insisted that the Russians were about to suffer a catastrophic defeat, after which the main German forces would redeploy and deal with the Western allies. All Kesselring had to do was hold on. How much of this Kesselring believed and processed through the generic optimism that gave him the nickname "smiling Albert" remains incalculable. What was certain was that the projected jump-off points for the attack kept falling into American hands before the Germans could get into position. First US Army made the subject moot on March 22 with an armored breakout to the northeast that joined 9th Army's spearheads to encircle the whole of Army Group B.

The Ruhr Pocket matched anything achieved by the Russians: over 300,000 Germans in some kind of uniform with some kind of military identity, ranging from schoolboys carrying bazookas to the remnants of famous divisions like 3rd Panzer Grenadier, 116th Panzer, and Panzer Lehr. An attempt at breakout failed when the Americans again overran the assembly areas. Lehr's records speak of "over-hasty withdrawals" and concede the division's fighting spirit was broken. By April 5, 15 AFVs remained. One battle group was built around four of them, three squads of bazooka men, a dismounted panzer grenadier company, and a local-defense pioneer company with all of its men over 50 years old.

Ten days later, as the Americans continued to carve up the pocket, the division staff concluded further resistance useless. The last rounds were fired off; the last armored vehicles destroyed; and what remained of Panzer Lehr waited for the Ami tanks to come and get them. Walther Model committed suicide on April 21 after telling a group of stragglers to go home and wishing them luck. When Germany surrendered, the German army in the West included three mechanized divisions: two armored, one panzer grenadier. The once mighty had fallen a long way.

The military bureaucrats responded to disaster by shuffling paper. In October 1944 a new type of panzer grenadier battalion was introduced on a scale of one or two to each army and Waffen SS division. Its rifle companies rode bicycles instead of trucks. In March the armored force introduced the Panzer Division 45. It created the "mixed panzer regiment," a battalion each of tanks and mechanized infantry plus support units: 40 tanks, half Panthers and half Panzer IVs. The other panzer grenadiers were now "partially motorized," a euphemism for the riflemen moving on foot. Panzer divisions unable to meet even these reduced standards were to be converted to "battle groups." Waffen SS panzer divisions lost two of their six infantry battalions, and two of the remaining four were to be equipped with bicycles. For practical purposes the new order remained a paper exercise. It nevertheless epitomized that demodernization of the Wehrmacht noted by so many scholars. And on March 28, Heinz Guderian was dismissed as Chief of Armored Troops and Acting Chief of Staff.

Guderian's position had never been exactly stable, despite his involvement in screening officers accused of complicity in July 20, his acceptance of the brutal suppression of the Polish Home Army and the destruction of Warsaw, and his tail-wagging support for the army's increasing Nazification. Requiring all General Staff officers to be "National Socialist officers" might be discounted as eyewash. But making the Nazi salute compulsory was more than a gesture—and was widely understood as such by all ranks.

After the war Guderian described his behavior as a set of compromises intended to encourage Hitler to listen to military reason. For Guderian that meant concentrating Germany's resources on the Eastern Front. He understood that this was the least worst alternative. But the Western allies had in fact halted their offensive, and been halted, short of the Rhine. Guderian shared a common German sense that Anglo-American fighting power was sufficiently mediocre that, for a while at least, High Command West could hold on with limited reinforcements. And at worst there was still some space in the west to trade for time. The Ruhr, Guderian argued, was finished: bombed out. The Silesian factories, in contrast, were still producing and must be defended.

German intelligence reported over 200 Soviet infantry divisions and two dozen tank and mechanized corps from the Baltic to the Carpathians—eleven-to-one odds in infantry, seven–to-one in tanks, plus the massive forces deployed in Hungary that through December continued the pressure on Budapest. Guderian responded on two levels. He began transferring mobile divisions eastward, with the intention of forming a central reserve strong enough to wage a maneuver battle on the Reich's frontier: the Lodz-Hohensalza area. That kind of fight, he argued, remained the strength of German soldiers and commanders. In any case it was the only chance for—what? Did Guderian share Hitler's hopes for the kind of miracle that had saved Frederick the Great? Was he playing out a bad hand because of professional pride? Or was he concerned with scoring points against his internal opponents?

What is known is that by mid-December Guderian had managed to reposition fourteen and a half panzer and panzer grenadier divisions. All were understrength. Most had been reconstructed like their counterparts remaining in the west, with replacements drawn from anywhere and equipment assembled ad hoc—not much for a front of 750 miles.

What is also known is that Guderian continued to argue in vain for the withdrawal of Army Group North from Courland, where its two dozen divisions were operationally useless, and to advocate equally in vain for a general shortening of the lines in the east—a position supported by Harpe and Reinhardt, the senior officers on the ground.

What is finally known—not least because Guderian was at pains to tell his version of the story in postwar safety—is that on Christmas Eve, New Year's Day, and January 9, Guderian met with Hitler, described the catastrophe looming in the east, and was blown off. Hitler dismissed the intelligence estimates as nonsense and ordered the responsible officer committed to an asylum. Guderian responded by calling the Eastern Front a house of cards that would collapse entirely if broken at any point. Hitler ended the dialogue by reasserting that the Eastern Front must make do with what it had.

When Guderian denounced the Führer's "ostrich strategy," he was being too generous. The ostrich is supposed to hide its head in the sand when confronting danger. Instead Hitler extended his neck—into Hungary. In early December, three rebuilt panzer divisions—3rd, 6th, and 8th—were dispatched to the theater as the core of a counteroffensive to recover ground lost in the autumn. That plan was forestalled first by predictable shortages of fuel and ammunition, then by a major Soviet offensive beginning in late December that set the stage for the war's final large-scale clash of armor.

Operationally Stavka's intention was to complete the capture of Budapest and open the way to Vienna. Strategically the aim was to fix Hitler's attention. Budapest would prove a difficult nut to crack, but the design's second half succeeded brilliantly. Hitler initially responded by sending south the two best divisions of Guderian's painfully assembled reserve, Totenkopf and Viking: IV SS Panzer Corps under Herbert Otto Gille. Gille is one of the forgotten generals of the Waffen SS— perhaps because he fits neither of the familiar physical stereotypes: barroom brawlers like Dietrich and Eicke or male models like Meyer and Peiper. Slightly built, wearing glasses, Gille looked like a middle-aged high-school science teacher. But he had commanded Viking for over a year and brought its survivors out of the Korsun Pocket, the first to wade into a flooded, freezing river at the head of a human chain. He led IV SS Panzer Corps ably in the autumn fighting around Warsaw, in the process winning Totenkopf's collective respect: neither an easy task nor necessarily a positive recommendation.

More than any of his senior counterparts in the Waffen SS, Gille eschewed ideologically connected behavior and rhetoric. He projected an alternate image with long and respectable antecedents in German military culture: a good comrade off duty but hard as he needed to be when it counted—a soldier doing a job. Now his job was to break through to Budapest. On the night of January 1 the panzers struck. Taking advantage of a collective post–New Year's hangover on the Russian side, IV SS Panzer Corps advanced 30 miles and knocked out over 200 tanks. But with half their strength still under way and only 100 Panthers and Panzer IVs between them, Viking and Totenkopf had no chance to break into the city directly. Finding that out cost them 3,500 men and 40 tanks and assault guns.

A simultaneous attack by III Panzer Corps similarly foundered against resistance too strong to be broken by the hundred-odd tanks available, even though 25 were Tigers. Gille's corps redeployed, went in again on January 9 around Esztergom, and broke into the rear echelons of the Soviets encircling Budapest. This time the SS got to within sight of the city towers. Gille called for a breakout. Hitler refused.

On January 12 the overextended SS again pulled back and shifted locations, this time south to Lake Balaton. On January 18 the corps attacked a third time, broke through on a 20-mile front, and advanced almost 40 miles the first day. The long 75s of "Guderian's Ducks" proved their worth as the panzers drove forward across open country on hard-frozen ground. On January 20 the Waffen SS reached the Danube, and this time came within 15 miles of Budapest before the surprised Russians concentrated enough force to stop what remained of them.

Taken together, the three attacks had been another bravura performance by Hitler's panzers, tactically on a level with the best of anything done in 1941–42. Gille and his men understood their efforts as a rescue mission, and had fought with reckless desperation even by Waffen SS standards. Once more, however, requests for a breakout were dismissed. Instead Hitler ordered the corps to withdraw.

The Führer saw Gille's operations as an initial step in driving the Red Army back from Budapest and securing the oil fields that were the Reich's last source of fuel. In mid-January he had begun removing SS divisions from the Ardennes for rebuilding. Most of what remained of Germany's arms production was poured into that process. Once again sailors without ships, airmen with neither planes nor bases, found themselves wearing SS runes. Guderian's expectation was that these refurbished shock troops would be transferred east. Instead, Hitler ordered 6th SS Panzer Army to Hungary for the offensive that, he informed

his generals, would decide a war that was essentially about controlling
resources.

Operation *Frühlingserwachen* (Spring Awakening) was the final
showcase and last stand of the panzers. Six Waffen SS divisions were
committed. Sixth SS Panzer Army had I SS Panzer Corps with Leibstandarte and Hitler Jugend: parent and child. The II SS Panzer Corps
included Das Reich and Hohenstaufen, old and new avatars of Himmler's personal army. Gille's corps was initially assigned to Balck's 6th
Army, alongside III Panzer Corps with two of the army's originals:
1st and 3rd Panzer Divisions. Put together, it added up to around 600
AFVs, the best available. Leibstandarte still boasted its battalion of 36
Tiger Bs. Hitler Jugend had an attached battalion of 31 Jagdpanzer IVs
and 11 Jagdpanther.

But the transfer of men and material was disrupted at every turn by
Allied air attacks, and the consequences of earlier attacks, on a railway
network no longer capable of sustaining the rapid, reliable, large-scale
troop movements of 1942–43. Not until March 6 was the main German
attack ready—and then almost 300 of its tanks and assault guns reached
the front only during the next week.

Hitler entertained hopes of not merely relieving Budapest, but
crossing the Danube, continuing into Romania, and recapturing those
oil fields as well. Reality was a last-ditch breakout attempt on February 11 by what remained of the city's garrison. Fewer than 1,000 men
reached German lines. The commander, seeking to escape through the
city sewer system, was driven to the surface by flooding and unheroic-
ally surrendered the next day.

At least with Budapest gone the panzers were free to concentrate on
their Soviet opponents—if they were able to reach them. The weather
had broken in late February. Rain and melting snow softened the
ground so badly that Balck established "road courts-martial," with the
power to execute out of hand anyone responsible for road maintenance
who failed in that duty. Morale did not improve. Nor did the offensive
make much initial progress as the heavier AFVs became bogged down
on roads Dietrich described as "catastrophic" or sank up to their turrets
in the marshy fields. The panzer grenadiers took heavy losses advanc-

ing on foot against a well-developed defensive system manned by no fewer than 16 rifle divisions. By the second day they had managed to open enough gaps for the panzers to move through. By the third day Hitler Jugend achieved a local breakthrough when a dozen of its heavy tank destroyers took out a Soviet antitank screen and the reconnaissance battalion's half-tracks machine-gunned and drove over the fleeing Russians in a style reminiscent of eighteenth-century cavalry. But the advance stopped at the Sio Canal, connecting Lake Balaton with the Danube.

In the absence of air and artillery support, the panzers were compelled to push right up to the canal banks to cover the infantry as they crossed. That brought them into killing range of Soviet antitank guns, and AFVs were no longer expendable assets. Where they were forced to retreat, the rubber boats of the assault troops were easy targets. Elsewhere Das Reich and Hohenstaufen were stymied. Leibstandarte managed to establish a bridgehead, and its pioneers managed to put a bridge across the Sio. But field bridging equipment had long since failed to keep pace with the panzers' increasing weight. The bridge promptly collapsed. Only heroic improvisation under heavy fire reopened it sufficiently to funnel forward tank destroyers able to counter the T-34/85s that for three days kept counterattacking what was in any case a foothold to nowhere. On March 15, Dietrich and his staff ordered a withdrawal, intending to shift the army's Schwerpunkt to II SS Panzer Corps. On March 16 it ceased to matter.

The Soviets had been able to contain Spring Awakening without committing their sector reserves. Instead those forces were concentrated west of Budapest, on the German left flank and rear. On March 14, Gille's corps reported the threat. On March 16, under cover of a heavy fog, a million men and 1,699 armored vehicles tore a 20-mile hole in the Axis defenses and kept going. Balck, an operational optimist, had been too engaged by Spring Awakening's chimerical prospects to retain deployable German armored reserves. By the time he, Dietrich, and Hitler could agree on the timing and direction of a counterattack, its prospects were long gone and the situation had deteriorated to *sauve qui peut.*

Viking was almost surrounded. Its CO pulled back in defiance of Hitler's order to stand fast, but it was Hohenstaufen's intervention that enabled Viking's remnants to withdraw. The IV and II SS Panzer Corps in turn held open a corridor long enough for most of the Germans cut off by the Soviet offensive to escape. That included all that was left of 1st Panzer Division—11,473 men and exactly one operational tank, as of April 1. Leibstandarte and Das Reich, the farthest east of the Panzers, managed to bring out the men able to walk.

Hohenstaufen's panzer regiment alone accounted for more than 100 verified kills in the course of the fighting. But 6th SS Panzer Army was reduced to fewer than 100 AFVs. More than 1,000 tanks and assault guns, Hungarian as well as German, fell to the Soviets. Relatively few had been knocked out. It was empty fuel tanks, engine breakdowns, and "General Mud" that finished off the panzers. The Russians captured enough usable tanks to put them into service against their former owners.

The German front in the south was never reestablished. For the next six weeks, operations amounted to a fighting withdrawal to, then past, Vienna. The Germans still had some sting in their tails. The last remaining tanks of Leibstandarte, predictably led in person by Peiper, retook a few villages around Sankt Pölten. For the panzers, SS or army, the primary mission nevertheless became covering the retreat as long as possible, then, wherever possible, pulling back quickly enough to surrender to the Americans. But the story of those final days is best expressed in the myth of the chamber pot.

On March 27, Hitler, enraged by the failure of his chosen troops in Hungary, ordered Leibstandarte, Das Reich, Hohenstaufen, and Hitler Jugend to remove the cuff titles bearing their division names. The alleged response exists in many versions involving combinations of a chamber pot full of armbands and high decorations being sent to the Führer's headquarters—sometimes accompanied by a severed arm, and sometimes by the injunction "kiss my ass."

Reality was predictably less spectacular. The most credible version has Dietrich saying with tear-filled eyes, "So this is the thanks for everything," and ordering the morale-killing message not to be passed to his men. The chamber pot and the epithet are gestures of defiance borrowed and adapted from Goethe's Sturm und Drang play *Götz von Berlichingen*—a bit of wishful thinking by postwar SS nostalgists. Ironically, the divisions had been ordered to remove their armbands for security purposes when sent to Hungary. Many replacements never even received them.

From Stavka's perspective, Hitler could not have been more obliging had he been on Stalin's payroll. The Soviet High Command's plan to finish the war dated from October, and involved two major offensives. The secondary attack would be mounted against East Prussia; the main one across Poland. In a decision with as many postwar implications as military aspects, Zukhov and Konev, personal and professional rivals since the war's early days, were each assigned command of a front under Stalin's direct command—objective Berlin.

Given the Soviets' overwhelming numerical superiority, developed operational effectiveness, and improving logistical capabilities, the Germans could do little but play out the hand, as a trumped bridge player tosses meaningless cards onto the table. Even before Gille was transferred to Hungary, Guderian's concept of a mobile defensive battle fought by a strong central reserve was arguably two years behind the times. Its potential was further diminished when the army group commanders concentrated four more mechanized divisions closely behind what they considered vital sectors. That approach, a variant of the Model model, was arguably only a year out of date. Its success depended on a far closer balance of quality and quantity than existed in 1945. The dispersed panzers were in fact a security blanket for an infantry who might stand to a finish—but whose chances of withstanding a major attack were limited to the point of being imaginary.

The main Soviet offensive made five miles in the first three hours of January 12. By the end of January 13, the breakthrough was 25 miles deep. The panzer divisions in its way were overwhelmed, able to do no more than fight for mere survival. Zukhov's 26th Guards Rifle Corps evoked the panzers' glory days by seizing a vital bridge before German engineers could throw the demolition switches. Warsaw fell on January 17, and Hitler's blind rage led him to turn Guderian over to the Gestapo for interrogation, albeit briefly. On January 20, Konev's spearheads entered Silesia. By January 31, Zukhov was on the Oder at Küstrin, 40 miles from Berlin.

The primary German response, initiated by Hitler, was to transfer the newly organized Grossdeutschland Corps from East Prussia. With Grossdeutschland, Brandenburg and Hermann Göring Divisions also under command, it went into action on January 16. But the trains carrying its rear echelon were intercepted by Soviet tanks; the best it was able to do was to serve as a rallying point for disorganized soldiers and fleeing civilians. Ever-dividing, ever-shrinking pockets, most coalesced around a couple of tanks, perhaps some half-tracks, and a company or so of panzer grenadiers, made their way toward the Oder, hoping above all to avoid attracting Soviet attention. The lucky ones beat Zukhov by a day or two.

To the north the Russian attack took five days to break through a German defense, enervated by the withdrawal of its armored reserve. As Russian tanks reached the Baltic, the Germans withdrew in the only direction open to them—eastward, into Königsberg. And the near-forgotten Courland Pocket, with its two forlorn panzer divisions, stood to, waiting for the Russians to finish it.

The Red Army's pause at the end of January was in part to refresh its logistics, in part to secure its flanks, and in part to structure its internal priorities. The attacks into Pomerania and Silesia in February and March scarcely make a footnote to the story of Hitler's panzers, apart from their success in screening a withdrawal-cum-evacuation into the relatively safe zone of the Sudetenland. The battle for Berlin was another matter. The Reich's capital was defended by the Wehrmacht's flotsam: boys and old men, convalescents and comb-outs, foreigners fighting with ropes around their necks, equipped with anything handy. Factories and rail sidings were full of armored vehicles that could not be moved for lack of fuel and fear of air attack.

Guderian's hopes of forming new reserves by transferring divisions from the West and evacuating Courland were not much less delusional than the Führer's. His plans for a local spoiling attack to disrupt the Russians on Berlin's doorstep primarily featured winning a screaming argument with Hitler. The attack itself collapsed within days—a predictable outcome given its limited striking power.

The final Russian offensive began on April 16. It was still a Zukhov-Konev derby, with the final prize the Reichstag. Familiar numbers flash across the screen: 21st Panzer Division, 25th Panzer Grenadier, LXVI Panzer Corps, 3rd Panzer Army, SS Northland Panzer Grenadiers. All by now were shadow formations exercising ad hoc command over constantly changing orders of battle that meant nothing except in a wire diagram. The tanks and assault guns that remained went down by ones and twos, on streets and in neighborhoods with names all too familiar.

No narrative of the Reich's final days can be called typical. Let one stand nevertheless for many. The 249th Assault Gun Brigade was evacuated from West Prussia, reorganized and reinforced, and picked up new guns in Spandau, at the factory itself. It went into action in Berlin on April 27. In three days it destroyed 180 Soviet AFVs—at least by its own reckoning—and had only nine guns left. They fought in the heart of Berlin: on Frankfurter Allee, around the Technische Hochschule, across Alexanderplatz. One of the officers was hanged by an SS flying squad, presumably for "cowardice." Another received the Knight's Cross for valor.

On May 5, Hitler's death was announced. The CO called his men together, and it was decided to break out toward the Elbe. In the darkness, the brigade lost contact. Half cut its way through to the Elbe. The other half, three guns, came under Russian fire. The lead vehicle took a direct hit. The next one got stuck. The third came to help, saw the second gun blown apart, and was itself disabled. Its crew escaped. The 249th had fought to the last gun and the last round. Adolf Hitler had long been aware the war was lost. Instead of a glorious final victory, he sought a heroic downfall, a Wagnerian Götterdammerung. What he achieved was in macrocosm the fate of this single small unit: downfall in chaos.

EPILOGUE

HITLER'S PANZERS ENDED their careers at random, wherever they had been washed up by the war's final tides. The 1st Panzer Division wound up in Austria and surrendered to the Americans. What was left of 2nd Panzer—200 men and seven AFVs—had been absorbed into a provisional brigade and surrendered in Plauen in the Vogtland—again to Americans. Fifth Panzer capitulated to the Red Army near Danzig. Seventh fought around Berlin and managed to deliver most of its men to the British. Fourth, 8th,13th, 20th, and 23rd Panzer Divisions were caught in the final Soviet offensives. Twelfth and 14th Panzer went under with the rest of the Courland Pocket; 29th and 90th Panzer Grenadier Divisons capitulated in Italy.

Ironically the bulk of 6th SS Panzer Army managed at the last minute to surrender to the Americans. A regiment of Das Reich brought a thousand-vehicle convoy of German wounded and civilians out of Prague and into the US 3rd Army's lines. Hitler Jugend, defiant to the last, refused to display white flags on their vehicles as ordered when they stampeded past a Russian tank column. Hohenstaufen surrendered en bloc. Frundsberg and Viking broke up and scattered. Totenkopf's CO negotiated with the Americans: surrender in return for disarming the guards at Mauthausen concentration camp. The division's 3,000 survivors were promptly turned over to the Russians—something about reaping what had been sown.

Most of the tankers who fell into Western hands demobilized themselves or were quickly released once it became clear that resistance to the occupation was limited and eroding. Some prisoners of the Russians returned home almost as quickly. Others disappeared into a postwar labor/penal system in a near-random process having nothing to do with individual behavior and little with unit identity—except in the case of Waffen SS. As many as a half million died; most survivors were held for around ten years.

More senior panzer officers faced trial than is sometimes understood. Hoth and Reinhardt each received 15 years in the High Command Trial held in 1948. A British tribunal sentenced Manstein to 18 years, essentially for failing to protect civilians in his areas of operation. Kurt Meyer and Jochen Peiper had death sentences commuted to life imprisonment. Guderian and Harpe were held by the US without charge or trial for three years, then released. Balck went underground as a day laborer until 1948 when he was arrested, tried, and convicted of ordering the drumhead execution of a subordinate for being drunk on duty. Raus, who remained below his own army's radar throughout the war, profited from his relative invisibility and was released after two years as a POW.

As in the case of their soldiers, there is no discernible pattern in the postwar treatment of the generals. What they have in common is the shortness of the time actually served relative to the sentences: six years for Hoth; four for Reinhardt and Manstein (the latter on health grounds!).

The generals' treatment is frequently dismissed as a revolving door farce inspired by the emerging Cold War and the perceived need for West German participation in a developing Atlantic Alliance. A more sinister variant asserts a comprehensive readiness to forgive and forget in the name of anti-Communism. Both were undeniable factors but played secondary roles. The Nuremberg Trials proper are best understood in the context of that variant of vigilantism which seeks to do justice according to existing generally accepted principles, in crypto-Hobbesian circumstances where an applicable legal apparatus does not exist. The tribunals' ultimate purpose was to establish precedents, not to replace one system of drumhead punishment by another.

In that context a major principle of selecting defendants was the potential for making an unchallengeable case. In the immediate postwar years, finding legally credible documentary or eyewitness evidence for specific criminal acts authorized or committed by senior officers was seldom easy. That was particularly true for field officers as opposed to occupation commanders—especially so for those whose primary service had been in Russia. Wilhelm Bittrich, for example, was convicted in 1953 by a French military tribunal of ordering the summary execution of Resistance members, but was later acquitted by a civilian court. Manstein's trial in the British system was sufficiently irregular to generate public protests from several generals—and from Winston Churchill, who denounced the process as politically inspired by a Labour government seeking to curry favor with the Soviet Union.

In the background lay as well the *tu quoque* argument that Allied forces had been guilty of similar behavior, ranging from Americans' shooting inconvenient prisoners in Sicily to mass rapes perpetrated by French *goumiers* in Italy and tolerated by the command structure. Nor, with effective deadly force in their own systems resting in the military, were governments especially enthusiastic about establishing the kinds of precedents involved in prosecuting senior officers for not denouncing and disobeying policies established by state authority.

In wider contexts, any hope of reconstructing a Europe devastated by war, occupation, and liberation depended heavily on restoring comity among states and peoples—especially given the obvious refusal of the British and Americans to consider anything but a limited occupation of "their" Germany. Even before the war, a major consideration in appeasing Hitler and seeking to integrate his Reich into Europe's order had been the sense that Germany's contributions to Europe's history, culture, and civilization were too seminal to be excluded at will and permanently.

Within what became the Federal Republic, Vaclav Havel's familiar argument against comprehensive punishment has retroactive force. Justice and reconciliation are concepts easier enunciated than implemented, especially in the context of the Third Reich. German society as a whole was complicit—arguably enthusiastically complicit—in Hitler's regime and Hitler's war. In practical terms, very few adult individuals were completely free of involvement. The nature of that involvement was such, moreover, that retribution involved half the German people perpetually sitting in judgment on the other half—with the halves differing for each situation. A reconstructed government and society would tear itself apart with new conflicts—unless it was created on what amounted to a totalitarian model.

That last was essentially the case in the Soviet Zone that became the German Democratic Republic. The experience of the Third Reich was addressed by fiat and implemented instrumentally: officially denying any connection between the "new" GDR and its immediate predecessor, and overlooking or redefining the awkward pasts of individuals useful to the new New Order.

"Collective amnesia" is too strong a term for what happened in the Federal Republic. *Stunde Null* (Zero Hour) is closer to the mark, if understood as drawing a line under the past for the sake of a present and a future. Memories remained so strong that one can best speak neither of denial nor repression, but rather of taboo: taboo against asking awkward questions in private and public. Beginning in the 1960s the memories have been eloquently evoked and comprehensively evaluated. In particular the concept that German soldiers remained free of the Reich's crimes and bore a "clean shield" as men fighting honorably for their country has been discredited beyond revival. But like drastic medical procedures and psychological processes, such voluntary fundamental reconstructions can only be performed effectively in a general context of health and stability. Without the "economic miracle" and the restoration of at least marginal international respectability, "mastering the past" was likely to have remained little more than a cosmetic project. Even then the examples of post–World War II Japan and post-Soviet Russia indicate that Germany's behavior remains more exception than rule.

During the 1950s most senior panzer officers found niches in a Federal Republic that was more a niche society than generally realized. Guderian and Manstein were by all odds the most visible, writing widely translated memoirs that continue to define many aspects of the tankers' war. Only a cut below these works in external influence is Friedrich von Mellenthin's *Panzer Battles*, a detailed, at times tendentious, operational/tactical analysis of his campaigns as a staff officer in North Africa and Russia. Fridolin von Senger und Etterlin made most of his reputation in Italy as a panzer general without armored troops. His *Neither Fear Nor Hope* probably ranks fourth in familiarity among English translations of tanker memoirs, probably because it is informed by a hostility to Nazism defined by Senger's Catholicism—which did not deter him from doing his duty to the German people by serving Hitler's Reich.

Other Panzermänner turned to the pen at home. Balck's *Ordnung im Chaos* presents the Russian front from the division and corps perspective. Kurt Mayer's *Grenadiere*, published in 1957 and later translated into English, has done much to confirm the image of the Waffen SS as a force of bold adventurers. History rather than autobiography was the preferred métier for more senior officers. Hoth published a narrative of his panzer group during Barbarossa. Raus authored a number of specialized reports for the US Army.

In wider contexts, Hasso von Manteuffel spent four years in the Bundestag as a Free Democrat, and was a guest lecturer at West Point. Herbert Gille became a journalist, founded a magazine for Viking's veterans, and actually owned a bookstore. Balck and Mellenthin made virtual second careers in the late 1970s as think-tank consultants advising the US Army how to fight outnumbered against the Soviet Union in the Fulda Gap and win panzer-style.

The panzers' direct influence on the emerging Bundeswehr was limited. Manstein served as Konrad Adenauer's senior defense advisor for a time, but the Federal Republic took extreme pains to keep out of leadership positions anyone whose attitudes or behavior might give the new armed forces a tone encouraging the denial of previous experiences. The ex-Wehrmacht officers accepted for service were almost all lower-ranking; major and below. Traditions were established *de novo*, in line with historian Manfred Messerschmidt's prescient warning against concentrating on achievements at the expense of intentions. Lines of heritage emphasized reformers and resisters. Unit designations were severely numerical. Naming buildings after former generals regularly generated criticism.

In operational contexts, the Bundeswehr in its developed form did closely replicate panzer formats and experience. Ten of its twelve divisions were armored or mechanized. Its Leopard tanks owed more in concept to the Panzer III and IV than the Tiger, and arguably the Panther as well, in their combination of gun power, mobility, and reliability. That was a sharp contrast to the British, for example, whose post-Centurion lines of tank development emphasized protection and hitting power in the fashion of the later panzer models. Its principal companion, the Marder, borrowed an old name for a development of the SdKfz 251: an armored personnel carrier that was a full-tracked fighting platform as opposed to a half-track battle taxi.

Politically the Bundeswehr was just as committed to a forward defense as had been its predecessor in Russia, albeit for essentially different reasons. With 30 percent of the Federal Republic's population and a quarter of its industrial capacity within 100 miles of the Eastern frontier, trading space for time in the Manstein/Guderian tradition was impossible. Analysis of the defensive operations in Russia between 1943 and 1945, however, strongly suggested that mechanized forces properly trained, equipped, and commanded retained the capacity to check effectively any conventional offensive in central Europe. Model and Raus became fashionable, albeit unacknowledged, mentors of a tactical doctrine calling for quick ripostes: trip-hammer blows executed at the lowest possible levels with the purpose of stabilizing the battle line to a point where nuclear escalation became a calculable option as opposed to a logical development.

The Bundeswehr's operational approach was never put to the test. Of arguably wider consequence was the effect of the panzer experience on Western, especially American, understanding of how World War II was fought on the Russian Front. It was thinly fictionalized in pulp magazines like the long-running weekly *Der Landser*, which endures in several variants and combines varying elements of pathos, nostalgia, and raw triumphalism. It was narrated in general-audience histories, and analyzed in sophisticated operational studies. The subtext was the same: German soldiers fought to the end in an honorable war against a brutal enemy. Russians were objectified as a faceless, soulless mass, a fundamental threat to Western civilization. Atrocities were the responsibility of the civilian party apparatus and the Waffen SS. The latter in turn sought to justify its war in a series of campaign and unit histories focusing on operational detail, many of them multivolume, increasing numbers translated into English by presses specializing in what is sometimes called "Wehrmacht porn."

This romantic/heroic self-image became the basis for presenting the Eastern Front in terms of a lost cause in language similar to the "gunpowder and magnolias" aura surrounding the Confederacy. Responding to a growing market, book clubs, magazines, and the History Channel, war gamers, military reenactors, and the Internet, contributed to a self-reinforcing popular myth that continues to flourish long after the reunification of Germany and the implosion of the USSR. Jacket blurbs, tables of contents, websites, and game designs combined to prevent any serious engagement with either the true nature of the war in the East, or the true extent of the suffering the Germans inflicted on tens of millions from the basest of motives.

The German monopoly of Eastern Front narrative was made possible in good part by the USSR's Cold War determination to control every aspect of the master story of the Great Fatherland Patriotic War. Entire campaigns, like the 1942–43 disaster at Rzhev, simply disappeared from the Soviet account. Ordinary soldiers' experiences were submerged in the Soviet aggregate. Most publication on the war was official, so turgidly propagandistic and hagiographic that it remained untranslated and unmarketed in the West. Heroic romanticizing had no effective competition, so, like Darwin's finches, it filled every interpretive niche.

The release of Russian primary sources since the fall of the Soviet Union has enabled balanced analysis at academic levels. David Glantz and Catherine Merridale are only two of a generation of scholars at this new cutting edge. Popular writers are beginning to follow. Availability of technical data, orders of battle, uniforms, and regalia have made the Red Army of World War II the latest thing in gamer chic and reenactor fashion.

Russia's war story nevertheless continues to emphasize the collective. In contrast, most German material is individual. Even unit histories, in contrast to their US counterparts, tend to be structured around biographies and personal narratives. This reflects a German cultural pattern of processing war as a Bildungserlebnis: a developmental experience. The German way to tell what Tim O' Brien calls "a true war story" in turn reinforces a central Western myth. From David and Goliath and the 300 Spartans to Tolkien's trilogy and *Buffy the Vampire Slayer*, heroism is defined as individual struggle against odds not only overwhelming but faceless, objectified, dehumanized. A difference in American perspectives on the Eastern Front is correspondingly likely to persist.

Americans do focus naturally and inevitably on the war in the West at the expense of Russia. Within that parameter, however, the standard works, from Stephen Ambrose's *Band of Brothers* through Audie Murphy's memoir *To Hell and Back* to long-running comics like *Sgt. Rock*, depict German soldiers, tankers in particular, not as romanticized role models but as dangerous and deadly enemies. *Hogan's Heroes* has arguably done more to foster an innocuous image of the Wehrmacht than all of the faux heroic stories with a Russian setting ever published in English.

Whatever their images, Hitler's panzers are best described and understood as a technocracy—not merely in terms of material but of mentality. Their history during World War II is of being set tasks beyond their means, arguably more so than any other element of the Wehrmacht. The resulting emphasis on operational proficiency reflected the sheer magnitude of their responsibilities, but also the lack of moral insight, of conscience, that informed their leadership.

Steadily escalating operational requirements were an analgesic, an excuse not to think beyond the next month, the next week, the next day. But war by its nature tends toward entropic violence without structure, purpose, or meaning. Effective war-making correspondingly depends on a comprehensive, definable, and specific culture. That culture is not merely utilitarian, something assumed and discarded at will or whim. The culture of war is an end in itself. Its traditions, rules, and conventions are part of the fighter's soul: a survival mechanism in a fundamental sense.

Call this honor. Call this as well something the panzers abandoned—from expediency, from ambition, from temptation—and not least from principle: the end justifying the means. Call this something that was expected to be reclaimed—sometime in an undefined future. Martin van Creveld offers two relevant consequences of honor's absence. One is the wild horde. Lawless and disorganized, committed to destruction for destruction's sake, it can neither give nor inspire the trust necessary for civilization. The other is the soulless machine. It makes war mindlessly and mechanically, never developing beyond an identity as a self-referencing, self-defined elite. Hitler's panzers incorporated both. Yet never did men fight better in a worse cause.

That said, individual and cultural identities can be fluid. Not every German soldier was an archetypical Nazi. Nor did Nazis always behave in character. Life happens in a gray middle that readily becomes muddled. Since 1945 Germans have sought to enunciate and internalize an important lesson from their past. That lesson remains best expressed by playwright Carl Zuckmayer: "Whoever was the Devil's general on this earth, and who bombed the path for him, has to be his quartermaster in Hell." It is a fitting epitaph for Hitler's panzers.

INDEX